The GI Offensive in Europe

The GI Offensive
in Europe
The Triumph of American
Infantry Divisions, 1941–1945

Peter R. Mansoor

 University Press of Kansas

Published by the University Press of Kansas (Lawrence, Kansas 66049), which was organized by the Kansas Board of Regents and is operated and funded by Emporia State University, Fort Hays State University, Kansas State University, Pittsburg State University, the University of Kansas, and Wichita State University

Library of Congress Cataloging-in-Publication Data

Mansoor, Peter R., 1960–
    The GI offensive in Europe : the triumph of American infantry
divisions, 1943–1945 / Peter R. Mansoor.
        p.   cm. — (Modern war studies)
    Includes bibliographical references and index.
    ISBN 0-7006-0958-X (cloth)
    1. World War, 1939–1945—Campaigns—Western Front.   2. United
States. Army—Infantry—history.   3. World War, 1939–1945—
Regimental histories—United States.   I. Title.   II. Series.
D769.M34   1999
940.54'1273—dc21   98-55249

British Library Cataloguing in Publication Data is available.

Printed in the United States of America

10 9 8 7 6 5 4 3 2 1

To the officers and soldiers of the Army of the United States, whose sacrifices made possible the victory of democracy over totalitarianism during World War II

Contents

Illustrations

PHOTOGRAPHS

Acknowledgments

Many people assisted in bringing this manuscript to completion. First and foremost, I express sincere appreciation to Professor Allan R. Millett for his guidance and mentorship over the past several years. Under his tutelage a generation of military historians have been educated, and I feel blessed to count myself among them. I also would like to thank Professor Williamson Murray, Professor John F. Guilmartin, Professor John C. Rule, and Dr. Joseph Kruzel for their support and encouragement during my studies at Ohio State University. Dr. Kruzel has since given his life serving his country in Bosnia, and we will all miss him greatly.

I gratefully acknowledge the assistance of archivists Dr. Richard Sommers and Dr. David Keough at the United States Army Military History Institute in Carlisle Barracks, Pennsylvania, and Dr. Timothy Nenninger and Mr. Richard Boylan at the National Archives in Washington, D.C. Without their professional assistance, I would not have been able to complete the research for this study. Lieutenant Colonel Jim Brown generously donated his time and expertise to translate selected documents from German to English. Ms. Debra DeRuyver of the Still Pictures Branch of the National Archives was most helpful in locating photographs that bring to life the experience of the American infantryman in World War II.

I appreciate the encouragement that my superiors in the Department of History at the United States Military Academy, Colonel Robert Doughty and Colonel Jim Johnson, gave me during my tenure as an assistant professor at West Point.

Dr. Christopher Gabel, Lieutenant Colonel Michael Doubler, and Professor Dennis Showalter gave invaluable suggestions for improving the manuscript during the editing process. I would also like to thank Lieutenant Colonel Rich Hooker and Lieutenant Colonel John Antal for their comments on the thesis, their lively and articulate criticism, and, most of all, their professional comradeship.

I corresponded with hundreds of infantry officers over several years of research. Where appropriate I have incorporated their comments into the manuscript. I am thankful for the time they took to answer my questions and provide their firsthand insights into various aspects of training in the United States and combat in North Africa and Europe during World War II.

I am indebted to Mike Briggs and his staff at the University Press of Kansas, who have performed minor miracles in preparing for publication the original rough manuscript I submitted for review some time ago. The quality of the final result would have been significantly diminished without their expert advice and assistance at every step of the way.

I am grateful to Jane Woebke and Mary Jane and Sam Barrow for providing a place to stay during my numerous research trips to the National Archives in Washington, D.C. I will forever treasure their love and friendship. As always, my wife, Jana, daughter, Kyle, and son, J. T., proved to be towers of support during countless hours of study, research, and writing.

1

Introduction

The landing craft bobbed uneasily in the choppy seas as the initial wave of the 1st and 29th Infantry Divisions headed for the Normandy coast. Inside the boats, weary and seasick infantrymen readied themselves for the moment when the ramps would drop and disgorge them onto the sand. Ahead of them, the bluffs overlooking the beach were eerily silent. The thousands of bombs and shells that should have obliterated the enemy machine gun and artillery emplacements by this time had largely missed their mark. As a result, the fate of the Allied invasion of France now rested firmly on the overloaded shoulders of the American soldiers packed together in cramped landing craft. Two and one-half years after the United States had entered World War II with the Japanese attack on Pearl Harbor, the quality of the army the nation had mobilized was about to be tested as never before. This was the crucible: D-Day, 6 June 1944.

OMAHA Beach was but a snapshot of America's army in action. All of the immense weight of matériel produced by the industrial strength of the United States was just so much junk without trained soldiers to operate it and bring it to bear against the enemy, a coherent doctrine for its employment, and leaders who could command the formations into which it was organized. From the deserts and hills of Tunisia, over the mountains of Sicily and Italy, and through the fields of France and Germany, American soldiers faced a multitude of challenges in a very short period of time. The task of mobilizing and training an army of eight million soldiers in four years was enormous. More impressive, however, were the results those soldiers achieved when pitted in combat against one of the most tactically proficient armies ever to exist. At locations hardly known and made famous only for a brief moment in time by the battles fought there—places such as the Sedjenane Valley, Gela, Troina, Anzio, OMAHA Beach, St.-Lô, Mortain, Aachen, Metz, the Vosges, Clervaux, Bastogne, Elsen-

1

born Ridge, St.-Vith, and Remagen—American soldiers proved their capabilities in battle, the ultimate test for an army and a nation.

A fashionable argument in the past two decades has been that the Allies won World War II only through the sheer weight of matériel they threw at the Wehrmacht in a relatively unskilled manner. This argument is actually a restatement of the theory put forward by German officers to explain their defeat, as evidenced by wartime interrogations and postwar manuscripts prepared by the defeated.[1] The more combat-effective German army was in the end bulldozed by less capable, but more numerous, enemies—or so the argument goes. This conclusion would have shocked the victors, especially the senior military leadership of the American army, who understood just how thin was the advantage they possessed in the numerical correlation between Western Allied and German ground forces in the crucial battles fought in France and Germany in 1944 and 1945.

History is replete with examples of a smaller, but more capable, army defeating a larger force: Alexander the Great's victory against the Persians, the Roman conquest of Gaul, Frederick the Great's ultimate triumph in the Seven Years' War, Napoleon's early successes against the coalitions arrayed against France, and the German victory over Russia in World War I are but a few. Fighting a coalition war made the task of the World War II Allies even more difficult. Napoleon understood the weakness of coalition operations when he answered a question once put to him regarding which European power he would like to fight next. His answer was unambiguous: "Allies."

Sheer numbers alone could not ensure the victory of the Allied coalition in World War II. Rather, the relative quality of the forces fielded by the Allied and Axis powers was crucial to the ultimate outcome. The combat effectiveness of these forces changed over time right up until the end of the fighting. In general, Allied combat effectiveness increased, while huge casualties and shortages of key resources eventually caused German effectiveness to decline. While the causes of the decay of the Wehrmacht are readily apparent, the reasons for the increase in Allied combat effectiveness are less well understood. Numbers are a part of the story, especially in the massive struggle in the East, but material superiority alone is an insufficient explanation for the ultimate triumph of the armies fielded by the United States in Africa, Italy, France, and Germany.

Analyzing the combat effectiveness of an army is no easy task, one made less so by the vagueness of the term. One military authority defines combat effectiveness as "a term used to describe the abilities and fighting quality of a unit. [Combat effectiveness is] the quality of being effective in combat."[2] This is obviously not a very helpful definition if one looks to analyze military organizations, especially for those wishing to quantify the capabilities of an army.

Since war involves the vagaries of human behavior under extreme stress, accurate quantification of combat effectiveness is not possible. But it is possible to examine successful military organizations to determine what makes them work, for in the end, success in war is the only standard by which to judge military organizations. A restated definition for combat effectiveness is the ability of a military organization to achieve its assigned missions with the least expenditure of resources (both material and human) in the shortest amount of time. Combat effectiveness encompasses many variables, not all of them under the control of the commander, but each vital to the ability of military organizations to accomplish their missions in an efficient and cost-effective manner. One can break these factors roughly into three groups: human, organizational, and technical. One factor that defies categorization is endurance, the ability of a military force to sustain its effort over time.

Human factors are the least easily quantifiable, but often most critical, aspect of combat effectiveness. Leadership is the glue that binds all elements of combat effectiveness together, for without competent leaders, a military organization will fail no matter how good or how numerous its soldiers, weapons, and equipment. Discipline, morale, and cohesion are the bedrock upon which military organizations are founded. Without these elements, units break apart under stress and cannot accomplish the difficult tasks involved in closing with and destroying the enemy.

Organizational factors are also vital to combat effectiveness. The types of weapons and equipment at an army's disposal are only one facet of its strength; another element, just as important, is how those weapons are organized and employed. Doctrine is the accepted norm for the planning and conduct of operations. Command and control refer to the methods by which leaders issue orders and supervise operations on the battlefield. Adaptability is the capacity of a military force to adapt to changing battlefield realities and to learn from its mistakes. Without this ability, a force will decay over time as the opposing forces improve their capabilities and adjust to their opponent's methods. Interservice cooperation is also a key component of military organizational effectiveness, for modern military operations nearly always require the joint coordination of ground, air, and naval assets to accomplish a mission.

Technical factors are another significant element of combat effectiveness. Technology, in terms of the weapons and implements that a military organization uses to accomplish its missions, is important to combat effectiveness, but it is not a decisive element if the technology of the opposing force is roughly equivalent. Intelligence gives a decided edge to the military force that both possesses it and can deny it to the enemy. Fire support—the use of artillery, close air support, naval gunfire, and electronic warfare to attack enemy units—is also crucial to the ability of a military force to destroy enemy forces. In World War II the most important aspect of tactical maneuver often was that it brought friendly units into a position where they could use fire support assets to destroy the enemy.

An often overlooked component of combat effectiveness is endurance, the ability of a military force to sustain itself over time. Any force that fails to do so dooms itself to attrition and eventual destruction over the long run. Personnel and logistical systems are often overlooked by military historians, if not by professional soldiers. They are essential components to the successful functioning of the huge apparatus that constitutes an army in wartime.

To complete the definition of combat effectiveness, some discussion regarding the role of time is necessary. Time is a sword with many edges for military organizations. An essential component of combat effectiveness is the ability to accomplish assigned missions in the least possible amount of time. Yet throwing hastily mobilized, inadequately trained organizations into combat is a sure recipe for disaster. Moreover, once entered into combat, military organizations must be sustained over time or their combat potential will deteriorate to the point where they become useless as instruments of national policy. Political leaders and their military advisers tread a fine line between committing forces to combat to achieve the desired ends of policy and allowing those forces the time to develop into effective organizations before doing so. During World War II the American people, and by extension their political leaders, demanded quick, decisive action to bring the war to a rapid conclusion. For over three years the Army of the United States was challenged not only to mobilize and train new units but also to sustain them in combat for extended periods. The American army's great accomplishment was its ability to achieve both of these ends while at the same time assisting in the destruction of one of the most tactically competent ground combat forces in history.

Comparing the American army and the Wehrmacht with the preceding discussion in mind, the difference between the two forces is more easily discerned. German ground combat units could perform in outstanding tactical fashion, but the Wehrmacht failed as a fighting organization because of its numerous deficiencies in other areas such as logistics, fire support, intelligence, and interservice cooperation, and its inability to adapt to the changing tactics and operations of its foes as World War II progressed. German units could maneuver well and generally had excellent leadership, discipline (however ruthlessly applied), unit cohesion, and training. The American army's strengths lay in its ability to adapt to changing conditions on battlefields across the globe, its use of intelligence, outstanding fire support, the ability to execute joint operations, and, most important, its endurance.

This study examines the evolution of combat effectiveness in the American infantry divisions that fought against Germany and Italy during World War II. The intent is not to slight the achievements of the armored and airborne divisions that fought on the same battlefields, for they have surely earned their rightful place in the history of the Great Crusade. Rather, exactly because there is much less disagreement regarding the quality of American armored and airborne divisions, this study focuses on the standard American infantry divisions that formed the bulk of the Western Allied forces by the end of the war. Allied commanders intent on victory in the West would have to craft their campaigns from these basic building blocks. If the standard American infantry division were a failure in combat, then no available amount of paratroopers dropping from the sky or Sherman tanks rolling across the countryside would be able to defeat the Wehrmacht.

American armored divisions, it might be noted, contained as many infantry battalions as tank battalions, and the typical corps in the European theater of operations (ETO) contained two infantry divisions for each armored division it possessed. Even with the standard attachment of a nondivisional tank battalion to each infantry division, a representative corps would consist of twenty-one infantry battalions and only five tank battalions. The tanks provided mobility, armored protection, and firepower that were important in close combat and essential in exploitation and pursuit, but victory or defeat more often than not rested on the shoulders of the infantry.

The formation of American infantry divisions from a common pattern and standardized training system was one of the greatest strengths of the Army of the United States. American corps and army commanders knew basically what to expect from their divisions on the battlefield. Beyond this baseline level of effectiveness, differences among divisions emerged as a result of the leadership of commanders and the combat experience of the soldiers. For an army whose strength was less than that of the Romanian army only a few short years before, perhaps the ultimate tribute was the fact that only one division out of eighty-nine completely failed the test of combat when the time came to prove their worth on the battlefield. American infantry divisions performed much better than both British and German military leaders believed they would. They became the essential components of the majority of the ground armies employed by the Western Allies in their quest to enter the heart of Germany and destroy its military forces.

The Army of the United States accomplished its mission in western Europe because it evolved over time into a more combat-effective force than Germany could sustain on the battlefield. Integral to this process was the ability of American military leaders to mobilize and train ground combat divisions that could close with and destroy enemy forces in a variety of combat environments. American citizen-soldiers proved to be adaptable to changing conditions and were often able to develop new tactics, techniques, and procedures in the midst of a campaign in order to accomplish their missions. The American army possessed great advantages in terms of superior intelligence and the ability to devastate opponents with the fire support means at its disposal. American military leaders were also able to plan and execute joint operations to a much higher standard than their adversaries.

The most critical factor, however, was the endurance of the American army once engaged in extended combat. American commanders in Europe rarely possessed the numerical superiority the revisionists claim overwhelmed the Wehrmacht in 1944 and 1945. Indeed, American commanders, strapped to maintain their divisions at something even approaching full strength, would have resisted the notion that they overwhelmed their adversaries with sheer numbers or material superiority. Instead, American leaders used the personnel and logistical systems they created to keep a relatively small number of divisions at a relatively high state of combat effectiveness. The ability of the American army to sustain its effort over an extended campaign tipped the balance in western Europe. What many critics of the Army of the United States fail to recognize is that its "tail," the combat service and combat service support organizations that constituted the majority of the force, was a large part of what made the American army the most combat-effective organization in World War II. To be sure, there were gross inefficiencies and excesses in American combat service support organizations, but in the aggregate these units were absolutely essential to the long-term effectiveness of the combat forces. In campaign after campaign the Army of the United States proved its ability to achieve its assigned missions, and if the expenditure of material resources was high, this was a more than adequate trade-off for the number of lives saved on the battlefield as a result.

The debate over combat effectiveness started early and has hardly waned since. The guns had barely cooled after the Allied victory in World War II when both participants and historians began to dispute the relative merits of the various armies. The victors wrote numerous memoirs and histories, which sometimes set off passionate arguments between British and American authors over their nations' contributions to defeating the Axis armies.[3] More recently, historians have focused on the tactical proficiency of the Wehrmacht in their effort to determine which army was the most combat effective. The accomplishments of the Army of the United States were fading into the background.

Context of writing

The assault on the reputation of the American army began early and came from an unexpected source. In 1947 Colonel S. L. A. Marshall, the deputy European theater historian during World War II, published *Men against Fire,* which called into question the quality of American infantrymen.[4] Marshall contended that fewer than 25 percent of American infantrymen fired their weapons in any given battle, a statistic he claimed was backed up by over four hundred company-level combat interviews gathered during the war. The inability of American infantry units to gain "fire superiority" over their adversaries was the primary reason for their failure to maneuver in order to close with the enemy and destroy him. Given the credibility of the source, for nearly four decades military officers and historians took Marshall's thesis as fact.

Three decades later another military historian, Trevor N. Dupuy, also cited statistics in his assertion of the inferiority of American combat units on the European battlefields of World War II. His work, *Numbers, Predictions, and War,* applied the techniques of quantitative analysis to the outcomes of eighty-one combat engagements in 1943 and 1944.[5] Dupuy attempted to isolate the variables surrounding tactical engagements: offensive/defensive posture, logistics, weather, terrain, communications, firepower, relative numerical strength, equipment, morale, and leadership. He then assigned numerical values to these variables and entered them into a mathematical equation he called the Quantified Judgment Model. After applying the model to selected tactical engagements, Dupuy concluded that German units were on the average 20 percent more effective than their British and American counterparts.[6] Dupuy believed some of the factors that caused this "superiority" could be better utilization of manpower, more experience, greater mobility, better doctrine, more effective battle drill, superior leadership, and inherent national characteristics.[7]

Dupuy was the vanguard of a group of historians who trumpeted the tactical superiority of the Wehrmacht at the expense of the American army. Russell Weigley gave the American army faint praise in his now-classic work, *Eisenhower's Lieutenants.*[8] Weigley claims that the American army in 1940 could not escape the influence of the western frontier heritage on its military thought. Although the Civil War taught the army the importance of power on a European-style battlefield, the frontier heritage emphasized the importance of mobility in tactical units. The result of this legacy was that American divisions lacked the staying power to fight a war of attrition against their German opponents, while the mobility of American units could not be used to the best effect in the slugging matches of France and Germany in 1944 and 1945. Furthermore, the quality of American infantry units was so poor that they could not routinely close with and destroy the enemy, relying instead on artillery fire to do the job. The pedestrian tactical abilities of inexperienced American generals resulted in a battle of attrition, waged by an army fashioned more for mobility than for staying power. Material resources, Weigley concludes, enabled the American army to "rumble to victory," despite its relative combat ineffectiveness against its German opponents.[9]

A year later Martin van Creveld made the most extreme case for the combat superiority of the Wehrmacht with the publication of *Fighting Power: German and U.S. Army Performance, 1939–1945.*[10] The Wehrmacht, van Creveld argues, "developed fighting power to an almost awesome degree" and totally outclassed the American army on the battlefield.[11] Van Creveld believes that the American army had a managerial view of war and treated its organizations as parts of a vast industrial enterprise.[12] The American emphasis on centralized planning, organization, and logistics relegated its soldiers to the status of cogs in a huge machine of war. By contrast, the German focus on small-unit cohesion, training, and tactics made German combat units much more effective on the battlefield. Van Creveld deplores the lack of attention paid by the American army to the needs of its fighting soldiers: primary group cohesion, promotions, decorations, military justice, and the treatment of psychiatric casualties. But he saves his harshest criticism for the American personnel replacement system. "Perhaps more than any other single factor," van Creveld argues, "it was this system that was responsible for the weaknesses displayed by the U.S. Army during World War II."[13] The American army, by attempting to maximize its efficiency in the numerical sense, ended up reducing its combat effectiveness by lack of attention to the psychology of the fighting man.[14] Finally, van Creveld dismisses the American officer corps of World War II as "less than mediocre."[15] Overall, van Creveld's assessment is a damning indictment of the American army of World War II.

Three British historians round out the field of authors who praise the combat effectiveness of the Wehrmacht at the expense of the victors of World War II. John Keegan, Max Hastings, and John Ellis all accept the arguments of Weigley and van Creveld without much alteration.[16] The German army, all three authors contend, was much more competent and combat effective than its Allied counterparts. The Allies won through brute force by bringing to bear the full weight of their material resources against the German military forces, which fought skillfully but unsuccessfully against overwhelming odds.

Historian Geoffrey Parker once noted that the half-life of a historical theory is roughly ten years, so it should not be surprising that scholars have not left the theory of German supremacy unchallenged. The first person to do so was John Sloan Brown with the 1986 publication of *Draftee Division,* a history of the 88th Infantry Division during World War II.[17] The 88th Infantry Division, commanded by Brown's grandfather, Major General John E. Sloan, earned an excellent reputation fighting in Italy from the spring of 1944 to the end of the war. The reason for the division's success, Brown argues, was that the War Department's Mobilization Training Program worked as long as a unit could stabilize its personnel early and keep them from being stripped away for other purposes. The 88th Infantry Division was one of the more fortunate units in this regard. With good leadership, sound training both in the United States and overseas, and a solid logistical structure behind it, the 88th Division was an example of the American mobilization system at its finest.

At the end of his book, Brown evaluates the work of Trevor Dupuy and finds it wanting. Dupuy's work, Brown contends, "simply demonstrates the intellectual intimidation wrought when complex calculations are unleashed upon a liberal arts community."[18] Not satisfied with Dupuy's "proof" of German prowess, Brown challenges his statistics. The sample of engagements, Brown contends, is skewed toward those battles in which the more elite German panzer and panzer grenadier divisions, which constituted only a small percentage of the Wehrmacht, participated. Dupuy thus compared the American army against the cream of the Wehrmacht. A second criticism is that Dupuy favored the defender in his model by underestimating the advantage possessed by the defender by a factor of two. Dupuy also rated the advantages of artillery and airpower too highly. Since the German army was on the defensive in most of the engagements Dupuy evaluated and the American army nearly always had the advantage in artillery and airpower, the shortcomings of Dupuy's model led to an overestimation of the fighting ability of German units. After reevaluating the factors, Brown recalculated Dupuy's statistics using the Quantified Judgment Model and found that American divisions were on the average more combat effective than most German units, panzer divisions being the exception. When properly analyzed, Brown concludes, Dupuy's historical data offer "convincing evidence that American divisions of 1943–1944 were more efficient than their German counterparts man for man, weapon for weapon, and asset for asset. . . . Colonel Dupuy's data [suggest] quantitative advantages were not sufficient to offset the difficulty of assigned missions, and Americans summoned up a qualitative edge as well."[19]

Taking a wider approach to the issue of military effectiveness, two years later Allan Millett examined the United States Armed Forces in World War II and concluded that the United States had done far better at generating combat-effective forces than was popularly believed.[20] Strategically, operationally, and tactically, American forces were well balanced and compared favorably with their adversaries on battlefields across the world. "Much like other American wartime forces," Millett writes, "the Second World War military needed only time, experience, and the human and material resources to forge armed forces of impressive scope and skill."[21]

Despite their contributions to the subject, Brown's *Draftee Division* was too limited in its scope and Millett's essay too limited in detailed evidence to come to any definitive conclusions about the combat effectiveness of the American army as a whole. Two more recent works have filled in some of the gaps in the history of the American army in World War II. In a study of the Seventh U.S. Army's campaign in the Vosges Mountains, Keith Bonn compares the strengths and weaknesses of the American and German armies that contended for the northeastern corner of France from October 1944 to January 1945.[22] Not only did the Seventh U.S. Army emerge victorious in this campaign; it did so without the aid of extensive logistical and close air support and in terrain and weather conditions that clearly favored a defensive stand by the numerically superior German forces. The divisions of the Seventh U.S. Army, Bonn argues, were more combat effective than their German counterparts in Army Group G. The American replacement system functioned better in maintaining those divisions at an adequate strength level, their uniform organization was superior to the ad hoc organizations employed by Army Group G, and American commanders were more tactically flexible and were able to use their initiative more often than their German counterparts. Army Group G was tenacious in delay, but it badly bungled the defense of the Vosges Mountains. Bonn concludes that in a campaign fought without the combat multipliers available to other American armies, without numerical superiority, and in atrocious weather and terrain conditions, the Seventh U.S. Army proved the superiority of American arms against its German counterpart—and it did so when the odds were even.[23]

Published the same year as Bonn's book, an impressive work by Michael Doubler examines how the American army was able to adapt to different conditions in its quest to close with and destroy the enemy in France and Germany in 1944 and 1945.[24] What was most impressive about the American combat performance, Doubler argues, was the Americans' ability to learn from their mistakes and adapt new tactics, techniques, and procedures in the face of unexpected conditions on the battlefield. Adaptability was crucial to the success of American combat units in the campaign for France and Germany. Doubler also argues that senior American commanders performed well, although an inadequate number of combat divisions and occasional shortages of manpower and supplies hampered their operations. After a period of adaptation, American divisions became effective instruments of national policy, able to close with and destroy the enemy in a variety of combat environments.[25]

In *Why the Allies Won,* Richard Overy tackles the commonly held view that the Allies defeated the Axis powers through the sheer weight of industrial abundance.[26] Although Allied victory in 1945 seems inevitable from the distance of half a century, it was not so clear to those nations that fought and won the war. The vast potential of Allied resources had to be turned into combat power. Victory depended not merely on material resources but also on the more intangible elements of leadership, fighting ability, and moral dimensions.[27] The gulf in fighting power, Overy argues, closed as the war progressed, with the Allies closing the qualitative gap with the German army by 1944. The German army, on the other hand, stagnated due to its unwillingness or inability to change. In the end, the Wehrmacht proved skillful in retreat, but withdrawals do not win wars. Overy concludes, "The Allies did not depend on simple numbers for victory but on the quality of their technology and the fighting effectiveness of their forces."[28] Imbued with the will to win and certain that their cause was just, the Allied nations turned their economic potential into combat power and thereby gained the ultimate triumph.

Historian Stephen Ambrose has used a large collection of oral histories to detail the accomplishments of the American soldier in the ETO during World War II in two books, *D-Day, June 6, 1944: The Climactic Battle of World War II* and its companion successor, *Citizen Soldiers: The U.S. Army from the Normandy Beaches to the Bulge to the Surrender of Germany.*[29] The quantity and quality of anecdotal evidence amassed in these volumes is impressive. The citizen-soldiers mobilized from the democratic society of the United States, Ambrose contends, were better than those who were indoctrinated with the fanaticism and racism of Nazi ideology. American soldiers fought because they had to, were held together by small-unit cohesion, and accomplished a difficult job under often brutal conditions.

As important as these works are, what is lacking in the argument for American combat effectiveness is a comprehensive approach to the subject. Revisionist historians have focused too heavily on the early struggles of the Army of the United States in World War II, such as the campaign in North Africa or the Normandy invasion, to the exclusion of later operations in 1944 and 1945. Additionally, some historians have mistaken Allied mediocrity in devising campaign strategy (the current doctrinal term is "operations") for tactical ineptitude at the division level and below. Due to decisions on allocation of resources made early in the war, American divisions operated with severe handicaps; nevertheless, nearly all American divisions developed into effective fighting organizations that accomplished their missions on battlefields literally oceans apart.

The United States mobilized an army of eighty-nine divisions during World War II, a decision based more on the erroneous belief that American industry could not give up more manpower to the military without incurring shortfalls than on any rational calculation of American needs on the battlefield. The official U.S. Army historian believes that the performance of its combat divisions on the field of battle in 1944–1945 "vindicated the bold calculation in Washington" not to produce more units.[30] This conclusion is highly debatable. One should not underestimate the achievement of the Army of the United States during World War II; the army, in conjunction with its sister services, did, after all, fulfill its mission of defeating the forces of Nazi Germany, Italy, and the Empire of Japan on the battlefields of Africa, Italy, France, Germany, and the Pacific. That achievement, however, should not blind one from observing that the victories did not come cheaply, and the provision of more combat divisions to the overseas theaters would have resulted in fewer casualties over the course of the war.

The decision to cap the army at eighty-nine divisions had ramifications beyond whether or not the United States and its allies would win the war. The limitation on the number of divisions, when combined with the inability of President Franklin D. Roosevelt and his chiefs of staff to adhere to the "Germany first" strategy, resulted in a shortage of divisions when the Western Allies conducted their crucial campaign in France in 1944. This situation forced American commanders to keep their divisions engaged in battle more or less continuously during the campaign.

As weeks and then months passed, the combat effectiveness of American divisions rose and fell as they lost men to enemy fire, disease, cold weather injuries, and exhaustion, and integrated hundreds of thousands of replacements into their ranks. A greater number of divisions would have enabled American commanders to rotate units more frequently for periods of rest, refitting, and retraining, thereby reducing the rate of casualties. Due to the ninety-division gamble and the employment of nearly one-third of the army along with all six marine divisions in the Pacific, however, systematic unit rotation was impossible in the ETO. American soldiers paid the price for the ninety-division gamble from Italy to Normandy, across France, along the West Wall, through the Ardennes, and into Germany.

Besides the numerical shortage of divisions, the performance of some American divisions, especially in their initial battles, left much to be desired. There were many reasons for the poor initial performance of these divisions, and high on the list is the quality of the personnel that the army assigned to its combat forces. Until 1944 the Army Air Forces (AAF) and Army Service Forces (ASF) had first priority on draftees with high Army General Classification Test (AGCT) scores or who had civilian skills that matched the needs of the service forces. The result of this system was the siphoning off of the most qualified inductees into almost any type of organization other than infantry, armor, and field artillery. Combat soldiers in the Army Ground Forces (AGF) were not only less educated than their service support counterparts but also physically less qualified.[31] By the time the War Department fixed the personnel selection system (if indeed it ever did), the AGF had already mobilized and trained the majority of its combat divisions.

Lack of personnel stability weakened many divisions, especially those mobilized after Pearl Harbor. These divisions endured high personnel turnover as the War Department stripped them for replacements to meet the pressing needs of overseas battlefields. Lack of personnel stability complicated the training of these divisions before their entry into combat, often forcing them to repeat basic training for new inductees at the expense of more advanced collective training for battalion and regimental combat teams.

Other factors also accounted for poor training. Due to the huge expansion of the army, many divisions lacked adequate leadership, particularly at the junior officer and noncommissioned officer level. Some of the best potential junior officers and noncommissioned officers ended up serving in nonflight positions with the AAF or participated in the Army Specialized Training Program (ASTP) until integrated as replacements—as enlisted soldiers—in 1944. Some field-grade officers were incompetent or past their prime, a result of the slow promotion system during the 1920s and 1930s. Recently formed divisions executed the mandates of the Mobilization Training Program as best they could with the men they had, but the quality of a division's leadership was a crucial determinant of its success in the endeavor.

Shortages of equipment also plagued the army in 1942 and early 1943, and many units trained with equipment different from that with which they went into combat. Training facilities were initially inadequate but were expanded rapidly as the army mobilized. Huge maneuver areas located across the United States allowed the army to conduct sustained large-scale, multidivision maneuvers for the first time in its history. Facilities and training improved as mobilization progressed and reached a peak in early 1944 as the army prepared for the invasion of France.

Army Ground Forces only partially met the goal of its commander, Lieutenant General Lesley J. McNair, of sending fully trained and combat-ready divisions into battle. Divisions attained various degrees of combat readiness based on numerous factors, and although most of them achieved an adequate baseline proficiency, the certification of some divisions as combat ready was a paper drill that masked their inadequacies. Not that the War Department had much choice in the matter; by the end of 1944 the need for divisions in Europe was so great that General George C. Marshall, the chief of staff, sent Allied commander General Dwight D. Eisenhower every division left in the strategic reserve, regardless of its state of readiness.[32]

With so few divisions in the line, the War Department worked hard to keep them at full strength. The army was able to avoid breaking up units for replacements, an expedient that plagued the American Expeditionary Forces in World War I. The army trained approximately 2,670,000 enlisted men as replacements from 1941 to 1945, more than twice the number of men assigned to the eighty-nine combat divisions at the end of the war.[33]

Replacements could keep a division numerically at the correct strength, but the proportion of well-trained and combat-experienced soldiers declined as minimally qualified replacements entered the ranks. Soldiers entering combat for the first time without adequate training and teamwork behind them experienced an inordinate number of casualties. As a result, a division suffered even more casualties in subsequent battles and required still more replacements to keep it at full strength. This vicious cycle was a direct result of the ninety-division gamble. Without enough divisions available to rotate units out of combat on a regular basis, there was no choice other than to integrate individual replacement soldiers into the combat divisions fighting on the front lines. The American army certainly could have administered its replacement system better, but given the assumptions underpinning the army's end strength, the decision to implement a system of individual replacements was the correct one.

Army Ground Forces worked instead to improve the training and quality of the replacements sent overseas, with mixed results. How replacements fared depended to a great extent on how receiving divisions treated them. Men who had time to train with their units, learn survival skills from combat-experienced veterans, understand their role in the team, and get to know their leaders had a better chance of surviving than those who were thrust into the front line immediately upon arrival.[34] The best divisions in the army learned this lesson early and treated replacements accordingly.

Compounding the difficulties many divisions faced in mobilization and training was the fact that only a few of them received any combat experience before wading ashore across UTAH or OMAHA Beach on or after D-Day. The fierce battles of attrition in Normandy pitted mostly untested Allied divisions, backed by a healthy superiority of artillery and airpower, against understrength German units leavened with combat-experienced leaders and possessing many technologically superior weapons. The Allies prevailed by wearing down the German army in bloody fighting among the hedgerows and then penetrating through the weakened German line with American armored and infantry divisions. The campaign was not pretty, but it was decisive.

The costly battle for Normandy has led in recent years to some revisionist thinking about the relative merits of the German and American forces that faced each other on the battlefield in 1944. These comparisons are misleading. Germany began its rearmament program in 1933 when Hitler came to power and enjoyed six years of peace in which to expand the hundred-thousand-man *Reichswehr,* but even that rather luxurious time interval strained the competence of the force.[35] The Wehrmacht seasoned its divisions in campaigns in Poland, Norway, France, the Balkans, Africa, and Russia prior to D-Day. The Germans suffered many casualties, but by June 1944 the Wehrmacht had combat veterans in command of the vast majority of its units. The Germans had an established, combat-tested tactical doctrine. Most German units had solid noncommissioned officer leaders and well-trained soldiers, kept in line through ideological indoctrination and rigid (and often brutal) discipline. German equip-

[handwritten margin note: German mob. adv.]

ment was among the most technologically advanced in the world, especially their tanks and machine guns.

The Army of the United States lacked most of these advantages when compared with the Wehrmacht. American rearmament began in June 1940 after the fall of France, and within two and a half years the first American divisions engaged in combat in North Africa against an experienced enemy. One wonders how the German army would have fared if forced into combat against the French in the Rhineland in 1936 under similar circumstances. Indeed, historian Williamson Murray concludes that "in nearly every respect, the Wehrmacht was not ready" to fight a major war even as late as 1938, five years after the beginning of rearmament.[36]

The United States rapidly produced an army of citizen-soldiers. Germany, on the other hand, had a long tradition as a military state, which eased its rearmament problems. As Manfred Messerschmidt of the *Militargeschichtliches Forschungsamt* states:

> The hundred-year tradition of compulsory military service, with its wide impact on society, state, and mind, prepared the ground for the *Reichswehr* and the *Wehrmacht.* This preparation represented a major asset for Hitler's success in Germany's rearmament program and preparations for war. Without this background, the German military would have enjoyed nothing like the speed of its expansion between 1933 and 1939. This backbone of remilitarization counted far more than the mere totals of divisions, aircraft, or submarines.[37]

Without this tradition of compulsory military service and obedience to the state, Americans struggled to form effective military units in a short period. Inevitably, problems arose, but the fact remains that the achievements of the Army of the United States in combat in World War II far outweigh its understandable deficiencies.

Few American divisions had received a baptism of fire before D-Day. Significantly, of those divisions sent to Normandy that had been in combat before (the 1st and 9th Infantry Divisions, the 82d Airborne Division, and the 2d Armored Division), all performed well. The army also still had to work out critical elements of its doctrine, such as antiarmor defense, at the unit level.[38] Most American divisions lacked combat-tested leadership, had not weeded out all of the incompetent leaders, and found training difficult due to the shortage of space in Great Britain.

Given these difficulties, the achievements of American combat divisions appear in a different light. By the late summer of 1944, the army had largely overcome its handicaps and had reached a high level of military effectiveness—superior to that of its enemies. A more balanced comparison of German and American forces would compare each organization at its zenith, say, the German army in June 1941 and the American army in April 1945.[39] I submit that one would be hard-pressed to choose between the two forces on the basis of technical or tactical proficiency at the division level. Given the pernicious ideological bias of many German units, however, the choice would in fact be easy to make for the people of a democratic society. The Army of the United States reached its zenith of combat effectiveness without the extensive ideological indoctrination and fear-based discipline that infused many German units with their will to fight.[40]

The foregoing discussion does not exonerate the Army of the United States from its faults, and it had many. The intent is to bring some balance back into the debate about the combat effectiveness of American infantry divisions in World War II. Despite the problems the army faced during its greatest period of expansion and the self-imposed handicap of the ninety-division gamble, most divisions developed into superb fighting organizations. Historians have yet to explore fully this development, although John Sloan Brown, Michael Doubler, and Keith Bonn have taken some healthy steps forward in this direction. An examination of American infantry divisions will help to isolate those factors that proved critical to the development of combat effectiveness in the American army between 1940 and 1945, and will put the achievements of the American soldier back into their rightful place in history.

The abundance of industrial resources gave the Army of the United States a large quantity of equipment and munitions, but army leaders still had to form units capable of using these weapons in an effective manner against enemy forces. The sheer magnitude of American industrial mobilization may cause one to overlook the quality of the end product. The success of American divisions on the battlefield was no accident. The Army of the United States contained a solid core of senior leaders who trained their units hard and learned from their mistakes. After an initial period of turbulence, most divisions eventually developed into lethal fighting organizations. The best units used their time out of combat wisely to train and to inculcate lessons learned from battle. Unfortunately, only airborne divisions routinely received all of the personnel and training resources they needed before continuing active operations. Nevertheless, during the critical battles in the fall and winter of 1944–1945, American divisions were able to sustain a high level of combat effectiveness, which they retained as they maneuvered to dismember the disintegrating Wehrmacht and overrun the ashes of the Third Reich.

Despite its late and hasty mobilization, the Army of the United States was able to develop combat-effective divisions that defeated their enemies on battlefields around the world. A handful of divisions were superb near the beginning of their introduction to combat; others took several months to develop their full potential. By the late summer of 1944, American divisions had enough time and combat experience behind them to reach a level of effectiveness that enabled them to defeat their foes from Germany and Japan. They proved the ability of American combat divisions to fight effectively on the battlefield and win. The American people asked of them nothing less, and the fate of the world's democracies required nothing more.

2

The Mobilization of the Army of the United States

The manner in which the War Department manned, organized, and trained its ground divisions was critical to the development of combat effectiveness in the Army of the United States during World War II. The eighty-nine divisions of the ground army used to fight the decisive campaigns of 1944–1945 emerged from a limited base of only twenty-seven understrength divisions in the summer of 1940. The creation of such a large number of new divisions required a massive organizational effort under the leadership of Lieutenant General Lesley J. McNair, commander of AGF. The critical factor in mobilizing forces was time, which was in short supply after the Japanese attack on Pearl Harbor. Scarcity of time and manpower limited the overall number of combat divisions mobilized and caused the army to rely heavily on the workings of a flawed replacement system to sustain its combat effectiveness overseas. The quality of the manpower assigned to combat divisions was also less than desirable. American divisions were bolstered by other sources of strength, such as firepower in the form of artillery and airpower, logistical plentitude made possible by the industrial capacity of the United States, and the fortitude and endurance of the American soldier, who triumphed despite adversity on battlefields spanning the globe. American combat divisions were eventually transformed into highly effective fighting organizations, but only after their entry into combat forced them to innovate and adapt to survive and accomplish their missions.

The quick and decisive German victory over France in May and June 1940 shook the United States out of its peacetime complacency. In theory, the National Defense Act of 1920 had created the Army of the United States, consisting of divisions of the Regular Army, the National Guard, and the Organized Reserves. In the summer of 1940 the tactical units of the Army of the United States existed largely on paper. The Regular Army consisted of eight understrength infantry divisions, one cavalry division, and one mechanized cavalry brigade. The eighteen divisions of the National Guard were neither trained nor manned for deployment in less than a year. Few units of the Organized Reserves existed, even in cadre strength. Field training of larger units, such as corps and armies, consisted of command post exercises and map drills.[1] The Louisiana maneuvers of 1940, which took place during the fall of France, were the first large-scale field exercises held in the United States, but they served mainly to highlight the weaknesses of the army. In 1940 the army needed dramatic expansion and improvement before it could match the awesome combat power of its potential adversaries.

After the fall of France, the War Department and the Roosevelt administration took several steps to improve the military readiness of the United States. On 10 July 1940 the War Department created a separate Armored Force to free the development of armored units and doctrine from the shackles of infantry and cavalry branch parochialism. On 26 July the War Department activated a General Headquarters (GHQ) under the command of the U.S. Army chief of staff, General George C. Marshall. GHQ controlled the four armies in the continental United States, GHQ Aviation, harbor defense troops, and the newly created Armored Force. General Headquarters was responsible for training field forces for combat. Marshall chose the commandant of the Command and General Staff School, Brigadier General Lesley J. McNair, as his chief of staff in GHQ. Since Marshall's other duties precluded his constant supervision of training, he gave McNair almost total control over the headquarters. The establishment of GHQ was another step in transforming the peacetime army into an effective wartime force.[2]

No other officer had as much influence on the development of American combat divisions in World War II as Lesley J. McNair. He was a member of the U.S. Military Academy Class of 1904 and was ranked eleventh in his class of 124. During World War I McNair earned the Distinguished Service Medal (awarded personally by General John J. Pershing) for his work as the senior artillery officer of the training section of General Headquarters of the American Expeditionary Forces. McNair and Marshall knew each other well from service together in World War I. McNair had been instrumental in the tests of the triangular division in 1937 before taking over as commandant of the Command and General Staff School at Fort Leavenworth. He was a rising star in the interwar army, but he did not seek the spotlight. He was soft-spoken and a tireless worker.[3]

General McNair put his imprint on almost everything the army did in the United States during World War II. He favored small staffs as inherently more efficient than large ones. A year after the activation of GHQ, his staff numbered a grand total of twenty-three officers, but these men managed forces numbering over a million soldiers at the time. Incurring the wrath of the branch chiefs, McNair insisted on the same basic training for every soldier in the army, regardless of eventual assignment. He spent more than half his time in the field and flew more than two hundred thousand miles in four years on a DC-3 to visit units in training. McNair championed the tank destroyer, one of the few doctrinal changes he got wrong. He died from friendly bombing during the Normandy campaign at the front, while observing the soldiers he had trained go into battle.[4]

General of the Army George C. Marshall, chief of staff, U.S. Army, poses for a photograph in the Pentagon in January 1945. Marshall was the guiding genius behind the success of the Army of the United States in World War II. (U.S. Army Signal Corps photo)

The U.S. Army that invaded the continent of Europe in 1944 was light-years away from the army of 1940. McNair's task was gargantuan. The Selective Service Act of 1940 provided large numbers of men for the army but magnified the already troublesome problem of creating combat-effective units. After the fall of France, the authorized strength of the Regular Army increased from 227,000 to 375,000 on 26 June 1940. Additionally, the president inducted the National Guard into federal service on 16 September 1940. By 1 July 1941 the U.S. Army had reached a strength of 1,326,577 men. General Headquarters consisted of twenty-seven infantry divisions, four armored divisions, and two cavalry divisions, divided into nine corps and four armies.[5] The army held the first maneuvers pitting two armies against each other in Louisiana and the Carolinas in the summer and autumn of 1941.[6]

This expansion did not come without a price. One of the fundamental problems GHQ faced was the dual focus of its mission, which entailed both readying existing forces for combat and creating new forces from scratch. Training had to take place simultaneously with the vast expansion of the army, which led to inevitable turmoil. Newly activated units drew many of their cadres from existing divisions, and the loss of these men lowered the readiness of the veteran units. Nearly every division sent overseas in 1942 had experienced significant personnel turnover in the months prior to deployment and entered combat with a less than cohesive organization. Given the huge expansion of the army, there was no immediate solution to this personnel turbulence. The army had to spread its scarce professional officers and noncommissioned officers around to take the lead in organizing and training new units.[7]

The largest single problem the army faced in its expansion was the lack of adequate officer and noncommissioned officer leaders. Many junior officers and noncommissioned officers lacked confidence; senior officers lacked experience in handling large units. A large proportion of National Guard officers (and many Regular Army officers as well) were overage or unqualified for the positions they held. After observing one National Guard division in training, McNair found the chief of staff and the G-3 (operations officer) unqualified for their positions: "The blind leading the blind," McNair remarked.[8] The problem involved contradictory needs: to provide adequate numbers of leaders for the force while at the same time eliminating many leaders unfit for positions of responsibility. The lack of adequate leadership explains the reason GHQ decided on a centralized training process, which took many decisions out of the hands of small-unit leaders. After one training inspection, McNair disparaged, "We have verified the inevitable—that inadequately trained officers cannot train troops effectively."[9]

To add to the turmoil, the U.S. Army changed the organization of every type of division in the force at least once after 1940. It converted infantry divisions from a "square" structure, with two brigades of infantry (each containing two regiments), to a "triangular" structure, which eliminated the brigade headquarters and grouped three infantry regiments directly under division headquarters. The intention behind this reorganization was to add flexibility to the infantry division by reducing a step in the chain of command, but it did so at the expense of staying power (due to the reduction by 25 percent of the number of riflemen in the division). The nine Regular Army infantry divisions officially converted to the triangular structure on 1 October 1940, but the eighteen National Guard divisions retained the square structure until early 1942.[10]

By late 1941 the army had come a long way, but its divisions were still

Lieutenant General Lesley J. McNair, commander of Army Ground Forces, in his office at Army Ground Forces Headquarters. No other officer had as much influence on the development of American combat divisions in World War II. McNair died from friendly bombing in Normandy on 25 July 1944, while observing the soldiers he had trained go into battle. (U.S. Army Signal Corps photo)

incompletely trained and inadequately equipped. The Louisiana and Carolina maneuvers showed the weakness of tactics, techniques, and leadership at the small-unit level. They also displayed the weakness of many senior officers in controlling large units on the battlefield. General Headquarters ordered remedial training for all units after the conclusion of the maneuvers, especially on unit skills below battalion level.[11] This order was overcome by events, as the expansion of the army after Pearl Harbor made small-unit training a lesser priority behind the mobilization of new units. The result was constant turmoil at the small-unit level that had an adverse impact on the performance of the Army of the United States in its first battles overseas.[12]

[handwritten margin note: training turmoil to battle turmoil]

The entry of the United States into the war on 7 December 1941 forced the War Department to accelerate an already rapid expansion of the army's strength. On 9 March 1942 the War Department reorganized itself for a multifront war. The War Plans Division of the War Department assumed the planning and operational functions of GHQ. The reorganization dissolved GHQ and created the Army Ground Forces (AGF) and Services of Supply (later redesignated the Army Service Forces [ASF]). AGF, under General McNair, continued the training function of GHQ and became responsible for the organization and training of units for deployment overseas.[13]

The War Department planned to activate three to four divisions per month beginning in March 1942 until it met the desired end strength, although at this stage in the war no one was certain how many divisions the United States needed to defeat its enemies. To speed up the process of mobilization of new units, the War Department bypassed the centralized replacement training centers for the basic training of draftees. Instead, inductees reported directly to their new divisions, where officer and noncommissioned officer cadres trained them under the guidelines of the Mobilization Training Program. The goal was to prepare a new division for combat within ten to twelve months of activation.[14]

In January 1942 GHQ published a plan for the creation of new divisions, and AGF largely followed this blueprint throughout the war. Primarily the creation of McNair's G-3, Brigadier General Mark W. Clark, the plan was a flowchart that guided the organization and training of divisions from their activation until their deployment to a port of embarkation. The initial step was the designation of the cadre for the new division. Clark (who was an infantryman) would work with the chief of infantry to select candidates to be infantry division commanders and assistant division commanders, while McNair (who was an artilleryman) would select the candidates to serve as division artillery commanders. General Marshall would make the final choices from the list of nominations submitted by AGF. Once the War Department had confirmed the division commander, Clark would call the nominee and get his input on key staff selections. McNair then chose the general staff section heads and key infantry and artillery officers. The Army Service Forces chose special staff officers and commanders of special units (medical, quartermaster, ordnance, transportation, signal, etc.). Army and corps commanders chose other officer cadres.[15]

The selection of the division commander was one of the most important decisions in the mobilization process. The ability of a division commander to form an effective command team and train his unit was a major factor in a division's ability to deploy overseas as a combat-effective organization. In this regard the record of the Army of the United States was solid, if not exceptional. Historian Martin Blumenson evaluates senior American commanders who fought in Europe as "generally workmanlike rather than bold, prudent rather than daring. . . . They showed a decided tendency to stay within the odds, the safe way of operating, and refrained from opting for the imaginative and unexpected. Very few of their operations were brilliant."[16]

The person responsible for the selection of division commanders was General Marshall. Over the course of his career, Marshall had noted those officers who, in his estimation, performed in an outstanding manner and merited promotion to positions of increased responsibility when circumstances warranted. The most favored were those officers who served under Marshall between 1927 and 1932, when he was assigned as the assistant commandant of the Infantry School at Fort Benning, Georgia. The lists of school instructors and students at the time read like a "Who's Who" of World War II division and corps commanders.

There were no institutional prerequisites for command, although in practice nearly all division commanders had completed the Command and General Staff School at Fort Leavenworth, Kansas. Most had also attended the Army War College in Washington, D.C. The education in military art and science acquired at these schools instilled in the future leaders of the U.S. Army the tactical and logistical fundamentals of large-unit operations and inculcated in them a common way of looking at military problems. The truly gifted leaders in the interwar army went beyond the institutional framework of learning by devoting themselves to an extensive program of self-study and reading.[17] These men were the exception in an institution that was notably anti-intellectual in its outlook.

A study of twenty-five representative division commanders who served during World War II is illuminating.[18] They were, on average, forty-seven years old and had been in the army for twenty-five years upon assumption of command; twenty-three of those years had been spent in the rank of lieutenant colonel or below. The lack of opportunity to command or work at higher levels in the interwar army resulted in the accumulation of a marginal set of credentials at best for the officers who would go on to command at the highest levels in the Army of the United States during World War II. The typical career of these officers in the interwar army rotated among troop duty, staff tours, schools (as either a student or instructor), and assignments overseas. More than half had previous combat experience in France during World War I; a like percentage were graduates of the U.S. Military Academy at West Point. All had attended the Command and General Staff School at Fort Leavenworth, and three out of four also had attended the Army War College. McNair preferred that an officer serve as an assistant division commander prior to division command, but it was not a prerequisite.[19]

Perhaps successful command of a battalion and a short stint as an assistant division commander provide adequate preparation for command at division level for some people, but for most officers they probably do not. American generals in World War II were hardworking, energetic men, mostly competent but hardly extraordinary. Criticism of their generalship, however, fails to take into account their background and experience. Historian Charles E. Kirkpatrick states:

> The astonishing thing, given their collective background, is that the average officers reared in the inter-war period could manage the fundamental tasks of higher command at all: to organize, train, supply, feed, equip, and move a formation with which they had no experience, at a level of command to which they had probably never aspired, under the stress of war, and then to meet even the most basic standards of tactical competence in maneuvering large units of which they had heard, but in which only a few had ever previously served, or even observed.[20]

The criticism also fails to take into account the ability of these men to learn from their mistakes and innovate to accomplish their missions. Whatever their initial shortcomings, over time American division commanders adapted to the realities of the battlefield and developed the ability to use both maneuver and firepower to defeat enemy forces and seize terrain.

If workmanlike performance characterized the tactical abilities of most American division commanders in World War II, however, one must look elsewhere for explanations of their units' success in battle. To many historians the answer is found in the logistical plentitude the American army enjoyed.[21] A better, if less obvious, reason is found in the organizational capabilities of the forces these men commanded.

The goal of the Mobilization Training Program was to ensure that every division was fully trained and combat ready prior to deployment overseas. Due to a variety of reasons discussed later, that goal was only partially met. The leadership exercised by senior commanders, however, was a critical element in the preparation of divisions for combat. Division commanders established the command climate under which their organization operated. They set the priorities, goals, and objectives for their commands. They were responsible for ensuring that regimental and battalion commanders trained their companies and platoons to standard. American general officers may have lacked experience and skill in handling large units in battle, but the vast majority knew the fundamentals of collective training necessary to prepare them for combat and could work within the guidelines of the Mobilization Training Program to do so. As in most areas involving human endeavor, there was wide variation in the skill and abilities of division commanders, but only a handful failed in their newfound and unexpected role.

The assignment of junior officers and noncommissioned officers was a different matter altogether. The bulk of the junior officers for the new unit came from the officer replacement pool, which by 1942 consisted mostly of graduates from officer candidate schools. A "parent" division provided trained enlisted cadres for the new division. The quality of the enlisted cadres depended on the professionalism of the commander of the parent division, who was supposed to give up his best soldiers but who often used the assignment of cadres as an opportunity to "clean house" and eliminate undesirable men from his unit. The total cadre numbered 172 officers and 1,190 enlisted men, but by August 1942 the War Department increased the cadre authorization to 216 officers and 1,460 enlisted men to provide more specialists to the new division (especially motor transport officers and mechanics).[22]

The cadre received two to three months of training prior to the division's activation. The division commander and his general and special staff officers attended a four-week course at the Command and General Staff School at Fort Leavenworth, Kansas; the assistant division commander attended a special course at the Infantry School at Fort Benning, Georgia; and the artillery commander attended a special course at the Field Artillery School at Fort Sill, Oklahoma. Separate unit commanders went to the appropriate branch school (infantry, artillery, engineer, quartermaster, medical, signal, cavalry). After this initial schooling, the cadre traveled to its new duty station, where the enlisted cadres and the remainder of the officer cadres joined them about three weeks prior to the arrival of the draftees.[23]

The new division spent the first two weeks organizing units and arranging the divisional living area. By then, it was hoped, a complement of training equipment constituting 50 percent of the Table of Basic Allowance had arrived so the division could begin basic training. The division used the War Department Mobilization Training Program as a guide to provide a weekly breakdown of training. The division spent the first seventeen weeks in basic and advanced individual training, followed by a test conducted by an army or corps staff. The division spent the next thirteen weeks in unit training, from company through regimental level. The army or corps would test selected units at the completion of this phase. During the next fourteen weeks, the division conducted combined-arms training, in which regimental combat teams or the entire division would train in large-scale exercises. The army or corps would again test selected units at the completion of this training. The plan devoted the final eight weeks of training to coordination with aircraft and mechanized forces and a review of selected topics. Training was progressive, and units were to repeat any training found deficient by the army or corps staffs. If all went well, by the end of the first year the division was ready to participate in large-scale, multidivision maneuvers, at the conclusion of which the War Department would designate the division as combat ready.[24]

Divisions training in the United States participated in a variety of exercises during and after the completion of their mobilization training. These included basic and small-unit training, collective training for regimental combat teams and divisions, and large-scale corps and army maneuvers in various areas across the United States. Forty-seven divisions and seventeen corps headquarters took part in maneuvers in 1943 alone at the height of the AGF mobilization program.[25] Too many of these exercises focused on training senior leaders and their staffs at the expense of the combat soldier. Writing after the successful completion of the Tunisian campaign in May 1943, Major General Omar Bradley reported to General Marshall:

> It seems to me that our large-scale maneuvers [in the States] are partially responsible for creating one frame of mind which must be corrected by special methods. In maneuvers, when two forces meet, the umpires invariably decide that the smaller force must withdraw, or if greatly outnumbered, it must surrender. And while the umpires deliberate, the men simply stand or sit about idly. No means are provided for giving proportionate weight to the many intangibles of warfare, such as morale, training, leadership, conditioning.[26]

The Third Army even coined a phrase, the "Louisiana Maneuver Complex," to describe the inclination to discard in large maneuvers those lessons that had been learned in earlier training.[27] The Army of the United States lacked appropriate training methods for small units. The army could subject the individual soldier and his small unit to the sights and sounds of battle, but it could not instill in him an appreciation for small-unit tactics and the disastrous consequences that awaited those who failed to master them.

Army Ground Forces attempted to measure the readiness of certain small units through administration of the Platoon Combat Firing Proficiency Test, based on an attack mission involving fire and maneuver; the Field Artillery Battery Test, which required units to move, occupy firing positions, and execute observed fires; and the Infantry Battalion Field Exercise Test, which required a battalion to plan, organize, and execute an attack against a defending enemy.[28] Although these tests provided a rough measure of unit proficiency, they lacked the three pillars of modern small-unit training: a highly trained opposing force to replicate the enemy, dedicated observer-controllers to facilitate training and conduct after-action reviews, and an instrumentation system capable of simulating combat outcomes. Army Ground Forces was also late in developing a well-conceived program for training nondivisional units, such as separate tank, tank destroyer, engineer, artillery, ordnance, and quartermaster battalions. The units that required the most supervision received the least detailed guidance on how to prepare for combat.

Divisions rarely met the optimistic timetable of the Mobilization Training Program, for personnel turbulence severely disrupted their training. The War Department's decision to have divisions, rather than replacement training centers, train draftees in basic skills meant that the process of selecting the best of these new men to attend officer candidate schools, specialist schools, or the

Army Specialized Training Program, or to transfer to the Army Air Forces occurred during the middle of the division's training cycle. As the best of the new soldiers departed, the recently formed division lost a valuable source of noncommissioned officers and the unit gradually became understrength. The provision of new, untrained personnel who arrived at spasmodic intervals to fill the division's shortages disrupted the training cycle. Many times the War Department waited until the division prepared for overseas deployment before filling it to complete strength. Divisions in training also lost men to provide cadres for newly activated units or to fill the need for replacements overseas. As a result, many divisions had to repeat training or deploy with a significant percentage of men who had not trained with their comrades, who did not recognize their leaders, and who did not identify with their new unit.[29]

The centralized nature of the training system in AGF also sapped the initiative of junior officers. Lieutenant Colonel Bryce F. Denno, an infantry battalion commander in the 66th Infantry Regiment, 71st Infantry Division, lamented the lack of initiative in training in a letter to the chief of infantry in April 1945:

> We have long recognized and preached the vital necessity for initiative and leadership on the part of junior officers; yet how can we demand so much of company officers, battalion C.O.s and regimental C.O.s when our training in the States is so centralized? In action, the lieutenant fights on his own; in the woods or in a town, with his platoon. Yet our training in the States forces him to spend every minute of his training time rigidly following a training directive from higher headquarters. In the States, all training revolves about the regiment; yet in action the battalion and the company is the fighting unit. My company commanders have improved a lot, yet their initial training in the States prompted them to look to me for every single piddling decision that had to be made.[30]

To be fair to AGF, a certain amount of centralization was necessary due to the huge scale of the mobilization effort required to produce eighty-nine combat divisions in less than four years. The best-trained units, however, realized that the training of small units and junior leaders was every bit as important as the training of regiments and divisions for large-scale maneuvers.

Lack of equipment and ammunition also hampered the training of new divisions. American industry produced limited quantities of new weapons as it geared up for war. The provision of equipment to Great Britain and the Soviet Union under the Lend-Lease Act siphoned off much of the available modern equipment.[31] Ammunition was in especially short supply, which limited the amount of live fire training that units could conduct. Many divisions lacked adequate training facilities, or units had to spend time building facilities before they could begin training. Lack of equipment and training facilities was especially critical in nondivisional organizations, where training in 1942 "represented a sequence of assumptions, simulations, and expedients."[32]

Equipment and ammunition shortages eased somewhat by 1943, which resulted in improved training. The combat experience gained by the Army of the United States in North Africa had a positive effect on training as AGF attempted to make training more like combat. McNair sent AGF observers out to North Africa to observe battle firsthand, a practice AGF later systematized and continued in other theaters throughout the war. They reported back that AGF training could never be too realistic. Army Ground Forces responded in February 1943 by mandating training courses in infiltration techniques, close combat, and city fighting. These courses featured movement over realistic, war-scarred terrain; the use of live ammunition (both by the men in training and around them to provide realism—machine gun bullets whistling overhead, explosives set off nearby, and overhead artillery fire); and a variety of surprise and moving targets at varying distances. Tanks were to run over men in field entrenchments; training was not to be restricted by unnecessary safety precautions. The applicable directive stated that "troops should be trained to the point that their final attitude toward tanks, planes and battlefield noises is one of fighting confidence."[33] During McNair's tenure as head of AGF, his units used 240,000 tons of ammunition just to familiarize troops with the sounds of battle.[34]

Army Ground Forces was never able to integrate adequately the Army Air

The Infiltration Course at Camp Roberts, California, June 1943. Trainees crawl under machine gun fire with explosions nearby to simulate incoming artillery and mortar fire to acquaint them with the sights and sounds of battle. (U.S. Army Signal Corps photo)

Forces into its training program, even though that was one of General McNair's primary goals for the training program in 1942. The shortage of planes and pilots contributed to this problem, but many officers in AGF correctly guessed "that more air could have been provided for joint training if the Army Air Forces in its thinking and planning had attached more importance to the technique and training necessary for close support of ground operations."[35] The logical outcome of this lack of emphasis on air-ground coordination was the absence of effective close air support in the army's initial campaigns in North Africa, Sicily, and Italy. The army had to learn on the battlefield—at great cost—what it had failed to learn on the training grounds of the United States.

Army Ground Forces developed several organizations for specialized training. These included the Airborne Command at Fort Bragg, North Carolina, established to train parachute and air-landing units; the Desert Training Center at Indio, California, which prepared units to function under desert warfare conditions; the Amphibious Training Center at Camp Edwards, Massachusetts (later moved to Carrabelle, Florida); and the Mountain Training Center at Camp Carson, Colorado (later moved to Camp Hale, Colorado), established to develop tactics and techniques for use in winter and mountain warfare. Army Ground Forces also controlled the activities of the Armored Force at Fort Knox, Kentucky; the Tank Destroyer Center at Camp Hood, Texas; the Replacement and School Command, which supervised training of replacement soldiers; and the Anti-Aircraft Command.[36] Operating under AGF, the Second and Third Armies controlled the troop units training in the United States and conducted large-scale maneuvers in training areas across the country. Gasoline and rubber shortages restricted the number of divisions and corps participating in maneuvers in 1942, but subsequent maneuvers became more sophisticated with the inclusion of river-crossing operations, armored divisions, and limited amounts of close air support.[37]

Army Ground Forces further improved maneuver training by converting the Desert Training Center (renamed on 20 October 1943 the California-Arizona Maneuver Area) in the Mojave Desert into a model theater of operations for corps-level exercises. With this conversion the Desert Training Center not only prepared men and units to fight under desert conditions but also provided advanced training in combined-arms combat. Army Ground Forces cycled twenty divisions through the area in 1943 for thirteen weeks of intensive training under realistic combat conditions.[38] Although the men who endured the harsh climate of the desert might have felt otherwise, fortunate indeed were those divisions that went to the California-Arizona Maneuver Area for this training. The Desert Training Center was the single most effective training resource that AGF mustered in fulfilling its mission of preparing units for combat, a resource that the historian of army ground combat training termed the "graduate school of combined training."[39]

Regrettably, conditions in 1944 relapsed into the confusion of 1942. Army Ground Forces had to close the California-Arizona Maneuver Area in April 1944 due to the lack of service units to support divisions in training. Army Ground Forces also canceled large-scale maneuvers due to the accelerated shipment of divisions overseas as the manpower crisis of 1944 hit the ETO. Thirteen divisions never participated in division-level maneuvers; as a result, the first time the commanders of those units had a chance to maneuver their force as a whole was in combat.[40] The results of all the efforts of AGF over the three years of mobilization were often disappointing. While all divisions received a year or more of training, many had turned into nothing more than training establishments for replacements. The 42d and 65th Divisions, for example, had never maneuvered as divisions, had no combined training of infantry regiments or artillery battalions, and had only 25 percent stabilization for the entire period of mobilization training.[41] By the time these divisions deployed overseas, they "were to a regretable [sic] extent crazy-quilt conglomerations hastily assembled from sundry sources, given only a minimum of training, and loaded on transports."[42] Their performance in combat reflected these deficiencies.

The combat effectiveness of even the best units degraded during overseas movement. "Preparation for Overseas Movement," or POM, was the army's term for bringing units to a final state of combat readiness, moving them to a port, and loading them on transports for shipment overseas. The system, especially in 1942 and early 1943, was dysfunctional. Due to chronic shortages of personnel and equipment, most units received a considerable slice of men and equipment only after they reached their port of embarkation. Most of the new men were only partially trained, and units had to integrate them as best they could before departure.[43] The equipment delivered to the port at the last moment was often of a different type than what the division had used in training. As a result, men trained in the use of carbines sometimes found themselves with 1903 Springfield rifles, and when the Services of Supply issued the new antitank rocket launcher (bazooka) to the troops in Task Force A participating in the invasion of North Africa, no one had ever seen the weapon before or knew how to use it.[44]

Due to the provision of new personnel and equipment at staging areas near the ports, divisions turned these areas into training establishments to acquaint men with new equipment, put replacements through firing courses, and maintain their units' training proficiency. Because of lack of shipping or poor scheduling, some divisions spent months in staging areas that the War Department had designed to hold units for a few weeks at most. The training facilities were inferior to those at divisional home stations. The situation got worse when units embarked, for there was little space or opportunity to conduct training aboard the crowded transports. As a result, combat readiness in most divisions deteriorated between the time they left their home stations and the time they arrived overseas.[45] Overseas theater commanders tried to give newly arrived divisions time to train for a few weeks before occupying a sector of the front. If the situation permitted, commanders would assign new divisions to a quiet part of the line, where the soldiers could gradually adjust to the rigors of combat. Some divisions, like the 106th Infantry Division, which the Germans destroyed during the Battle of the Bulge, were not so lucky.

Personnel of the 36th Infantry Division arrive at Oran, Algeria, aboard the transport *Brazil*, 13 April 1943. Crowded conditions during transport significantly limited training and degraded physical conditioning in transit, causing combat skills to decay. (U.S. Army Signal Corps photo)

The situation improved somewhat after the publication of a War Department directive on 16 January 1943 dealing with the organization, training, and equipment of units deploying overseas. Only replacements who had completed basic training and marksmanship courses could join divisions once they had left their home station. The Army Service Forces could not equip deploying units with new or different weapons from the ones the unit had used in training. The division was to spend no longer than two weeks in a staging area before embarkation. In practice, the army did not always observe these restrictions, but the situation improved in relation to the earlier chaotic conditions.[46]

The War Department never solved the problem of personnel turnover. Too many units deployed to staging areas with large numbers of partially trained men. The result was a frenzied effort, largely on paper, to qualify the men for overseas service at the last minute. The system sacrificed team building, cohesion, and effective training to bureaucratic requirements, as recorded by one official army historian:

A common sight in almost any AGF camp in the spring and summer of 1944 was a group of lieutenants herding a batch of recent arrivals from the Army Specialized Training Program, low-priority units, or converted organizations through weapons-firing and combat courses so that they might be put down as "qualified" and taken to port with the unit. Frequently these newcomers were so ignorant of tactics and so unaccustomed to firearms that the lieutenants dared not permit freedom of maneuver, but felt constrained instead to coach them through the exercises, with frequent admonitions to "get back in line" and "don't fire till I tell you." Circumscribed to this extent, the well-conceived processing became an empty ritual.[47]

One does not have to look much further to understand why some American infantrymen lacked initiative in combat or failed to execute aggressive fire-and-maneuver when faced with opposition in battle. Another reason for the lack of aggressiveness in American infantrymen was their lack of numbers. The ninety-division gamble was a decision that cost the lives of numerous servicemen—primarily infantry replacements—in Europe in 1944 and 1945. Divisions were so scarce that American commanders routinely employed them at the front long after they should have been withdrawn to retrain and integrate new replacements. The lack of divisions meant that units had to accomplish these tasks at or near the front, which resulted in a high rate of casualties among the new personnel. Some divisions literally fought themselves out in constant operations; even the best American divisions, such as the 1st and 9th Infantry Divisions, experienced collective exhaustion when they had been in the line too long. Additional divisions would have allowed for more frequent unit rotations, but due to a series of crucial decisions made by the War Department in 1943, by the end of 1944 no more divisions were available in the strategic reserve.

The Victory Program in the fall of 1941 projected an army of 215 divisions and 8,795,658 men at full strength.[48] The author of the Victory Program, Major Albert C. Wedemeyer, assumed that the United States and Great Britain would have to defeat Germany without the help of the Soviet Union, which was on the verge of collapse at the time. When the Soviet Union proved its ability to remain in the war and tie down large numbers of German divisions, Secretary of War Henry L. Stimson and General Marshall decided that the War Department could safely reduce the number of divisions in the wartime army.[49] In a memo to the Joint Chiefs of Staff (JCS) on 24 August 1942, Marshall proposed a force structure for the army for 1943 of 7.5 million men organized into 111 combat divisions and 224 combat air groups. The intent was to create new units at a rate that would conform to estimated shipping capacity through 1944.[50] On the same day, President Roosevelt requested the JCS to make an exhaustive study of the troop basis for 1943.

The JCS referred the issue to the Joint Planning Staff (JPS), whose report proposed a 1943 troop strength of 10,894,673 men (8,208,000 army; 2,151,975 navy; 360,215 marine; 174,433 coast guard). The planners ran into opposition from Paul V. McNutt, chairman of the War Manpower Commission, who estimated that the armed forces could induct no more than 9 million men by 31

December 1943 without jeopardizing essential war production.[51] The War Department estimated that 10.5 million men would be available by the end of 1943 and 13.5 million when the nation was fully mobilized.[52] The planners considered the War Department figures on available manpower as more accurate. "In the final analysis," they wrote, "the eventual number of men which must be mobilized in the Armed Forces is that number which is required to prosecute the war successfully and, regardless of how great this ultimate figure may be, the economy of the Nation must adjust itself to conform thereto."[53]

The planners estimated that the army could maintain forty-eight divisions overseas in 1943 and eighty-eight in 1944, assuming a convoy turnaround time of two and one-half months and a loss rate of 2 percent. The planners did not believe that shipping capacity should govern the size of the army, however. Divisions not shipped overseas in 1943 or 1944 could continue their training and enter combat in 1945 better prepared. "On the other hand," the planners concluded, "to have need for such divisions and not to have them available would represent criminal lack of foresight and would adversely affect the outcome of the war."[54] The JCS approved the report of the JPS on 29 September and forwarded it to the president. The following day, President Roosevelt approved the troop basis for 1943 as proposed by the JCS.[55]

Despite the president's backing, manpower was clearly becoming a limiting factor in the mobilization of the armed forces. On 5 November 1942 the JCS met with Claude R. Wickard (secretary of agriculture), Donald M. Nelson (War Production Board), Paul V. McNutt (War Manpower Commission), Major General Lewis B. Hershey (director of Selective Service), Elmer Davis, and James F. Byrnes (future head of the Office of War Mobilization) to discuss manpower shortages. The JCS showed Paul McNutt the approved troop basis for 1943, which he had not yet seen. McNutt said the 1.8-million-man difference between the troop basis and what the War Manpower Commission considered the upper limit of acceptable military manpower "would be a matter of vital importance." General Marshall made several suggestions to alleviate the shortages, to include accepting more women into the armed forces and war industries, reducing interior guards within the United States, and adopting a longer workweek for civilians. McNutt pointed to serious objections of some employers to hiring more women. Admiral William D. Leahy stated that the best way to force the issue was to induct more men into the military and force industry to cope by hiring more women.[56]

As the manpower pool dried up, the services fought vigorously to protect their allocations. On the whole, the navy, Marine Corps, and Army Air Forces fared much better than the army in receiving manpower to fill their needs. The dominating size of the army made it a tempting target for cuts, especially early in 1943 when public and congressional opposition to increasing the size of the armed forces heated up. Manpower allocations were the subject of several congressional hearings and numerous editorials during this period.[57] To alleviate the criticism, the War Department undertook a public relations campaign to justify the army's mobilization plan. General Marshall stated publicly:

> There is a feeling in some quarters that we are building too large an Army—that we could not transport it to active theaters even if we had it— in short, the belief that we do not know what we are doing or where we are going. I realize that in a few quarters this reaction may be stimulated by an ulterior motive, a willingness to wave the flag but a reluctance to accept the hardships when the shoe pinches. . . . The assumption that we have not even calculated our ways and means necessarily implies a serious doubt as to our competence to direct military operations.[58]

In the end, Congress proved unwilling to alter the troop basis and risk public wrath in the event of defeat. Nevertheless, the public pressure caused the JCS to review the mobilization program more closely.

The JPS met in April 1943 to begin planning the troop basis for 1944. The planners recommended stabilizing army strength at its 1943 level, while the navy, Marine Corps, and Coast Guard would increase to crew ships under construction and to provide more amphibious forces in the Pacific. Unlike the previous report, the planners now recognized shipping as a limitation on army strength.[59] The JPS forwarded its report to the JCS on 5 May 1943 but noted in the minutes of its discussion the increasing friction between the army and navy over manpower issues now that a ceiling had been reached.[60] Indeed, a special army committee noted a month later, "The Marine Corps has become essentially a land army and such an increase in strength, when the ground forces projected for the Army are being reduced or curtailed, cannot be reconciled."[61] As the war continued, the drain of qualified personnel into marine divisions became a continual source of frustration for army leaders in their quest to field effective divisions, a debate that spilled over into the postwar period with a vengeance.

General Marshall realized the army had reached a crisis over the manpower issue. In May 1943 the Operations Division of the War Department formed a committee (Colonel Ray T. Maddocks, Colonel Edwin W. Chamberlain, and Lieutenant Colonel Marshall S. Carter) to review the current mobilization program and the projected number of combat divisions "in the light of the strategical situation with a view toward their downward revision, with proposals for preliminary checks on scheduled expansions."[62] In its report the committee stated that if the Soviet Union could continue to contain the majority of German air and ground forces (a correct assumption) and if the Combined Bomber Offensive reduced the capacity of the German people for resistance (an incorrect assumption in 1943), then the United States would ultimately need 100 combat divisions and supporting units to defeat the Axis. The committee recommended that the Army Air Forces complete its 273-group program, but that the army should freeze its mobilization at eighty-eight combat divisions for the remainder of 1943. It recommended that the War Department defer the mobilization of the other twelve combat divisions until the first half of 1944 to "permit more orderly organization and training during the remainder of the year and afford opportunity to correct mistakes and deficiencies which now exist." Deferment of the twelve divisions would also reduce the time between the completion of their training and their introduction into combat.[63] General Marshall and Secretary of War Stimson both approved the report, and the War Department published a lowered troop basis in July.

The committee report made sense in the short term. For instance, the decision to postpone the invasion of Europe until 1944 and to begin the Combined Bomber Offensive (Operation POINTBLANK) in 1943 meant that the army needed fewer combat divisions and more air wings overseas in the early stages of the war. Combat divisions stacked up in the United States in 1943, and training space was at a premium. In the long run, however, once the War Department turned off its mobilization spigot, it could not turn it back on. The difficulties experienced by the AGF in completing the training of those divisions already activated, the increased tempo of operations in the Pacific, the formation of B-29 squadrons, and the shortage of replacements combined to doom the activation of any new combat divisions in 1944.[64] After the Allies invaded Normandy, the shortage of infantry replacements further reduced the pool of available manpower.

General Marshall did what he could to remedy the shortage of troops. In February 1944 he cut back the ASTP to 30,000 men, thereby releasing 120,000 high-quality men for the army. Marshall persuaded President Roosevelt to pressure the War Manpower Commission and Selective Service to reduce the induction backlog.[65] Even then, the new personnel only backfilled vacancies in existing units, and the army ended the war with eighty-nine divisions (Table 2.1). As a result, the Allies faced the German army in France in 1944 with only a 1:1 ratio of combat divisions and virtually no strategic reserve. Maurice Matloff, one of the official historians of the Army of the United States, concludes:

> It will long be a question whether the photofinish in World War II reflected an uncommonly lucky gamble or a surprisingly accurate forecast. But few would deny that, in their performance on the field of battle in the critical campaigns of 1944–45, the hitherto still largely untested divisions of the U.S. Army, so largely a product of General Marshall's own faith and struggles, vindicated the bold calculation in Washington.[66]

Whether due to bold calculation or to happenstance, the shortage of combat divisions put more pressure on the few that fought the nation's battles. The formation of another fifteen to twenty combat divisions would have been a small price to pay to provide not just sufficiency but overwhelming power in one of the most crucial military campaigns in the history of the United States. As historian Russell Weigley has concluded, the creation of "a ninety-division army for the Second World War was not an altogether impressive performance for a superpower."[67]

Table 2.1   The Activation of U.S. Army Divisions for World War II

Year	Infantry	Cavalry	Armor	Airborne	Total
1940	20	1	2	0	23
1941	9	0*	3	0	12*
1942	27	0	9	2	38
1943	11	0*	2	3	16*
1944–1945	0	0	0	0	0
Total	67	1*	16	5	89*

*Does not include the Second Cavalry Division, which the War Department activated and deactivated twice.
Source: William R. Keast, Robert R. Palmer, and Bell I. Wiley, *The Procurement and Training of Ground Combat Troops* (Washington, D.C.: Office of the Chief of Military History, 1948), 492.

The mobilization of divisions was not a linear process. The requirement to support an early invasion of Europe in 1942 (Operation SLEDGEHAMMER) or 1943 (Operation ROUNDUP) caused the War Department to activate a large number of combat divisions in 1942. After the Combined Chiefs of Staff made the decision to invade North Africa (Operation TORCH), execute the Combined Bomber Offensive against Germany, and postpone the invasion of Europe until 1944, the need for ground combat forces decreased in the short term. The extended Allied line of communication into the Mediterranean theater of operations (MTO) required a large number of service units to support a relatively small number of combat divisions in the theater. At the same time, the increased tempo of operations in the southwest Pacific also required the activation of a large number of service units to support a small number of combat divisions.

By the time the Allies invaded Normandy on 6 June 1944, the Army of the United States had to provide service forces for five major theaters of operation: Europe, the Mediterranean, China-Burma-India, the southwest Pacific, and the central Pacific. Three of these theaters had little connection with the war against Nazi Germany. The inability of the United States to adhere to the "Germany first" strategy created a shortage of ground combat forces in 1944, when the United States committed its forces to the decisive campaign in western Europe. In nearly every personnel decision made during the crucial months of mobilization after Pearl Harbor, the War Department cut the AGF in favor of more service forces and air units. The total army manpower grew much faster than the number of divisions in the force (Table 2.2). Part of the explanation is

Table 2.2   Increase in Army Personnel and Division Strength, 1941–1945

	31 Dec 1941	31 Dec 1942	31 Dec 1943	31 Mar 1945
Personnel*	1,303,231	3,796,959	5,186,083	5,848,573
% increase		191%	37%	13%
Divisions	36	73	90	89
% increase		103%	23%	–1%
Percentage of Army manpower in combat divisions	41%	29%	26%	23%

*Does not include the Army Air Forces.
Source: Kent Roberts Greenfield, Robert R. Palmer, and Bell I. Wiley, *The Organization of Ground Combat Troops* (Washington, D.C.: Office of the Chief of Military History, 1947), 161, 203.

the pooling of combat and combat support units above division level, but of even greater significance was the growth of the army's service establishment. On 31 March 1945 army strength reached 8,157,386 officers and enlisted men.[68] Subtracting the 2,308,849 men and women in the Army Air Forces and the Women's Army Corps, 5,848,537 men were serving in the army at that time.[69] Of these soldiers, only 2,711,969 (46 percent) served with combat, combat support, or combat service support units; the remainder belonged to service forces, training establishments, replacement depots, and other miscellaneous functions.[70] The number of enlisted men assigned to the eighty-nine combat divisions did not differ significantly from the number of men assigned to the seventy-three combat divisions in existence in December 1942 (1,125,000 versus 1,056,000); the War Department had increased the number of divisions by reducing their authorized strengths.[71] To put it another way, of the 1,966,000 men added to the authorized strength of the army after 1942, only 124,000 ended up in combat units.[72] The proportion of men assigned to combat divisions dropped from 41 percent in 1941 to 23 percent in 1945.

Army Ground Forces recognized the problem but could do little to solve it. After the War Department decision to cap army strength in 1943 at eighty-eight divisions, General McNair wrote the War Department to express his concern. McNair stated "that the proposed distribution of manpower within the Army indicates a serious condition which warrants radical corrective action to effect the assignment of a much greater proportion of the manpower to units designed for offensive combat."[73] McNair made several suggestions to reduce the number of men needed to support each combat division, to include eliminating unnecessary antiaircraft units, using civilian labor instead of army service troops wherever possible, reducing services in second- and third-line defensive bases and defense commands, and better control of theater requests for service troops and overhead allotments. Despite his best attempts, however, McNair could not bring the situation under control.

The War Department abandoned the attempt to raise twelve more divisions in 1944 due to the increasing demands of the service forces and air forces for personnel. The War Department activated the last division (the 65th Infantry Division) in August 1943, and the army had to make do with what it had from that point on. Even then the AGF had difficulty in filling units to full strength. Part of the problem was the sheer magnitude of the wartime undertaking; the War Department never could manage to reduce the number of people listed as "overhead" and "miscellaneous." "I doubt," wrote General McNair in February 1944, "that the troop basis can be balanced because there is an insufficient allowance for the pipeline—the invisible horde of people going here and there but seemingly never arriving."[74] On 30 June 1944, in fact, 456,032 enlisted men served in Zone of the Interior jobs within the United States, a number that exceeded the 445,007 men assigned as infantry soldiers in the Mediterranean and European theaters at the time.[75] The War Department had added men to the air forces, service forces, replacement organizations, training establishments, and the hospital population, but combat divisions received little of the three-million-man increase in end strength after 1942.

McNair emphasized offensive capability and flexibility; small, efficient staffs; the assignment of only those types of units that a division needed at all times, with all other types pooled at corps or army level; and as few links in the chain of command as possible.[76] The overall impact of these ideas made American combat divisions in World War II flexible and mobile but also more reliant on outside support.

Army divisions needed many attachments to function effectively in combat. By the end of 1944, 1,541,667 men served in nondivisional combat and combat support units (separate tank battalions, tank destroyer battalions, artillery battalions, engineer battalions, etc.) as compared with 1,174,972 men serving with combat divisions.[77] One drawback to the pooling of nondivisional units at higher headquarters was the lack of unit cohesion that it engendered, since nondivisional units did not always train or operate with the same division. Corps and armies attempted to compensate for this by habitually assigning the same nondivisional units to support a specific division, but this was not always possible. McNair pooled nondivisional units because he did not think that every division needed these types of units at all times. The AGF could therefore save manpower by creating fewer of them. During the campaign in France, however, commanders found out that every infantry division required the support of a nondivisional (GHQ) tank battalion and tank destroyer battalion at all times, but there were not enough of these units to go around. The infantry divisions operated as best they could with what they got.

To squeeze the last ounce of manpower from the army, on 2 October 1942 the War Department ordered the AGF to streamline the tables of organization of the various types of divisions in the force. The goal was to cut the manpower of each division by 15 percent and the number of vehicles by 20 percent, without cutting combat power or forcing an alteration in doctrine for the employment of the army in combat. McNair directed the work of the AGF Reduction Board, and the revised divisional structures bore the imprint of his ideas on combat organization.

The AGF Reduction Board sat from November 1942 to June 1943 and largely achieved its goals. The board cut personnel from the service and support echelons of the force and trimmed headquarters personnel. The board cut vehicles by providing more trailers for hauling bulk supplies. Complaints from the field about the severity of the reductions resulted in the elimination of some of the proposed cuts, but in July 1943 the War Department issued revised tables of organization for most units in the army.[78]

The cuts of the AGF Reduction Board, as modified by the War Department, reduced the strength of the infantry division by 1,261 men (Table 2.3). The board slightly reduced the strength of the twenty-seven rifle companies that formed the heart of the division, but it compensated by adding a fourth artillery battalion to the organization. Since there were sixty-three infantry divisions in

Table 2.3   Authorized Strength of the Infantry Division, 1941–1945

	1 Jun 1941	1 Aug 1942	15 Jul 1943	24 Jan 1945
Strength	15,245	15,514	14,253	14,037
Rifle Co. Strength (27 Total)	6,021	5,346	5,211	5,211
Howitzers, 105mm	36	36	54	54
Howitzers, 155mm	12	12	12	12
Vehicles	1,834	2,149	2,012	2,114

Source: Kent Roberts Greenfield, Robert R. Palmer, and Bell I. Wiley, *The Organization of Ground Combat Troops* (Washington, D.C.: Office of the Chief of Military History, 1947), 274–275.

the force at the time the War Department issued the revised tables of organization, the total savings was 78,750 men, or enough to fill another five and a half infantry divisions. The board was less successful in cutting the number of vehicles in the division, which was not necessarily a drawback. The large number of vehicles enabled American infantry divisions to dispense with horses, which the German army still used in great numbers. American infantry divisions could conduct rapid, mobile operations when necessary through the attachment of only six truck companies.[79] Even without attachments, infantry divisions could move quickly by shuttling their infantry forward in trucks taken from within the division organization (usually from the artillery).

The infantry division as organized on 15 July 1943 remained basically unchanged until the end of the war. It consisted of three infantry regiments, the division artillery consisting of one battalion of 155mm howitzers and three battalions of 105mm howitzers, a combat engineer battalion, reconnaissance troop, medical battalion, signal company, ordnance (light maintenance) company, quartermaster company, military police platoon, the division band, and a headquarters and headquarters company. Tank battalions, tank destroyer battalions, antiaircraft artillery battalions, 4.2-inch chemical mortar battalions, heavy artillery battalions, and specialized engineer units (such as bridging units) were pooled at corps or army level and could be attached to infantry divisions as needed. In normal operations, divisions would parcel out combat support and service support assets to the infantry regiments, which would function as semi-independent regimental combat teams (RCT). This mode of operations extended to logistics as well. Divisions were not intended to be in the chain of supply except in emergencies.[80]

Each infantry regiment consisted of three infantry battalions, a cannon company (six 105mm, short-barreled howitzers), an antitank company (twelve towed 57mm antitank guns and a mine-laying platoon), a service company, a medical detachment, and a headquarters company. Each infantry battalion was composed of three rifle companies; a heavy weapons company (six 81mm mortars, seven antitank rocket launchers, three .50-caliber machine guns, and eight water-cooled .30-caliber machine guns); and a headquarters company, which included an antitank platoon (three 57mm antitank guns) and an intelligence and reconnaissance platoon. Rifle companies contained 192 men grouped in three rifle platoons; a weapons platoon (three 60mm mortars, three antitank

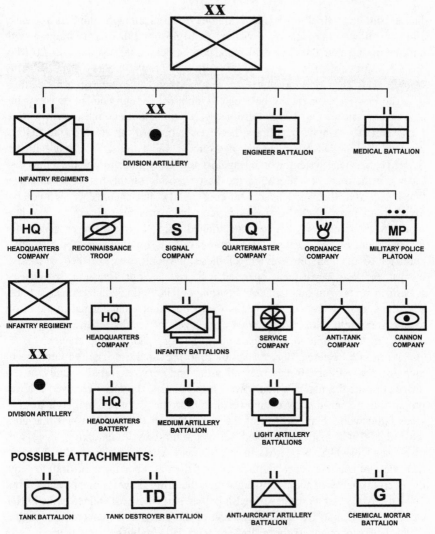

Infantry Division Organization, 1943

rocket launchers, and two .30-caliber machine guns); and a headquarters section. The smallest element was the rifle squad, three of which formed a rifle platoon. Each squad contained twelve men, ten armed with M-1 Garand rifles, one with a Browning automatic rifle, and one with a M-1903 Springfield rifle intended for use as a sniper weapon.

The War Department did not use the economies created by the reorganizations of 1943 to activate new divisions. Instead, it used the manpower saved to redress existing shortages within divisions already activated and to create non-divisional and service units. The tanks and personnel released by the reorganization of the armored divisions, for example, ended up in GHQ tank battalions.

These battalions finally became available in large enough numbers by early 1944 to allow some infantry divisions to begin combined-arms training with tanks, training that the AGF had mandated as "essential" as early as 20 May 1942.[81] Regrettably, the training was too little and too late. The First U.S. Army would invade Normandy woefully unprepared to fight a combined-arms battle.[82]

The War Department not only had to mobilize enough combat divisions but also had to ensure that those divisions were competent enough to win battles. Many national manpower policies, however, hampered the effort of the AGF to improve the combat effectiveness of ground combat units. Problems with the Selective Service System worked against the army in favor of the other services. Furthermore, in allocating the best portions of the nation's manpower that it received, the War Department consistently shortchanged ground combat divisions in favor of the Army Air Forces and Army Service Forces. Furthermore, even for properly formed and trained units, flaws in the procedure for moving them overseas caused numerous problems for divisions about to enter combat. To maintain the strength of those divisions over extended periods of combat, the War Department operated a flawed personnel system that infused American units with hundreds of thousands of individual replacement soldiers over the course of the war. Divisions were consistently challenged in the effort to integrate these men and maintain high levels of combat effectiveness while conducting continuous operations against a tough and capable enemy.

While the Selective Service Act of 1940 provided the required numbers of men for the military forces, not all arms and services fared equally in the distribution of the nation's manpower. In particular, the army received a lower proportion of high-quality manpower than did other services, and combat divisions fared worse than the rest of the army. Part of the problem was that until the end of 1942, many men opted out of the draft by volunteering for assignments with the U.S. Navy, Marine Corps, and Army Air Forces. Most volunteers were of above-average intelligence, and their absence from the draft lowered the overall quality of the pool from which the army drew its manpower.[83] Until 1944 the Army Air Forces received a higher percentage of inductees in AGCT categories I, II, and III than did the rest of the army. The noncombat branches of the ASF siphoned off those draftees who had established trades or skills in civilian life, and whose experience was useful to quartermaster, transportation, signal, military police, engineer, medical, and other types of units. These personnel were also mostly of high caliber.[84] The problem was that infantrymen had no counterpart in civilian life.

A War Department inspector general's report in November 1942 brought the issue of quality manpower to General Marshall's attention. One survey of 7,426 privates in the Army Air Forces found 2,717 (19.2 percent) of them to be either category I or II. Of these privates, over half (1,561) served on "ordinary duty" (positions such as messengers, warehousemen, clerks, guards, orderlies, truck drivers, firemen, and cooks). The inspector general recommended the use of quotas levied against the Army Air Forces to force reassignment of those privates with AGCT scores greater than 100 to Officer Candidate Schools for the AGF and ASF.[85] The report also noted that the army rejected too many inductees classified as "limited service" when their physical defects could be treated (venereal disease, bad teeth, etc.) or compensated for in assignment.

In 1942 and 1943 over 150,000 of the brightest inductees participated in the ASTP, which allowed them to begin or continue their college studies. Of those high-quality men who remained, many left their units after a few weeks or months to volunteer for officer candidate school or aviation cadet training. During the most critical period of mobilization, therefore, the combat divisions drew their manpower from a pool already greatly reduced at the top end (Table 2.4). Since officer candidates had to come from AGCT categories I or II, and most noncomissioned officer candidates came from AGCT category II, the result of these personnel policies was a shortage of qualified officer and noncommissioned officer candidates available to combat divisions as the force expanded.

Certain divisions fared better than others. Those divisions mobilized before Pearl Harbor did not suffer the problems of manpower quality to the extent that many newly formed divisions did from 1942 onward.[86] In addition, the newly created airborne divisions received permission on 18 September 1942 to reduce the number of AGCT category IV and V men in their units to the army average.[87] Since the army average included the AAF and ASF, the airborne divisions ended up with a higher-quality force than other divisions in the AGF. All replacements for the airborne divisions were volunteers with better than average physical qualifications. The 10th Mountain Division, activated in 1943, also had a high number of intelligent and physically superior men. It drew the bulk of its manpower from the skiers and mountaineers of the Mountain Training Center, which had called for (and received) experienced outdoorsmen-volunteers upon its formation in 1941.

Many divisions experienced an acute shortage of leadership, a problem directly attributable to the inequitable division of the more intelligent and skilled portions of the nation's manpower pool. Army Ground Forces required category I and II soldiers to fill its requirements for officer candidates, certain enlisted specialties of a technical nature, airborne volunteers, and noncommissioned officer cadre for activating units. Those soldiers who remained with a division after all of its quotas were filled were, according to one of the official army historians, "a very much picked-over lot."[88] The inability or unwillingness of the War Department to fill its combat divisions with quality manpower reduced the

Table 2.4   Distribution of Draftees by AGCT Score, 1943

	Category I/II	Category III	Category IV/V
Ground Combat Arms	29.7%	33.3%	37.0%
Army Service Forces	36.5%	28.5%	35.0%
Army Air Forces	41.7%	31.3%	27.0%

Source: William R. Keast, Robert R. Palmer, and Bell I. Wiley, *The Procurement and Training of Ground Combat Troops* (Washington, D.C.: Office of the Chief of Military History, 1948), 18.

effectiveness of the Army of the United States in its battles overseas. Only belatedly did the War Department come to this conclusion, and by that time there was little it could do to rectify the situation.

The War Department did what it could in 1944 to improve the quality of the manpower funneled into the army's combat divisions. In February 1944 the department developed the Physical Profile Plan, which classified soldiers on the basis of general stamina, upper extremities, lower extremities, hearing, vision, and emotional stability. Physicians graded soldiers from 1 (highest) to 4 (lowest) in each area. A 1 or 2 in all categories qualified the soldier for combat duty, a 3 limited the positions he could fill, and a 4 disqualified him from service. By June 1944 all reception centers, hospitals, and redistribution stations used the physical profile system in an attempt to send the fittest soldiers into the combat arms. Even so, the pool of available manpower had shrunk so much by this time that even with the physical profile system in place, the army received 5 percent fewer men in AGCT categories I and II than in 1943.[89]

The War Department further nullified the effects of the system by prohibiting eighteen-year-old inductees from serving overseas. Only half the inductees at this stage of the war were over nineteen years old, and since the overseas theaters clamored for replacements, nearly all of the men in this age-group found themselves trained as combat soldiers, regardless of physical ability. The War Department reversed its policy on the use of eighteen-year-old soldiers in combat on 1 November 1944, when the need for replacements became so great that it could no longer keep this age-group out of the replacement stream. The physical profile system made little difference by then, since the War Department had to funnel 90 percent of inductees into the AGF anyway, to make up for the casualties sustained by combat divisions—particularly infantrymen—overseas.[90]

In 1944 the War Department also finally realized that such programs as the ASTP had become a luxury. In response to a memo from General Marshall, in February 1944 Secretary of War Stimson reduced the number of men in the ASTP from 150,000 to 30,000, and thus a large number of young, intelligent men became available to fill combat divisions that the War Department had gutted to send replacements overseas.[91] With the invasion of France approaching, the War Department also reduced the aviation cadet training program to provide more manpower for the ground forces. The transfer of these men had an immediate impact on the AGF. Thirty-five divisions benefited from an infusion of an average of 1,500 ASTP students each, and twenty-two divisions each received an average of 1,000 aviation cadets.[92] The divisions assigned the bulk of these men to the infantry, and training and morale—by no coincidence—soon improved. The War Department also combed out about 200,000 enlisted men from the ASF and AAF in the Zone of the Interior in 1944 and 1945 and transferred them to the AGF.[93]

These actions came much too late. The transfer of men from the ASTP, the aviation cadet program, and the Zone of the Interior service establishments improved the quality of the personnel in the divisions still in the United States, but these men had only a limited amount of time to train with their new units before deployment overseas. If the War Department had assigned these men to combat divisions in the first place, many of them already would have filled positions of leadership in their units. By 1944 the soldiers quickly released from ASTP and other programs were just more "warm bodies" needed to fill gaps in the ranks. As matters stood, many qualified leaders ended up serving in their new units under less-qualified officers and noncommissioned officers.[94] Many ASTP soldiers rose to positions of leadership despite a late start. The 102d Infantry Division, for instance, received 2,750 ASTP soldiers before deployment; about 100 of them eventually earned battlefield commissions after rising to noncommissioned officer leadership positions in battle.[95]

One wonders how many more of these men would have assumed positions of leadership within their units if they had been assigned to combat divisions earlier in the mobilization process. Had the quality and quantity of men who became available to the AGF in 1944 and 1945 been available in 1942 and 1943, the combat divisions deployed overseas almost certainly would have been more effective. The inability of the War Department to focus its efforts on ensuring that a fair share of the highest-quality draftees fought in combat units resulted in a shortage of good junior leadership in the infantry divisions of the Army of the United States.

The problem of quality manpower extended to the issue of replacements. The quality and training of replacements was an acute problem for the AGF throughout the war. Replacements received thirteen weeks (increased to seventeen weeks in mid-1943) of basic and specialized training at a replacement training center, then moved to a replacement depot for shipment overseas. Upon arrival in theater, the men stayed in a series of replacement depots until assigned to a unit. The amount of time spent at replacement depots and in transit after the conclusion of training was variable, but it could amount to several months. In the ETO in 1944–1945, the average combat replacement spent several weeks in four different depots before being assigned to a unit.[96] By the time a replacement soldier arrived on the front line, his physical condition had deteriorated and he usually had forgotten at least a portion of his training, which a unit could inculcate only by repeated drill. Some replacement soldiers did not even know how to fire their weapons.[97] If a replacement soldier was immediately assigned to a force engaged in combat, as often happened, he was likely to become a casualty before he proved of any value to his new unit.[98] By the end of the war, the replacement system had become the focus of endless recrimination and bitterness on the part of the soldiers who endured its workings.

In 1941 and 1942 the army had focused its efforts on building new units. Although it did not ignore the replacement issue, the capacity of the replacement training centers was inadequate to keep pace with losses after the invasion of North Africa in November 1942. Three problems emerged. Initially, demand for replacements led to shipping of soldiers who had not been properly screened in the United States. Some units received replacements whom they had rejected as unfit for duty during the POM process. Second, theater replacement pools were not properly organized. As a result, men spent too much time sitting in depots instead of training, and widespread misassignments occurred. Major General Walton H. Walker, an AGF observer in North Africa, wrote on 12 June 1943: "At the present time, the most pressing question with reference to replacements is the deterioration in the morale, discipline, training, and physical condition of men from the time they leave replacement centers until they arrive at their final destinations."[99] Finally, AGF came to the late realization that thirteen weeks of training for a replacement was insufficient to prepare him for combat.

Theater commanders complained that enlisted replacements were unsatisfactory in regard to physical standards, discipline, and training.[100] The theaters themselves were not blameless; AGF inspection teams found widespread abuse of the replacement system overseas. The biggest problem was misassignment of replacements into specialties other than those for which they had been trained. Some replacements were used to activate new units (often service support organizations) in theater rather than to fill existing units to full strength. Nevertheless, AGF took action to improve replacement training by expanding it to seventeen weeks in the fall of 1943.[101]

The problem with the replacement system was not the use of individual replacements per se but the poor administration of the system. The army recognized the weaknesses of the replacement system and eventually took measures to improve it. Most replacement depots developed training programs to occupy soldiers while they awaited assignment, but the quality of these programs often left much to be desired. Although the administration of the replacement system improved somewhat as the war progressed, successful divisions took matters into their own hands by creating effective systems to integrate new soldiers into units. The problem of replacing inexperienced junior leaders plagued the army to the war's end, ameliorated only somewhat through battlefield commissioning of experienced noncommissioned officers.[102]

By the end of the war, the United States had committed all but two of its ground divisions to combat. In Europe, commanders had kept most of them at the front without relief for extended periods. Extended fronts, continuous combat, and the lack of an organized system of relief or rotation strained the scarce combat resources of the triangular infantry divisions and small armored divisions. To make up for the lack of divisions, the War Department counted on the replacement system to keep American divisions at full strength. As the official army historian states, "The replacement stream became in effect the reserve of the ground combat forces."[103]

Due to the inadequate capacity of replacement training centers to furnish infantrymen, the army ended up stripping many units in training to meet the replacement needs of overseas theaters. These units then had to begin the training cycle over again with a fresh group of draftees. Exactly one year before the invasion of Normandy, the G-3 of AGF, Brigadier General John M. Lentz, wrote to Brigadier General Floyd Parks, assistant division commander of the recently activated 69th Infantry Division, "No matter what strength you attain you will be drilling recruits again before too long."[104] The effect of this expedient was to turn the infantry divisions of AGF into replacement training centers. The 69th Infantry Division earned the dubious distinction of being the most stripped unit in the Army of the United States, with 1,336 officers and 22,235 enlisted soldiers pulled from it between its activation in May 1943 and its deployment overseas in late 1944.[105] In effect, the commanders and staff of the 69th Infantry Division had trained two divisions' worth of replacements and a third division, which they took into combat.

The individual replacement system had its drawbacks. A study conducted by the surgeon general in the Mediterranean theater in the spring and summer of 1944 concluded that the psychiatric casualty rate of men in infantry battalions could reach as high as 120 to 150 percent annually, compared with less than 3 percent in units of other arms.[106] Prolonged exposure to the stress of combat and harsh field conditions, relieved only by death or wounds, cracked even the hardiest soldier, usually weakened by fatigue and nagging illnesses, if he was kept in the line for too long. Individual replacement of casualties as opposed to rotation of units aggravated this situation. Newly assigned replacements did not have an attachment to their units, did not know their leaders, and made many basic errors in combat that usually led to their early demise. Individual replacements were much more effective if integrated into their units behind the front, put through a period of training, and given an opportunity to get to know their leaders and comrades before going into combat. The most effective way to accomplish these goals is to rotate units periodically out of the line. Only in the Pacific theaters did the army achieve this optimum rotation system, and then only by coincidence.

In World War I the United States opted to create large divisions and to keep them on the front for extended periods. Under the square structure, these large divisions had plenty of internal resources from which to draw in order to rotate men out of the trenches at regular intervals. In World War II the War Department, specifically General McNair, decided to create smaller divisions in order to increase their flexibility and mobility on the battlefield. The new division was a good organization, as long as army group commanders had enough divisions to rotate them out of the line at regular intervals for rest, retraining, and refitting. American commanders in Europe never had enough divisions for this purpose and ended up keeping their divisions in the front too long. They took solace in the fact that the replacement system could keep the divisions at full strength, but this was of small comfort to the men who fought, suffered, and often died in combat.

Where could the army have obtained additional manpower to create more combat divisions? The most unlikely possibility was that the War Department could convince the president and Congress to increase the share of national manpower allocated to the army. General Marshall and Secretary of War Stimson did not do this, for they realized that an upper limit of about eight million men was all they could expect without disrupting the wartime economy or impinging on the needs of the other services. Another way was to economize within the army structure to use manpower more efficiently. This was the purpose behind the AGF Reduction Board of 1943. The changes in the unit tables of organization did save manpower, but at the expense of combat divisions, not the fast-growing service establishment.

Other possibilities existed. The army used over three hundred thousand women in noncombat roles and could easily have used more. Of the twenty-two million Selective Service registrants as of 31 December 1942, over six million received deferrals and nearly five million had been rejected on physical grounds.[107] Hundreds of thousands of these men could have been used for limited service within the training and service establishments, thereby releasing more fit soldiers for combat duty. The army could have done better in culling its bloated supply and service organizations, especially within the United States. The cancellation of the ASTP before it got started would have ensured that high-quality leaders would have been available to assume leadership positions within the army when needed.

The army also did not capitalize on the potential of African-American soldiers (then called Negroes or colored troops). Although the official policy of the War Department stated that colored troops would be inducted proportional to their percentage of the population, in fact the army never reached the goal it set for itself in that regard (10.6 percent of army strength). The 1943 Troop Basis provided for 416,898 Negro soldiers out of an army total of 7,533,000 men, which even on paper failed to give African-Americans equal representation in the service.[108] In reality, the various major commands resisted the inclusion of more Negro manpower. As a result, African-American manpower in the army remained below the target goal for the entire war (Table 2.5).

Racism was the predominant factor in the underutilization of minority soldiers in World War II. In 1943 the G-3, War Department General Staff, wrote to AGF: "To organize additional non-divisional combat units with Negro per-

Table 2.5   Participation of African-American Soldiers in the Army of the United States, 1941–1945

	African-American	Total Army Strength	Percentage
Dec. 1941	99,206	1,685,403	5.88
Jun. 1942	178,708	3,074,184	5.81
Dec. 1942	399,454	5,397,674	7.40
Jun. 1943	555,176	6,993,102	7.94
Dec. 1943	633,448	7,482,434	8.47
Jun. 1944	698,911	7,992,868	8.74
Dec. 1944	691,521	8,052,693	8.59
Jun. 1945	694,818	8,266,373	8.41

Source: Ulysses Lee, *The Employment of Negro Troops* (Washington, D.C.: Office of the Chief of Military History, 1966), 415.

sonnel will further reduce support already inadequate, since Negro combat units admittedly are not of the same quality as similar white units."[109] This was an interesting statement, for at the time the army had not yet employed an all-black unit in combat. The bias was equally strong in the ASF, which wrote that the "efficiency of the Quartermaster service as a whole will suffer considerably and [it] will not be able to maintain its place in the team with the other services" unless the War Department reduced the number of Negroes allotted to the branch.[110] Again, this statement stands in stark contrast to the performance of African-American soldiers in quartermaster units in France in 1944. The rejection rate for African-Americans at induction stations in 1943 was 53 percent, versus 33.2 percent for whites.[111] There is evidence to indicate that blatant racism was the cause of the higher rejection rate for African-Americans, which caused the shortfall in Negro inductees that year.[112]

By 1944 the War Department G-3 gave up its attempt to ensure that African-Americans were proportionately represented throughout the army, to include service with combat units. From that point on, the army used African-Americans primarily to man battalion-size or smaller combat service support organizations, with only a small representation in the combat and combat support branches.[113] The meritorious service of African-Americans in the war in Europe shows that the army seriously underestimated their potential during World War II. In listing the reasons for the critical manpower shortages in the army in 1943 and 1944, one must include racism as a contributing factor.

The army also expended too much of its manpower on certain types of units, such as tank destroyers and antiaircraft artillery. The latter category alone claimed 557,000 men by the end of 1943.[114] Since the attainment of air supremacy by the Army Air Forces was a precondition to a cross-Channel invasion, one wonders if the need for antiaircraft units was not overstated. In the campaign for France and Germany, 12th Army Group cannibalized many of these units for infantry replacements. Likewise, the need for tank destroyer battalions would have been eliminated had the army paid attention to the lessons of the Eastern Front and North Africa and had armed at least a portion of its Sherman tanks with a 90mm gun, thereby allowing them to take over the role of the poorly protected tank destroyers in combat.

Eighty-nine combat divisions were sufficient to defeat Germany without excessive casualties only if the United States had strictly adhered to the "Germany first" strategy as agreed to by the Combined Chiefs of Staff at the ARCADIA Conference in December 1941.[115] The provision of more divisions and service troops to Europe would have proved instrumental in reducing the casualties sustained by American forces there. Although the United States could have conducted a scaled-back counteroffensive in the Pacific with the four marine and nine army divisions stationed there at the end of 1942, denuding the Pacific theaters of more combat divisions was not politically possible.[116] Doing so would have released at least thirteen divisions and their associated slice of combat service and support units for use in Europe, since by September 1944 the various Pacific theaters of operation had laid claim to twenty-one divisions.[117] The curtailment of the dual offensive in the Pacific also would have released large numbers of service troops for conversion to combat units.[118]

Politically, however, the "Germany first" strategy was unacceptable to the vast majority of Americans, who wished to punish Japan for the attack on Pearl Harbor. The provision of twenty-one army divisions, in addition to six marine divisions, to the Pacific left the American army in Europe barely adequate to complete its mission. The increased combat burden on the infantry divisions fighting Germany led to the physical and mental exhaustion of the troops and increased casualties. The ambitious dual drive in the southwest and central Pacific in 1944 allowed the United States to defeat Japan and Germany simultaneously, but at a cost. Americans sustained more casualties on the battlefield in Europe than they would have had more of the manpower sent to the Pacific theaters been placed at Eisenhower's disposal instead.

The creation of the armed forces of the United States, which played such a large role in the Allied victory over the Axis powers, was one of the greatest achievements in the history of the American Republic. Of the twelve million men and women who served in the armed forces in 1945, nearly six million served in the ground forces of the Army of the United States, which centered its efforts on fielding combat divisions capable of defeating the forces of Italy, Germany, and Japan on battlefields literally oceans apart. This was achievement on a vast scale, tempered in part by the natural inefficiencies such a massive undertaking entailed. One major flaw in mobilization was the failure of the War Department to ensure that combat units received their fair share of quality manpower and replacements. Another defect was the lack of attention paid by AGF to the cohesiveness and training of small units at battalion level and below. Large-scale exercises such as corps and army maneuvers trained higher-level commanders and their staffs, but they were meager fare for small-unit leaders and their soldiers. Despite the successes of the mobilization system used by the United States during World War II, too many organizations entered the combat arena deficient in the cohesiveness, teamwork, and skills that generally make small units successful in battle. Too often companies and battalions were forced to adapt on the battlefield to achieve the level of combat effectiveness that ideally should have come from progression through the Mobilization Training Program.

3

Citizens to Soldiers: Precombat Training

By 1944 the American army was composed overwhelmingly of citizen-soldiers, men and women who only a few short months or years before had had almost no contact with the military whatsoever. The great triumph of the Mobilization Training Program was to fashion capable military forces from these soldiers given the meager resources provided by the small but competent interwar army. Rapid expansion did not come without a price, however. Continual culling of divisions for cadres to create new units turned many Regular Army and National Guard divisions into little more than individual training establishments until the AGF decided to stabilize them prior to overseas deployment. This process, along with the infusion of draftees provided by the normal workings of the Selective Service System, diluted the distinct character and flavor of Regular Army and National Guard divisions over time. Although these organizations continued to pride themselves on their heritage, by the end of the war factors such as leadership, training, and combat experience had as much or more to do with the distinctions that existed among divisions as the origin of the divisions themselves.

The new "draftee divisions" of the Organized Reserves and the Army of the United States, mobilized after the outbreak of war, faced a wholly different set of challenges. Although these divisions did not incur as much culling for cadres as their Regular Army or National Guard brethren, they were continually called upon to provide replacements for overseas theaters. If the divisions had time to ingest and train new inductees, then this process was harmful but not fatal to their combat effectiveness. When a division did not have time to integrate new soldiers into its ranks, the results could be disastrous. Once deployed overseas, divisions rarely had the time or training facilities available to remedy deficiencies in their stateside preparation before entry into combat.

In World War I the United States shipped hastily organized divisions overseas to France, where the American Expeditionary Forces trained them for their role in trench warfare.[1] The Army of the United States enjoyed no such luxury in World War II. The only areas available outside the Mediterranean for staging American divisions overseas before D-Day were Great Britain, Northern Ireland, and Iceland. The United States sent forces to all three locations in 1942, but the limited space on these islands made large-scale training impossible. The only option left to AGF was to train American divisions to combat readiness in North America prior to their shipment overseas.

Construction of new training facilities took time and energy away from mobilization training. The United States was largely devoid of large-scale training areas prior to 1940. World War II caused the army to expand existing installations or construct new facilities across the country. Between 1940 and 1945 the army conducted exercises in five massive maneuver areas located in Louisiana, the Carolinas, Tennessee, Arizona-California, and Oregon.[2] Individual divisions, however, needed more permanent locations in which to organize and train. Some divisions had to live in tents for the first few months of their existence as they struggled to plan and build training facilities.[3]

Regular Army divisions generally fared better in the mobilization and training process than did National Guard or Organized Reserve divisions.[4] Since Regular Army divisions either were already in service in 1940 or were activated that year, the War Department had a large pool of experienced Regular Army personnel from which it could select commanders and cadres. General George C. Marshall assigned some of the best general officers in the army to command these units. In addition, the divisions received experienced junior officers and noncommissioned officers from the interwar army and some of the best graduates from the Reserve Officers' Training Corps (ROTC). Although subsequent War Department levies on these divisions for cadres to form new units hurt readiness, lengthy prewar training and early combat experience were key factors in making regular divisions generally more effective upon their entry into combat.

The history of the 1st and 9th Infantry Divisions prior to their participation in Operation TORCH illustrates the advantages of the Regular Army divisions early in the war. The 1st Infantry Division, the "Big Red One," is the oldest infantry division in the U.S. Army. The War Department activated the division on 24 May 1917 and never deactivated it after World War I. The 1st Division participated in all major American offensive operations of the Great War, to include the Aisne-Marne, St.-Mihiel, and Meuse-Argonne campaigns.[5] This distinguished battle tradition resulted in a great deal of pride and a certain amount of hubris among the soldiers of the Big Red One in World War II.

The 1st Infantry Division was one of the first divisions converted to the triangular configuration, which eliminated infantry brigade headquarters and reduced the number of infantry regiments in the division from four to three. The reduction of support services created an organization designed to operate as a component of a larger organization. In combat, the division would receive additional combat, combat support, and combat service support assets from corps or army pools.[6] The War Department used maneuvers in Louisiana in May 1940 as a means to test the new triangular structure of its divisions. The War Department recognized the potential significance of the triangular division in combat when it specifically asked commanders to comment on "the tactical mobility of the division" and "the capacity of the division for sustained action."[7]

The report of the 1st Infantry Division on the Louisiana maneuvers of 1940 attested to the utility of the triangular division in mobile operations:

> Organized into balanced and compact combat teams, the division is poten-tially a highly efficient battle unit. It exemplifies speed, power, maneuver-ability. As organized and trained it is highly mobile and may be adapted to a variety of tactical situations. Although not completely motorized, maxi-mum use (in time and space) of its available motors enhances the opportu-nities for success by means of its attacks. Its armament with the ammunition carried will enable the division to sustain combat—limited only by its insufficient available manpower.[8]

In a single paragraph the 1st Infantry Division recognized both the strengths and the weaknesses of the triangular infantry division, which would manifest themselves on the battlefields of France and Germany four years in the future. Specifically, the division report stated, "The commander who fails to grasp the great changes caused by the introduction of the motor and who does not use these motors to the maximum, is bound to fail."[9] On the other hand, the divi-sion also noted that after subtracting those elements of the infantry regiments not normally used in battle (cooks, drivers, headquarters personnel, etc.), the divi-sion had only approximately sixty-five hundred men available to fight. The 1st Infantry Division did not think the number sufficient to sustain combat operations.[10]

The War Department earmarked the 1st Infantry Division along with the 3d Infantry Division for amphibious training early in the mobilization process. As a result, both divisions received excellent and continuous training between 1940 and 1942 as the United States mobilized its ground army for upcoming operations.

The first major amphibious exercise involving the 1st Infantry Division began in December 1940 with preliminary training near Edgewood Arsenal, Maryland. The division used advance copies of FM 31–5, *Landing Operations on Hostile Shores,* to train its combat teams.[11] The division task force sailed on 17 January 1941 and reached Culebra, Puerto Rico, nine days later. There the division conducted joint landing exercises with the navy and three marine com-bat teams. The division continued its amphibious training in the summer of 1941 at New River, North Carolina. The maneuvers were of great benefit in teaching the 1st Infantry Division the basics of amphibious operations, espe-cially the doctrine developed by the Marine Corps during the 1920s and 1930s.[12]

The next major training exercise for the 1st Infantry Division was the Carolina maneuvers of October and November 1941.[13] The division learned many useful lessons in these maneuvers but also noted problems with infantry-

tank cooperation, air-ground liaison, poor radio equipment, vehicle maintenance, inadequate cold weather uniforms, and the capabilities of antitank guns.[14]
Interestingly, the 1st Infantry Division concluded that tank destroyers should
have a superior gun and equal mobility and protection to that of the tanks they
would engage. "This leads to the conclusion that the tank attacker should be a
specialized type of tank armed with the 75mm or a 105mm gun."[15] The War
Department would have done well to heed the advice.

Finally, the division noted that the large-scale training of army-level maneuvers did not improve the tactical capabilities of small units. Its report recommended, "All large maneuvers should be immediately followed by training
of the small units in the details and technique which are quite often slurred in
large maneuvers due to the rapidity with which they move and a constant
tendency of all echelons to develop a maneuver technique as opposed to a war
technique."[16] Lieutenant General Lesley J. McNair and GHQ intended to remedy the lack of small-unit training with a four-month remedial training program
beginning in December 1941. This program was the first of many that had the
effect of consolidating training standards under the supervision of GHQ and its
successor, the AGF.[17] By an untimely coincidence, a little more than a week
after the conclusion of the Carolina maneuvers the Japanese bombed Pearl
Harbor and the United States found itself at war. For most divisions, plans for
retraining fell by the wayside as the War Department ravaged them for cadres
to mobilize new units.

The War Department largely spared the 1st Infantry Division from providing cadres in favor of more amphibious training. The War Department was
fairly sure that any combat operation conducted in 1942 would begin with an
amphibious landing on a hostile shore. The army needed at least one or two
units at full strength and efficiency to execute such an operation.

Immediately after the conclusion of the Carolina maneuvers, the 1st Infantry Division began planning for amphibious training at Cape Henry, Virginia,
which took place in January 1942. Colonel Norman D. Cota, the division G-3,
noted in his after-action report that all echelons from company through division
showed a much better understanding of amphibious operations compared with
the exercises of the previous year. The biggest problems the division noted
were the failure of the landing craft to deliver the troops to the correct landing
beaches and inadequate air and naval gunfire support—deficiencies that the
army and navy still had not corrected when the division landed on the beaches
of Normandy over two years later. The division also emphasized the necessity
of employing tanks in the leading waves of the assault, since their firepower
and shock action would provide "immeasurable assistance" in securing the
beach. Colonel Cota recommended more night training and a joint air-naval-
ground rehearsal prior to actual operations.[18]

The 1st Infantry Division rounded out its training prior to combat in Camp
Blanding, Florida, and Indiantown Gap, Pennsylvania. Before going overseas,
however, the division received a new commanding general. Major General

Donald Cubbison, who commanded the division from July 1941 to May 1942, was one of the numerous generals in the army whom Marshall deemed too old to command a division in combat. The colorful and combative Major General Terry de la Mesa Allen took command of the Big Red One at Camp Blanding. Thus began a love affair between Allen and the 1st Infantry Division that would cause much controversy in the North African and Sicilian campaigns.

Terry Allen was born on 1 April 1889, the son of a charismatic and successful Regular Army officer, Henry T. Allen.[19] He grew up on various army posts, largely in the Midwest and Southwest. Allen entered the United States Military Academy in 1907 but failed his second year. He received another chance but failed again in 1911 and left West Point for Catholic University in Washington, D.C. After earning his degree, Allen took and passed the competitive examination for a commission as a cavalry officer in the Regular Army. He served with the 14th Cavalry on the Mexican border before deploying overseas in 1918. Allen served as an infantry battalion commander in World War I with the 90th Division, which was commanded by his father. He fought in the St.-Mihiel and Meuse-Argonne offensives, where he was wounded twice and earned two citations for bravery. Allen later attributed his emphasis on night operations to his experiences with the 90th Division in the Meuse–Argonne Forest.[20]

Terry Allen cultivated his skills as a polo player while serving with various cavalry regiments in the Southwest between 1922 and 1940. During this period he also attended the Cavalry and Infantry Schools, the Command and General Staff School, and the Army War College. During the mobilization of the army in 1940, the War Department promoted Allen from lieutenant colonel to brigadier general. He served with the 2d Cavalry Division, the 4th Infantry Division, and the 36th Infantry Division prior to assuming command of the 1st Infantry Division in June 1942. Allen was an exceptional division commander who displayed intense loyalty to his soldiers, and they returned his confidence in them through their performance in combat. "Never in my life have I seen a man so worshipped as Terry was and is not only by his men in the First but by every war correspondent who has ever come in contact with him," wrote reporter Quentin Reynolds.[21]

When the 1st Infantry Division deployed to Great Britain in August 1942 in preparation for its role in Operation TORCH, the invasion of North Africa, it could proudly claim to be the best-trained and best-led division in the Army of the United States. This statement is not meant to denigrate the other units of the army but instead reflects the advantages the Big Red One enjoyed as a result of its early designation by the War Department as one of the first combat divisions intended for overseas action. As a result, the 1st Infantry Division enjoyed a high percentage of Regular Army leadership at all levels, low personnel turnover, and good training as it prepared for combat. This was not the case with most other divisions—including many Regular Army divisions—prior to their introduction into combat. The 9th Infantry Division is a case in point.

The War Department activated the 9th Infantry Division on 1 August 1940 at Fort Bragg, North Carolina, as part of the expansion of the Regular Army to 375,000 men. The newly created division received a strong cadre that formed a solid basis on which to build a quality unit. A total of 1,881 officers and men arrived from posts in twenty-four states, to include many noncommissioned officers who were technical specialists in various fields.[22] Volunteer recruits followed shortly to flesh out the cadre for the new division. The cadre's first task was to convert a pine-covered wilderness into a military camp. The men lived in a tent city until Christmas, when they moved into new, wooden barracks. The engineers built numerous roads and training facilities. The experienced cadre trained the new recruits on fundamental soldier skills, with time left over for organized athletics and weekend recreation.[23]

The division suffered a tragic loss on 20 September 1940 when its commander, Brigadier General Francis W. Honeycutt, died in an airplane crash en route from Fort Bragg to corps headquarters in Atlanta. To replace him, the War Department assigned Major General Jacob L. Devers as the commanding general. Devers was a 1909 graduate of the United States Military Academy. He missed combat during World War I, which he spent in training at Fort Sill, Oklahoma. Between the wars, Devers commanded several field artillery units and had a normal range of staff assignments. He was a distinguished graduate of the Command and General Staff School (1925) and a graduate of the Army War College (1933). Prior to his assignment as the commander of the 9th Infantry Division, he had been the chief of staff of the Panama Canal Department. Devers would remain with the division for a little less than one year, but he gave the unit strong leadership and a good start in its formative months.

On 16 January 1941 the first group of draftees arrived to bring the division to full strength. Unlike the divisions activated in 1942 and 1943, draftees composed less than half of the 9th Infantry Division.[24] The cadre trained the new inductees in basic and advanced soldier skills. Within a few months the division had assimilated the draftees and began to grow into a cohesive and capable organization. Training activities included road marches, rifle marksmanship, grenade exercises, calisthenics, close-order drill, bayonet training, and numerous inspections. The division spent the summer of 1941 in extensive field training exercises, to include regimental maneuvers against the 44th Infantry Division.[25] Despite shortages of modern equipment, the division developed tactics and techniques in accordance with the latest doctrine.[26] General Devers left the division on 31 July 1941 to assume command of the Armored Force at Fort Knox, Kentucky. Major General Rene E. DeRussey Hoyle, the commander of the division artillery, took command and led the division through army maneuvers.[27]

The 9th Infantry Division finished its mobilization training by participating in the Carolina maneuvers, one of the two great GHQ maneuvers held in the summer and fall of 1941. The maneuvers began with division-versus-division and corps-versus-corps exercises in October and early November, followed by army maneuvers from 16 to 28 November. The 9th Infantry Division was part of Lieutenant General Hugh A. Drum's First Army, a traditional infantry-heavy force of eight infantry divisions and six regimental-size antitank groups.[28] "These were the days of simulated artillery fire, flour-sack bombs, broomstick guns and beer-can mortar shells," according to the divisional history.[29] The army-level maneuvers were somewhat anticlimactic for the 9th Infantry Division. Drum kept the division in army reserve during the first phase of the maneuvers.[30] In the second phase, the division attacked as part of Major General Lloyd R. Fredendall's II Corps. After two days the division was pinched out of the line, and Drum again pulled it into army reserve.[31] He used the division to defend against an armored breakthrough and temporarily motorized it to conduct another attack. The maneuvers did little to improve the state of training or readiness of the average soldier.[32] More important was the staff practice gained in the coordination of larger combat units in battle.[33]

At the conclusion of the Carolina maneuvers, the 9th Infantry Division returned to Fort Bragg. On 3 December 1941 General Hoyle congratulated the division on its performance. "We have fought a good fight," Hoyle stated; "the 9th Infantry Division is ready for anything."[34] It would have to be, for four days later the United States was unexpectedly at war. In the frenzied atmosphere, the 9th Infantry Division dispersed throughout North Carolina to guard power plants, dams, and bridges.

The 9th Infantry Division was a victim of the dichotomy of the mission of GHQ in early 1942. The division not only had to train for war but also lost many valuable men to provide cadres for newly activated units. General Headquarters planned to use the 9th Infantry Division as one of the first assault elements in any expeditionary force operation, so in January 1942 it assigned the division to the Amphibious Force, Atlantic, for amphibious assault training.[35] The division began training in loading and unloading from ships with mock-ups, rope ladders, and small boats representing transport vessels and landing craft. The division also continued routine garrison and field training to maintain its proficiency as a fighting organization. Due to excessive personnel turnover, however, the division found it impossible to sustain its training level of the previous year.

The ordeal of the 9th Infantry Division was representative of the turmoil that many units (the 1st Infantry Division being a notable exception) experienced in the hectic months of mobilization that followed Pearl Harbor. In January 1942 the War Department ordered the 9th Infantry Division to prepare and train a cadre for the 82d Infantry Division, which the War Department would soon activate at Camp Claiborne, Louisiana. Unlike some divisions, the 9th Infantry Division took its role as a "parent" unit seriously. "This cadre consisted of some of our most experienced noncommissioned officers and a thorough program of training was prepared for them," recorded one unit historian in 1942.[36] The quality of the 82d Infantry Division, soon to provide the basis for both the 82d and the 101st Airborne Division, attests to the abilities of the cadre provided by the 9th Infantry Division.

The provision of a cadre for the 82d Infantry Division in February 1942

88th, \ pull from
r 82nd, \ 9th
101st

did not end the exodus of trained personnel from the 9th Infantry Division. As soon as the cadre for the 82d Infantry Division departed, the War Department ordered the 9th Infantry Division to prepare another cadre to form the nucleus of the 88th Infantry Division, which the War Department planned to activate in the summer at Camp Gruber, Oklahoma. The 9th Infantry Division again sent some of its best personnel to the new division. The fact that Major General John E. Sloan, commander of the 88th Infantry Division, and Brigadier General Stonewall Jackson, the assistant division commander, were friends with many senior officers in the 9th Infantry Division helped to expedite the cadre selection process.[37] The 88th Infantry Division went on to establish a reputation in Italy as one of the best American infantry divisions in World War II, another indication of the high quality of cadres provided by the 9th Infantry Division in 1942.

The 9th Infantry Division also provided numerous cadres for nondivisional organizations and replacements to fill units deploying to the Pacific to fight the Japanese, as well as training a cadre for the newly activated 78th Infantry Division. The drain of experienced manpower from the division degraded its overall readiness, even with the increased tempo of training now that the nation was at war. As the division's amphibious training reached a peak during the summer of 1942, there was little the units could do about the personnel turnover except train the new inductees they received in exchange for the experienced personnel they lost. The trade was not fair, but it was necessary if the army were to expand into the huge force envisioned by the Victory Program of 1941.

In the summer of 1942 the 9th Infantry Division began full-scale amphibious exercises off Solomon's Island in Chesapeake Bay and New River, North Carolina. The amphibious training ended in early September, when preparation for overseas deployment began. By September the War Department had filled the division to complete strength in preparation for Operation TORCH, but the training of the soldiers varied widely. Even so, the 9th Infantry Division fared better than those organizations remaining in the United States. The demands of the TORCH forces caused the War Department to strip men and equipment from many divisions left behind.[38]

The 9th Infantry Division would enter combat under new leadership. On 24 July 1942 Brigadier General Manton S. Eddy assumed command.[39] Eddy had received a direct commission into the army in 1916 and fought with the 39th Infantry Regiment, then part of the 4th Division, in France during World War I. He served with a machine gun detachment and was wounded, but he decided to continue in the service after the war. During the interwar years, Eddy served in various assignments as an ROTC instructor, assistant operations officer in the Hawaiian Department; he also spent six years in Fort Leavenworth as both student and instructor. On 16 March 1942 he reported to Fort Bragg as the assistant division commander of the 9th Infantry Division. On 9 August the War Department promoted Eddy to major general. Eddy proved to be an outstanding division commander during the war; his leadership was a key factor in the success of the 9th Infantry Division in combat.

Due to personnel turnover, the 9th Infantry Division was less than a fully cohesive and capable force when it embarked for French Morocco in the fall of 1942. Nevertheless, with a solid core of Regular Army cadre, the division would eventually develop into a fine fighting force after suffering through its first, dismal combat actions. The experiences of the 1st and 9th Infantry Divisions proved that the army could build quality units from its small, interwar foundation. For the massive effort required to win a war against Germany and Japan, however, the nation would need every combat division at its disposal. In World War II the National Guard divisions would receive their first substantial test as a component of the Army of the United States.

When President Franklin D. Roosevelt began the induction of the National Guard into federal service on 16 September 1940, its eighteen divisions were poorly trained and woefully understrength.[40] The Selective Service Act, passed by Congress on the same date as the induction of the National Guard into federal service, provided fillers to bring National Guard units along with Regular Army divisions to full strength. Large numbers of untrained personnel, however, were worthless unless the army could provide the experienced cadres to train them to standard. Although the National Guard provided over twenty-one thousand officers, less than a third of them had completed a course of instruction in a service school, such as the Infantry Officers Course at Fort Benning, Georgia.[41] Too many National Guard divisions foundered in 1940 and 1941 as a result of poor leadership. Discipline and morale in National Guard units were poor, staff work was weak, and senior National Guard commanders were slow to adapt themselves to the changing concepts of warfare. Marshall and McNair acted after the Louisiana maneuvers of 1941 to purge National Guard divisions of the incompetent and unfit.[42]

To be fair to the senior National Guard leadership, none of the Regular Army division commanders in 1940 went on to command divisions in wartime either, although three of them were promoted and commanded at higher echelons. The problem was that the interwar promotion system produced division commanders who were simply too old to function well under the strain of combat. Unfortunately for National Guard senior leaders, when General McNair nominated replacements to command divisions, he naturally dipped into the pool of talent with which he and General Marshall were most familiar—the Regular Army officers with whom they had served for three decades. As a result, only in rare instances did National Guard officers rise above the rank of colonel and command of a regiment. By the end of the war, only one National Guard division—the 37th Infantry Division from Ohio—was commanded by the same person who had commanded it in 1941 (Major General Robert S. Beightler).[43]

This failure to promote National Guard officers to command of divisions was the result of extensive discussions between Marshall and McNair. On 7 October 1941 McNair wrote a memorandum to Marshall in which he gave his assessment of National Guard division commanders:

26th—Eckfeldt, Mass.—50—live but green; may learn; one of the few promising ones.

27th—Haskell—63—should go out for more than age.

28th—Martin, Pa.—62—no question but that he should go.

29th—Reckord, Md.—62—good administrator but should go.

30th—Russell, Ga.—52—pleasing; leader of a sort; but not a military comdr. Should go sooner or later.

31st—Persons, Ala.—53—comds effectively; question is whether he has sufficient military background; one of the most promising ones.

32d—Fish, Wis.—62—fine man; experienced in Nat. Gd., but believed lacking in military knowledge; should go sooner or later, preferably sooner.

33d—Lawton, Ill.—57—dubious; performance thus far shows force, but not too well directed; military knowledge too limited.

37th—Beightler, Ohio—49—One of the best Nat. Gd. comdrs if he stays with the job.

41st—White, Ore.—61—Strong comdr, but military knowledge none too full. However, one of the best.

44th—Powell, N.J.—48—Incompetent; Fredendall said would be reclassified.

45th—Key, Okla.—52—Forceful; impressive; and that's about all. Dubious for the long pull.[44]

McNair followed this memorandum with another on 24 October 1941 in which he stated:

I am unalterably opposed to promoting any NG brig gen now on the horizon to maj gen and assigning him to comd a NG div.... "token" promotions by way of appeasement will harm rather than improve the situation. ... The situation today, as I see it, is not the same as in the World War, when div had merely to "go down the alley." Today the tempo of all operations is speeded tremendously, but the difficulty is that the upper story of our comdrs is not speeded correspondingly.[45]

Did McNair have a bias against senior National Guard officers? Undoubtedly. Was it justified? Given the lack of training in the National Guard during the interwar years and therefore the lack of experience and professional qualifications of National Guard officers, probably. General Marshall summed up the feelings of most Regular Army officers when he wrote to Under Secretary of War Robert P. Patterson, "The RA units are not bothered by poor morale because the officers have attained professional knowledge either at schools or through practical exp. NG officers have not had these opportunities, and the morale of their units reflects the deficiency."[46]

General Beightler may have survived because he was not afraid to remove incompetent officers of his own division without prodding from above.[47] Many National Guard divisions, however, suffered from a severe case of the "good old boy" syndrome. Colonel (Ret.) Robert C. Works, who as a major served as operations officer of the West Virginia Maneuver Area and was able to evaluate six reserve and National Guard divisions during training, relates an experience in which a National Guard regimental commander asked him to rate the officers under his command. Major Works thought that most of them were good, with the conspicuous exception of the regimental adjutant, a captain. When Major Works gave his evaluation, the regimental commander stated that he knew of the problem but could not relieve the adjutant since the captain's father owned the only bank in the regimental commander's hometown. "This nepotism was typical of the 4 or 5 NG regiments I observed in this tough training area," Colonel Works states.[48]

In the midst of the chaos of mobilization, most National Guard divisions slowly improved their capabilities. Many of these divisions would go on to earn excellent reputations for their performance in combat in 1944 and 1945. How did the army transform them into effective combat units? An examination of the mobilization and training of the 29th and 30th Infantry Divisions shows in part how the process worked.

The War Department inducted the 29th Infantry Division, nicknamed the "Blue and Gray" Division because its component units came from Virginia, Maryland, and Pennsylvania, into federal service on 3 February 1941 at Fort Meade, Maryland. The interwar period had not been kind to the division. Like other National Guard divisions, the component units of the Blue and Gray Division "functioned as best they could with civilian volunteers handicapped by a public imbued with a disarmament psychology and apathetic to any form of military endeavor."[49] The division trained as best it could during limited weekend drills and two-week summer training camps, but these were insufficient preparation for combat.[50] The order bringing the division into federal service set off a "frantic scramble and hasty and makeshift preparation" as civilian-soldiers "who had dabbled in the military life of their communities" now faced the ultimate reason for their division's existence.[51]

To make up the shortfall in commissioned officers, the division commander, Major General Milton A. Reckord, established a ten-day officer candidate school in Baltimore in January 1941.[52] The men who went through this course received their commissions in the Army of the United States on 3 February 1941, but one wonders how prepared they were to take up their responsibilities after such a short training period. In the 29th Infantry Division, however, seasoned soldiers were a scarce commodity.[53]

The division faced two major personnel tasks simultaneously. First, it had to weed out the incompetent and physically unfit officers and men in its ranks. Second, it had to fill its ranks with replacements brought into service through Selective Service and train the new men in the fundamentals of soldiering. The draftees began to arrive at Fort Meade in April.[54] The purge would take longer.

Throughout the spring and summer of 1941, the 29th Infantry Division conducted basic and unit training at Fort Meade. Meanwhile, the division attempted to cope with a basic problem of the National Guard system. The draftees and officers who had come into the division after mobilization felt the National Guardsmen kept them from advancing, while the National Guardsmen felt the Regular Army officers at higher levels discriminated against them. The division historian felt that this friction "was ironed out . . . through common experience. Most of this was cleared up in the mud and dust of the field."[55] The division historian was somewhat optimistic in his outlook, for the ill feelings generated between the "ins" (National Guardsmen) and the "outs" (everyone else) in the division would last until the crucible of combat forged them all into one team.[56]

The 29th Infantry Division moved to Fort A. P. Hill in Virginia for field training in September prior to its participation in the Carolina maneuvers. The division—especially the higher-level commanders and staff officers—benefited from the training received before and during the maneuvers. At lower levels the training was of lesser value. One participant recalled:

> The maneuvers, at my level, were a huge, uncomfortable, motorized camping trip. The antitank platoon, now equipped with inadequate 50-caliber machine guns, shifted from place to place, ostensibly protecting the 2d Battalion from trucks bearing signs designating them as "tanks," which never appeared. The top commanders and staffs that supplied and ordered us about may have received useful training, but I learned nothing I did not already know breathing dust and sleeping on the ground.[57]

Despite the poor training at lower echelons of the command, after the Carolina maneuvers the division was at a higher state of readiness than it was upon activation. After 7 December 1941, however, the needs of national defense and mobilization would combine to actually lower the readiness of the division.

In the wake of the Japanese attack on Pearl Harbor, the War Department scattered the division from Pennsylvania to North Carolina to guard key installations. A month later, General Reckord took command of the III Corps Area, an administrative command. General Marshall wanted younger generals to command American divisions in combat, and Reckord's advanced age (sixty-one) marked him for relief. The division's new commander, Major General Leonard T. Gerow, was a Regular Army officer. As a 1911 graduate of the Virginia Military Institute, Gerow was a popular choice among the many Virginians in the division.[58]

Gerow had served four tours during the interwar period in the War Department, mostly on the planning staff. His final assignment in the War Department was as an assistant chief of staff in the War Plans Division, where he was succeeded by Brigadier General Dwight D. Eisenhower. General Gerow went on to command V Corps during the Normandy invasion and throughout the campaign for France and Germany in 1944 and 1945. He was fifty-three years old when he took command of the 29th Infantry Division and was considered by some officers to be the best infantry tactician in the U.S. Army.

In February 1942 the War Department reorganized the division into a triangular configuration. Although the reorganization streamlined the division, the process involved a short-term dislocation while units adjusted to the new configuration. The War Department stripped a total of eighty-six officers from the division between April and June to augment cadres in other units.[59] Finally, the division supplied nearly sixteen hundred men to officer candidate schools before deploying overseas.[60]

In May 1942 the 29th Infantry Division moved permanently to Fort A. P. Hill, which had better training facilities than Fort Meade. Gerow worked his division hard in training in preparation for the VI Corps maneuvers in the Carolina Maneuver Area. The maneuvers ran from July to August and involved the 4th Motorized Division, the 29th and 36th Infantry Divisions, and the 2d Armored Division. Afterward, the 29th Infantry Division was ordered to Camp Blanding, Florida. Before the division left the Carolinas, however, the War Department transferred nearly the entire 2d Battalion, 175th Infantry, from the division to the Army War Show for the purpose of touring the United States to stimulate the sale of War Bonds.[61] In the midst of another change of station, the division coped yet again with a major reorganization to reconstitute the lost battalion.

The 29th Infantry Division closed on Camp Blanding by 19 August. In the finest army tradition, within three weeks of arrival the division was alerted for overseas service. A week later the War Department ordered the division to Camp Kilmer, New Jersey. The orders caught the division by surprise, and units scrambled to get men back from leave.[62] Despite the frantic pace of the movement, the division executed the transfer smoothly. At Camp Kilmer the division received new equipment and supplies, but it remained over three thousand men understrength.[63]

The division embarked from New York harbor in two elements. The first sailed on the *Queen Mary* on 26 September, the second on the *Queen Elizabeth* on 5 October. Units conducted the movement from Camp Kilmer to the harbor under cover of darkness. Most of the men were nervous.[64] They did not realize they would wait another year and a half before seeing combat.

The fast passenger liners made the journey to Great Britain in only a week. Their speed allowed them to dispense with the slower convoy procedure that most vessels used. The *Queen Mary* went a little too fast, in fact; the ship damaged her bow when she rammed and sank a Royal Navy corvette as she steamed toward an anchorage in the Firth of Clyde, Scotland.[65] The soldiers, intent on their games of craps and poker in the lounges, paid little attention.

The 29th Infantry Division finally settled down in Tidworth Barracks in Hampshire, west of London. Here the division found itself on Salisbury Plain, the best military training area in England. General Gerow took advantage of the facilities to train his men hard. On 5 January 1943 the Blue and Gray Division was still short over thirty-five hundred enlisted men and faced a period of training replacements.[66] Training took place seven days a week until late January 1943, when the pace throttled back to six days a week as it became clear that the division would not deploy to North Africa.

Small-unit training occupied the division's attention early in 1943. Each platoon underwent a combat proficiency test. Every soldier had to complete a twenty-five-mile march. Those who dropped out were given a physical examination; those who failed the physical were transferred from the division.[67] General Gerow went on an inspection of the U.S. II Corps in Tunisia and witnessed a portion of the battle for Hill 609, the famous "Longstop Hill" on the road to Bizerte. Upon his return to England, Gerow transmitted to the officers of the division the combat lessons he acquired during his trip.[68]

In late May and early June the 29th Infantry Division moved to Devonshire and Cornwall, where it took over the mission of the British 55th Division to defend the area. Intensive training continued in the murky moors of southwest England. Replacements came in to bring units up to strength.[69] The move also brought the division closer to the Amphibious Assault Training Centers near Barnstaple on the north coast of Devon and at Slapton Sands on the south coast. Here the division could conduct realistic amphibious training prior to the invasion of the Continent. General Gerow, however, would not remain with the division to oversee its amphibious training. On 17 July 1943 the War Department promoted Gerow to command of V Corps. The 29th Infantry Division would serve in V Corps under a new commander, Major General Charles H. Gerhardt.

Gerhardt was born on 5 June 1895 in Lebanon, Tennessee, the son of an infantry officer who was a graduate of the United States Military Academy.[70] He grew up in military life at army posts in the United States, Alaska, and the Philippines. He entered the Military Academy in 1913 but graduated early, on 16 April 1917, due to the outbreak of war. Gerhardt ranked fiftieth out of a class of 139 and was commissioned in the cavalry.

During World War I Gerhardt served as aide to Major General W. M. Wright, commander of a training group in the Vosges Mountains and later commanding general of the 89th Division. Gerhardt served with the occupation forces in Germany until 1919. His interwar service included troop duty with cavalry regiments in Texas, Iowa, and California; instructor duty at Fort Leavenworth and tactical officer duty at the Military Academy; attendance at Command and General Staff School; and overseas duty as G-1 (personnel officer) of the Philippine Department. In the Philippines Gerhardt received the attention of some future superstars. His commander was General Douglas MacArthur, Major Dwight Eisenhower was the chief of staff, and Major J. Lawton Collins was the G-3.

In 1940 and 1941 Gerhardt served in GHQ under General McNair and earned his first star. Gerhardt commanded the 2d Brigade, 1st Cavalry Division, in the Louisiana maneuvers of 1941. He performed well enough that in May

1942 General Marshall gave him command of the 91st Infantry Division. Gerhardt activated and trained the division until it passed its AGF tests. Marshall then sent him to England to take over the 29th Infantry Division.

General Gerhardt liked what he saw when he arrived in England. "The special staff was especially strong and the infantry regiments, particularly the 116th, were in good shape, and the artillery under [Brigadier] General [William H.] Sands was superior," he would write later.[71] The command team got even stronger in mid-September 1943 when Brigadier General Norman D. Cota, the combat-experienced chief of staff of the 1st Infantry Division, replaced Brigadier General George M. Alexander as the assistant division commander. Cota liked working with troops and shied away from spending long hours in division headquarters.[72] Gerhardt immediately put him to work running battalion training exercises similar to AGF tests.[73]

General Gerhardt earned the admiration and respect of many officers and men in the 29th Infantry Division, but his personality had an abrasive side that probably prevented him from being loved the way the 1st Infantry Division loved Terry Allen. One battalion commander who served in the 29th Infantry Division later recorded his impressions of Gerhardt:

> A gutty, pushy, arrogant little bastard, admired and respected by many . . . hated by probably a greater number. He knew his stuff, was aggressive, and took care of the men he knew to be loyal to him. . . . He was also impatient of inability or slowness. . . . My net impression of Charlie is that he was a very fine, egocentric little bastard with a Napoleonic complex, and that if he had had a bit more judgment he would have been a great leader.[74]

Another officer had this impression of Gerhardt:

> Physically and by temperament, he conformed to General Philip Sheridan's specifications for a cavalryman, which he had been before the war: short, wiry, daring, and quick. Everything about him was explosive: speech, movements, temper. He dominated the division by knowing exactly what he wanted done, discarding those who failed to produce it, and rewarding those who did.[75]

Gerhardt proved to be a capable division commander in combat. In the near term, however, he had cause for impatience with some of his subordinates, for despite Gerow's best efforts, the Blue and Gray Division was still not a cohesive fighting team when Gerhardt took command.

Contrary to the statement of the division historian that the infighting between the National Guardsmen and the rest of the division ended in training, much animosity still existed in the fall of 1943. The War Department devised the National Guard system based on the idea that men from the same area would function as a cohesive team in combat. During World War II, however, the normal functioning of the mobilization and replacement system of the Army of the United States caused all National Guard divisions to be filled mostly with personnel outside the unit's home area. The National Guardsmen resented the newcomers, especially Regular Army officers who took over coveted positions of leadership and command.[76]

On the other hand, newcomers to the division often felt shunned by the National Guard clique. One officer from the 3d Battalion, 115th Infantry Regiment, penned some confidential notes on the state of morale in the division at the time.[77] The officer based his conclusions on observations of his own regiment and from talks with officers and men throughout the division. "The 'home town boy' still gets the breaks," the officer stated. "The favoritism is a morale-lowering factor. Many competent and patriotic officers and men have been thwarted, frustrated, harried, [and] persecuted at every turn when they have tried to remedy the situation." National Guard officers also sometimes had trouble instilling discipline in their units, since after the war they had to go back and live with the people whom they would punish.

When Gerhardt took command, the officer noted a marked change for the better in morale. General Gerhardt encouraged the rise of competent officers and noncommissioned officers, regardless of their source of commission or regional affiliation. "Everyone gained a very favorable opinion of Gerhardt when he first took over," the officer wrote. "In everyone's opinion he's a 'soldier's soldier.' . . . He's been a tonic for most of the men in the Division." Nevertheless, the officer still felt the problem of morale was "critical." The problem stemmed from the company and battalion commanders, most of them National Guardsmen, who the officer felt were "fundamentally unqualified for their jobs." Finally, the officer complained about inequitable punishment given to draftees and reserve officers compared with that given to National Guardsmen for real or imagined offenses.

The result of the National Guard system in the 29th Infantry Division was a lack of initiative at lower levels:

> Restricted, parochial, small town outlooks on the part of these commanders [have] also resulted in many officers being unwilling to attempt to better the type of training received by the men because they knew their COs would not sanction anything but the old, tried-and-true routine. . . . Many officers—in fact, this has happened on many occasions in *every* company—have been practically shut out of the running of their companies, because company commanders have preferred to take their old-line NG [National Guard] NCOs into their confidence while leaving out their junior officers.[78]

The leadership problems of the division adversely affected its preparation for combat. The officers and men who were not National Guardsmen felt discriminated against by those "in the favored graces of state politics." Although Gerhardt instituted changes for the better, much still remained to be done "to eliminate the remaining jealousy and favoritism." Despite its problems, however, the officer felt the division would give a good account of itself in combat, for the competent officers and enlisted men would "not be hindered by mistakes or stupidities when the chips are down."[79]

General Gerhardt had the best tonic for the situation—hard training. He was ruthless toward his subordinate officers and demanded a high state of discipline and competence from his soldiers.[80] Aside from the infantry battalion training exercises and tests, each infantry regiment underwent intensive amphibious training at the Assault Training Center on the north coast of Devon in November 1943.[81] Here the army practiced the basic techniques it would use in the upcoming cross-Channel invasion.

In 1944 training intensified as the invasion drew nearer. The 175th Regimental Combat Team (RCT) participated in Exercise DUCK from 29 December 1943 to 4 January 1944 at Slapton Sands. The results of Exercise DUCK were not good. Seasickness in some units reached 50 percent; the assault battalions showed a lack of initiative, aggressiveness, and teamwork on the beach; and combined-arms teamwork was poor. Wave after wave piled up on the beach, and units advanced only after much confusion. Officers and noncommissioned officers exhibited a lack of leadership and a basic knowledge of tactics.[82] The after-action report concluded, "Had this been an actual operation, it is extremely doubtful if many men would have left the beach alive."[83]

General Gerow, the V Corps commander, summed up his thoughts on the exercise as follows:

> After watching this exercise and similar ones at the A.T.C. [Assault Training Center], I am convinced that a successful daylight landing on a well-defended beach is dependent on such a thorough saturation of the beach area by bombing . . . that wire, mines and gun emplacements are largely demolished and the defenders' morale shaken. . . . Deliberate removal of wire, mines and other obstacles on open beaches cannot be done by foot troops in the face of heavy aimed fire.[84]

Despite these dire predictions, none of the favorable conditions Gerow described would prevail on OMAHA Beach on 6 June 1944. In the end, the skill and bravery of the troops mattered as much as the massive firepower assembled behind them in the English Channel. Gerow did get one thing right, however—the need for more practice in landing operations.[85]

Perhaps because of the poor performance of the 175th RCT during Exercise DUCK, General Gerhardt subsequently designated the 116th RCT as the lead assault element of the division for Operation OVERLORD. The 116th RCT participated in three major amphibious training exercises: DUCK 2 (7–15 February), FOX (9–12 March), and FABIUS I (2–5 May), the latter two in conjunction with the 1st Infantry Division. DUCK 2 went much more smoothly than DUCK. The chief umpire of DUCK 2 noted, "The 116th Infantry and attached and supporting units did a fine job. The landing, the assault of the beach defenses, and the attack inland to the division beachhead line [were]

Rocket-launcher teams cover the movement of infantry off the beach at the Assault Training Center in Devon, England, 23 October 1943. The reality on D-Day in Normandy seven and one-half months later was quite different. (U.S. Army Signal Corps photo)

aggressive. The team work between the infantry and supporting arms deserved commendation."[86] However, the soldiers still displayed characteristics of units unseasoned by combat: bunching up, improper use of cover and concealment, men standing upright in the face of enemy fire, and poor flank security.[87]

Alarmingly, the Ninth Tactical Air Force participated in neither DUCK nor DUCK 2, so the division was not able to test its air-ground coordination system. Furthermore, naval gunfire did not destroy the pillboxes and gun positions on the beach prior to the landing. The after-action report attributed the problem not to poor accuracy but to the low volume of fire used.[88] The 29th Infantry Division thus missed a major lesson in the preparation of beaches for amphibious invasion: the need for highly accurate fire to destroy point targets.

Exercises FOX and FABIUS I were dress rehearsals for the invasion of OMAHA Beach, with both the 116th RCT from the 29th Infantry Division and the 16th RCT from the 1st Infantry Division taking part. V Corps received both naval and air support for the exercises, to include the use of rocket-firing landing craft, naval gunfire, and air missions from B-26 bombers and P-47 fighter-bombers.[89] Even so, air support was still limited, as one can see from the comments of the Ninth Air Support Command spokesman at the after-action review:

I would like to admit that our extent of participation in amphibious exercises of this type is rather limited. We participated in Exercises "DUCK" and "FOX," and were conspicuous by our absence. The only people actually knowing and seeing us were the SOS [Services of Supply], when we hit their chow line, and the Navy, when we ate their white bread.[90]

The result of the lack of air-ground training in Exercise FOX was the inability of combat forces to receive on-call close air support when they needed it badly on the beach. D-Day would be no different.

One of the problems that continued to haunt the ground forces in amphibious training was landing on the wrong beaches. The commander of the 6th Engineer Special Brigade in FOX stated, "I think we can never get just at the point where we are sure we will land on the right beaches, but we can get just as close as possible. In the event we do land on the wrong one, we will discover the error right away."[91] The commander declined to speculate on what would happen once the error was discovered. The commander of the 116th Infantry Regiment, Colonel Charles Canham, noted:

In my opinion, there is too much landing on wrong beaches. The last assault company landing on Baker Red was taken approximately 1200–1500 yards south of their beach. Other units were landed in the 16th Infantry area. It seemed to be the rule to get them on the wrong beach. . . . If you can't get in on the right beach in daylight, God knows, they might land you in Russia in the real thing.[92]

Little did the commanders realize how close Exercise FOX would come to the "real thing" on 6 June 1944.

The 29th Infantry Division was as well trained as General Gerhardt and the army could make it when it embarked for the invasion of the Continent. The soldiers were in good physical condition and confident from their long period of intensive training. One officer remarked on the condition of his battalion as it moved to its marshaling area, "I was impressed that the battalion was at its peak, as ready as an outfit could be. . . . I was not aware of it, but we were never to look exactly that way again. Battle turned sleekness to a wary, worn look; after D-day, the companies became a kaleidoscope of changing faces."[93] The division lacked one major ingredient in shaping an effective unit—combat experience. Almost none of the officers and men in the division had been under enemy fire before D-Day. The men of the Blue and Gray Division would receive that experience in spades in the Normandy beachhead.

The experiences of other National Guard divisions sometimes mirrored those of the 29th Infantry Division and sometimes diverged considerably. The 30th Infantry Division, initially composed of National Guard troops from the Carolinas, Georgia, and Tennessee, entered federal service earlier and combat later than the 29th Infantry Division. The division earned a reputation for dependable performance in combat. European theater of operations deputy historian S. L. A. Marshall rated it as the best division in the ETO.[94] What accounts for the division's performance in battle?

The War Department activated the 30th Infantry Division, "Old Hickory," on 16 September 1940 over the protests of the War Plans Division. General William K. Harrison Jr., who was in the War Plans Division at the time and later served as the assistant division commander of the 30th Infantry Division, states:

> It [the 30th Infantry Division] was a guard outfit from the Carolinas, Tennessee, and Georgia, and when they put it in federal service in 1940, we protested in War Plans because all the inspection reports showed it was pretty near the lousiest in the country. The people were okay, but you know, they had these political commanders. I think they had a guy named Russell [Major General Henry D. Russell, the brother of a Georgia senator; commanded the division from 31 December 1940 to April 1942] who was the commander of it; he may have been a very estimable gentleman and a lawyer and all that, but he wasn't a soldier. Anyway, it took not quite two years to get rid of him.[95]

Meanwhile, at Fort Jackson, South Carolina, the 30th Infantry Division received replacements through Selective Service and established a divisional replacement training center to put them through thirteen weeks of basic training.[96] The division also worked to rebuild the old World War I camp and erect new structures to accommodate two divisions (the 8th Infantry Division was also stationed there at the time).

In June 1941 the division participated in Second Army maneuvers in the Tennessee Maneuver Area along with the 5th and 27th Infantry Divisions and the 2d Armored Division. The maneuvers allowed army leaders to continue working out the problem of integrating armored divisions into the army's training. With Major General George S. Patton Jr. in command of the 2d Armored Division at the time, the armor performed very well in a mobile environment, as one might suspect. Like the other corps and army-level maneuvers held in the United States during World War II, however, senior commanders benefited most from the training and enlisted men the least.[97] Lieutenant General Ben Lear, the Second Army commander, noticed problems at the lower command levels.[98] His concerns echo the statement by Harrison regarding the young leaders in the 30th Infantry Division: "Those were fine young men, many of them good leaders naturally, but they didn't know anything. And this is what a lot of people forget; those are good guys, but you must train them."[99]

Training was not exactly the strong suit of some army units in 1941. Letters from draftees to their congressmen complained of wasted training time, poorly planned exercises, inadequately explained maneuvers, lack of confidence in officers, illiterate and unintelligent noncommissioned officers, and the lack of opportunity to progress.[100] Although some of the letters undoubtedly reflected personal dissatisfaction with the service or a particular unit or leader, others contained some truths about the general condition of the army at the time. The critical challenge posed to division commanders was to improve the training and leadership of their organizations. The 30th Infantry Division underwent good training in the Carolina maneuvers of October and November 1941 but could not correct observed deficiencies prior to the outbreak of war.

By this time the 30th Infantry Division was clearly in trouble. Training in the division was poorly organized and haphazardly conducted. Ten out of twelve of the division's field artillery battalions failed firing tests. The commander of I Corps, Major General C. F. Thompson, wrote a long memorandum to General Russell in which he cataloged in excruciating detail the failures of the 30th Infantry Division to progress with its training. The primary cause of the failure, according to the memorandum, was the unwillingness of the division commander to relieve incompetent subordinates from their positions of leadership. Russell did not relieve a single senior officer from his division in its first year of active federal service. Upon the retention of the National Guard in federal service beyond the one year initially announced, he "expressed an opinion that operation of [the age-in-grade] policy would correct most of the deficiencies in leadership of the 30th Division without recourse to measures which would create ill will without certainty of accomplishment." In other words, Russell did not want to antagonize officers from the National Guard with whom he had served during the interwar period.[101] This failure to eliminate officers unfit for combat duty and training deficiencies in the division contributed to his relief early in 1942.

As was the case with the 29th Infantry Division, the declaration of war a week after the Carolina maneuvers dealt a blow to the readiness of the 30th Infantry Division as it reconfigured to a triangular structure and gave up cadres and trained replacements to form new units. The division also lost men to officer candidate schools. By the fall of 1942, the division artillery, engineer battalion, and reconnaissance troop had less than 50 percent of their authorized strength. Even worse, in the summer of 1942 the division lost the 118th Infantry Regiment and the 115th Field Artillery Battalion to foreign service. To replace the lost regiment, the division used cadre drawn from the 117th and 120th Infantry Regiments to activate the 119th Infantry Regiment on 7 September 1942. The division then stripped soldiers from the 120th Infantry Regiment to fill the 117th Infantry Regiment, which the War Department detailed to Fort Benning for four months to act as school troops. The 119th and 120th Infantry Regiments were little more than shells after these moves.[102]

By this time the regional character of the 30th Infantry Division was seriously diminished, and it more closely resembled a newly created Organized Reserve division. The division moved to Camp Blanding, Florida, in October, where it received over ten thousand replacements. On 7 December 1942, one year after Pearl Harbor, the 30th Infantry Division began mobilization training from scratch.[103]

Meanwhile, the division went through several changes of command. Major General William H. Simpson, the future commander of the Ninth U.S. Army, took command in May 1942, but he left the division in July for higher-level assignments. The division finally received a permanent commander on 11 September 1942 when Major General Leland S. Hobbs took command.

Leland S. Hobbs was born in Gloucester, Massachusetts, on 24 February 1892.[104] He graduated from the United States Military Academy in 1915, ranking sixty-eighth out of a class of 168. Hobbs joined the infantry and served with the 63d Infantry Regiment in France during World War I. During the interwar years he served as a tactical officer at the Military Academy, commanded an infantry battalion in Hawaii, served in the Office of the Chief of Infantry in Washington, and was G-4 (logistics officer) of the IV Corps area and chief of staff of the Third Army in Atlanta. He attended the Infantry Officers Course, Command and General Staff School, the Army War College, and the Naval War College.

In May 1942 Hobbs assumed duties as the assistant division commander (ADC) of the 80th Infantry Division. After only four months in that position, he received his second star and command of the 30th Infantry Division. Hobbs was a big, blustery, bombastic man with a stubborn streak, traits reflected in his leadership style.

Hobbs chose Brigadier General William K. Harrison Jr. to be his ADC. Harrison, the son of a U.S. Navy officer and grandson of a Confederate cavalry general, graduated from the United States Military Academy in April 1917 and was commissioned in the cavalry. He had a normal range of assignments and schools in the interwar period and served on the War Department General Staff from 1939 to 1942. The slightly built, Christian, composed Harrison could not have been more different from the large, theatrical, profane Hobbs. Even though the assignment worked to the best interests of the division, the respect between the two general officers was anything but mutual. Harrison later recalled:

> When he [Hobbs] said he had asked for me and I was coming to his outfit, oh, I could have wept. I just didn't like to serve with a guy that I didn't really respect as a soldier. He might have been good at something else. His idea of running a war was to do it by telephone. Well, you can't push a telephone line, you know what I mean? You can't push a string.[105]

Hobbs put his new ADC to work improving the division's training. Harrison began by training the staff and regimental commanders in map maneuvers and command post exercises, then began improving the quality of lower-level units.[106] Harrison became the heart and soul of the 30th Infantry Division, both in training and in combat.

The 30th Infantry Division slowly emerged as a trained division, and it made this transformation without large numbers of Regular Army leaders. "We never had more than 31 Regular officers in the division, but they were all in key spots and as soon as I found one that couldn't hack it, we got rid of him," Harrison later recalled.[107] At the same time, he forced the junior National Guard and reserve officers to develop a sense of responsibility for their units.[108] The division contained some quality senior National Guard leadership. The commander of the division artillery, Brigadier General Raymond McLain, was the most outstanding senior National Guard officer of the era. McLain would later assume command of the 90th Infantry Division late in the Normandy campaign and ended the war as commander of XIX Corps.

In May 1943 the 30th Infantry Division moved to Camp Forrest, Tennessee, where it underwent AGF battalion field exercise tests. Eight out of nine infantry battalions passed the tests; the one unsatisfactory battalion subsequently passed after a period of retraining.[109] The division then continued unit and combined-arms training until the beginning of army-level maneuvers. In September and October the division participated in Second Army maneuvers in the Tennessee Maneuver Area along with the 94th and 98th Infantry Divisions and the 12th Armored Division. General Harrison recalled, "I was told after the war, by a fellow who had been in McNair's headquarters that the 30th Division was reported by Ben Lear's headquarters as the best division they ever had in the maneuvers—but I think it was because of the training."[110]

At the conclusion of maneuvers in early November, the 30th Infantry Division moved to Camp Atterbury, Indiana, where it put the finishing touches on its training and prepared for overseas movement. On 22 January 1944 the War Department ordered the division to move to a staging area at Camp Myles Standish, Massachusetts. The division moved to the port of Boston on 11 February and sailed for Great Britain the next day on board the *John Ericsson, Brazil,* and *Argentina.* The three ships joined a convoy that arrived in Great Britain ten days later, and the division moved by rail to its final destination, Chichester Barracks on the south coast of England.[111]

How well trained was the 30th Infantry Division for combat? Extremely well, if one judges by the results it achieved. The early training in 1940 and 1941 probably was not a crucial factor in preparing the division for combat, since the War Department stripped the division so heavily in 1942 and changed much of the senior leadership. In 1943 the War Department pretty much left the "new" 30th Infantry Division alone to train and develop as a team. Good leadership, along with this lengthy period of undisturbed training, allowed the division to progress rapidly and transform into a quality unit. Training in England, limited to small combat team problems, some live fire, physical training, and whatever units could accomplish in their garrisons, merely maintained the level of training the division had attained after the 1943 Tennessee maneuvers. When the 30th Infantry Division embarked from Southampton on 9 June 1944 and headed toward OMAHA Beach—nearly four years after activation into federal service—it was finally ready for war. By then, due to the normal workings of the Selective Service System, Old Hickory hardly resembled a traditional National Guard division. In June 1944 the 117th Infantry Regiment, for example, was composed of soldiers from every state and had twice as many officers from New York and Ohio as from Tennessee; half of its enlisted personnel hailed from states outside the South.[112]

The Regular Army and National Guard together would not give the United States the number of divisions it would need to fight another world war. In December 1941 the Army of the United States consisted of 29 infantry divisions, 5 armored divisions, and 2 cavalry divisions. Clearly, this total would not be enough to defeat the forces of the Axis powers on battlefields across the globe. To win the war, the United States would have to generate massive amounts of additional combat power. The Victory Program of 1941, written by Major Albert C. Wedemeyer of the War Plans Division, envisioned a total of 215 maneuver divisions in the Army of the United States.[113] Although the army never remotely approached this number, it nearly tripled the number of divisions by the end of the war. The only way to expand this rapidly was to cause major dislocation to existing units by pulling cadres and trained personnel from them to activate new divisions.

These new divisions of the Army of the United States activated after the outbreak of war would provide the bulk of the combat power necessary to achieve victory over the Axis armies on the battlefields of Europe, Africa, and Asia. If the army could not prepare them for combat prior to deployment overseas, they would have great difficulty in combat with more experienced enemy forces. How well did the army prepare the newly mobilized divisions of the Army of the United States for the ultimate test of battle?

As a general rule, the divisions activated in 1942 fared much better than those activated in 1943. The reasons are not hard to explain. First, sixteen of twenty-eight infantry divisions activated in 1942 received their cadres from Regular Army divisions, which meant the cadres were more experienced and contained a higher percentage of noncommissioned officers with prewar military experience (Table 3.1). All of the fourteen infantry divisions activated in 1943 received cadres drawn from organized reserve divisions or training centers. Since these cadres were withdrawn from their parent division after only five months of training, they were much less experienced than the cadres provided by Regular Army divisions. Second, divisions activated in 1942 received more time to train and were able to participate in army maneuvers in one of the large training areas in the United States. Divisions activated later in 1943 were often just reaching their collective training cycle when the great replacement crisis of 1944 hit them with unrelenting force. The history of the 42d Infantry Division is a case in point. The division was activated on 15 July 1943 and completed all phases of individual training on 8 January 1944 with a rating of "very satisfactory." From that date until the infantry regiments embarked for overseas duty in November, the division lost 17,970 men to the replacement stream. The division never held collective maneuvers until 6 February 1945, when it assembled in Alsace for the final drive into Germany.[114]

A study of three newly mobilized reserve divisions—the 90th, 104th, and 106th Infantry Divisions—provides some insight into the varied quality of pre-combat training in the Army of the United States between 1942 and 1944. The 90th Division had a proud history in World War I. After the war it returned to

Table 3.1 Cadre Plan for New Infantry Divisions

Division	Activation	Cadre Source
1–3 Infantry	1917	RA Units
4–9 Infantry	1939–1940	RA Units
10 Mountain	Jul 1943	Mtn Trng Center
11 Airborne	Feb 1943	88th ID
13 Airborne	Aug 1943	11th Abn/78th ID
17 Airborne	Apr 1943	101st Airborne
23 Inf (Americal)	May 1942	Composite
24 Infantry	Oct 1941	Hawaii Division
25 Infantry	Oct 1941	Hawaii Division
26–41, 43–45 Infantry	Sep 1940–Mar 1941	National Guard
42 Infantry	Jul 1943	102d ID
63 Infantry	Jun 1943	98th ID
65 Infantry	Aug 1943	104th ID
66 Infantry	Apr 1943	89th ID
69 Infantry	May 1943	96th ID
70 Infantry	Jun 1943	91st ID
71 Infantry	Jul 1943	Mtn Trng Center
75 Infantry	Apr 1943	83d ID
76 Infantry	Jun 1942	1st ID
77 Infantry	Mar 1942	8th ID
78 Infantry	Aug 1942	Composite
79 Infantry	Jun 1942	4th ID
80 Infantry	Jul 1942	8th ID
81 Infantry	Jun 1942	3d ID
82 Infantry/Airborne*	Mar 1942	9th ID
83 Infantry	Aug 1942	2d Cav Division
84 Infantry	Oct 1942	4th ID
85 Infantry	May 1942	2d ID
86 Infantry	Dec 1942	79th ID
87 Infantry	Dec 1942	81st ID
88 Infantry	Jul 1942	9th ID
89 Infantry	Jul 1942	6th ID
90 Infantry	Mar 1942	6th ID
91 Infantry	Aug 1942	1st Cav Division
92 Infantry	Oct 1942	93d ID
93 Infantry	May 1942	Composite
94 Infantry	Sep 1942	77th ID
95 Infantry	Jul 1942	7th ID
96 Infantry	Aug 1942	Composite
97 Infantry	Feb 1943	95th ID
98 Infantry	Sep 1942	82d Airborne
99 Infantry	Nov 1942	7th ID
100 Infantry	Nov 1942	76th ID
101 Airborne	Aug 1942	82d ID/Abn
102 Infantry	Sep 1942	2d ID
103 Infantry	Nov 1942	85th ID
104 Infantry	Sep 1942	90th ID
106 Infantry	Mar 1943	80th ID
1 Cavalry	1921	RA Units
2 Cavalry	Feb 1941	RA Units
2 Cavalry	Feb 1943	9th/10th Cav Regts

*Designated an airborne division in August 1942.
Source: HQ, AGF, 320.2/9 (Inf)(R)-GNG-CT, 10 Sep 1942, SUBJECT: Cadre Personnel for New Divisions, National Archives, Record Group 337, Entry 24, Boxes 1–7, plus various unit histories.

its home in Texas and reverted to little more than a cadre of reserve officers and soldiers. The division's patch displayed a "T-O" insignia, denoting the division's origins in Texas and Oklahoma. Later in World War II, after massive replacements had diluted the original geographic background of the personnel, soldiers in the division would claim the T-O stood for "Tough 'Ombres." Indeed, the 90th Infantry Division emerged from the war with an excellent combat record that justified the soldiers' claims. The success of the T-O Division, however, did not come immediately upon its entry into combat, and the price of glory was high.

The most recent work on the 90th Infantry Division in World War II, written by John Colby, is an excellent unit history written from the perspective of the men who fought in the division.[115] Colby combines personal narratives, letters, diaries, unit journals, and unit histories with analysis to form his conclusions regarding the combat effectiveness of the 90th Infantry Division. The evaluations of the senior officers in the division are blunt and frank; indeed, Colby blames most of the division's early problems on inadequate senior leadership, especially at division level.

In Normandy the 90th Infantry Division fared poorly in its initial battles. Lieutenant General Omar N. Bradley considered breaking it up and using the men as replacements for other units. Colby writes: "During our initial, confusing days of combat we were hesitant and unaggressive—we were green; after crossing the beaches, we had to regroup and organize for the execution of a complex, demanding campaign; our first two Division commanders and some regimental and battalion commander[s] proved to be weak or futile; and a veteran enemy was strongly deployed through hedgerow terrain."[116] Yet many other divisions in Normandy faced these same obstacles. Why did the 90th Infantry Division have so much more difficulty overcoming them?

Colby does not believe that training was the primary cause of the problems: "Our infantry had bad habits at the squad/platoon level, derived from sloppy conduct of these small units in large-scale maneuvers. More importantly, we were not alerted to or trained for the awful difficulties of hedgerow fighting—an intelligence failure of immense consequence. However, on balance, it remains difficult to ascribe our poor performance primarily to training inadequacies."[117] Indeed, Colby states that "the Division had been well trained, by the standards of its day."[118] He concludes by blaming the poor performance of the division on its leadership. "Any objective appraisal indicates that our Division's early leadership was critically weak, especially at the two most important command levels in an infantry division—Commanding General of the division and the commanders of the nine infantry battalions."[119]

How fair is this assessment? The leadership of the 90th Infantry Division in Normandy was clearly inadequate, but the leadership failures did not just manifest themselves in combat. The poor leadership also affected the 90th Infantry Division's preparation for combat. The soldiers in the division were no better or worse than those in other infantry divisions, but their inadequate training in the United States set them up for failure on the battlefield. In time the 90th Infantry Division, under a new set of leaders, would emerge as a quality division in the battles for France and Germany in 1944–1945. Regrettably, poor precombat training meant that the soldiers had to learn their profession at the sharp end of combat. As a result, they experienced high casualties in their first two months of battle.

The War Department reactivated the 90th Infantry Division on 25 March 1942 at Camp Barkeley, Texas, one of the first three divisions formed after Pearl Harbor. The cadre came mostly from the 6th Infantry Division, but most of the enlisted fillers were originally from Texas and Oklahoma.[120] Major General Henry Terrell Jr. commanded the 90th Infantry Division from its activation until January 1944. His influence, more than that of the commander who followed him (Brigadier General Jay W. McKelvie), determined the quality of training the division received prior to its deployment overseas and entry into combat.

Terrell, a native Texan, entered military service by competitive examination in 1912 and joined the 22d Infantry at Fort Bliss, Texas. He served in World War I as an officer in the 39th Infantry Regiment and took part in the Second Battle of the Marne, the St.-Mihiel offensive, and the Meuse-Argonne campaign, where he received the French Croix de Guerre for heroism. Terrell commanded the 9th Infantry Regiment at Fort Sam Houston, Texas, in 1940. After serving in the personnel division of the War Department General Staff, he received his first star and served with the 8th Infantry Division at Fort Jackson, South Carolina, until his appointment as commander of the 90th Infantry Division.[121]

The 90th Infantry Division went through the standard seventeen-week basic training cycle from April through July 1942. The cycle was not even complete, however, before the War Department ordered the division to give up a cadre of over thirteen hundred officers and enlisted soldiers to form the 104th Infantry Division.[122] The fact that the 104th Infantry Division performed superbly in combat reflects well on the soldiers the 90th Infantry Division sent to Oregon as cadres. Like other parent divisions, the 90th Infantry Division underwent short-term disruption as a consequence. It probably could have recovered from this disruption during the unit training cycle, which began in August 1942, except for a decision by the War Department to reorganize the division.

The War Department interrupted unit training when it designated the 90th Infantry Division a "motorized" division on 15 September.[123] For the next several months, division training was in turmoil as the units adjusted to their new roles. General William E. Depuy, who served in the 357th Infantry Regiment during the war, later recalled:

We were motorized by that time, and all the energy and imagination in the division was totally absorbed in how you could get a regiment to mount up in trucks and go down the road and not be lost and get there on time. We spent months just learning how to do that. Whereas, we should have spent months learning how to fight. But the reason for that was that the division commander, the regimental commander and the battalion commanders were able intellectually to cope with a truck movement, but they weren't intellectually able to cope with training for combat because it was more complex. So, I really didn't think much of the training.[124]

Furthermore, the leadership of the 90th Infantry Division did not take advantage of lessons learned from North Africa to improve the division's training.[125]

General Depuy's comments are borne out by the evaluation the division received during AGF tests administered by VIII Corps in December 1942 and January 1943. Nearly every mistake the division made in these tests it repeated in combat in Normandy. A representative sampling of the umpire comments are enlightening:

> None of the enlisted men or NCO's of the 359th Infantry questioned knew anything at all about the situation or mission. Some of them didn't even know their individual sector of fire. They didn't know why they were there or what they were doing.[126]

> The Division plan was to jump off with two regiments abreast. The 359th Inf. . . . jumped off in column of companies; with companies in column of platoons; and platoons in column of two's, closed up tight on the road. In this formation, the Battalion advanced . . . until the head of the column was fired on by two machine guns at a range of about 100 yards. This would have caused great losses.[127]

> 90th Division Headquarters failed to supervise the formation of the plans of subordinate units. It permitted lower units to promulgate plans which were tactically unsound, although ample time was available for modification before jump-off.[128]

> The movement of the Blue forces [358th Infantry] . . . showed a lack of aggressive action. There was a tendency to remain on the vehicles and move close to the enemy before dismounting to fight on foot.[129]

> In a deployment on the morning of January 11th, the 2d Bn., 359th Infantry, advanced without knowing the location of other units of their own regiment. As a result, a portion of their troops opened fire on the 3d Bn., 359th Infantry, which was deployed to their front and engaged with the enemy. The 3d Bn. was thrown into some confusion.[130]

> The men bunch up too much during the attack and control over companies is lacking. Platoons advance without knowledge of terrain and without proper use of scouts. . . . Men are allowed to advance by fire and movement . . . the movement being standing, when they should be crawling (3d Bn., 357th Infantry).[131]

On the other hand, the umpires praised the ability of the division to conduct road marches and establish assembly areas, just as one might expect from General Depuy's comments on the training emphasis of the division. The umpires also noted the excellent morale of the soldiers of the division and believed they "will make a good showing if properly led and supervised."[132] Overall, one must agree with Depuy's assessment that "there wasn't much conviction about tactics" in the division.[133]

After the completion of division tests, the 90th Infantry Division deployed to the Louisiana Maneuver Area to take part in Third Army maneuvers against the 77th Infantry Division. The maneuvers ended in late March and the division returned to Texas, only to have the War Department convert the unit back to a standard infantry division. The division, which had learned how to conduct long, motorized movements so well, now faced a period of training in the more basic tasks of close combat. The division established courses in attack of fortified areas, village fighting, close combat, and day and night infiltration techniques.[134]

The next major maneuver the division participated in was better suited to the training of a motorized unit than a standard infantry division. The 90th Infantry Division deployed to the Desert Training Center in Arizona and California in September 1943 and trained there for three months. Maneuvers against the 93d Infantry Division in the desert conditioned the 90th Infantry Division for long, sweeping movements.[135] They did little, however, to correct the deficiencies in training at the small-unit level or to prepare the division for combat in Normandy.

The 90th Infantry Division deployed to Fort Dix, New Jersey, from 26 December 1943 to 8 January 1944. There the division integrated replacements (stripped from the 63d Infantry Division) to bring it to full strength and received new clothing and equipment. On 23 January 1944 Brigadier General Jay W. MacKelvie assumed command of the division, and General Terrell left to take command of XXII Corps at Camp Campbell, Kentucky.[136] MacKelvie took the 90th Infantry Division to Great Britain in late March. Quartered in the Midlands near Birmingham, England, the division waited for the next move that would take it into combat.

General MacKelvie was a native of South Dakota who had enlisted in the 7th Cavalry in 1913 and had participated in the Punitive Expedition to Mexico in 1916. In 1917 he received a commission and served in the 78th Field Artillery in World War I. He served in various artillery units during the interwar period, attended the Command and General Staff School and the Army War College, and served in the War Plans Division and in the Office of the Chief of Field Artillery. MacKelvie commanded the 85th Division Artillery from May 1942 to September 1943 and the XII Corps Artillery for four months before assuming command of the 90th Infantry Division.[137]

General Depuy recalls, "MacKelvie's nickname was the 'Oral Null' because to the best of anybody's knowledge, he never said anything during the entire time he commanded the division. He certainly didn't say it to any troops."[138] John Colby is even more critical in his assessment of MacKelvie. "Careful analysis of all available comments from a large number of veterans finds not a single favorable note," Colby writes. "Shortfalls included: no apparent knowledge of infantry tactics or battlefield leadership; unwillingness to accept sound advice from his knowledgeable subordinates, . . . was distant, cold, and remote in personality. . . . He rapidly disintegrated within four days of actual combat stress. . . . Indeed a sad picture, but it can be painted in no kinder colors."[139] Simply put, MacKelvie lacked the ability to remedy the defects in the division's training. Poorly trained and woefully led at the higher echelons of command, the 90th Infantry Division was headed for disaster in Normandy.

In contrast to the 90th Infantry Division, few divisions in the Army of the United States were as well trained prior to entering combat as the 104th Infantry Division. Activated on 15 September 1942, the "Timberwolves" (the division adopted this nickname to reflect its origins in the Northwest) managed to escape the period of high personnel turbulence that affected other divisions in the first half of 1942. The War Department did not deploy the division overseas until August 1944, so it missed the grueling battles of attrition in Normandy. Finally, the Timberwolves entered combat under the command of Major General Terry de la Mesa Allen, one of the few combat-experienced division commanders in the army. The combination of a long period of training, good leadership, and entry into combat under favorable circumstances led to the division's success on the battlefield.

The War Department organized the 104th Infantry Division in July 1921 as a reserve division under the provisions of the National Defense Act of 1920.[140] Known until 1942 as the "Frontier Division," the reservists assigned to the division in the first two decades of its existence constituted little more than a caretaker cadre. After activation in the fall of 1942, officers and enlisted men arrived from all over the United States to bring the division to full strength. Most of the cadre came from the 90th Infantry Division, then stationed at Camp Barkeley, Texas. Under the command of Major General Gilbert R. Cook, the 104th Infantry Division underwent its mobilization training at Camp Adair, Oregon, a post it shared with the 96th Infantry Division. Three months of maneuvers in the Oregon Maneuver Area from August to October 1943 capped the division's mobilization training. During this period the division passed its "D" series maneuvers and took part in IV Corps' maneuvers with the 91st and 96th Infantry Divisions.

General Cook had taken the Timberwolves through the mobilization process, but he would not take the division into combat. General George C. Marshall knew that Major General Terry de la Mesa Allen, who had been relieved of command of the 1st Infantry Division during the Sicilian campaign, was too valuable a resource to leave out of combat. On 6 October 1943 Cook departed the 104th Infantry Division to take command of the XII Corps area, and nine days later Allen assumed command of the Timberwolves.[141] The match proved to be a good one.

Allen put his indelible stamp on the 104th Infantry Division. He turned the Timberwolf Division into an organization that in many ways resembled the Big Red One. In North Africa, Allen wrote, "Nothing in hell must stop the First Division" on the initial operations order he issued. He now transferred that motto to the 104th Infantry Division by proclaiming, "Nothing in hell must stop the Timberwolves." Allen also wrote and distributed to his officers and noncommissioned officers pamphlets entitled "Combat Leadership," "Directive for Offensive Combat," and "Night Attacks." These publications formed the basis for his training and leadership of the division.[142] On one occasion a visiting inspector general asked Allen who paid for the publication of these "irregular manuals." When Allen replied that the division financed them through the proceeds from two nickel slot machines located in the officers' club, the officer "went off complaining that there was too much levity in this 'dizzy Timberwolf outfit.'"[143]

Allen forced the 104th Infantry Division to become proficient in night operations. "Night Attacks" was largely based on a similar pamphlet Allen had used as commander of the 1st Infantry Division. The pamphlet contained concise information on the utility of night attacks and the preparation, direction, and control of forces operating in darkness. Units were to conduct night attacks on a narrow front in column formation to facilitate command and control. The pamphlet concluded, "The skillful use of night attacks indicates smart, aggressive leadership. Properly executed night attacks will frequently attain difficult limited objectives, with comparatively few casualties. *The attacking troops must be highly trained and imbued with a determination to close with the enemy and destroy him with the bayonet.*"[144] In a handwritten note at the end of the pamphlet Allen added, "The 104th Div will learn this dope and *do* it."[145]

Allen also transferred his experience in combat to his division. In "Directive for Offensive Combat," Allen stressed the need for simplicity in combat operations, the value of night operations, gaining and maintaining contact with the enemy through good reconnaissance, fixing him with field artillery fire and infantry support weapons, and the use of fire and maneuver to destroy enemy forces. Allen knew the value of supporting fire and stressed that "fire superiority is largely gained by the intensive use of close supporting weapons. *For attacking rifle units to attempt to secure fire superiority by building up a firing line at long range, results in delay and unnecessary exposure to enemy fire.*"[146] He also understood German doctrine:

> *German infantry invariably counter-attacks very promptly.* By anticipating and preparing for such counter-attacks, heavy losses may be inflicted on the enemy. American artillery has been particularly effective in this respect. During the Tunisian campaign in North Africa, field artillery units of the First Infantry Division killed more Germans in repelling enemy counter-attacks than in all other types of fire combined.[147]

For an untested division, Allen's ability to inculcate lessons learned in combat was an invaluable asset.

Allen understood the value of unit cohesion. He felt that this cohesion came from two sources: the commander and the pride of soldiers in their unit. "American combat units all have the same potential capabilities," Allen wrote. "Their combat efficiency and esprit will depend on the leadership of their commanders. A 'sorry outfit' means a 'sorry commander.'"[148] Allen later thanked the soldiers for adhering to the four primary objectives of their training: discipline, training, physical fitness, and belief in their units. "In this last item particularly, our division has been most outstanding as we all feel completely assured that we are second to none as an American combat unit."[149]

Unlike many divisions that went into their first battles with no combat-experienced leaders, the 104th Infantry Division gathered more than a few combat veterans into its ranks from an unexpected source. Many officers and noncommissioned officers in the 1st Infantry Division who rotated back to the United States due to wounds or War Department policy managed to arrange an assignment to Allen's new division.[150] They helped to leaven the newly trained Timberwolves. Additionally, the assistant division commander, Brigadier General Bryant E. Moore, and the artillery commander, Brigadier General William R. Woodward, had both served combat tours on Guadalcanal. These officers and noncommissioned officers brought the reality of combat into the division's training. "The 104th Division trained under my command for a year before going into combat," Allen later wrote. "They learned all the combat tricks of the old First Division and acquired many new tricks of their own, particularly in night combat."[151]

The 104th Infantry Division rounded out its training at the Desert Training Center in Arizona and California in late 1943 and early 1944 before deploying to Camp Carson, Colorado, for the remainder of its stay in the United States. In April 1944 the division integrated approximately four thousand new soldiers who had been released from the ASTP.[152] The Timberwolves worked hard to train and integrate their ASTP transfers prior to departure overseas. In mid-August the 104th Infantry Division traveled by train to Camp Kilmer, New Jersey, in preparation for overseas deployment. The division sailed in the first convoy to travel directly from the United States to the port of Cherbourg in France, where it landed on 7 September 1944.[153] The Timberwolves were ready for the test of combat.

In contrast to the experience of the 104th Infantry Division, the mobilization and training of the 106th Infantry Division showed what could go wrong with the divisions of the Army of the United States when they lacked solid leadership or were too heavily stripped to provide replacements for units overseas. The War Department activated the 106th Infantry Division on 15 March 1943 at Fort Jackson, South Carolina, with a cadre provided by the 80th Infantry Division. The division commander was Major General Alan W. Jones.

Jones was commissioned in 1917 through competitive examination, but he missed combat during World War I.[154] He served in a variety of infantry regiments in the United States and the Philippines until 1924, when he attended the

Infantry Officers Course at Fort Benning, Georgia. From 1925 to 1929 he taught in the Weapons Department at the Infantry School during the "Benning Renaissance," which brought him to the attention of Colonel George C. Marshall, the assistant commandant. Jones served in the Office of the Chief of Infantry in Washington for three years before attending the Command and General Staff School at Fort Leavenworth. He then served with the 7th Infantry Regiment in Vancouver Barracks, Washington, in 1936 and 1937; his brigade commander there was Brigadier General George C. Marshall. As a field-grade officer on a small post, Jones undoubtedly had many dealings with the future chief of staff of the U.S. Army.

Two assignments with Marshall in the interwar period practically guaranteed Jones a choice assignment in the Army of the United States during World War II. In theory all senior officers had an equal opportunity for promotion and command during the war, but in practice division commands went to officers associated with either General McNair or General Marshall. Jones's two tours with Marshall marked him as a potential commander in an expanded Army of the United States. Jones's selection as a division commander later proved that the "system" used by the army in World War II to select division commanders was really no system at all. Connections mattered almost as much as competence. Although the army on the whole ended up with a decent set of commanders, the use of centralized command selection boards most likely would have resulted in some changes among division commanders in the Army of the United States. "For every person entered in Marshall's notebook," writes historian Martin Blumenson, "there were probably a dozen, perhaps more, who were every bit as good as the ones he listed. The others were simply unfortunate because they had failed to come within Marshall's orbit and ken."[155]

Jones attended the Army War College in 1937–1938. He served with the 19th Infantry Regiment in Hawaii until 1941, when he was transferred to Washington for duty with the Training Branch, G-3, War Department General Staff. He moved over to the headquarters of AGF in 1942, where he worked under General McNair. Jones's connections with Marshall and McNair paid off in June 1942, when he received his first star and became assistant division commander of the 90th Infantry Division, a position he held until his selection as division commander of the 106th Infantry Division in 1943. He would enter combat in 1944 as green as his division, a not uncommon experience in the Army of the United States during World War II.

The 106th Infantry Division went through mobilization training at Fort Jackson before departing for the Tennessee Maneuver Area in January 1944. There the division took part in maneuvers with the 26th and 78th Infantry Divisions and the 17th Airborne Division. By the conclusion of the maneuvers in March 1944, the 106th Infantry Division was an average, trained division and ready for combat.[156]

When the division moved to Camp Atterbury, Indiana, in late March 1944, the personnel raids began. Although the War Department did not require the

"Golden Lions" to furnish a cadre to form another division, it combed the personnel of the 106th Infantry Division for overseas replacements. Between March 1943 and October 1944, AGF stripped 1,215 officers and 12,442 enlisted soldiers from the 106th Infantry Division, most of them in the first half of 1944.[157] The challenge facing Jones and his leaders was to train the men sent to fill the division before it left the United States for overseas duty. These men came from ASTP, the ground establishment of the AAF, antiaircraft and coastal artillery units, and the ASF.[158]

The 106th Infantry Division never recovered from the raids upon its personnel. When Lieutenant General Ben Lear, commander of AGF since Lieutenant General McNair's tragic death in Normandy in July 1944, and his staff inspected the unit in September 1944, they found a division unprepared for combat. Lear stated:

> The division has not yet reached the peak of its training or its efficiency. You haven't much time left, and you must get busy with tank-infantry as well as all other forms of training. If you do not, you will ruin the reputation of your division. Wonderful things were expected of your division. We have had too much to complain about. It's your fault.[159]

General Lear was only partly correct, however. The 106th Infantry Division had already reached the peak of its training during the Tennessee maneuvers. Due to the stripping of its personnel in the interim, however, the division needed to repeat much of its earlier training to indoctrinate the thousands of new inductees received since then. This training would take time. When the War Department alerted the division for overseas movement in October 1944, time ran out on the Golden Lions.

Personnel turbulence created by the overseas replacement crisis was a problem, but alone it is an inadequate explanation for the problems of the 106th Infantry Division. Nearly every other division still in the United States in 1944 sustained personnel transfers of equal magnitude. The 100th Infantry Division, for example, which was activated on 15 November 1942 and took part in the Second Army maneuvers in Tennessee a year later, lost 14,636 enlisted men and hundreds of officers to the replacement stream in 1944. "With most of these losses occurring in the infantry for overseas shipment," the division recorded, "this meant that the Century Division had supplied well over one full division of infantrymen for combat."[160] Despite these losses, the 100th Infantry Division managed to integrate thousands of ASTP men, transfers from the Army Air Forces, and antiaircraft artillery soldiers reclassified as infantrymen into the division before departure from New York on 6 October. "At the end of this period," the division historian concludes, "the Century Division, despite its shifting population, was ready to take the field in combat."[161] Reinforcing that assessment, the division launched a major attack in Alsace a little over a month later, with impressive results. One must conclude that the quality of a division's leadership mattered a great deal in its training and preparation. The circumstances under which the division entered combat also had an important impact on its development.

Due to the chaotic mobilization of the American army for war, only a few of its divisions reached a high level of effectiveness before their entry into combat. Regular Army units fared better than National Guard divisions and divisions of the Organized Reserves created on the outbreak of war, but due to massive culling of personnel to create cadres for new units and provide replacements for the overseas theaters, divisions of the Army of the United States faced an uphill struggle in their efforts to become cohesive, trained organizations. The most important factor in this process was the leadership provided by the division, regimental, and battalion commanders. The training programs they established were absolutely critical to the performance of their units. Divisions that failed to supplement division, corps, and army maneuvers with demanding training that focused on units at battalion level and below inevitably fared poorly when subjected to the rigors of combat against a tough and capable enemy. Nevertheless, the vast majority of divisions reached an acceptable—if not optimal—level of proficiency prior to their entry into combat. Those divisions that failed to do so paid the price in blood for their lack of competence.

4

First Battles: North Africa and Sicily

In North Africa and Sicily in 1942 and 1943, American divisions learned many tough lessons in their first and subsequent battles with seasoned German units. The cost was often high in terms of soldiers wounded and killed, and in a few cases the toll was exorbitant. Nearly every military organization has problems upon its initial entry into combat; however, American divisions proved that they could successfully cope with the shock of battle and integrate the hard lessons learned into their future operations. The campaigns in the North African and Mediterranean theater of operations gave the Army of the United States much-needed combat experience upon which it could build for the future. Many divisions that fought in these battles went on to establish solid reputations, among them the 1st, 3d, 9th, and 45th Infantry Divisions, the 2d Armored Division, and the 82d Airborne Division, all of which eventually transferred to the ETO to fight the Wehrmacht in the climactic campaigns for France and Germany in 1944 and 1945. Combat operations in North Africa and Sicily also seasoned American commanders: Eisenhower, Bradley, Patton, Truscott, Allen, Eddy, Middleton, Ridgway, Harmon, and others all gained valuable experience during these operations. Although Army Chief of Staff General George C. Marshall was not enamored with the diversion of American combat power to secondary theaters of operation, the combat experience gained by American forces and leaders in North Africa and Sicily in 1942 and 1943 later proved crucial to the successful prosecution of the Normandy invasion in 1944.

The invasion of North Africa—Operation TORCH—was the result of President Franklin D. Roosevelt's desire to see American ground forces engaged in combat against Axis troops somewhere in Europe or North Africa before the end of 1942, coupled with British unwillingness to consider a cross-Channel invasion before 1943 at the earliest. President Roosevelt feared that unless American forces became involved in a campaign against Germany soon, public pressure in the United States would force the diversion of more military assets to fight the Japanese in the Pacific. The British did not believe a cross-Channel invasion was either possible or desirable until attrition on the Eastern Front and on the periphery of Europe had reduced the quantity and quality of German forces available to defend France. Operation TORCH was therefore a compromise between military reality and political expediency.[1]

The decision to invade North Africa in 1942 probably saved Allied forces from catastrophe had they invaded France in 1943, for Operation TORCH uncovered serious weaknesses in joint and combined operations, combined-arms training, and small-unit leadership. Had the French army put up serious resistance, American forces would have been hard-pressed to establish themselves ashore. Except for isolated incidents, resistance was light, and the French quickly agreed to an armistice. For the men of the 1st, 3d, and 9th Infantry Divisions, the invasion provided valuable if limited experience. Nevertheless, the invasion hardly went smoothly for the American forces, whose weaknesses became all too apparent in the first battles in Tunisia several months later.

The 1st Infantry Division began its journey to North Africa in Scotland, where the division conducted an amphibious landing exercise on 18 and 19 October 1942. The Big Red One embarked on twenty ships and sailed from the Clyde on 26 October with a British naval escort. After an uneventful voyage, the division landed without serious opposition on "Y" and "Z" beaches to the west and east of Oran, respectively, in the early morning darkness of 8 November. The 18th Infantry Regiment ran into stiff French resistance at St.-Cloud, which Major General Terry de la Mesa Allen quickly ordered contained by one battalion and then bypassed. Two days later, American troops entered Oran, and the French agreed to a cease-fire.[2]

The 3d and 9th Infantry Divisions, along with elements of the 2d Armored Division, were part of Major General George S. Patton's Western Task Force, which embarked from the east coast of the United States. The 3d Infantry Division, under the command of Major General Jonathan W. Anderson, had undergone its amphibious training on the west coast of the United States in conjunction with the 2d Marine Division. As the key component of Task Force BRUSHWOOD, its mission would be to land at Fedala in French Morocco and then attack south to seize the port of Casablanca. Upon landing at 0500 hours on 8 November, the "Rock of the Marne" lost a large percentage of its landing craft due to a high surf and rocky beach, which slowed the division's buildup and delayed the attack toward Casablanca.[3] Despite this setback, the 3d Infantry Division managed to push south to the outskirts of the city by 10 November. A day later the French agreed to an armistice that ended hostilities.

The plan for Operation TORCH did not envision the use of the 9th Infantry Division as an integral unit. Instead, the plan broke the division into RCTs, which normally consisted of an infantry regiment, a field artillery battalion, an engineer platoon, and a medical collecting company.[4] American planners provided substantial reinforcements to strengthen the standard combat teams with tanks, reconnaissance troops, antiaircraft guns, signal units, aviation, military

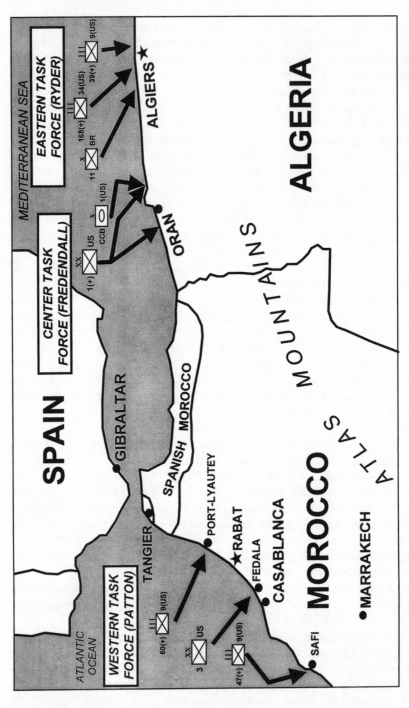

Operation TORCH, November 1942

intelligence, and civil affairs personnel. These RCTs would invade North Africa under the command of task force commanders: the 39th RCT would form part of the force gathered to invade Algiers in the Mediterranean Sea, while the 47th and 60th RCTs were part of the Western Task Force that would invade French Morocco from the Atlantic Ocean.

After deploying to Great Britain shortly before the invasion, the 39th RCT had a rough voyage to Algiers. On 7 November a torpedo hit the USS *Thomas Stone,* which carried the 2d Battalion, 39th Infantry Regiment. The remainder of the combat team landed on the beaches at Ain-Taya, fifteen miles east of Algiers, on 8 November. The boat waves lost all semblance of organization; soldiers and equipment ended up strewn over three different beaches.[5] The farther down the chain of command one went, the more critical were the officers of the results of the operation. Second Lieutenant G. B. Beasley noted, "There was too much confusion and congestion when we first got on the beach. There were too many men giving orders which confused the soldiers and they didn't know who to follow."[6] Many units spent several hours just sorting themselves out after the navy landed them haphazardly on the beaches.

Even after the battalions established themselves ashore, their performance was far from sparkling. A few French soldiers held up the 3d Battalion for several hours, and when the battalion attempted to bypass the resistance at night, it got lost.[7] The overall success of the operation, however, boosted morale. Second Lieutenant Bernie L. Bogue summed up his feelings at the moment: "Morale is still high. We are very thankful and pleased that we are here, that we are alive, that we are Americans."[8]

The other two combat teams of the 9th Infantry Division departed for Norfolk, Virginia, in mid-October, loaded aboard transports, and sailed for a convoy rendezvous in Chesapeake Bay. The 47th RCT formed part of Sub–Task Force BLACKSTONE, with the mission of seizing the port of Safi, French Morocco. The 60th RCT formed part of Sub–Task Force GOALPOST, under the command of Brigadier General Lucian K. Truscott Jr. His force's mission was to seize Port Lyautey, French Morocco. Upon reaching Solomon's Island in Chesapeake Bay, Truscott had his men rehearse the landing operation in conjunction with the crews of the transport vessels. The rehearsals exposed many faults in the organization and training of the transport crews and assault force, and commanders were able to make some corrections prior to sailing overseas.[9] On 23 October the Western Task Force departed from the United States in convoy, bound for North Africa.

The 47th RCT, under the command of Colonel Edwin H. Randle, conducted the smoothest landing in the invasion at Safi, French Morocco. Companies K and L landed between 0435 and 0445 hours directly in the harbor of Safi from the decks of the destroyers *Bernadou* and *Cole,* surprised the French defenders, and quickly took possession of the harbor facilities. The remainder of the regiment landed behind schedule during the morning hours. By midafternoon the 47th RCT had subdued all organized French resistance in Safi. The tanks of the 2d Armored Division began to unload, and reconnoitered east toward Marrekech.[10]

The 60th RCT met the toughest resistance of any unit in the 9th Infantry Division during Operation TORCH. Like the other units in the division, the 60th RCT landed late on its beaches west of Port Lyautey, French Morocco. The assault ships had lost formation at night; consequently, the navy had difficulty forming the correct landing waves according to the invasion plan. Wave commanders had problems finding the correct beaches. Instead of advancing toward their objectives in darkness, the disorganized American forces ended up conducting a daylight assault. "This loss of direction and control by assault waves made the whole landing operation a hit or miss affair that would certainly have spelled disaster against an alert and well armed enemy," the regimental after-action report noted.[11] The combat team encountered severe resistance from French infantry and tanks and did not secure its objectives until 10 November.

Perhaps because the 60th RCT had the toughest combat, it learned the most from its experience. Communications from ship to shore were inadequate, radios drenched by salt water worked poorly or not at all, and commanders had to exercise personal control on shore to be effective.[12] The combat team learned the value of close cooperation between tanks and infantry as the armor of the 70th Tank Battalion proved its worth in many actions. The units began to appreciate the destructive firepower of artillery, self-propelled guns, naval gunfire, and aircraft. The 2.75-inch rocket launcher was a welcome addition to infantry squads, since it provided a lightweight, mobile source of fire support for small units. Support troops learned the importance of infantry training, as commanders often used them as reserves during critical points in the fighting.[13]

The combat team also learned a great many lessons about amphibious operations, although the division did not participate in another seaborne assault during the war. One of the critical lessons was the impact of unit cohesion on an amphibious landing. "When a soldier lands," the after-action report stated, "after a long sea voyage, on a strange beach, in utter darkness, he should be surrounded by men he knows and under leaders he has learned to respect and trust. Leaders of all ranks should know their personnel from long association and training."[14] Regrettably, hasty mobilization precluded many divisions from achieving a period of "long association and training," which the 9th Infantry Division found so helpful in combat.

The 1st Infantry Division also learned important lessons from TORCH, which proved the soundness of the division's previous training in amphibious operations. Planners would subsequently ignore some recommendations, such as the need to reduce the amount of equipment carried by individual soldiers in the initial landing waves and the need for waterproof casings for radio sets.[15] A year and a half later in Normandy, both problems would again plague the division on D-Day. General Allen also noted "certain weaknesses in the proper employment of fire and movement for infantry units," a problem that existed throughout the army.[16] In addition, Allen stated, "The present prescribed system of securing air support through the higher echelons is too cumbersome and too slow."[17] The provision of close air support to army ground forces would remain inadequate throughout the North African campaign. Indeed, the Army Air Forces would not fix the system until after the invasion of Normandy in June 1944.

After the successful invasion of North Africa, Allied troops attacked east in a race to seize Tunisia. The Germans won the race in December, which forced Allied troops to halt while their commanders accumulated supplies and reinforcements for another offensive to seize the ports of Bizerte and Tunis. The enemy struck first, however, on 14 February 1943 along the eastern dorsal of the mountains in central Tunisia. The resulting Battle of Kasserine Pass was the worst defeat suffered by American ground forces in World War II, but the battle ended without the Germans gaining a clear operational or strategic advantage. For American forces, the battle served as a brutal schooling in the essentials of combat against an experienced enemy.[18]

The experience of the 34th Infantry Division exemplified the problems of the hastily mobilized, inadequately trained American infantry at Kasserine Pass. The "Red Bull" Division, composed of units recruited from the upper Midwest, was a typical National Guard division. Supply problems and inadequate training facilities hampered the mobilization of the division upon activation in February 1941. The division soon moved to Camp Claiborne, Louisiana, for mobilization training, but personnel turnover limited the effectiveness of the training program. During the Louisiana maneuvers in the fall of 1941, the division spent nearly the entire time in V Corps reserve. Combined-arms training was inadequate. Only partly trained, poorly equipped, and in the midst of reorganization to a triangular configuration, the 34th Infantry Division deployed to the United Kingdom between January and May 1942. Lack of equipment and training areas and the siphoning of hundreds of the best soldiers to form the first Ranger battalions hampered the division's readiness prior to its deployment to North Africa.[19]

The 168th Regiment of the 34th Infantry Division participated in Operation TORCH at Algiers, but it learned little from its brief entry into combat. Two days prior to the beginning of the Battle of Kasserine Pass, the regiment received 450 poorly trained replacements and its first shipments of the 2.75-inch antitank rocket launcher (bazooka). Needless to say, the regiment had assimilated neither the new soldiers nor the new equipment when the battle began. The Germans quickly surrounded the 2d and 3d Battalions along with the regimental headquarters, which surrendered on 17 February. The regiment lost 2,200 men, 1,400 of whom were taken prisoner. "It took the remnants of the 168th Regiment a month to rebuild, refit, and process replacements," writes one historian. "In essence, it became a new unit; the 168th Regiment of the Iowa National Guard was destroyed."[20] This process repeated itself sooner or later—to a greater or lesser degree—in every National Guard division in the Army of the United States. By the end of the war, there were no appreciable differences in the personnel composition of the sixty-seven standard American infantry divisions.

The debacle at Kasserine Pass damaged the reputation of the American army in the eyes of its British allies, but the U.S. II Corps recovered quicker than the British opinion of it. Lieutenant General George S. Patton Jr. took command of the corps in place of Major General Lloyd R. Fredendall and immediately began its rehabilitation. One immediate change was the consolidation of American divisions; no longer would they fight with their various components parceled out piecemeal across the desert countryside.[21]

A month after Kasserine, II Corps attacked toward El Guettar to draw off enemy reserves facing the British Eighth Army in southern Tunisia. On the morning of 23 March, the *Afrika Korps* counterattacked with the 10th Panzer Division against the southern flank of the 1st Infantry Division. The Big Red One not only held off the enemy attack but also inflicted substantial tank and personnel losses on the enemy force.[22] The 18th RCT jubilantly reported, "Our artillery crucified them with HE [high explosive] shells and they were falling like flies."[23] Allied air support was much improved from Kasserine, although the enemy still had air parity and was able to use dive-bombers to strike forward positions. The bombing had little effect on the soldiers of the 1st Infantry Division, who proved that well-trained and well-led American soldiers could succeed in their first battles if employed properly.

Regular Army divisions also had their problems upon entry into combat. As other Allied forces advanced into Tunisia, the 9th Infantry Division settled down in Morocco and Algeria to guard lines of communication and train. When the German forces attacked and overran several American units in the Battle of Kasserine Pass, the Allied command ordered the artillery of the 9th Infantry Division to march to Tunisia to reinforce the fires of II Corps. After an epic 735-mile march over a period of four days, in weather conditions that included rain and a snowstorm, the artillery arrived on the battlefield in time to play an important role in halting the German attack, a feat for which the division artillery earned a Distinguished Unit Citation.[24]

The other elements of the 9th Infantry Division moved to Tunisia in the artillery's wake. On 28 March the division's mission was to attack the German positions east of El Guettar in conjunction with the 1st Infantry Division. For the next ten days the II Corps fought for control of the high ground against well-fortified German resistance. Only the success of the British Eighth Army finally forced the Germans to retreat from their positions.[25]

The 9th Infantry Division's performance in the Battle of El Guettar left much to be desired. The 39th RCT had recently rejoined the division after an absence of nearly six months. The employment of the 39th RCT as a guard force in the two months after TORCH did nothing to develop the combat effectiveness of the organization. The 39th Infantry could not even train to assimilate the lessons learned from the brief period of combat it had witnessed. The division also lacked adequate maps for the El Guettar area, and the sheets that were available contained many inaccuracies. On the first morning of the

Troops of the 2d Battalion, 16th Infantry Regiment, 1st Infantry Division, march through Kasserine Pass, Tunisia, 26 February 1943. The Army of the United States received a sharp but temporary setback in its first major battle against the Wehrmacht, but it learned significant lessons during combat in North Africa that improved its operations on the continent of Europe. (U.S. Army Signal Corps photo)

attack, the lead battalion of the 47th Infantry Regiment reported inaccurately that it had reached its objective. When the Germans entrenched on the actual objective halted progress, the 2d and 3d Battalions maneuvered to outflank the enemy from the south. The 3d Battalion captured the ridge, but elements of the 10th Panzer Division caught the 2d Battalion in the open in front of their defensive positions and destroyed Company E. The remainder of the battalion lost contact with the division for thirty-six hours. When Major General Manton S. Eddy committed the 1st Battalion, 39th Infantry, to extend the envelopment even farther to the south, it too became lost.[26]

The next day, 29 March, the situation grew even worse. The Germans ambushed the 2d Battalion, 39th Infantry, as it moved forward in trucks along the El Guettar–Gabes road. The battalion sustained heavy losses and became badly demoralized. The 1st and 3d Battalions, 47th Infantry Regiment, could not dislodge the German defenders from their positions. The 1st Battalion, 39th Infantry, and the 2d Battalion, 47th Infantry, remained out of contact. The division regrouped during the night and finally made contact with the two "lost" battalions. On 30 and 31 March, Eddy and his troops made little progress. II Corps was out of touch with the situation, for on 1 April Patton ordered the 9th Infantry Division to proceed with the second phase of the corps plan, which called for the 1st Armored Division to pass through the 9th Infantry Division after the latter had opened a hole wide enough for exploitation. But until the Americans controlled the high ground around Hills 369 and 772, the armor would go nowhere.[27]

On 3 April Patton placed the entire corps artillery under the control of the 9th Infantry Division. A massive barrage hit the German positions on Hill 369, but the 47th Infantry Regiment was slow to follow the artillery preparation and failed to take the hill. The next day the 47th Infantry tried to infiltrate the German positions under cover of darkness, but it again failed to dislodge the defenders. Only after the Germans withdrew from their positions on 6 April did the division make any progress. Soon thereafter, II Corps received replacements of men and equipment in preparation for a move to the north for its final operation in North Africa, an attack toward Bizerte.[28]

The 9th Infantry Division's introduction to combat was neither easy nor cheap. Not counting the casualties sustained by the detached 60th RCT, the division lost 120 killed, 872 wounded, 316 missing, 186 injured, 207 exhaustion cases, and 111 nonbattle casualties. Since 425 men returned to duty within thirty days, the net loss for the division was about 10 percent of its strength. The 39th and 47th Infantry Regiments sustained 98 percent of these losses. Five out of six infantry battalion commanders in these two regiments were out of action (two wounded, one case of combat fatigue, one captured, and one missing). Of 207 men affected by combat fatigue, only about 40 percent returned to their units after the battle.[29]

The division learned basic, but crucial, lessons in the Battle of El Guettar. Commanders need to perform reconnaissance early and then take the time to perfect their plans and issue orders. II Corps rushed the 9th Infantry Division into battle, which meant that the division had to rely on intelligence gathered by the 1st Infantry Division, most of which was outdated or incorrect. During its attack the 9th Infantry Division failed to take the dominating high ground. As a result, German artillery observers poured fire onto the attackers, and the division ended up assaulting enemy positions frontally. Artillery fire alone could not dislodge the defenders from their well-fortified positions (some of which the Germans had blasted into solid rock). Infantry needs to follow closely behind its artillery preparation, a basic lesson from World War I that American soldiers had to relearn in World War II. Despite these deficiencies, the division after-action report ended on a positive note: "Opposing crafty and veteran soldiers, our troops showed courage and ability. With one battle behind them, they were now ready to enter the next operation a wiser and more able fighting unit."[30] The battle was a costly lesson in the basics of modern warfare.

The 1st Infantry Division also learned important lessons at El Guettar. The division's after-action report noted, "Germans are a tenacious group of fighters and organize small islands of resistance which include mostly machine guns and machine pistols, well wired in. They are well supported by mortars and artillery and cannot be attacked frontally. They must be fixed by fire and out-flanked. . . . The German soldier is a determined fighter under almost all con-ditions."[31] The tactics needed to overcome a well-entrenched German defense required a high level of small-unit leadership, but until American units gained combat experience, aggressive leadership was not always forthcoming. The division report continued:

> The American soldier has had his first real fight with a determined enemy; his mistakes were many as were his attributes. His use of cover which was poor initially became excellent after the first skirmish. The use of a base of fire with a maneuver unit was not properly employed initially, but as time went on and the futility of frontal attacks was impressed on each soldier, groups as small as two men would apply the basic principle of using one man to fire while the other got behind. The use of mortars and automatic weapons by the enemy taught our soldiers lessons the application of which increased the efficiency of the close infantry support weapons tremendously.[32]

The great advantage formations such as the 1st and 9th Infantry Divisions had over most other American units in Europe is that they were able to learn such basic lessons of combat before they landed in Normandy in June 1944. *learn before D-Day*

Like the 1st and 9th Infantry Divisions, the 34th Infantry Division also learned valuable lessons upon its entry into combat. Finally assembled as an entity in March 1943, the Red Bull Division suffered a serious setback during its first battle as a complete unit. German positions in the Fondouk Gap had been blasted into solid rock, with clear fields of fire and strong wire and mine obstacles. The 34th Infantry Division's attack was unimaginative, basically amounting to a frontal assault in the face of withering machine gun fire. After the battle, the division withdrew to conduct remedial training, with special emphasis on night attacks and infantry-artillery cooperation. The division would put these lessons to use in its next operation, with much-improved results.[33]

After El Guettar, II Corps, under the command of Major General Omar N. Bradley as of 15 April, moved into northern Tunisia and prepared for its upcoming attack toward Bizerte. The 1st and 9th Infantry Divisions were to attack on line, but due to the terrain and road networks there was only a tenuous connection between the two units.[34] The 1st Infantry Division, whose mission was to seize the high ground astride the upper Tine River Valley (an area dubbed "The Mousetrap"), would conduct the main attack. II Corps reinforced its four divisional artillery battalions with six light (105mm) and five medium (155mm) artillery battalions. Behind the Big Red One, the 1st Armored Division waited to exploit any penetration toward Mateur. The 34th Infantry Division was initially in corps reserve.

Following an intensive artillery preparation on the morning of 23 April, the soldiers of the 1st Infantry Division attacked the heavily fortified enemy positions along the chain of hills covering the road to Mateur. Lieutenant General Lesley J. McNair, commander of AGF, was wounded by artillery fire while observing the attack of the 16th Infantry Regiment.[35] After three days of heavy fighting, the German defenders fell back four miles but still had good positions on high ground with interlocking fields of fire.[36] To put more strength behind the attack, on 26 April General Bradley inserted Major General Charles W. Ryder's 34th Infantry Division between the 1st and 9th Infantry Divisions. Ryder's mission was to seize Hill 609, the key position in the German defensive network.

The Germans used a reverse-slope defense to protect their positions on Hill 609, thereby negating any firepower advantage the American forces might have while attacking the forward slope of the hill. Timely enemy counterattacks often forced American troops to relinquish hard-won objectives.[37] On 29 April the 3d Battalion, 135th Infantry Regiment, followed a rolling barrage onto the southwestern slope of Hill 609. To overcome resistance on the remainder of the hill, American infantry units needed a more mobile, direct fire weapons system to support their attacks. The Sherman tank was the logical choice for this role. Reinforced by a company of medium tanks from the 1st Armored Regiment, the 1st Battalion, 133d Infantry Regiment, was able to gain the summit of Hill 609 on 30 April after only four hours. The seizure of Hill 531 and Hill 455 during the night by the 1st Battalion, 135th Infantry Regiment, completed the mission.[38] Sadly, the lesson in tank-infantry coordination was lost on the army as a whole. Not until several weeks into the Normandy campaign would the army put much-needed emphasis on infantry-tank training in combined-arms attacks.

With the high ground in American possession, the artillery of the 1st and 34th Infantry Divisions shattered enemy attempts to counterattack the next day.[39] General Bradley then unleashed Major General Ernest N. Harmon's 1st Armored Division, which seized Mateur on 3 May. The honor of taking Bizerte, however, would fall to the 9th Infantry Division and attached French forces, which fought a skillful battle in the northern portion of the II Corps' zone to open the way to the city.

The 9th Infantry Division faced fortified German positions on two hill

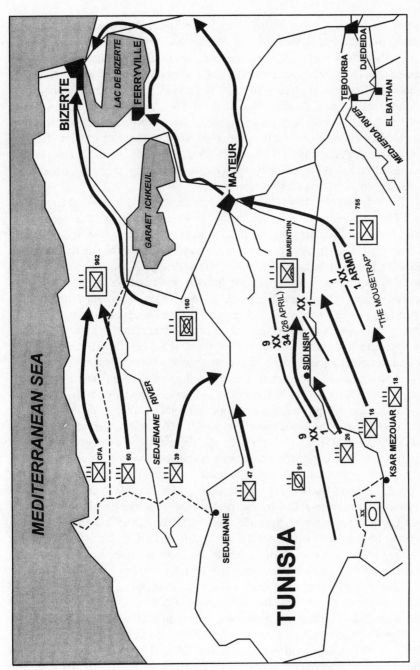

II Corps Operations in Tunisia, April–May 1943

masses (nicknamed "Green Hill" and "Bald Hill") that dominated the road leading to Mateur and Bizerte. The British had unsuccessfully attempted to assault these hill positions frontally three times already. General Eddy had learned enough from El Guettar not to make a fourth effort. Instead, he planned to hold the Germans in place with the 47th Infantry Regiment, while maneuvering the 39th and 60th Infantry Regiments through the extremely rough terrain of the Sedjenane Valley to the north of the German positions. Eddy decided that the potential benefits of the operation were worth the risk of moving the division out of communication with its supply and service organizations. He felt that the division could surprise the German defenders with the unexpected maneuver through "impassable" terrain.[40]

The 9th Infantry Division and its commander had learned their lessons well. The division made a meticulous study of the terrain and the enemy, and then completed a comprehensive plan, which commanders thoroughly briefed to their men. The division obtained three hundred mules for supply and evacuation in the mountainous terrain. Between 19 and 21 April, the 60th RCT moved during hours of darkness north into the Sedjenane Valley, unobserved by German forces. The attack began on 23 April. The 47th and 60th Infantry Regiments reached their initial objectives with little opposition, but the 39th Infantry Regiment met stiff resistance. When the commander of the 39th Infantry Regiment lost control of his forces, General Eddy relieved him. Brigadier General Donald A. Stroh, the assistant division commander, temporarily assumed command of the regiment and got it moving again. During the next several days, the division advanced to the east, slowed by steep hills, thick vegetation, and enemy resistance. Supply difficulties were acute.[41]

On 30 April the 39th Infantry took Hill 406, which overlooked the area behind Green and Bald Hills. Before the regiment lay a variety of German supply dumps and command and control installations. The 26th Field Artillery fired over four thousand rounds in a single day with devastating effect on the German rear area. Outflanked, the Germans pulled off the Green and Bald Hill positions and withdrew. During the next several days the division reached the final German positions in the hills west of Bizerte. The 1st Battalion, 60th Infantry, forced the Germans off the key terrain of Djebel Cheniti on 6 May by attacking in the best fashion of the Great War with bayonets fixed one hundred meters behind a rolling artillery barrage, thereby opening the way to Bizerte. On 7 May the first American units entered the city, only to withdraw again to allow French units to claim the liberation. On 8 May French forces entered Bizerte, and the North African campaign came to a close.[42]

The Sedjenane Valley campaign was a brilliant success for the 9th Infantry Division. The division suffered a net loss of 1,114 men, fewer than at El Guettar, and had accomplished all of its missions in outstanding fashion. The division's after-action report stated:

The 9th Division had demonstrated that it was able to take advantage of the lessons learned at El Guettar. It had substituted sweat for blood. It had maneuvered the Germans out of one position after another. The wide envelopment to the north undoubtedly came as a complete surprise to the enemy. . . . commanders were given ample time to make detailed plans and reconnaissance.[43]

The division used ample amounts of firepower; the artillery expended a total of forty-seven thousand rounds of 105mm and 155mm artillery shells during the operation. Staff sections improvised as necessary to make the plan work. The quartermaster foraged for 22,977 pounds of hay and 85,416 pounds of barley for the mules. The signal battalion laid huge amounts of wire, which was essential because radio communications were spotty at best due to the terrain. At times there were twelve hundred miles of wire on the ground. Engineers built seventy miles of roads for the artillery and supply vehicles. The medical battalion used mules to evacuate casualties and improvised a "casualty train" along a railroad track by removing the tires from a truck and placing the truck on the rails. In short, the division was learning its business.[44]

As much as combat itself, the digestion of combat experience during a period of training afterward and the internalization of lessons learned through thorough after-action reviews made the 1st and 9th Infantry Divisions into two of the best units in the army. The capable leadership of Eddy and Allen also had much to do with their divisions' successes. In his memoirs Omar Bradley showered praise on Eddy:

> There are few distinguishing characteristics of a successful division commander. Success comes instead from a well-balanced combination of good judgement, self-confidence, leadership, and boldness. . . . of all these commanders, none was better balanced nor more cooperative than Manton Eddy. Tactically he performed with classical maneuvers such as the one he employed at Jefna [Sedjenane Valley]. Yet though not timid, neither was he bold; Manton liked to count his steps carefully before he took them.[45]

Eddy did not hesitate to act when necessary, but his success depended as much on his ability as a trainer and administrator as it did on his competence as a tactician. Eddy was a well-balanced general officer, an excellent choice to lead a division in combat.

General Allen and his assistant division commander, Brigadier General Theodore Roosevelt Jr., also proved effective in combat, but their leadership style differed a great deal from that of the unassuming Eddy. Roosevelt was a famous man in his own right: son of former president Theodore Roosevelt, World War I hero, and former commander of the 26th Infantry Regiment. Allen and Roosevelt were nearly identical in temperament: fearless, aggressive, unconventional, and fiercely loyal to the soldiers under their command. Their parochialism and personality conflicts with General Bradley would result in their relief in Sicily in August 1943. One story relates that "in North Africa a general was heard to complain that Roosevelt and Allen 'seem to think the United States Army consists of the 1st Division and 11 million replacements,' which caused T.R. to retort, 'Well, *doesn't* it?' "[46] For his part, Terry Allen's leadership of the Big Red One in North Africa earned him both the ire of Bradley and a place on the cover of *Time* magazine.[47]

The Army of the United States as a whole also learned a great deal from the campaign in North Africa. Immediately upon the cessation of hostilities, Allied Forces Headquarters (AFHQ) ordered each division involved in the campaign to submit a thorough report on combat experiences and lessons learned for training purposes. AFHQ published excerpts of these reports as AFHQ Training Memorandum No. 44 on 4 August 1943. The War Department reprinted the memorandum as a training manual entitled *Lessons from the Tunisian Campaign* on 15 October 1943 and distributed it to divisions still training in the United States. Battle experience, AFHQ and the War Department concluded, had validated existing training literature and doctrine. "Failures or tactical reverses have resulted from misapplication of these principles, or from lack of judgement and flexibility in their application, or from attempts to follow book rules rigidly without due consideration of their suitability to existing situations."[48] Not all observers would agree with that conclusion. Especially in the area of antiarmor tactics, North Africa proved that American doctrine could not always stand up to the rigors of modern combat.[49]

Many of the lessons learned repeated fundamental training concepts that units relearned the hard way on the battlefield. These lessons included the use of fire and maneuver to advance against enemy positions, the importance of combined-arms coordination, the need to train and fight at night, the use of smoke to obscure movement, and the importance of small-unit training.[50] The report of the 9th Infantry Division stressed the most important lesson learned— seize and take the high ground. "We learned that to live we must take to the ridges and advance along them, avoiding the natural 'avenues of approach' up the valleys. . . . Taking to the ridges was tedious, strenuous business but it saved hundreds of lives and gave physical possession of the high ground."[51] Possession of the high ground afforded observation for forward observers, who could call in deadly artillery strikes against enemy positions. American artillery performed superbly in North Africa, as it did throughout the war. Its flexibility and ability to mass fires made American artillery a formidable weapon of destruction.[52]

On the other hand, air support of ground forces proved to be disappointing. Close air support was "not close enough." There was an excessive delay between request and execution of air missions, which caused the support to be ineffective. "The Air Corps complained on several occasions that there were no enemy where we reported them, yet their planes flew over the indicated target two or three hours after the request was made—Enemy troops move," one report stated.[53] Shamefully, the Army Air Forces did nothing to fix the close air support system, and the Sicilian and Italian campaigns again highlighted its faults. Not until the breakout from Normandy in late July 1944 did the close air support system become responsive to the needs of the ground forces.

North Africa was also a proving ground for the logistical apparatus of the new triangular infantry division. The most important lesson learned was that the division quartermaster company was a key link in the chain of supply. Due to the extended distance of supply dumps from the front in Tunisia—often seventy miles or more behind the lead divisions—the forty-eight trucks of the division quartermaster company often traveled great distances to keep the unit supplied with essentials such as food and fuel.[54] This lesson would be lost on AGF in the 1943 redesign of the infantry division. Lieutenant General McNair decentralized the responsibility of food and fuel supply to infantry regiments and separate battalions. In theory, these subordinate units would pick up supplies directly from army supply points, thereby eliminating the division as a middleman. The trucks of the division quartermaster company were to be used as a logistical reserve.[55] Fortunately, AGF did not cut out the quartermaster company entirely, and the War Department restored the service platoon (a pool of soldiers used to load and unload trucks) to the table of organization before approving the new division design. In the campaigns to come, the quartermaster company would prove absolutely critical to the successful functioning of the American supply system at division level and below.

German Field Marshal Erwin Rommel gave high marks to the ability of the American units to learn from their mistakes. Rommel stated:

> In Tunisia the Americans had to pay a stiff price for their experience, but it brought rich dividends. Even at this time, the American generals showed themselves to be very advanced in the tactical handling of their forces, although we had to wait until the Patton Army in France to see the most astonishing achievements in mobile warfare. The Americans, it is fair to say, profited far more than the British from their experience in Africa, thus confirming the axiom that education is easier than re-education.[56]

This comment is enlightening in view of the severe criticism some historians level on the tactical abilities of American units, both in North Africa and later in the war. Apparently, some German commanders at the time thought differently.

Finally, successful combat operations in the latter part of the North African campaign engendered confidence among the divisions involved. The 2d Battalion, 168th Infantry Regiment, 34th Infantry Division, one of the units so badly mauled at Sidi-bou-Zid, recorded in the division history: "It was in the engagements at Hills 473, 375, and 609 that men found themselves. They had proved to themselves that they were a much superior soldier in comparison to the invincible German. They had become veteran troops overnight."[57] After the seizure of Bizerte, the 1st, 9th, and 34th Infantry Divisions no longer viewed the Germans as either superior or invincible. Successful operations breed confidence, and confidence is an important factor in a unit's performance in battle.

American infantry divisions continued to improve in their next operation, the invasion of Sicily. Operation HUSKY grew out of decisions made by the Allies six months earlier at the Casablanca Conference. At the conference Prime Minister Winston Churchill of Great Britain argued that the Allies should finish the campaign in North Africa and then strike at the "soft underbelly" of the Axis in the Mediterranean, with Sicily, Italy, and the Balkans as potential targets for future operations. Due primarily to the ongoing Allied operations in North Africa, which created a momentum of their own, Churchill's position prevailed. The Allies agreed to invade Sicily at the conclusion of the Tunisian campaign, an agreement that effectively postponed a cross-Channel invasion into France until 1944.[58] Aside from strategic considerations, continued operations in the Mediterranean gave American forces more time to digest lessons learned, to train, and to gain combat experience prior to the decisive cross-Channel invasion.

Training for the invasion of Sicily began as early as March 1943 when regiments of the 3d Infantry Division began cycling through the Fifth Army Invasion Training Center at Arzew Beach in Algeria. Training stressed physical conditioning, combined-arms coordination, assault against fortifications, removal of mines and obstacles, and ship-to-shore movement. A complete rehearsal, Operation COPYBOOK, took place from 20 to 26 June. Lack of waterproofing materials allowed for only limited vehicle debarkation from the landing craft, but the exercise was as close to a full-scale rehearsal for the upcoming invasion as possible.[59]

In the early morning hours of 10 July 1943, British and American forces stormed ashore across the beaches of southeastern Sicily. Seven Allied divisions (three American, three British, and one Canadian) composed the seaborne echelon of Operation HUSKY, the code name for the operation, as opposed to only five in the more famous Operation OVERLORD that would take place less than a year later in Normandy. The initial landings were remarkably successful due to the absence of any stiff opposition from Italian coastal divisions in the area. Despite this initial victory, the Allies would take over a month to secure the remainder of the island against stiff resistance from three German panzer grenadier divisions. Sicily was a bitter victory for the Allies, but the campaign resulted in Italy's surrender and took the Allies one step closer to Berlin.[60]

In the American zone of attack, the 3d Infantry Division landed at Licata, while the 1st and 45th Infantry Divisions landed near Gela. All three divisions were well trained and capably led. General Allen's 1st Infantry Division had extensive combat experience in North Africa. The other two divisions had seen little or no combat but would soon prove themselves in battle.

The 45th Infantry Division, the "Thunderbird" Division, was a National Guard unit from the American Plains and Southwest under the command of Major General Troy H. Middleton. As the youngest colonel in the American Expeditionary Forces, Middleton had commanded an infantry regiment in the Meuse-Argonne offensive in World War I. He had left the U.S. Army in 1937

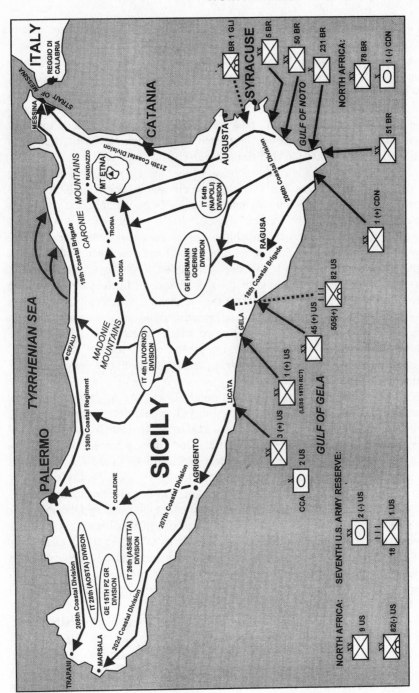

The Sicilian Campaign, July–August 1943

as a lieutenant colonel to take a position as dean of administration and director of student personnel at Louisiana State University. When the Japanese bombed Pearl Harbor, he offered his services to the War Department, which reinstated him in his former grade. A competent leader, Middleton rose in rank quickly. By June 1942 he was a brigadier general and assistant division commander of the Thunderbirds; by the fall he was a major general and the division's commanding officer. According to Lieutenant General Lesley J. McNair, when the 45th Infantry Division departed the United States in June 1943, it was "better prepared than any division that has left our control to date."[61]

General Middleton was more critical of the division's amphibious training and deployment overseas. From the time the division debarked from the United States on 28 May 1943 until its landing in Sicily on 10 July, the troops remained embarked except for one week in North Africa. "This long period during which troops were aboard ship needs no comment," Middleton bitterly remarked in his report.[62] Furthermore, he felt the division could have received better amphibious training had it deployed earlier to North Africa instead of training on the eastern seaboard of the United States. "In the case of the 45th Division," Middleton remarked, "I believe we could have accomplished in two weeks in North Africa more than we accomplished the entire time at Solomons, Maryland. In Africa there were beaches on which the entire Division could be landed. Furthermore, away from home troops are closer to the war atmosphere."[63] Despite these drawbacks in their training and deployment overseas, the Thunderbirds performed well in Sicily.

The 3d Infantry Division had had minimal exposure to combat in Operation TORCH, where it performed sluggishly. It would enter combat in Sicily under a new commander, Major General Lucian K. Truscott Jr., an exceptional leader and trainer and one of the finest division commanders in the war. Truscott had spent over six years as a student and instructor at the Command and General Staff School at Fort Leavenworth in the 1930s and was only a major of cavalry when France fell in June 1940. His outstanding abilities carried him to the rank of lieutenant general and command of the 3d Infantry Division, U.S. VI Corps, and the Fifth U.S. Army by the end of the war. Truscott was instrumental in the formation of American Ranger battalions in 1942, personally observed the tragic Anglo-Canadian raid on Dieppe, and had commanded a sub–task force under General Patton in Operation TORCH. As a division commander, Truscott would set a high standard for training, planning, and combat leadership.[64]

Truscott put a high premium on physical conditioning, especially marching. The normal rate for infantry marching was two and one-half miles per hour. Truscott felt he could nearly double that figure with proper conditioning. "I had long felt that our standards for marching and fighting in the infantry were too low," Truscott wrote later, "not up to those of the Roman legions nor countless examples from our own frontier history, nor even to those of Stonewall Jackson's 'Foot Cavalry' of Civil War fame."[65] The soldiers of the 3d

Infantry Division soon dubbed the new marching speed of four miles per hour the "Truscott Trot." The commander of the 3d Battalion, 7th Infantry Regiment, during Operation HUSKY, Lieutenant Colonel John A. Heintges, credits good training, thorough rehearsals, and physical conditioning for the Marne Division's success in Sicily. "They [the soldiers] were capable of a hell of a lot more than they thought they were. . . . We practiced the 'Truscott Trot,' and this is why our battalions made such long moves, as much as 34 miles in one day, and fought at the other end, and had a couple of little battles on the way."[66] As a result of the Truscott Trot, the 3d Infantry Division was the most foot-mobile regular infantry division in the Army of the United States.

Truscott was a cavalryman at heart, which influenced the speed at which he conducted operations. In Sicily the 3d Battalion, 7th Infantry Regiment, once scaled a difficult mountain trail reportedly heavily defended by the enemy only to find Truscott standing on a rock at the summit in his brown leather jacket with his white neckerchief fluttering in the wind. His presence was a subtle reminder to the battalion commander that his unit was moving too slowly.[67]

The only serious challenge to the landings of the Seventh U.S. Army in the Gulf of Gela came from a counterattack by the Hermann Goering Panzer Grenadier Division and the Italian Livorno Division. In fierce fighting the 1st and 45th Infantry Divisions, the Ranger Force, and elements of Colonel James M. Gavin's 505th Parachute Infantry Regiment held off enemy attacks with help from tanks of the 2d Armored Division, artillery, and naval gunfire support. The heavy pounding American forces inflicted on the attackers destroyed the Livorno Division as a fighting unit and severely weakened the Hermann Goering Division.[68] Predictably, airpower played almost no part in the battle as the air forces decided to place most of their resources into interdiction missions. Furthermore, the system for requesting close air support remained cumbersome at best.[69]

After beating off the German counterattack, Allied forces began the slow drive north toward the crucial port of Messina in northeastern Sicily. General Bernard L. Montgomery's British Eighth Army conducted the main attack along the direct route up the eastern coast, but the Germans tenaciously defended this obvious avenue of approach and slowed the British attack to a crawl. Lieutenant General George S. Patton's Seventh U.S. Army had the mission of defending the Eighth Army's flank, but remaining passive in a flank guard role went against Patton's aggressive nature. Sensing an opportunity, Patton ordered his army to conduct a "reconnaissance in force" northwest to seize the port of Palermo.[70]

While Bradley's II Corps (1st and 45th Infantry Divisions) attacked across the center of the island, a provisional corps under the command of Major General Geoffrey Keyes consisting of the 3d Infantry Division, the 2d Armored Division, the 82d Airborne Division, and Task Force X (two Ranger battalions and the 39th Infantry Regiment of the 9th Infantry Division) drove toward Palermo. The attack began on 19 July, and on 22 July American troops entered the city. "It was here that the Truscott Trot really came into its own," claimed William B. Rosson, S-3 (operations officer) of the 7th Infantry Regiment. "The troops were in very good condition and they were pushed hard."[71] As a result, the infantrymen of the 3d Infantry Division advanced a hundred miles in three days and reached Palermo at the same time as the 2d Armored Division with its tanks and half-tracks.[72]

The seizure of Palermo was a great propaganda victory for Patton and his army, but it would be a meaningless triumph unless it also led to the seizure of Messina, the only really important strategic objective in Sicily. As the Seventh U.S. Army swung east to drive toward Messina, however, Patton's forces met with the same stubborn German delaying efforts that had stalled Montgomery's forces on the Catania Plain south of Mount Etna. Bradley's II Corps faced especially difficult terrain in the mountainous interior of Sicily.[73] Middleton's 45th Infantry Division attacked east along Highway 113, the coastal road leading to Messina, while the 1st Infantry Division fought along Highway 120, the mountainous route to the same objective. Both divisions made only slow headway against the delaying German 15th and 29th Panzer Grenadier Divisions.

The 1st Infantry Division fought a particularly bitter battle for the town of Troina on Highway 120. During most of July the German defenders had delayed from ridgeline to ridgeline in the harsh terrain of northeastern Sicily, causing American forces to deploy to envelop successive defensive positions in time-consuming and costly maneuvers. The delay ended when the German commander in Sicily, *General der Panzertruppen* Hans Valentin Hube, decided that his forces would defend Troina as the anchor of the entire German defensive line.[74] On 1 August the 39th Infantry Regiment, attached to the 1st Infantry Division, ran into the strong German defenses around Troina. General Allen committed the rest of his division to penetrate the German line. For five days the division battered itself against the German defenses built into the formidable terrain around Sicily's highest city. On the morning of 6 August, the Big Red One occupied a devastated Troina.[75] The battle was to be the division's last until the morning of 6 June 1944.

Major General Terry de la Mesa Allen's reward for taking Troina was to be relieved of his command.[76] General Eisenhower and General Patton felt that Allen was tired and needed some time away from combat. Eisenhower decided to relieve Allen (and his assistant division commander, Roosevelt) "without prejudice," so they could rotate back to the United States and assume duties at an equivalent level of command. The conclusion of the battle for Troina was an appropriate time for a change of command, but the order effecting Allen's relief came through normal administrative channels instead of personally from Patton or Bradley. As a result, rumors flew that Allen had been relieved for ineffective command. Nothing could be further from the truth, despite Bradley's lukewarm appraisal of Allen in his memoirs.[77] There is little doubt that a personality conflict existed between Bradley and Allen, and Allen made no effort to conceal his lack of respect for his corps commander.[78] Allen would go on to

Lieutenant General George S. Patton Jr., commander of the Seventh U.S. Army, discusses the situation near Troina, Sicily, with Brigadier General Theodore Roosevelt Jr., assistant division commander of the 1st Infantry Division, 4 August 1943. A few days after this picture was taken, Roosevelt and his division commander, Major General Terry de la Mesa Allen, were relieved of duty. Both went on to serve with distinction in other divisions. (U.S. Army Signal Corps photo)

command the 104th Infantry Division with distinction and would prove his worth once again as a combat leader. Roosevelt would invade Normandy as the assistant division commander of the 4th Infantry Division less than a year later, where he earned a Medal of Honor and died of a heart attack.[79]

After Allen's relief, Major General Clarence R. Huebner assumed command of the 1st Infantry Division, with Brigadier General Willard G. Wyman as his assistant division commander. Allen did what he could to make the transition a smooth one. In what must have been a difficult gesture, Allen personally escorted Huebner around the division and introduced him to the regimental and battalion commanders.[80]

Under Huebner the Big Red One would rise to new levels of combat effectiveness and fight its most impressive battles. He had served with the 1st Infantry Division in every grade from private through colonel and had earned the Distinguished Service Cross with palm, two Purple Hearts, the Croix de Guerre, and a Distinguished Service Medal while serving in its ranks during World War I. Nevertheless, the men of the division treated Huebner as an outsider for many months, in large measure because his command style was so different from Allen's. Huebner was a very tough commander, a strict disciplinarian who preferred formality in his relationships with subordinates. Upon his assumption of command, Huebner immediately enforced high standards of discipline and military courtesy. Training events that included marksmanship and close-order drill earned the ire of jaded combat veterans, who only slowly learned the value of such activities. Near the end of the war, Huebner observed of the men of the Big Red One: "They respected me; they loved General Allen."[81]

The 1st and 45th Infantry Divisions began the attack toward Messina; the 3d and 9th Infantry Divisions would finish it.[82] Truscott's men conducted a series of amphibious envelopments along Sicily's northern coast while the 9th Infantry Division fought through the mountains. After the battle for Troina, the 9th Infantry Division passed through the 1st Infantry Division to continue the attack east. Based upon two excellent tactical terrain studies and intelligence reports, General Eddy decided to repeat the tactics used successfully in the Sedjenane Valley. The 47th Infantry Regiment would pin the Germans from the front, while the 60th Infantry Regiment maneuvered through the mountains around the German northern flank.[83] Once again, the substitution of sweat for blood saved men and gained ground. In a nine-day operation, the 9th Infantry Division advanced to Floresta and Randazzo, the last German positions before Messina. There the 3d Infantry Division and the British 78th Division pinched the 9th Infantry Division out of the line.

The terrain was again the biggest obstacle, but the engineers, medics, and quartermaster units overcame severe handicaps to keep the 60th Infantry supplied and on the move. The 60th Infantry had become proficient in infiltrating enemy positions through mountainous terrain. The unit marched one hundred hours, mostly at night, over mountain slopes with minimal supplies, with only the light of a full moon to show the way.[84] The division lost 1,201 men in the operation, but it again proved that the best way through enemy positions is to go around them, no matter how difficult the terrain.[85]

The 3d Infantry Division fought a similar battle against terrain on the coastal road leading to Messina. German demolitions and mines continually blocked the road and in places dropped parts of it off the face of the cliffs along which it ran. When this happened, the 10th Engineer Battalion ended up blasting a new road into the face of the cliffs. When German units contested the road, General Truscott either sent forces inland to envelop the enemy positions or used small battalion task forces in short amphibious turning movements to force the enemy to vacate his positions.[86] The division also made several night assaults, one of the keys to winning the battle for Sicily.

General Patton's forces won the "race" to Messina by a matter of hours, but the triumphal American entry was meaningless in military terms, for the German forces had already escaped intact across the Strait of Messina into the "toe" of Italy. Nevertheless, the seizure of Sicily on 17 August 1943 opened the Mediterranean shipping lanes to unhindered traffic and gave the Allies a springboard for further operations in the region. The most important result of the campaign, however, was the removal of Mussolini's fascist government from power. Italian troops had done little to hinder Allied offensive operations in Sicily. As one division history stated, "The Italian was not a good soldier, had no stake in the war, and no interest in continuing to fight it."[87] When given the slightest pretext to do so, Italian soldiers surrendered in droves. Mussolini's successor, Field Marshal Pietro Badoglio, agreed to surrender terms within three weeks after the fall of Sicily, an event that led to the Allied invasion of the Italian mainland and the beginning of a long, difficult campaign to pierce the "soft underbelly" of Hitler's Fortress Europe.[88]

The Sicilian campaign had at least two major effects on the Army of the United States. First, the campaign allowed American commanders—among them Patton, Bradley, Allen, Truscott, Eddy, Middleton, Major General Hugh J. Gaffey (commander of the 2d Armored Division), and Major General Matthew B. Ridgway (commander of the 82d Airborne Division)—to continue to gain much-needed experience in the conduct of battles and campaigns. Second, the campaign provided an opportunity for American divisions to gain further combat experience prior to the cross-Channel invasion in 1944.

All divisions continued to draw lessons from their experiences, and these lessons became more sophisticated as the units mastered the basics of combat. The 9th Infantry Division learned the need to maintain contact with retreating enemy forces at all costs, to prevent them from reestablishing a coherent defense (a lesson the division would put to good use in the Cotentin Peninsula in June 1944). The 45th Infantry Division felt the best way to keep pressure on the enemy was through the employment of successive night attacks. Infantry units recognized the need to keep troops moving through artillery fire, rather than halting and giving the enemy artillery a fixed target at which to shoot. Once again, artillery proved to be the most effective and deadly weapon in the American ground arsenal. Other lessons dealt with the need for commanders to place themselves forward, where they could personally observe the battle, training in mine and booby trap removal, the use of heavy weapons in infantry battalions, the need for engineers to repair roads and bridges quickly, and the use of pack mules in mountain operations.[89]

American infantrymen cross a blown-out roadbed during operations in Sicily, 14 August 1943. Extensive demolitions slowed the Allied advance across the island. (U.S. Army Signal Corps photo)

The Sicilian campaign continued to prove the inadequacy of Allied air support of ground operations. Airpower should have been one of the decisive elements of the campaign; instead, the emphasis air commanders put on the independent mission of interdiction as opposed to close air support limited the role of airpower in several important battles. Truscott complained that despite repeated requests, the Army Air Forces did not even provide an officer to help plan air support for the amphibious invasion.[90] As a result, almost no close air support was available to help repel the initial enemy counterattacks on the beaches at Gela. The 1st Infantry Division was also critical of the quality of close air support; fratricide from the air was a problem singled out by the Big Red One as a particular concern.[91] The report concluded, "The morale effect on the American soldier in seeing air that is supporting him in his small battle and the devastating effect it has on the German soldier makes every effort for close coordination of the infantry and air arm a matter of utmost importance."[92] Not until the division received pilots with radio communications that enabled them to communicate directly with attacking aircraft did close air support improve, but the Army Air Forces were tardy in systematizing the procedure.

Logistically, the invasion of Sicily provided two important firsts for the

American army. One development that proved its worth was the use of the DUKW—a six-wheel, 2.5-ton amphibious truck—to carry supplies from cargo vessels to the beach and beyond.[93] One hundred forty-four DUKWs worked at off-loading cargo and equipment for the 1st Infantry Division at Gela. They were indispensable, since sandbars offshore prevented LSTs (landing ship, tank) from off-loading cargo directly onto the beach.[94] A second improvisation that worked well in Operation HUSKY was the 45th Infantry Division's use of wooden pallets to configure supply loads that could be carried by a DUKW and quickly off-loaded using a forklift or crane. One quartermaster officer sent to observe the operation credited the pallets with a 50 percent increase in the rate of delivery of supplies from ship to inland dump.[95]

The Allied command, however, did not heed one of the most important logistical lessons learned by the 9th Infantry Division. The movement of the division from North Africa to Sicily went smoothly because the division combat-loaded on transports and put first priority on maintaining unit integrity. Vehicles carried their full combat loads; the division did not crate any equipment. This allowed for rapid unloading in Palermo, and the division was ready for combat quickly after arrival.[96] Regrettably, logisticians gained the upper hand in planning the use of shipping space for the Normandy invasion. The result was the sacrifice of unit integrity for maximization of the use of cargo space on the transport vessels. This caused chaos on the beaches, with units searching for men and pieces of equipment for days after arrival. Invasion planners did not heed the lesson that what really matters is not the number of units transported to the beachhead but the number of combat-ready units available to the field commander upon debarkation.

By contrast to its experience in Sicily, shortly after D-Day in Normandy the 9th Infantry Division moved across the Channel in small loads distributed among forty-seven Liberty ships, eight LSTs, and twelve LCTs (landing craft, tank), integrated with loads from four other divisions and miscellaneous corps units. As a result, the 9th Infantry Division took four days to disembark. Even then, small detachments continued to come ashore for several more days.[97] A less ambitious loading plan emphasizing unit integrity would have brought more useful combat power ashore in less time. The turnaround time to England was short; the transports could have made a few more trips to compensate for the fact that a specific unit could not use every last square foot of cargo space on its assigned ship.

The G-3 Training Section of Allied Force Headquarters compiled a list of lessons learned and published them on 25 October 1943 as "Training Notes from the Sicilian Campaign."[98] The purpose of the document was to provide training lessons for units that had not yet entered combat. Even though Sicily presented a unique set of problems involving mountainous terrain with few roads and an enemy that used extensive mines and demolitions to delay attacking forces, many combat experiences were transferable to other situations. The campaign as a whole validated American ground combat doctrine and lessons learned in Tunisia, especially the vitality of the infantry-artillery team.

Operations in North Africa and Sicily proved a necessary intermediate step in the development of combat effectiveness in the Army of the United States. During these campaigns American leaders and units garnered valuable experience that would not go to waste in future operations. Although early reverses at Kasserine Pass demonstrated the initial difficulties American commanders had in orchestrating combat operations, American doctrine on the whole proved sound, with two notable exceptions. Antiarmor doctrine and the composition and use of tank destroyer units proved woefully inadequate to the needs of the battlefield. Likewise, the planning and execution of close air support constituted a major weakness that would not be quickly or easily remedied. Despite these two concerns, the lessons learned in North Africa and Sicily filtered back to units training in the United States and Great Britain. Combat-experienced commanders stressed the importance of fire and maneuver, combined-arms coordination, night combat, use of terrain and smoke during battles, and the critical nature of small-unit training. Army Ground Forces heeded these lessons by mandating more small-unit training, including courses in attack of fortified areas, village fighting, close combat, and day and night infiltration techniques. Planners also gained experience and were able to build on lessons learned during two major amphibious invasions.

The only combat-experienced American divisions in Normandy in 1944 gained that experience in North Africa and Sicily. Four of the six American divisions that fought in Sicily also fought in Normandy: the 1st and 9th Infantry Divisions, the 2d Armored Division, and the 82d Airborne Division. The other two American divisions that battled for possession of the island—the 3d and 45th Infantry Divisions—would fight in Italy before invading southern France in August 1944. These units brought a wealth of experience to the American forces engaged in the decisive campaigns for France and Germany in 1944 and 1945. The difference in combat effectiveness between these battle-tested units and the remainder of the Army of the United States in the ETO would become readily apparent after the invasion of Normandy on 6 June 1944. These divisions proved, however, that American combat forces could quickly adapt to the realities of the modern battlefield and after a short period in combat match or exceed the capabilities of the enemy forces arrayed against them.

Despite expelling German forces from Sicily, the Allies were not successful in destroying large numbers of enemy troops. The Germans skillfully used the rugged Sicilian terrain, mines, demolitions, and booby traps to delay Allied forces. When German units took up strong defensive positions such as at Troina, the cost of dislodging them was high. Firepower alone could not force the deeply dug-in defenders from their positions. Three German panzer grenadier divisions managed to delay two Allied armies for over a month in the mountainous terrain. The struggle for Sicily should have provided a warning to Allied leaders: the results they could expect from a campaign in Italy would not be commensurate with the effort involved. Nevertheless, buoyed by the Italian surrender and the end of the Sicilian campaign, Allied forces soon plunged into what proved to be anything but the "soft underbelly" of Hitler's Fortress Europe.

5

The Long Road to Germany: The Italian Campaign, 1943–1944

The Army of the United States exhibited both strengths and weaknesses during the Italian campaign. Achieving the mission of seizing terrain and destroying enemy forces was difficult at best against an enemy who proved extremely adept at carving out defensive positions in the mountains of the Italian peninsula. Poor tactics led to high casualties in some operations, such as the assault by the 36th Infantry Division across the Rapido River in January 1944. The senior American commander, Lieutenant General Mark Clark, proved unable or unwilling to use success to destroy the German army in Italy when the opportunity presented itself during Operation DIADEM, instead opting for a symbolic political victory in the seizure of Rome in June 1944. Problems with the individual replacement system, such as the misassignment of soldiers into positions other than that for which they had been trained and the poor training and conditioning of replacements, plagued the Fifth U.S. Army. On the other hand, the personnel system was able to keep American divisions in the fight by continuously reconstituting losses. The American supply system proved capable of maintaining supplies at a high level through the proficient use of all transportation means at its disposal. American artillery proved its superiority over the enemy through the effective massing of fires. Finally, the newly created divisions of the Organized Reserves, the "draftee divisions," received their baptism of fire in Italy in the spring of 1944. Their achievements boosted the morale of the American people and increased the confidence of the American army prior to the Normandy invasion in June.

The Allied invasion of Italy in September 1943 grew out of the successful seizure of Sicily during the previous two months. The capture of Sicily created a momentum of its own, one that the British hoped to use to expand operations in the Mediterranean. More important, the attack on Sicily caused the downfall of Mussolini's fascist government in Italy. The decision by Mussolini's successor, Field Marshal Pietro Badoglio, to agree to surrender terms led to the Allied invasion of the Italian mainland and the beginning of a long, difficult campaign to seize Rome and advance north up the mountainous peninsula. For the Allied divisions involved, the Italian campaign was an endless morass of mud, mountains, and frustration. Locked in a seemingly interminable struggle against both the elements and the enemy, American infantry divisions in Italy adapted as best they could to the exigencies of the moment.

The Allies hoped to advance rapidly up the Italian "boot," but the Germans reacted quickly to the Italian collapse and soon had reinforcements in place to take over the defense of the peninsula.[1] The British Eighth Army, commanded by General Bernard L. Montgomery, crossed the Strait of Messina into the "toe" of Italy on 3 September and moved slowly north up the Calabrian Peninsula. Six days later the Fifth U.S. Army, commanded by Lieutenant General Mark W. Clark, landed in the Gulf of Salerno south of Naples. After an interval of twenty-five years, American forces once again found themselves fighting on the continent of Europe.

The invasion of Salerno, code-named AVALANCHE, was a near disaster. Clark's plan was to land two British divisions and the American 36th Infantry Division, spearheaded by Rangers and Commandos, on opposite sides of the Sele River with a gap of ten miles between them.[2] The terrain behind the invasion beaches rose rapidly in a line of steep hills that gave the defenders a decided advantage. The redeployment of combat troops to Great Britain in preparation for the cross-Channel invasion and the lack of assault shipping limited the reinforcements available to Fifth Army.[3]

While still at sea the Allied soldiers heard the announcement of the surrender of Italy. If the troops thought the surrender would make the invasion easy, they were sadly mistaken. The German 16th Panzer Division resisted fiercely, although the Allied divisions managed to claw their way ashore. The next day the 45th Infantry Division landed to reinforce the attack. By 12 September, Fifth U.S. Army had managed to carve out a beachhead forty miles long, but only seven miles deep. As with most military operations, the weakest point was at the boundary; the Allies had still not closed the interval between the British X Corps and the U.S. VI Corps along the Sele River.[4]

As the Allied troops fought their way inland on 13 September, the Germans launched a massive counterattack with elements of four panzer and panzer grenadier divisions into the gap between the British and American forces. The next forty-eight hours were critical, but hard fighting and quick reinforcements salvaged the Allied cause. The 36th and 45th Infantry Divisions rallied to save their precarious beachheads, but at one point Clark ordered his staff to work on a contingency plan to withdraw VI Corps from south of the Sele River. The commander of the 45th Infantry Division, Major General Troy Middleton, would have none of it. "Put food and ammunition behind the 45th," he scolded Clark. "We are going to stay."[5]

What the Fifth U.S. Army needed was reinforcements. Although General Sir Harold Alexander, commander of the 15th Army Group, rushed the 3d

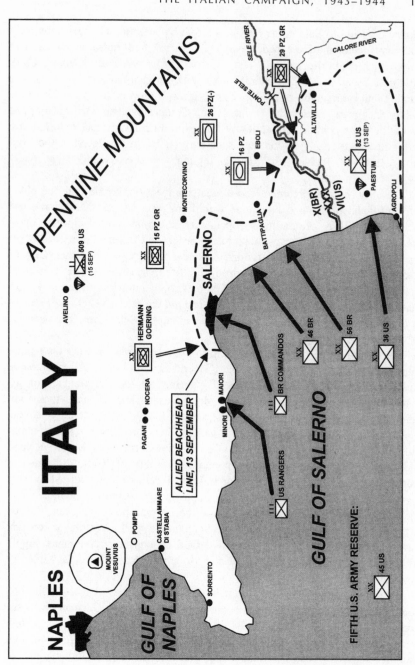

Operation AVALANCHE, September 1943

Infantry Division to Salerno as fast as possible by sea, the only real hope for a rapid reinforcement of the beachhead lay with the 82d Airborne Division in Sicily, which could drop at least two regiments in by parachute. General Clark sent a note by air to Major General Matthew B. Ridgway asking him to drop a regiment that same night. "Can do," was Ridgway's reply.[6] The 504th Parachute Infantry Regiment, under the command of Colonel Reuben Tucker, dropped into the beachhead at midnight, and by early morning Tucker had reported into Clark's headquarters. "As soon as assembled you are to be placed in the front lines," Clark told Tucker. "Sir," Tucker replied, "we are assembled and ready now."[7]

The airborne reinforcement had a greater impact on morale than the physical reinforcement by two battalions would suggest. The German attack had reached its zenith before the paratroopers entered the line on the morning of 14 September, but the American troops in the beachhead received a needed boost at a critical period of the operation. The next night Colonel James Gavin's 505th Parachute Infantry Regiment dropped into the beachhead. The balance of the battle shifted noticeably. With the German counterattack repulsed and additional units at its disposal, VI Corps could resume the offensive. On 17 September the Americans and British closed the gap along the Sele River. The next day the Germans withdrew.[8]

The 82d Airborne Division could help save the beachhead, but not the reputation of the VI Corps commander, Major General Ernest Dawley. After the battle Clark relieved Dawley as a sacrificial offering for the deficiencies of his command, perceived, real, or otherwise.[9] Major General John P. Lucas took command of the VI Corps, only to meet the same fate five months later at Anzio.

Ultimately, the Allies succeeded in landing their forces on the Italian mainland and seized the major port of Naples, but the Germans withdrew in good order to prepared positions in the Winter Line south of Rome. Terrain and weather dominated the rest of the war in Italy. Torrents of rain turned the fine clay soil of the river valleys into near-impassable quagmires. Swollen rivers blocked the few valleys that led north into the German positions. Rain washed out tactical bridging. Snow capped the heights and made frostbite a constant danger. Poor roads, turned into rivers of mud by constant rain, made supply difficult at best. For the Fifth U.S. and British Eighth Armies, a winter of discontent lay ahead.

By mid-November 1943 the combat divisions of the Fifth U.S. Army had been bled white in repeated frontal assaults against the tough German positions. Cold, wet weather also caused a loss of stamina and recuperative power among both officers and men of frontline units. The rate of evacuation for nonbattle casualties such as pneumonia and trench foot rose sharply. Shorter periods of frontline duty and regular rotation of units to the rear for rest could alleviate the situation, but the Fifth U.S. Army lacked sufficient divisions to rotate units on a regular basis. Instead, personnel managers sent individual replacements to the front to maintain units at full strength. A replacement crisis inevitably arose.

Army Ground Forces and the personnel managers in the MTO had not made sufficient allowances for the large number of infantry casualties that the Fifth U.S. Army incurred. As a result, AGF stripped units still in training in the United States to maintain an adequate replacement flow overseas.[10] Overseas, commanders of replacement depots, under pressure to fill existing shortages of infantrymen, diverted replacement soldiers trained in a wide range of skills to infantry units. In October the 1st Battalion, 26th Infantry Regiment, then stationed in Great Britain, received forty replacements to refill a company decimated by losses. The battalion requested riflemen but received the following instead: 2 riflemen, 3 basics, 3 dishwashing machine operators, 8 antiaircraft gunners, 14 truck drivers, 2 radiomen, 1 artilleryman, and 7 other men with miscellaneous skills. One replacement asked, "What do you do with a grenade?"[11]

The poor replacement situation led General Clark to convene a board of officers in December to look into the problem. The board's findings were an indictment of the replacement system as it existed at the time. Replacements were in poor physical condition, mainly because they had not received proper training once they left their replacement training centers or divisions in the United States. The replacements had spent almost as much time traveling to Italy (twelve to sixteen weeks) as they had training since entering the army (thirteen to seventeen weeks). As a result, their skills had eroded. Since training at the replacement depots en route to the theater was inadequate or nonexistent, replacements entered combat poorly prepared to assume their duties. The quality of these soldiers was not high. Of the 17,698 replacements received in Italy between 9 September and 6 December 1943, 1.5 percent were category I, 14.5 percent were category II, 38.8 percent were category III, 40.9 percent were category IV, and 4.3 percent were category V.[12]

The 3d, 34th, and 45th Infantry Divisions, heavily committed during the fall, were forced to integrate their replacements into combat units directly at the front. The 36th Infantry Division, in reserve for much of this period, was able to give its replacements a two-week training course before assigning them to their regiments. Replacements integrated at the front experienced a much higher proportion of casualties than veteran soldiers—as much as three times as high.[13] The board recommended holding replacements in depots in Italy for two weeks of physical conditioning prior to shipping them to divisions. Rather than releasing replacements in large increments, the board favored a steady flow of small numbers on a daily basis to allow divisions to assign replacements only to units in reserve. Finally, the board recommended attaching combat-experienced officers and noncommissioned officers to replacement depots for two-week periods to improve the training offered there.[14]

One can hardly overstate the deleterious impact of the personnel situation on the combat divisions. In December 1943 Major General Lucian Truscott ordered the 3d Infantry Division's adjutant general to examine the impact of the replacement situation on the fighting strength of his division. The division entered Italy on 18 September more or less at full strength due to the transfer of 2,000 replacements from the 1st and 9th Infantry Divisions before their departure to Great Britain. After fifty-nine days of consecutive combat, the division was relieved from action on 17 November 1943. During this period it sustained 3,144 battle casualties and 5,446 nonbattle casualties, but it received only 4,118 replacements and 2,213 returned to duty from hospitals. As a result, the division was short about 2,200 soldiers when it went into reserve to prepare for the Anzio invasion.[15]

Aggregate numbers told only part of the story. Personnel losses devastated the three infantry regiments. In two months of combat, the infantry regiments lost nearly 70 percent of their strength to battle and nonbattle casualties as they sustained 93 percent of the division's total battle casualties. The infantry sustained six battle losses for every one suffered by other divisional elements. Nonbattle casualties were twice as great in infantry regiments due to their habitual exposure to the elements with little chance to rest, warm up, or dry out. The adjutant general noted that "from the first day of serious combat on 18 September to relief on 17 November, the trend of this [the division's] effective strength curve is downward."[16] Casualties were particularly high among junior leaders, which caused "a gradual reduction in combat efficiency due to the loss of experienced leaders and a lack of opportunity to train and indoctrinate new leaders."[17] The adjutant general concluded:

> Infantry combat requires great exertion, is subject to greater risk, and imposes greater hardship than any other branch. Certainly no combat imposes greater mental and physical strain on individuals than does infantry combat. Infantry, therefore, requires the highest physical standards and replacements must be in the highest degree of physical condition.[18]

As discussed earlier, the army's personnel policies effectively reversed the priorities called for by this report.

General Truscott made some basic, sensible recommendations when he signed the report. He recommended the organization of replacement pools based on actual loss rates by specialty and grade, maintenance of replacement battalions closer to supported divisions, better training of replacements under combat-experienced leaders, automatic supply of small numbers of replacements to committed divisions on a regular basis, return of recovered soldiers from hospitals back to the units from which they came, greater pay for soldiers exposed to greater hazards, and a distinctive insignia for combat infantrymen.[19] In time, the army would act on many of these suggestions, such as the creation of the Combat Infantry Badge for infantrymen who had engaged in combat.

In addition to manpower problems, combat divisions in the Fifth U.S. Army had difficulties with supply and transportation. Moving supplies forward required a herculean effort. In one month alone, the 45th Infantry Division had four of its bridges over the Volturno River wash out.[20] Vehicle losses from constant use in the difficult driving conditions were high. Trails and narrow passes required innovative methods of supply, such as the use of pack mules, dubbed the "3d Division Cavalry" by Truscott's men.[21] By the end of the war, the Fifth U.S. Army was using over forty-five hundred mules grouped in fifteen pack companies to deliver supplies to otherwise inaccessible areas. Each company, manned by Italian personnel or disbanded elements of the 2d Cavalry Division, could support the needs of an infantry battalion in combat.[22]

The trucks of the division quartermaster company played a crucial role in the combat effectiveness of American infantry divisions. "In the Mediterranean theater as in all others," the official U.S. Army historian noted, "it was hard to say which was more important—the gun that fired the ammunition at the enemy or the truck that brought the ammunition to the gun position."[23] As American divisions discovered in North Africa, General McNair's theory of army quartermasters delivering supplies directly to regiments failed the test of combat. Division quartermasters merely ignored AGF doctrine and placed themselves in the supply chain. Trucks of the division quartermaster company were instrumental in supplying the needs of the infantry regiments on a daily basis, not just in emergencies as envisioned by AGF planners.[24]

Other facets of quartermaster operations still fell short of expectations, however. Although the service platoon survived the reorganization of the quartermaster company in July 1943, the tasks of loading, unloading, and distributing supplies to using units were more than it could handle without augmentation. General Truscott noted the lack of a laundry and bath unit in the division's logistical structure, an omission remedied by the 34th Infantry Division when it created its own system for bath and clothing exchange.[25]

As Allied forces tried to penetrate the various belts of the Winter Line, operations degenerated into actions by regiments and battalions to run the ridges and seize high ground for observation. The problem with combat in Italy was that there was too much key terrain for an attacker to seize. If the Allies forced the Germans off of one ridge or mountain, the Germans simply moved back to the next one and the process started over. The German commander in Italy, Luftwaffe Field Marshal Albert Kesselring, who had spent most of his career as an artillery officer, understood the nature of defensive warfare in the mountains of Italy. He was determined to hold the Allies south of Rome.[26]

By mid-December the Allies came up against the toughest part of the German defenses, the Gustav Line anchored on the town of Cassino and the Rapido River at the southern end of the Liri Valley. Under pressure from Prime Minister Winston Churchill to seize Rome, Field Marshal Sir Harold Alexander and General Dwight Eisenhower planned an amphibious turning movement around the Gustav Line at Anzio, a small port south of Rome.[27] Alexander gave the mission of planning and executing Operation SHINGLE to Clark and the Fifth U.S. Army. Due to lack of landing craft, only two divisions could participate in the initial landing. Churchill and Alexander assumed that a two-division landing would be enough to force the Germans either to weaken the Gustav Line to the point where the Fifth U.S. Army could penetrate it or withdraw their forces altogether to confront the VI Corps in their rear.[28] Kesselring had other ideas.

As a prelude to the invasion, General Clark ordered the 36th Infantry Division to attempt an assault crossing of the Rapido River on 20 January 1944. The purpose of the assault was to draw German reinforcements to the Cassino front and enable the invasion forces to establish their beachhead at Anzio with less resistance. A successful assault might even allow the Fifth U.S. Army to penetrate the Gustav Line and link up with VI Corps at Anzio.[29]

One could hardly conceive of a more difficult mission and a more challenging piece of terrain upon which to execute it. Fall and winter rains gorged the fifty-foot-wide river with water flowing at ten miles per hour. The Germans had diverted water to flood the approaches to the riverbank, then liberally sowed both sides with mines. The veteran 15th Panzer Grenadier Division tenaciously defended the sector of the river at the mouth of the Liri Valley.[30]

The 36th Infantry Division was not in great shape to tackle the task ahead of it. In December 1943 the division had taken over three thousand battle and nonbattle casualties in the grueling Battle of San Pietro. The division needed time to rest and to integrate replacements to fill its depleted ranks. The division commander, Major General Fred L. Walker, was hardly enthusiastic about the mission.[31] The biggest problem, however, was poor staff work and planning, which failed to synchronize the various arms involved in the crossing and left the Texas Division short of fire support at critical moments in the battle.

The plan entailed a night assault by the 141st and 143d Infantry Regiments north and south of San Angelo to establish a bridgehead through which the 1st Armored Division would pass to continue the attack. Engineers would have to clear paths to the riverbank in darkness, since German guns dominated the approaches to the river. The engineers would mark paths clear of mines with white tape, but no one questioned how the troops would see this tape at night. Other engineers would handle the boats used in the crossing. Troops would have to negotiate over a mile of open, muddy swamp with their heavy loads just to get to the river. Once across, strong German fortifications and mined ground awaited them.[32]

When the assault commenced at 2000 hours on 20 January 1944, almost everything that could go wrong did. Engineers guiding the assault troops got lost and led units into unmarked minefields. German artillery and mortar fire caused numerous casualties and delays as the assault troops moved across the open ground to the river. Engineers and infantrymen who had never worked together before failed to coordinate their efforts effectively. Terror and confusion reigned supreme at the river. By daylight the division had established only two footbridges across the Rapido, but it had to abandon these bridges almost immediately due to accurate German artillery fire that blanketed them. Portions of two battalions made the crossing to the west bank of the river, but the 143d Infantry Regiment withdrew its forces before the enemy annihilated them completely. This withdrawal left scattered elements of one infantry battalion in the 141st Infantry Regiment across the Rapido on 21 January.[33]

The next night the 141st Infantry Regiment attempted to reinforce the precarious bridgehead with its other two battalions, while the 143d Infantry Regiment again attempted to cross the river. The failure to complete a vehicular bridge, however, doomed the infantrymen on the far side. The inability of division and corps artillery to silence the enemy guns also contributed to the attack's failure. After beating off several enemy counterattacks and enduring heavy artillery, mortar, and machine gun fire, the men of the 36th Infantry Division on the west side of the Rapido finally collapsed on the night of 22 January.[34] They were victims of a poor plan badly executed.

The division sustained over two thousand casualties in the two-day attack. Its combat effectiveness was so poor at the end of January that the intelligence officer of the 143d Infantry Regiment concluded sarcastically, "The Germans can hold and occupy their present positions or they can withdraw or they can occupy our positions."[35] In the next few months, however, the 36th Infantry Division showed the resilience of the American infantry division in World War II. By the time of the breakout from the Anzio beachhead four months after the Rapido fiasco, the Texas Division had fully reconstituted and was ready to play a key role in the attack on Rome.

36th turnabout

Two days after the failure of the Texas Division to cross the Rapido, the 34th Infantry Division attacked the Gustav Line north of Cassino. The German positions were exceptionally strong and included bunkers reinforced with concrete and railroad ties, wire and mine obstacles, and other fortifications with overhead cover that protected the troops underneath from artillery fire. After five days of tough fighting, the Red Bull Division successfully crossed the Rapido River and seized a series of hills on the far bank, but the decisive terrain of Monte Cassino remained in enemy hands, skillfully defended by German paratroopers. To sustain itself in the mountains, the division used eleven hundred mules and seven hundred litter bearers over and above the normal allotment of transportation and medical personnel. Bridges across the Rapido came under constant enemy bombardment; the torn debris of modern war mixed with the stench of rotting mule carcasses to complete the Dantesque scene. The 133d Infantry Regiment fought a brutal battle for the town of Cassino, locked in close combat with its German defenders. After three weeks of intense combat in harsh winter conditions on mountainous terrain, the troops of the 34th Infantry Division had reached the limits of human endurance.[36] On 14 February the 4th Indian Division relieved the 34th Infantry Division, which retired for rest and refitting. Like the Texas Division, the Red Bull Division would also be reconstituted with replacements and new equipment in time to play a major role in the breakout from the Anzio beachhead.

The failure of the 36th Infantry Division to cross the Rapido and the 34th Infantry Division to seize the heights of Monte Cassino meant that VI Corps at Anzio could expect little immediate reinforcement from the Fifth U.S. Army. This caused no little consternation, since preparations for Operation SHINGLE did not go well. The rehearsal for the landing, code-named WEBFOOT, between 13 and 18 January 1944 was a disaster. None of the infantry battalions in the exercise landed on time, in formation, or on the correct beach. No antitank guns, artillery, tanks, or other heavy weapons were in position ashore by daylight. Ship-to-shore communications were poor or nonexistent. The navy launched the landing craft so far from shore that the 3d Infantry Division lost an entire battalion's worth of artillery along with signal and other equipment. "We had the damnedest foul-up in that thing I've ever seen any time," one participant recalled.[37] General Truscott concluded, "No military force can hope to assault a defended beach with prospects of success unless it can be landed on shore in tactical order and proper condition to engage in combat. Exercise just concluded this date disclosed so many deficiencies in these respects that the need for additional Naval training and improved organization is perfectly obvious."[38] Clark was unwilling to delay the invasion. Truscott yielded.

Despite the poor rehearsal, nearly everything went right on the day of the actual invasion. The soldiers of VI Corps achieved complete surprise when they waded ashore at Anzio on 22 January 1944. Landings by the U.S. 3d Infantry Division, British 1st Infantry Division, 504th Parachute Infantry Regiment, and Commandos and Rangers were virtually unopposed; by nightfall the Allies had landed over thirty-six thousand troops and three thousand vehicles with negligible losses.[39] The corps commander, Major General John P. Lucas, was determined to build a solid defensive line before proceeding farther toward operational objectives, however. By the time he was ready to exploit off the beachhead, Field Marshal Kesselring had elements of ten divisions either at Anzio or on the way there. The Allied attack to reach Campoleone and Cisterna in late January failed; the Germans completely eliminated two Ranger battalions as they attempted to infiltrate enemy positions along the Pantano Ditch. Recriminations flew. Prime Minister Churchill stated, "Instead of hurling a wild cat on to the shore all we got was a stranded whale and Suvla Bay over again."[40] Lucas mused, "This whole affair had a strong odour of Gallipoli and apparently the same amateur was still on the coach's bench."[41]

The Allied beachhead was now clearly in trouble. Kesselring assembled a massive force and counterattacked in early February. His forces had the advantage of holding the key terrain along the high ground ringing the Allied positions. German artillery could pound Allied units from the dominant hills overlooking Anzio. The combination of the Italian winter, heavy artillery fire, and static positions made Anzio resemble the western front of World War I more closely than any other battle in World War II. The divisions of VI Corps shared a miserable existence in damp and dismal holes and trenches, under constant observation and bombardment from enemy artillery and aircraft. General Clark had little choice but to reinforce the beachhead to prevent a complete collapse. Before long the American 45th Infantry Division (now under the command of Major General William W. Eagles, formerly the assistant division commander of the 3d Infantry Division), the elite Canadian-American First Special Service Force, and the British 56th Infantry Division deployed to Anzio.[42] By the time of the breakout from the beachhead in May, VI Corps numbered six infantry divisions and one armored division. Had this force been available when the Allies launched SHINGLE, there is little doubt that VI Corps could have achieved the great things expected of it. Instead, the Allies at Anzio had to fight for their lives in one of the most miserable, disheartening battles of the war.

Four things saved the Allies from disaster. First, the British and American infantrymen at Anzio, fighting on the defensive, displayed a high capacity to endure in the toughest of conditions. Second, Allied artillery, despite the disadvantage of being positioned on lower ground, soon gained the upper hand over the German gunners. Third, the Allied logistical apparatus continued to function even in the dangerous and confined conditions in the beachhead. Fourth, the outstanding leadership of Major General Lucian Truscott, who replaced Lucas when Clark relieved the latter of command, imbued VI Corps with a will to win. The ultimate victory at Anzio was his greatest achievement.

Truscott took command of VI Corps on 23 February at the conclusion of the largest German attack to collapse the beachhead. He brought to Anzio the same lead-from-the-front style of leadership that he had used as commander of the 3d Infantry Division. Lucas had located VI Corps headquarters in tunnels beneath the ground; Truscott established his command post aboveground to share the perils of enemy fire with his soldiers. The corps staff was not confident in planning or directing operations. Truscott eliminated the debating-society atmosphere and replaced it with firm, military decision-making procedure. Lucas had alienated the British commanders and staff officers at Anzio; Truscott, used to working with the British since his assignment with Admiral Lord Louis Mountbatten's Combined Operations Headquarters in Great Britain in 1942, mended fences. The Fifth U.S. Army had numerous combat service support assets at Anzio, and morale in many of these organizations was low. Truscott brought them under effective supervision. Most important, Truscott reorganized the VI Corps fire support assets—primarily its heavy artillery—to mass fires on any endangered point in the beachhead. "The beachhead had come close to disaster," Truscott later wrote. "Unnecessarily so, since we had demonstrated that we had sufficient means to stop the German offensive much earlier had we adequately organized, properly coordinated, and effectively employed our resources."[43]

Artillery was the Allies' greatest asset at Anzio; indeed, artillery was the American army's greatest asset in World War II. The creation of the infantry-artillery team in the Army of the United States was an outgrowth of the battles of attrition on the western front in World War I, coupled with technical improvements made during the interwar period. The Second Battle of the Marne and the battles at Cantigny, St.-Mihiel, and the Meuse-Argonne proved to American officers that infantry needed massive fire support to succeed on the modern battlefield. The problem with artillery in World War I, however, was its

Major General Lucian K. Truscott, commander of VI Corps, in his aboveground headquarters near Anzio, 20 May 1944. This photo was taken three days prior to the Allied breakout. Truscott took command of VI Corps during the crisis of the German counteroffensive in February 1944. He not only saved the beachhead but also led the Allied forces in Anzio to decisive victory three months later. (U.S. Army Signal Corps photo)

inflexibility. Due to lack of adequate communications, most fires were preplanned. Although massive, artillery barrages were mostly hit-or-miss affairs, since artillerymen lacked the means to adjust fires rapidly. Artillery pieces also lacked the mobility to move forward quickly when they needed to displace to keep up with the attack.[44]

Three developments in the interwar period solved these problems. The first was the creation of centralized fire direction centers, which could synchronize fires from numerous artillery battalions simultaneously onto a single target. The second was the emergence of forward observation teams equipped with radios. Forward observers could call fire missions on targets as they appeared on the battlefield, which eliminated the need for much of the elaborate planned fires used previously. Light aviation observation squadrons, mounted in Piper Cub aircraft, took this development one step further as they flew over the battlefield and called in fires on targets of opportunity. The third development was the manufacture of guns with split trails capable of being towed by motor vehicles and other artillery pieces that were completely self-propelled. As a result, American artillery entered World War II with the most advanced fire control system in the world and the mobility to keep pace with motorized and mechanized forces.[45]

At Anzio, VI Corps did not use its artillery to full effect until Truscott took command. "General Truscott realized the capabilities and limitations of his artillery," stated Lieutenant Colonel Harry Lemley, S-3 of the 18th Field Artillery Brigade at Anzio, which Truscott transformed into his corps artillery. "He was demanding of it."[46] When Truscott arrived at VI Corps, he found the artillery poorly coordinated. He called on Major Walter T. Kerwin Jr., S-3 of the 3d Infantry Division Artillery, to fix the system. Truscott ordered Kerwin to accompany the VI Corps Artillery officer, Brigadier General Carl A. Baehr, on a mission to organize the corps artillery fires as he had done in the 3d Infantry Division.[47] Major Kerwin centralized fire direction in the beachhead to enable VI Corps to mass its fires. Soon the corps was able to mass all its fires—over a thousand tubes counting tanks and antiaircraft guns—at any given moment on any single target in the beachhead.[48] The technique used was time-on-target, or TOT. When the corps artillery officer decided an important target required the concerted fires of the entire beachhead, he would transmit the code word "BINGO" to all artillery units, followed by the coordinates and the time of attack.[49] The fire direction centers would compute data for each gun so that the shells landed on the target nearly simultaneously. The effect was nothing less than devastating.

The new artillery fire control system received its first major test on the morning of 29 February. The previous evening VI Corps had received intelligence that the Germans were preparing an attack for early the next day. General Truscott ordered a massive artillery counterpreparation for 0430 hours by all guns in the beachhead. "We would have every gun in the beachhead pound these troop assembly areas, reserve positions, artillery locations, and tank concentrations for a full hour before they could begin their attack," Truscott wrote later. "It was possible, I thought, we might completely disrupt the German strategy."[50] The artillerymen worked hard to pull the mission off. "I'd really never done anything quite like that before, but I was able to pull things together because by this time we had a single artillery headquarters integrated with the corps headquarters and as a result, a much better feel for the situation and much better control over our units and a much better coordination with the divisions," Lemley stated later.[51] The tactic worked; the German assault barely made a dent in Allied lines. The Allies destroyed half the German tanks in the attack and took over a thousand prisoners.[52]

German artillery overlooking Anzio was not as effective as American artillery. The Germans had the advantage of position and range, but their fire control technique lacked the sophistication of the Allied system. "I don't believe the Germans knew how to [mass fires]," Lemley stated. "In fact, I'm sure that's true because after the war, I took it upon myself to interrogate a number of German artillery generals and their concepts at the end of the war were not much further than mine when I started out."[53] As a result, German commanders relied on the ability of their infantry and tank units to break through Allied lines with superior tactics. Hitler sent his elite Parachute Demonstration Battalion to Anzio; accurate artillery fire destroyed half the battalion in its first assault.[54] A similar fate befell the vaunted Infantry Lehr Regiment, an infantry demonstration regiment rushed from Germany to participate in the battle.[55] A simple comparison of artillery expenditures in the 45th Infantry Division shows the magnitude of the effort. During four months in combat on the Fifth U.S. Army front in Italy, the Thunderbirds fired 167,153 rounds. At Anzio during the single month of February 1944, the division fired 129,732 rounds.[56] Not for the first nor the last time in the war, German attempts to maneuver foundered due to Allied firepower. The beachhead at Anzio held.

The Allied ability to reinforce the beachhead with men and matériel was also a significant factor in the outcome of the battle. The most important innovation was the use of the LST to ferry preloaded trucks to and from the beachhead. Each truck would be loaded with one type of supply at army dumps in Naples, then drive onto an outbound LST. At Anzio the trucks would drive off the LST onto shore and proceed to VI Corps supply dumps in the beachhead. Using this roll-on, roll-off method of supply, an LST could be off-loaded in one hour, compared with twelve hours for a bulk-loaded LST.[57]

For the next eleven weeks, Allied and German forces maintained a precarious stalemate at Anzio while the Fifth U.S. Army prepared an offensive to penetrate the Gustav Line, break out of the beachhead at Anzio, and seize Rome. Activity in the beachhead was confined to patrolling, small raids, and artillery and mortar fire. General Truscott rotated his divisions out of the line for short periods of rest, reequipping, and training.[58] "To men confined to foxholes by day and limited movement at night," the 30th Infantry Regiment reported, "a 48 hour rest period improved morale immeasurably."[59]

The divisions badly needed the break. During the period from 22 January to 28 March 1944, the 3d Infantry Division sustained 5,475 battle and 5,441 nonbattle casualties, over two-thirds of its authorized strength.[60] In sixty-six days of combat, the division lost 116 percent of its riflemen, over 70 percent to the effects of enemy artillery fire.[61] Major General John W. "Iron Mike" O'Daniel, who took over the Marne Division from Truscott, reported,

Sherman tanks debark from an LST in Anzio Harbor, 27 April 1944, in preparation for the spring offensive in Italy. The innovative use of the roll-on, roll-off capabilities of LSTs to ferry supplies and equipment from Naples to Anzio enabled VI Corps to hold the beachhead and eventually break out. (U.S. Army Signal Corps photo)

> The battle and non-battle loss rates at Anzio, if continued, is [sic] equivalent to the replacement of an entire division with new troops and hospital returnees every 94 days and of the infantry regiments alone every 74 days. Judging by the casualty statistics of the Anzio operation and the first phase [of the Italian campaign], over 90 percent of battle casualties will be infantry and future replacement requirements should be weighted accordingly.[62]

In short, infantry divisions could enter combat at full strength and with well-trained personnel but could not maintain a higher state of training than the standard held by the replacement stream.

In Italy the replacement system could not react fast enough to the demands placed upon it. For the spring offensive, however, the Fifth U.S. Army tried a different technique to keep units functioning. Before the beginning of the offensive, each division received several hundred infantry replacements above the division's authorized strength. The 750 replacements in the 34th Infantry Division were placed with infantry companies at the front for training and "battle inoculation." After an interval, they were withdrawn and placed in replacement pools at regimental level. During the attack, losses were replaced quickly from these pools, keeping the infantry regiments at a higher state of effectiveness for a longer period.[63]

Reinforcements arrived in both VI Corps and the Fifth U.S. Army in preparation for the spring offensive, code-named DIADEM. The U.S. 34th and 36th Infantry Divisions and the U.S. 1st Armored Division arrived at Anzio to give VI Corps the ability to resume offensive operations. To take their place on the Fifth U.S. Army front, the first Organized Reserve divisions arrived in Italy. The 85th and 88th Infantry Divisions were activated in May and July 1942, respectively. After more than a year of training in the United States, the divisions deployed to North Africa in late 1943 and to Italy in early 1944. Although they assumed defensive positions on the Fifth U.S. Army front in March 1944, DIADEM would be their first taste of offensive combat. Their performance would validate the method used to raise and train new combat divisions after Pearl Harbor.[64] Fittingly, General Clark would see his system of building new divisions tested for the first time in the army under his command.

The 88th Infantry Division was one of the more fortunate of the new draftee divisions in the Army of the United States. Its commander, Major General John E. Sloan, was a 1910 graduate of the United States Naval Academy who had transferred to the Coast Artillery in 1911 and then to the Field Artillery during World War I. Although he did not get overseas during that war, Sloan had extensive troop-leading experience during the interwar period. He attended the Command and General Staff School in 1926 and the Army War College in 1932. He also taught extensively, first as an ROTC professor at Texas A&M, next as an instructor at Fort Leavenworth, then during a tour as professor of military science and tactics at Oregon State College. Like General George C. Marshall, Sloan organized and commanded a Civilian Conservation Corps camp. Everything about Sloan's career suggested he would do well in raising and training a new unit composed primarily of untrained draftees.[65] Like many other officers in his generation, nothing in his career pointed to how he would perform in combat. In Italy Sloan would prove his competence as a division commander.

The 88th Infantry Division received a quality cadre from the 9th Infantry Division and its fair share of the draftee pie. What allowed the division to coalesce was the stability of its personnel. It escaped large drafts for officer candidate schools, the ASTP, or to provide replacements for overseas units.[66] As a result, the training program progressed smoothly, and within sixteen months the 88th Infantry Division had embarked for overseas, a record exceeded by only one other division in World War II.[67] When the division occupied a sector of the U.S. II Corps front near Minturno on 4 March 1944, it was as well prepared as any draftee division would be to assume its duties in combat. The 85th and 88th Infantry Divisions used the lull of the next two months to season their troops and prepare for the upcoming offensive.

The experienced divisions in VI Corps also used the relative lull in combat to train for offensive operations. The 3d Infantry Division in particular reached a peak of efficiency under its new commander, Major General O'Daniel. "He was just like Truscott, and Truscott was just like Patton," stated John A. Heintges,

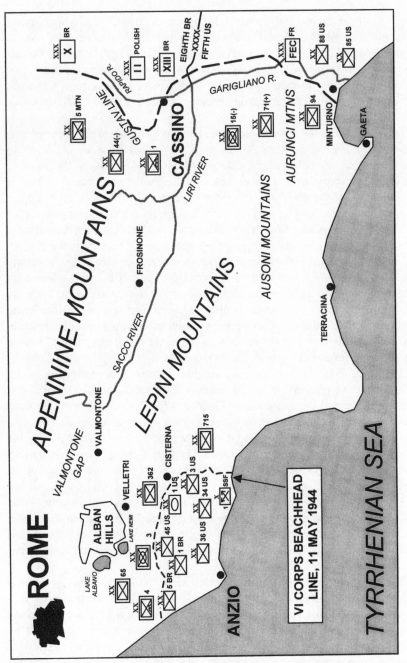

The Italian Campaign, Spring 1944

executive officer of the 30th Infantry Regiment at Anzio. "You know, move, move, move, move."[68] O'Daniel, nicknamed "Iron Mike" because of his booming voice, exuded confidence and professionalism. "They [Truscott and O'Daniel] were hard men to please and let you know in no uncertain terms when you were not performing to their standards, but they were a pleasure to serve under," Heintges recalled.[69] The training program under O'Daniel hardly missed a beat.

One area the new division commander was determined to improve was combat patrolling. In the static situation at Anzio, patrols were necessary to keep the enemy off balance and take prisoners for information. The loss of experienced personnel during the defensive battles in February caused a drop in the proficiency of the division's patrols. Inexperienced soldiers could not operate effectively in the dark as part of a small, cohesive team. To compensate for the loss of experienced personnel, O'Daniel ordered each regiment to form a battle patrol group of combat-experienced volunteers. The groups were quartered in the regimental service company areas, where they received rest and hot food. They also trained hard to become patrolling specialists and conducted all of the combat patrol missions for the battalions. At the service company area, the battle patrol groups had time to plan, organize, and rehearse before being sent forward on a mission. These groups raised patrolling standards and executed their missions with fewer losses than under the previous system of having each battalion form and organize its own patrols.[70]

The training in the 30th Infantry Regiment gives some indication of the level of expertise reached by the 3d Infantry Division during this period. For three weeks prior to the execution of Operation BUFFALO, the breakout from Anzio, the regiment conducted intensive training in the beachhead. The regiment indoctrinated replacements and corrected deficiencies noted during the previous combat period. "There still exists a lack of training in basic leadership among junior officers and NCO's," the regiment noted in its after-action report. "The present soldier [a draftee replacement] must be *led*. Older officers and NCO's must closely supervise, control and train the new replacements. This process is continuous and must be done even in battle."[71] Individuals and teams went through live fire exercises with all of their weapons. The regimental staff made plans, issued orders, developed mock-ups of the attack zone, and conducted rehearsals.

The regiment also stressed coordinated tank-infantry training, something most new divisions neglected until bitter experience proved its necessity. "In a fast moving attack and pursuit in which Infantry, Tanks and TD's are working in teams, wire communication is not practicable because of damage to wire by armored vehicles. Radio and officer liaison were found to be the most effective means of control, but even they were not entirely satisfactory," the regiment noted. "Much thought must be given to the solution of this problem."[72] The 7th Infantry Regiment echoed the concern of its sister regiment: "It was found that a definite means of communication, possibly SCR 300 radio, between tanks and infantry, down to include the rifle platoon working with the tanks, is essential."[73] Deplorably, the rest of the army gave almost no further thought to the problem of infantry-tank coordination until near disaster in Normandy forced divisions there to improvise better means of communication. The experience was just one more indication that in World War II, the Army of the United States usually adapted itself to combat at the division level.

DIADEM began on 11 May 1944. The first three days of the battle were a bitter slugfest for II Corps. Neither the 85th nor the 88th Infantry Division fully achieved its objectives on the first day of the attack, but the German defenders suffered irreplaceable losses. The 85th and 88th Infantry Divisions fought well for new divisions but sustained hundreds of casualties. One battalion S-3 in the 88th Infantry Division lamented his unit's losses: "Two years of training [have] gone up in smoke."[74] What the major could not see was the resilience of the replacement system behind his battalion. The two infantry divisions in II Corps began DIADEM with an overstrength in personnel. The excess men formed replacement detachments at division level. These soldiers trained with their divisions prior to the commencement of the offensive and thus were more easily integrated during pauses in combat. When the two divisions attacked again on 13 May, they did so with nearly the same strength as they had two days earlier.[75]

As a result of the breakthrough of the French Expeditionary Corps (FEC) and the pressure exerted by the 85th and 88th Infantry Divisions, the German defense in front of II Corps soon crumbled. By the morning of 16 May, both the French and the Americans had broken the Gustav Line in their zones. While the FEC assisted the British Eighth Army by enveloping the Hitler Line, II Corps advanced north toward linkup with VI Corps at Anzio. The 85th and 88th Infantry Divisions had sustained over three thousand casualties in six days of battle, but they had helped to break the back of German resistance.[76]

Along the way, they had proved that the new American "draftee divisions" could perform well in battle. "It was the events of May and June," writes the historian of the 88th Infantry Division, "that were particularly held by the nation's leadership, the War Department, the newspapers, and the draftees themselves to have proved the mettle of the draftee division. The toughness of the 88th Infantry Division was no longer a question."[77] One cannot overestimate the boost in confidence that the success of Operation DIADEM gave to the Army of the United States. The entry of the draftee divisions into combat came approximately four weeks before the cross-Channel invasion of France. Other new divisions would be tested in the hedgerows of Normandy, as the 85th and 88th Infantry Divisions had been tested in the mountains of Italy. Upon the outcome of their struggles to succeed would rest in part the fate of the free world.

On 23 May VI Corps launched Operation BUFFALO and joined in the Allied offensive to shatter German defenses in southern Italy. The brunt of the assault fell to O'Daniels's 3d Infantry Division and Major General Ernest N.

Soldiers of the 88th Infantry Division wind their way across a small valley high in the mountains near Itri, Italy, 18 May 1944. The success of the "draftee divisions" in Operation DIADEM calmed anxious minds in the War Department and buoyed the spirits of a nation starved for news of victory. (U.S. Army Signal Corps photo)

Harmon's 1st Armored Division. At 0545 hours the beachhead shook as the VI Corps artillery pounded German positions in front of Cisterna, the town that had eluded the grasp of the Rangers and the Marne Division in their ill-fated attack four months earlier. Enemy positions were heavily fortified, and mines were thickly sown on all avenues of approach. At 0630 hours the infantry attacked and ran into strong opposition from the entrenched enemy. Cisterna was the key to enemy defenses at Anzio, and the Germans knew it. They defended the town tenaciously.[78]

After three days of vicious fighting, which included one of the few documented bayonet assaults by American troops in World War II, the 3d Infantry Division seized the shell that had once been Cisterna in house-to-house fighting. Along the way four of the division's soldiers earned the Medal of Honor, two posthumously.[79] The 3d Infantry Division sustained fourteen hundred killed and wounded. The Germans had suffered much worse. The attack by the 3d Infantry Division, 1st Armored Division, and the 1st Special Service Force destroyed the German 362d Infantry Division and severely damaged the 715th Infantry Division.[80] The loss of Cisterna and Cori opened the way to Valmontone and the line of communication of the German Tenth Army, still fighting in the Gustav and Hitler Lines to the south. General Truscott now pointed the spearhead of VI Corps toward this terrain feature, the jugular vein of the German army in Italy.

At this point in the battle, Clark intervened to order Truscott to change the direction of his attack. Clark was concerned that the British would seize the glittering prize of Rome while American units were tied up in the Valmontone Gap.[81] He therefore ordered Truscott to proceed directly north to the Eternal City. "Such was the order that turned the main effort of the beachhead forces from the Valmontone Gap and prevented the destruction of the German X Army," sighed Truscott.[82] Clark's change of mission necessitated extensive shifts among the units in the beachhead. The 3d Infantry Division attacked toward Valmontone alone, while the 34th, 36th, and 45th Infantry Divisions attempted to penetrate the still-formidable German defensive positions in the Alban Hills. The 1st Armored Division had to retrace its steps to prepare to exploit any penetration to the north. "Considering the congested area and restricted road net available for these preparations, a more complicated plan would be difficult to conceive," wrote Truscott. He added, "It was practicable only because staff preparation was thorough and complete and it was carried out by well trained, and disciplined troops; and because enemy capabilities for interference were limited."[83]

To his credit, Truscott expressed public enthusiasm for Clark's plan even while seething privately. He would obey Clark's orders, and he expected his division commanders to do the same.[84] The new plan called for the 34th and 45th Infantry Divisions to attack on a narrow front to penetrate German positions in the Caesar Line. As Truscott expected, the German defenses in this area were too strong for the two divisions to penetrate them quickly. After two days of fighting, VI Corps was still short of its immediate objectives and had not broken the enemy line.[85] Nevertheless, Truscott committed the 1st Armored Division to the attack on 29 May. It, too, failed to penetrate the German defenses.

The unit that would break the stalemate, ironically, was the same division that had received one of the worst defeats in the Italian campaign during the abortive attack across the Rapido River back in January. The 36th Infantry Division had discovered a two-mile gap between the I Parachute Corps and the LXXVI Panzer Corps along the slopes of Monte Artemisio on 27 May.[86] General Walker proposed to penetrate the gap with his division, and Truscott agreed to the plan. In a night assault beginning at 2300 hours on 30 May, two regiments of the Texas Division quickly scaled the heights of Monte Artemisio and took them without firing a shot. When daylight came, forward observers on the heights had a field day shooting at the lucrative targets that opened up below them.[87] The attack by the 36th Infantry Division effectively enveloped the German positions along the Caesar Line south of Rome and made possible a renewed effort by the 34th and 45th Infantry Divisions and the 1st Armored Division. The Texas Division proved that it had learned a great deal during its previous battles. For the men of the division, Monte Artemisio was not just a battle—it was justice.

The 36th Infantry Division's exploitation of the Monte Artemisio gap into the Alban Hills caused the German defenses south of Rome to crumble. As the Germans began to withdraw, General Clark brought II Corps abreast of VI Corps for the final drive on the Eternal City. Divisions from both corps entered Rome on 4 June, two days before the long-awaited commencement of Operation OVERLORD, the cross-Channel invasion of France. A week later, the VI Corps headquarters and the 3d, 36th, and 45th Infantry Divisions dropped out of the pursuit of German forces in Italy to begin training and preparations for an invasion of southern France. For nearly a year the Italian campaign had been the key project for British and American ground combat forces. With Rome in Allied hands, the campaign would become a sideshow to more significant events elsewhere.

The Army of the United States endured great hardship in Italy, but it had much to be proud of as well. The infantry divisions of the Fifth U.S. Army adapted themselves to combat against a skilled enemy in some of the most rugged terrain in the world. American infantry divisions learned from their mistakes and increased their combat effectiveness despite the inefficiencies of the replacement system on which they depended so heavily. The American logistical system proved it could keep pace with the demands of modern combat, even if the end of the logistical pipeline proved to be a pack train of mules. The Allied intelligence system, firmly based on ULTRA code-breaking efforts and air reconnaissance, demonstrated its effectiveness during numerous operations. American artillery proved its technical superiority in the Anzio beachhead and beyond. Finally, American divisions proved themselves to be flexible, resilient, and capable of functioning at a high level of effectiveness over extended periods in combat.

Other facets of the American performance in Italy deserve more criticism. Senior American leadership, with certain exceptions like Lucian Truscott, often proved incapable of exploiting opportunities as they arose. Air-ground coordination was abysmal. Finally, the personnel system of the Army of the United States was proving inadequate to the demands of the World War II battlefield. Although American senior leadership was gradually seasoned in battle and air-ground cooperation improved, the Army of the United States was burdened to the end of the war with a replacement system it could never fully fix. As with so many other problems faced by the American army in World War II, the burden was placed on division commanders to improvise solutions to the replacement problem. Their solutions would be sorely tested in the campaign for France and Germany in 1944 and 1945.

6

Normandy: Graduate School in the Hedgerows

The Normandy invasion was the most complex undertaking executed by the Army of the United States in World War II. To crack the Atlantic Wall, planners scheduled the use of all the fire support assets that American industry could provide, to include heavy and light bombers, naval gunfire, and amphibious tanks. Poor weather, however, caused most of the bombs and shells fired at the American invasion beaches to miss their targets. On OMAHA and UTAH Beaches, American infantrymen had to wrest their beachheads from the German defenders by infiltrating behind German strongpoints to attack them from the rear. Despite the massive amounts of firepower available to the assault forces at OMAHA and UTAH Beaches, the invasion succeeded primarily due to the skill and bravery of the soldiers in the three infantry divisions who waded ashore under their heavy burdens on D-Day. The training in England had focused on this one event, but it did not prepare the soldiers for the confusion they experienced that day. Initiative at the small-unit level and some outstanding leadership by officers and noncommissioned officers enabled American forces to establish their beachheads despite the overly complex plan for the invasion that failed the test of combat. D-Day was the greatest triumph of the American mobilization system to date. It showed that an army of democracy, citizens turned into soldiers in a short period of time, could improvise and prevail against the supposedly superior military system of the Wehrmacht. For Nazi Germany, D-Day was a harbinger of disaster.

Since the beginning of active American involvement in World War II in December 1941, General George C. Marshall had pushed hard to get the Allies to agree to a cross-Channel invasion of France at the earliest opportunity. The British preferred a strategy of peripheral operations in the Mediterranean and a Combined Bomber Offensive that attacked Germany directly from the air. Behind these strategies lay a long history that distinctly separated the British and American approaches to war. In the nineteenth century the British defeated

Napoleon through a blockade of the European continent, monetary support of Continental allies, and a peripheral campaign in the Iberian Peninsula. During World War I the British rejected this approach, committed a large army to the battles of attrition in France, and lost the flower of British manhood in bloody trench warfare. Battles such as Ypres and Passchendaele seared the memories of Prime Minister Winston Churchill and his military advisers. Their proposals for the invasions of North Africa, Sicily, Italy, the Balkans, and even Norway reflected their reluctance to put the British army into position to fight a decisive, but undoubtedly costly, campaign against the German army in France.

History had cast the American army in a different mold. During the climactic struggle of the American Civil War in 1864 and 1865, the commander of the Union armies, Ulysses S. Grant, launched his forces directly at the Army of Northern Virginia and the Army of Tennessee. His strategy resulted in both huge casualties and decisive victory. In World War I the American Expeditionary Forces attacked directly into the teeth of German defenses in the Argonne Forest. Once again, the American army exited the conflict with both huge casualties (more Americans died in the seven weeks of the Meuse-Argonne offensive than during years in Korea or Vietnam) and victory. In World War II the American army again decided that the quickest way to achieve victory was to implement a strategy of annihilation by attacking into the strength of the German army in France. In spirit if not in body, the American army of World War II landed in Normandy alongside its Civil War and Great War brethren.

Theoretically, the American army assembled in Great Britain for the cross-Channel invasion had many advantages that both its ancestors and the German army lacked. Since mid-April 1944 the Allied air forces had attacked rail networks in western Europe to degrade the enemy's ability to transport reinforcements to France. Hundreds of bombers flew sorties on D-Day in an attempt to destroy or neutralize enemy coastal fortifications prior to the landing of the first wave of troops. Dozens of battleships, cruisers, and destroyers supported the invasion armada with naval gunfire. An Allied deception plan code-named FORTITUDE fixed the German Fifteenth Army in the Pas-de-Calais, the most direct avenue of approach into France from the Channel. These advantages would prove their worth in time.

On D-Day, 6 June 1944, they did not provide the decisive advantage that invasion planners had hoped. Air interdiction could slow, but not halt, the German reinforcement of the Seventh Army in Normandy. None of the thirteen thousand bombs dropped by B-17 and B-24 bombers hit their targets on the beach. Poor weather caused the bombardiers to delay release for fear of hitting friendly troops, with the result that their bombs hit as far as three miles inland.[1] Preinvasion naval gunfire support failed to destroy enemy fortifications sited to cover the beaches as opposed to the sea approaches. German guns concealed from seaward observation survived to pin American troops on the beach in a deadly crossfire.[2] Finally, although the German Fifteenth Army remained fixed in the Pas-de-Calais, the German Seventh Army in Normandy was able to utilize both man-made and natural obstacles and fortifications to augment its still-considerable fighting power in a defensive battle.

One of the reasons for the failure of Allied air and naval power to prepare the invasion beaches adequately was the unwillingness of army leaders in Europe to learn lessons from the amphibious invasions in the Pacific. In November 1943 the 2d Marine Division invaded Tarawa in the central Pacific and took the island at the cost of over three thousand casualties. The marines quickly learned the value of coastal fortifications and the need to suppress them with pinpoint bombing and naval gunfire missions. Saturation bombing devastated Tarawa but did little to affect the well-fortified Japanese defenders.[3] The army forces in the Pacific put these lessons to good use in subsequent amphibious operations, such as the assault of Kwajalein atoll in the Marshall Islands by the 7th Infantry Division on 31 January 1944. The conquest of Kwajalein was nearly flawless. As a result, General Marshall ordered the commander of the 7th Infantry Division, Major General Charles H. "Pete" Corlett, to report to Great Britain to command one of the corps in the First U.S. Army and to lend his expertise to the planners of Operation NEPTUNE, the code name for the amphibious portion of Operation OVERLORD. General Dwight D. Eisenhower, Lieutenant General Omar N. Bradley, and their staffs chose to ignore Corlett's advice and instead dismissed the Pacific experience as "bush league."[4] In Normandy air and naval forces resorted to saturation bombing in the preparatory bombardments of the beaches, with negligible effects on the German defenders.[5] As a result, the outcome of the most critical Allied joint operation in World War II depended on the ability of the infantry and airborne divisions committed on D-Day to establish a beachhead with less than adequate fire support.

The three American infantry divisions that landed on D-Day—the 1st, 4th, and 29th Infantry Divisions—operated according to a plan over which they had little control. "Until the troops actually got ashore the tactical commanders had no control over when they would be put in the water or how they would be beached," stated Major General Charles H. Gerhardt of the 29th Infantry Division, "and although the plan was meticulous in its detail the practicalities of the situation made necessary many command changes on the spot by the people most interested, the tactical commanders concerned."[6] Indeed, the plan for Operation NEPTUNE was too detailed. Major Carl W. Plitt, the operations officer of the 16th Infantry Regiment, which landed on OMAHA Beach, reported after the operation, "There was continual interference by higher echelons in detailed matters to such an extent that at times, the [regimental] planning staff wondered where in the 'Hell' they stood. Craft were loaded with vehicles and diagrams made before personnel were assigned and to get some semblance of order and a tactical situation out of the mess called for a certified public accountant."[7] In an attempt to orchestrate the landings of different units to the exact minute, the planners failed to account for the inevitable fog and friction of war on the beaches.

On OMAHA Beach almost nothing went right for the 1st and 29th Infantry

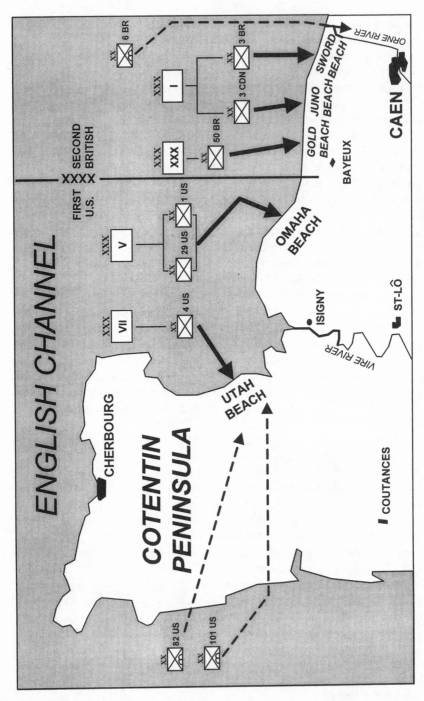

Operation OVERLORD, 6 June 1944

Divisions on the morning of D-Day. Of the thirty-two amphibious tanks of the 741st Tank Battalion that were supposed to land ahead of the 16th Infantry Regiment in the zone of the 1st Infantry Division, twenty-six sank due to high seas and the decision of the navy to launch them over six thousand yards from the beach.[8] The tanks attached to the 29th Infantry Division fared better, but the division lost nearly the entire 111th Field Artillery Battalion when its DUKWs swamped in the rough seas on the long journey to the beach.[9] An unexpected tide and poor observation caused many units to land hundreds or even thousands of yards east of their objectives and intermixed different units in a jumble of confusion.[10] The 116th Infantry Regiment of the 29th Infantry Division was affected the most by the poor landings, since many of its units ended up in the zone of the 16th Infantry Regiment to the east. Casualties among the infantry in the first wave—hit by withering fire from numerous machine guns—were horrendous, in many companies exceeding 50 percent. Most landing craft grounded on sandbars fifty to one hundred yards from shore, which made the assault troops easy targets as they slowly waded to dry ground. Seasick and burdened by too much equipment, the soldiers of the first wave were exhausted by the time they reached the beach.[11]

The inadequate preinvasion bombardment, the unexpected discovery of the German 352d Infantry Division in the area, and poor weather combined to make a shambles of the carefully choreographed plan for the landings on OMAHA Beach. As succeeding waves—which included many combat service support units—landed according to the predetermined timetable, they only added to the confusion on shore. Only the initiative of a few officers and noncommissioned officers prevented the Germans from hurling the invasion force back into the sea and saved the American forces from a devastating defeat. As soldiers clustered behind the seawall and shingle embankment that protected them from enemy fire, a few brave leaders managed to coax them forward to attack the German defenses. One salutary consequence of the naval bombardment was the numerous brushfires that erupted on the bluffs overlooking the beach. Under the concealment of the smoke from these fires, several groupings were able to cross the beach and ascend the bluffs beyond.[12] The heroic efforts of several destroyer captains, who brought their ships to within several hundred yards of the shore to blast enemy strongpoints, also assisted the assault echelons.[13]

Although all of the combat actions on OMAHA Beach were important, the assault from Easy Red Beach that opened up the E-1 and E-3 draws turned out to be absolutely critical, since it provided an avenue inland for reinforcements. Here the 2d Battalion of the 16th RCT managed to work its way up the bluffs between the E-1, E-3, and F-1 draws. The success was the result of initiative provided by the leaders of the Big Red One at the small-unit level.

The experience of Company E is illustrative of the effort exerted on OMAHA Beach by the American infantrymen. Company E landed in the first wave at 0630 hours approximately one thousand yards east of its intended objective on Easy Red Beach. Men exited their landing craft into shoulder-high water laced

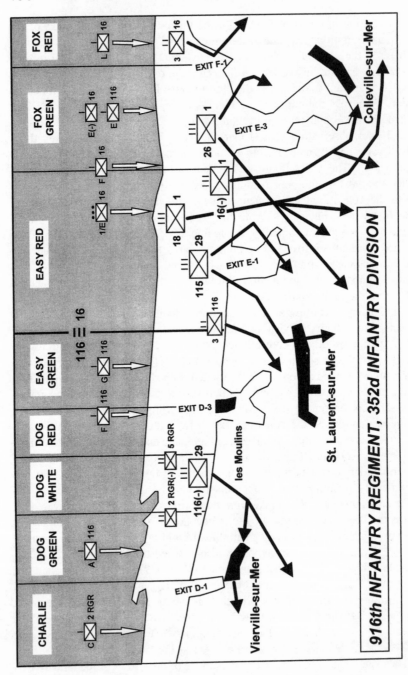

OMAHA Beach, 6 June 1944

with German automatic weapons fire. Soldiers vomiting from seasickness and intake of salt water slowly waded ashore under their heavy loads; many of those hit in the water drowned. Isolated sections of the company took a good hour to reach the protection of the shingle embankment. Weapons jammed with sand refused to fire; soldiers fieldstripped their weapons and cleaned them under fire.[14]

Junior leaders stepped forward to accomplish the mission. On Easy Red Beach, Second Lieutenant John Spaulding's 1st Platoon of Company E was one of the few units to land intact in the first wave. After arriving at the shingle embankment, the platoon sergeant, Technical Sergeant Phillip Streczyk, had one of his men blow a gap in the enemy wire. Second Lieutenant Spaulding led his men through the gap and up the bluffs between the E-1 and E-3 draws. The platoon worked its way up a small trail and emerged in the rear of the enemy entrenchments guarding the bluff. Spaulding's men infiltrated through the German trenches and attacked them from the rear. The action neutralized the strongpoint facing the E-1 draw, which allowed succeeding waves to land with fewer casualties than the first wave. Company E began the day with 183 men and lost 104 of them on the beach; the attack inland cost the company only one casualty.[15]

In the second wave, Company G also landed largely intact and advanced up the bluff to positions near Colleville. The gaps opened up by these actions became a funnel for reinforcements. Senior leaders such as Colonel George A. Taylor, commander of the 16th Infantry Regiment, and Brigadier General Willard G. Wyman, the assistant division commander of the 1st Infantry Division, pushed units forward off the beach.[16] The 18th, 26th, and 115th Infantry Regiments all poured through Easy Red and Fox Green Beaches by the evening of D-Day. Vehicles clogged the beach and jammed Exit E-1, but they were finally moving inland.

In the west, the 29th Infantry Division also managed to claw its way ashore in the face of bitter enemy resistance at Les Moulins and Vierville. The first wave of the Blue and Gray soldiers and troops of the 2d Ranger Battalion suffered miserably. Company A, 116th Infantry Regiment, was one of the few units to go ashore where it was supposed to land—right in front of the D-1 draw north of Vierville on Dog Green Beach. The Germans in the fortifications there, barely touched by the preinvasion bombardment, massacred the men of the company as they disembarked from their landing craft. Company A lost 96 percent of its soldiers killed, wounded, or missing on D-Day—the highest rate of loss of any unit in the invasion.[17]

Providentially for the men of the 116th Infantry Regiment, most of them landed to the east of their assigned objectives, where enemy fortifications were not as numerous or strong as in front of the D-1 and D-3 draws. Men overloaded with sixty- to seventy-pound packs slowly made their way to the protection of the seawall. There they were safe from enemy fire, but they were also disorganized and confused. Within the first five minutes of landing, the plan for the invasion had to be discarded. There was no way to dislodge the German defenders from their fortifications in front of Vierville and Les Moulins with frontal assaults. As was the case in the zone of the 1st Infantry Division, junior leaders stepped forward to improvise an attack up the bluffs between the German strongpoints. Their actions stemmed from common sense. To stay on the beach meant death; if they advanced up the bluffs, the soldiers had a chance to live.[18]

Aided by fire from destroyers, which hammered enemy strongpoints, and smoke from grass fires, which partially obscured their movement, soldiers of the 116th Infantry Regiment and 2d and 5th Ranger Battalions scaled the bluffs of OMAHA Beach. By the end of D-Day they had taken Vierville and isolated the German defenders in the D-1 and D-3 draws. The assistant division commander, Brigadier General Norman D. Cota, seemed to be everywhere—leading, cajoling, inspiring, directing, and organizing. When Company C finally arrived in Vierville after moving up the bluffs, the men "met Cota walking down the narrow main street, twirling a pistol on his index finger like an Old West gunfighter. 'Where the hell have you been, boys?' he asked."[19] Cota led a group of soldiers down the D-1 draw to seize it from the rear and then organized an operation to open the exit to vehicular traffic.

At a cost of three thousand casualties, U.S. V Corps had managed to carve a shallow beachhead extending approximately a mile and a half into France.[20] The assault at OMAHA Beach had succeeded, but probably not in the way that any of the planners had envisioned back in Great Britain. On a day when the Allies dropped tens of thousands of tons of high explosive in Normandy, ironically—but predictably—the key events on OMAHA Beach took place with rifles and grenades at the company and platoon level.

In comparison to the attack on OMAHA Beach, the assault by the 4th Infantry Division on UTAH Beach went smoothly. While the 82d and 101st Airborne Divisions fought to secure the causeways over the flooded ground behind UTAH Beach, the 4th Infantry Division waded ashore nearly unmolested. Air support by B-26 medium bombers had been more successful on UTAH Beach than the heavy bombers had been on OMAHA. Although the strong tide and obscuration of the beach by smoke and dust caused the assault force to veer off course to the south of its objective, the enemy was not present in strength in the area where the force landed. Brigadier General Theodore Roosevelt Jr., the assistant division commander, and Colonel James Van Fleet, the commander of the 8th Infantry Regiment, adjusted their plans to the situation and soon had their units attacking inland to secure the area behind UTAH Beach.[21] By the evening of D-Day the 8th Infantry Regiment had made contact with elements of the 101st Airborne Division. Flooded ground and enemy resistance prevented linkup with the 82d Airborne Division until the following day. The entire 4th Infantry Division had landed in less than fifteen hours at a cost of fewer than two hundred casualties.[22]

Roosevelt played a key role in the success of the 4th Infantry Division in Normandy. He loved soldiers, had an aggressive spirit and an acute tactical

American troops wade ashore at UTAH Beach on D-Day, 6 June 1944. (U.S. Army Signal Corps photo)

sense, and generated high morale in the division. While the 4th Infantry Division was in its marshaling area, General Bradley came to give the officers a pep talk. "Gentlemen," he began, "this is going to be the greatest show on earth, and you are honored by having grandstand seats." Hearing that, Roosevelt whispered out in his deep bass voice, "Hell, goddamn it! We're not in the grandstand. We're down on the gridiron." The comment lightened the mood and left Bradley somewhat flustered.[23] Roosevelt would die of a heart attack in Normandy, but the army awarded him a Medal of Honor as a result of his heroic service there.[24]

The task before the Americans was now clear: expand the beachhead, land reinforcements, gather supplies, and break out of Normandy. Allied leaders would soon learn the effectiveness of the relatively untested American army in combat against a bloodied, but still-experienced, foe.

For a week after landing at OMAHA Beach on D-Day, the 1st and 29th Infantry Divisions attacked to enlarge the beachhead south and to link up with the 101st Airborne Division near Isigny and Carentan to the west. V Corps also committed the 2d Infantry Division and 2d Armored Division to the battle when they landed. The 2d and 29th Infantry Divisions, still new to combat, made some mistakes but adapted quickly. The 2d Infantry Division had difficulty in its first attack on Trevieres, mostly due to the fact that its heavy weapons were still entangled in the mess on OMAHA Beach.[25] Despite the difficulty of its hasty attack immediately upon debarkation, the 2d Infantry Division recovered well after its first day of battle and went on to seize the Cerisy Forest on 10 June. The 29th Infantry Division also continued to learn from its errors. On 9 June the 2d Battalion, 115th Infantry lost 150 men in a German ambush due to poor security in its night defensive position. The resilience of American logistics and administration became evident after this disaster. The next day, the 2d Battalion received 110 replacements and new equipment and moved back into the line.[26] The attack ground on.

Air interdiction of the transportation network in France hampered German reinforcements moving to Normandy and greatly assisted the Allies in their efforts to expand the beachhead.[27] The priority of German effort went to holding the key road center of Caen in the British zone of operations. As a result, German strength in the Cerisy Forest–Caumont area was not sufficient to hold the line. The veteran 1st Infantry Division penetrated the weak enemy front and seized Caumont on 13 June.

The First U.S. Army was on the verge of decisively rupturing the enemy front, but General Bradley did not take advantage of the Big Red One's success. Instead, on 13 June he ordered V Corps to halt offensive operations and defend in sector, activated U.S. XIX Corps to enlarge the Isigny-Carentan corridor, and shifted priority of effort to the U.S. VII Corps in the Cotentin Peninsula.[28] Until Major General "Lightning Joe" Collins's forces took Cherbourg and the logistical situation improved, the advance south of OMAHA Beach would have to wait. The battle would resume on 7 July against a heavily reinforced German front. The ensuing battle among the hedgerows would prove once again that, in combat, good things do not necessarily come to those who wait.

The terrain in Normandy—the area the French referred to as the *bocage*—provided the defender with a marked advantage. The *bocage* is a mass of small, irregularly shaped farm fields separated by hedgerows that have grown over the centuries into formidable barriers. The hedgerows consist of earthen banks several feet high topped with a mass of tangled vegetation. Each hedgerow forms a natural breastwork and obstacle to movement. Sunken roads often run between hedgerows, thus channelizing vehicular movement. The *bocage* provided natural cover, concealment, and ready-made engagement areas—a patchwork quilt ideal for the defense. Soldiers dug fighting positions directly into the base of hedgerows, and commanders positioned automatic weapons at the corners of adjacent fields to cover the approaches. Antitank guns covered openings in the hedgerows and the roads between fields. Hedgerows served as natural antitank obstacles, limited observation and fields of fire, and cut the battlefield into a series of disjointed fights in which the attacker often found it difficult to bring his numerical superiority to bear.[29]

American divisions struggled to find an adequate solution to attacking hedgerows without taking exorbitant casualties. Armies in World War I learned that operational-level maneuver was simply not possible until they overcame the tactical impasse of trench warfare.[30] A similar situation arose in Normandy in 1944, where American leaders chafed at their inability to maneuver against the German army. Attacking hedgerows created numerous problems. Each field bordered by hedgerows, properly organized for the defense, formed a fortified position that an attacking force had to assault individually. Units could not maintain contact with their neighbors in the advance, since the hedgerows between fields limited observation and communication, except by radio. The excellent cover and concealment of the hedgerows provided the defender with the advantage of surprise, and the poor observation afforded by the terrain limited the effectiveness of supporting heavy weapons and artillery. Tanks were of limited value until the American army developed a solution that allowed them to penetrate through hedgerow walls. As a result of these factors, coordinated attacks above the company level were difficult if not impossible.[31]

The American army had not trained adequately before D-Day to cope with combat in the *bocage,* despite available evidence that should have suggested the need to do so.[32] Combat in the hedgerows required the close coordination of all arms at the small-unit level and maximum individual initiative from small-unit leaders. The after-action report of the 9th Infantry Division for June 1944 stated, "The entire operation resolved itself into a species of jungle or Indian fighting, in which the individual soldier or small groups of soldiers play a dominant part. Success comes to the offensive force which employs the maximum initiative by individuals and small groups."[33] Only a few American units, however, possessed the experience and leadership at the small-unit level to achieve the "maximum initiative by individuals and small groups" called for by the division's after-action report. Faced with an unexpected situation for which they were not prepared, American infantry divisions struggled to accomplish their missions while adjusting their tactics to the situation on the ground. For many American infantrymen, Normandy was a Hobbesian universe where life was solitary, poor, nasty, brutish, and often short.

The 90th Infantry Division suffered as much as any American division in the *bocage* and more than most. With the 4th Infantry Division tied up in fighting to the north of UTAH Beach, the VII Corps commander, Major General J. Lawton Collins, committed the 90th Infantry Division in an attack to the west of the 82d Airborne Division's bridgehead over the Merderet River on 10 June. The commander of the 90th Infantry Division, Brigadier General Jay W. MacKelvie, attacked with the 357th and 358th Infantry Regiments shortly after first light. Before even completing the passage of lines, soldiers from the division fired on soldiers of the 325th Glider Infantry from the 82d Airborne. Once through friendly lines, the 90th Infantry Division's attack went nowhere against opposition from the German 91st Division.[34] "One of the regiments had a battalion that was out in front of us there, in a clearing—milling around—without any leadership apparently at all," Teddy H. Sanford, the commander of the 1st Battalion, 325th Glider Infantry Regiment, stated later. "The damnest situation we had ever seen, a desperate situation. We sent people over there and got them lined up and marched them back through our lines."[35] The division continued attacking for several days and incurred hundreds of casualties for minimal gains. Poorly trained and led, the 90th Infantry Division failed miserably in its first combat. On 13 June General Collins relieved MacKelvie along with two of his regimental commanders.[36]

The situation forced Collins to revise his plan of attack. On 14 June the 9th Infantry Division passed through the 90th Infantry Division to assume the main effort in the attack west. Collins ordered the 82d Airborne to attack to the south of the 9th Infantry Division. Both divisions made headway through the difficult terrain and captured bridgeheads over the Douve River. On 17 June the 47th Infantry Regiment moved southwest and passed through the positions held by the 82d Airborne Division at St.-Sauveur-le-Vicomte. By 2200 hours the 1st Battalion had severed the last German-held road leading to Cherbourg. The next day the 9th Infantry Division reached the sea on the western side of the Cotentin Peninsula, thereby isolating Cherbourg.[37]

Elements of the trapped German 77th Division attempted to break out, but

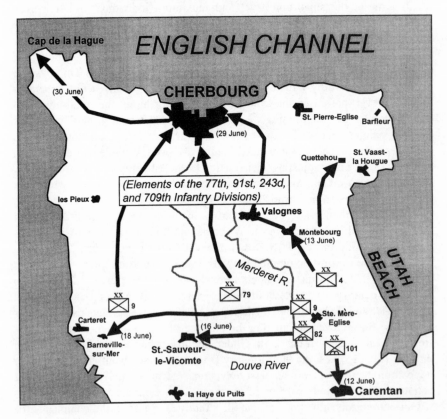

The Seizure of Cherbourg, June 1944

the 9th Infantry Division destroyed a large part of the enemy force. The 9th Infantry Division's operations report describes the action:

A column of vehicles, infantry and artillery attacked the 1st and 2nd Battalions, 60th Infantry. A fierce artillery concentration from all available guns [known in the division as a ZOMBIE] was brought down by Division Artillery on the head of this column. . . . The concentration then was adjusted so as to creep up the congested road inch by inch from the crossroads to a point 5 miles to the northwest. The infantry completed the devastation with small arms and anti-tank fire.[38]

Destroyed German vehicles and dead bodies littered a five-mile stretch of road. The division parried other breakout attempts during the day, even while Major General Manton S. Eddy wheeled his unit ninety degrees to face north in preparation for an attack on Cherbourg. Only a handful of divisions on either side could have performed this feat; the 9th Infantry Division was one of the best.

On 19 June the 9th Infantry Division attacked north toward Cherbourg in conjunction with the 4th and 79th Infantry Divisions, reaching the outer perimeter of the port defenses the next day. The divisions used 21 June to reconnoiter and plan an assault, which began the next day with a massive aerial bombardment on the fortifications of the city. Despite the bombing, German resistance was stiff. Infantry followed closely behind artillery concentrations, but tank destroyers and artillery fire were necessary to reduce individual strongpoints. The fighting continued in the city until 26 June, when the 39th Infantry Regiment captured the German fortress commander and his staff. The 4th Infantry Division took charge of the city on 27 June, and the 9th Infantry Division moved to clear enemy forces from the Cap de la Hague Peninsula. By midday on 1 July, the 9th Infantry Division had completed its mission and moved to an assembly area to integrate replacements, train, and take a well-deserved rest.[39]

The 9th Infantry Division successfully improvised tactics and techniques to overcome the obstacles in its path. Besides having troops that were combat experienced and well trained in the tactics of fire and maneuver, the division also learned to supplement its infantry regiments with additional firepower. Regiments routinely used tank destroyers and self-propelled artillery to augment their organic assault guns in support of infantry attacks. Although the tank destroyers were too lightly armored to be used continuously at the front, they could add much-needed offensive firepower to an attack as long as friendly infantry cleared their route of march. Additionally, the division found that the 4.2-inch chemical mortar was an effective indirect fire weapon when used in the same manner as the organic 81mm mortars of the infantry battalions.[40]

The contrast between the performance of the 9th and 90th Infantry Divisions during the operations to isolate and seize Cherbourg could not have been more stark. In the Cotentin Peninsula the 9th Infantry Division performed like the experienced, veteran division that it was. Correspondent Ernie Pyle wrote:

American soldiers escort German prisoners after seizing Cherbourg, 28 June 1944. (U.S. Army Signal Corps photo)

> The Ninth was good. In the Cherbourg campaign, it performed like a beautiful machine. Its previous battle experience paid off. Not only in individual fighting but in the perfect way the whole organization clicked. . . . The Ninth did something in that campaign that we hadn't always done in the past. It kept tenaciously on the enemy's neck. When the Germans would withdraw a little the Ninth was right on top of them. It never gave them a chance to reassemble or get their balance.[41]

Pyle's observation is not hard to explain. The 9th Infantry Division had merely applied the lessons it had learned in Africa, in Sicily, and in training. Other infantry divisions, with the exception of the 1st Infantry Division, learned through on-the-job experience. Given enough time, most would become as proficient as the veteran divisions.

The performance of the 90th Infantry Division in its first battles, on the other hand, caused the First U.S. Army staff to consider breaking up the unit and using its soldiers as replacements.[42] One can ascribe the poor performance of the division to two causes: poor leadership and poor training. General William E. Depuy later recalled the division's first attacks in Normandy:

> At first, we just attacked straight ahead because that's the way we had been trained, two up and one back. . . . But what we finally learned, which is

what all soldiers finally learned, is don't attack them where they are. The way we cracked those positions was simply by finding a hole somewhere around the flank. Find a hole and get in their rear, and the whole bloody thing would collapse. Then you'd have them in the open. That's the kind of thing I wished that we had learned in the two years in the United States and the three months in England. . . . We learned that the hard way and from then on to the end of the war, all the good commanders fought all their battles by looking for a way around, and practically never went straight forward. Every time you had to go straight forward, you took high casualties.[43]

Units fight like they train; the 90th Infantry Division fought poorly in large part because it trained poorly prior to entering combat.

The other problem with the 90th Infantry Division was its leadership. John Colby, author of *War from the Ground Up,* a recent and thoughtful history of the 90th Infantry Division, believes that poor leadership, not training deficiencies, caused the majority of the division's problems in Normandy.[44] The first two division commanders, General MacKelvie and his replacement, Major General Eugene Landrum, receive exceptionally sharp criticism. According to Colby, MacKelvie "should never have been given command of a division" and was "critically weak in all aspects of leadership, command, and tactics."[45] Landrum, later relieved of command on 25 July, was "short, fat, uninspiring" and "commanded the Division from an arm chair in a cellar."[46] Colby berates five of the nine original battalion commanders for poor leadership abilities. Depuy thought his regimental commander, Colonel P. D. Ginder, was "a horse's ass of the worst order. Goddamned fool. And didn't know anything about anything, but he was very ambitious and a wild man. . . . he was a disaster."[47] Depuy goes on to say that Landrum "had no impact on the division other than through the command post and distant orders. He just wasn't a good leader. . . . He was no tactical general. He was a map general."[48]

Given these training and leadership deficiencies, the amazing thing about the 90th Infantry Division was not how much it suffered in Normandy but how quickly it recovered and turned itself around. Commanders who survived training but failed in combat did not last long. More able men rose within the division "through an arduous process of combat selection."[49] Many of the battalion and regimental commanders who finished the war with the division—such as Depuy—began the Normandy campaign as captains.

The most important change came on 25 July when Brigadier General Raymond S. McLain took command of the division. McLain was a banker from Oklahoma City and the only National Guard officer promoted to command a corps during World War II. Previously he had commanded the artillery of the 45th Infantry Division in Sicily and Italy, and he held the same position in the 30th Infantry Division in Normandy. His impact on the 90th Infantry Division was salutary and immediate. Depuy states:

We had confidence in McLain. He wasn't asking us to do stupid things.

And he visited all the time. . . . He knew what troops could do and couldn't do, and he told us we were okay, but the leadership had been bad. And he was right. So what happened? We had some successes . . . and success fed on itself until . . . we were beginning to feel that we were soldiers. In Normandy the division had no pride, because it had no successes to be proud of. . . . victories provided confidence and confidence made a good division. And I think that happened to dozens of divisions. But we needed it more than most.[50]

McLain had the advantage of starting with an almost clean slate of subordinate leaders when he took command of the division; most of the incompetent officers had been weeded out. In addition to changes at the top and middle levels, skilled small-unit leaders also began to emerge through the crucible of combat. Soldiers learned the grim business of killing at the sharp end of fighting. In addition, when McLain assumed command, the worst of the hedgerow fighting was over, so initial success came easier. By the time the 90th Infantry Division left Normandy, it was already a capable combat organization. By the end of the war, Eisenhower, Bradley, and Patton all listed it as one of the best divisions in the ETO.[51]

With Cherbourg in American hands, General Bradley could shift the main effort of the First U.S. Army. Allied leaders now focused on expanding the beachhead to a point where the ground forces could attack decisively to rupture the German front line irreparably. To accomplish this goal, the forces south of OMAHA Beach had to attack to seize the crucial communications center of Normandy at St.-Lô. The resulting clash was the most bitter, hardest-fought battle of the Normandy campaign for the American army.

The German army defended Normandy tenaciously. Hampered by lack of air support and an antiquated logistical system, it took advantage of the terrain, established defensive doctrine, and its qualitatively superior weapons to exact a heavy toll on the attackers. German defensive doctrine was an outgrowth of trench warfare in World War I. In the fall of 1916 the German army adopted a new defensive doctrine in response to the Allied attacks that year. Described as an "elastic defense-in-depth," the doctrine stressed flexibility in the use of terrain, maximum use of automatic weapons and artillery to break up attacking formations, and immediate counterattacks to take advantage of the attacker's confusion upon reaching the main defensive line.[52] This doctrine had changed little by 1944.

In Normandy, the *bocage* facilitated the construction of defensive positions in depth. Often an attack would falter upon reaching only the advanced position *(Vorgeschobene Stellung)* or outpost zone *(Gefechtsvorposten)* of the German defensive line. The enemy soldiers in these positions, armed with automatic weapons, could hold up an attacking force for hours before withdrawing to the main line of resistance, which the Germans often sited on the reverse slope of a hill or ridge.[53] If a force succeeded in penetrating the main defensive position,

German doctrine called for an artillery barrage to annihilate the enemy forces, followed by a counterattack to retake the position.[54]

The German army compensated for its lack of manpower by arming its troops with increasing numbers of automatic weapons. By 1944, German infantry divisions numbered only 12,500 men, a reduction of 4,500 soldiers from earlier in the war.[55] In Normandy most German divisions could not even muster this much strength. The number of automatic weapons, however, increased from 700 submachine guns and 643 machine guns in the old division to 1,503 submachine guns and 656 machine guns in the 1944 organization. Parachute divisions, such as the one that defended the approaches to St.-Lô, contained 3,026 submachine guns and 1,110 machine guns.[56] In contrast, American infantry divisions in 1944 fielded only 243 automatic rifles, 157 light machine guns, and 236 heavy machine guns.[57] While nearly every German squad carried at least one machine gun, American infantry companies with an authorized strength of 193 men were only allotted a total of two .30-caliber machine guns. In short, American infantry battalions in France were heavily outgunned by their German counterparts.

German machine guns, moreover, were of much higher quality than their American counterparts. The deadly German MG 42 had a rate of fire of 1,200 rounds per minute, whereas the American M1919 Browning fired only 500 rounds per minute.[58] While the predominant German submachine gun, the MP 40, had a short range and a tendency to jam, it was an excellent weapon for use in the confined hedgerow territory.[59] The American Browning automatic rifle (BAR) was an excellent weapon (although it, too, had a tendency to jam), but there simply were not enough of them around. Not until 1945 did the American army increase the authorization of the BAR from one to two per squad, although many squads acquired extra automatic rifles on their own initiative.[60] In the meantime, the American commanders relied on the 6,518 M-1 semiautomatic rifles in the infantry division to provide the direct small-arms fire necessary to engage enemy forces in close combat.

Gaining a firepower advantage over the German defenders in Normandy was easier said than done. In theory, an American infantry unit would establish a "base of fire" with artillery, mortars, machine gun, and rifle fire to pin down enemy defenders, which would allow a maneuver element to close with and destroy the enemy at close range. Some commanders, such as Bradley and Patton, advocated "marching fire," whereby infantry units would advance and fire simultaneously to keep the defenders' heads down.[61] This technique was usually suicidal to the force that attempted it in closed terrain; it therefore had very little utility in Normandy.

In practice, American units relied on artillery fire to suppress enemy positions, since they lacked the number of automatic weapons necessary to accomplish this task with direct fire.[62] In Normandy, however, the hedgerows protected the Germans from the worst effects of American artillery, although the use of aerial observers operating in Piper Cub aircraft allowed American artillery units

An 8-inch gun fires in support of U.S. forces in France, 4 July 1944. The quality and quantity of artillery support gave American forces a decided advantage over their adversaries during World War II. (U.S. Army Signal Corps photo)

exceptional targeting information on uncamouflaged or moving enemy forces. The close ranges and limited visibility made difficult the adjustment of artillery close to friendly lines; mortars often were the indirect fire weapon of choice in the *bocage*. The demand for mortar ammunition was so great that shortages existed until the breakout from Normandy in August.[63] Only slowly did the American army learn that suppression of enemy positions required the close coordination of all arms at the small-unit level. Even a lone surviving German infantryman, armed with his squad's MG 42 and adequate ammunition, could hold up an unsupported American infantry company in the advance for hours.[64] "The rank and file combat GI and company officer had a distinct respect for the German infantry, his '88' artillery [*sic*], his MG 42 and his panzers," states Colonel Warren A. Robinson, who commanded the 314th Infantry Regiment of the 79th Infantry Division.[65] They all presented a difficult problem for the American army in Normandy.

These were the challenges that faced the First U.S. Army in its attack to seize ground more suitable for launching a large-scale offensive to break out of Normandy. After a three-week hiatus while VII Corps cleared the Cotentin Peninsula, Major General Troy Middleton's U.S. VIII Corps began the "Battle of the Hedgerows" on 3 July with an attack from the base of the Cotentin

Peninsula south toward Coutances.[66] The 79th and 90th Infantry Divisions and the 82nd Airborne Division made only slow progress against heavy resistance and under poor weather conditions, which kept air support grounded for much of the time.[67] General Collins's VII Corps, now redeployed to the east of VIII Corps, joined the attack south on 4 July with the 83d and 4th Infantry Divisions, but it too made little headway in the narrow neck of dry land crowded between the Taute River bottomlands and the swamps of the Seves River.[68]

Decades after the war, historians would decry the inability of American infantry divisions to gain ground more rapidly, but at the time the report of the German Seventh Army in Normandy credited American commanders "with facility in tactical maneuver and with being quick to exploit favorable situations."[69] On 10 July the intelligence officer of Army Group B reported, "The enemy fights in the broken terrain of the hedgerow country of Normandy exceptionally well. All units were carefully schooled in similar terrain in England."[70] Although the report was incorrect as far as preinvasion training was concerned, the respect of Army Group B for its adversaries in Normandy clearly stands out.

On 7 July General Corlett's U.S. XIX Corps opened its attack with an

A soldier grimaces as a 4.2-inch mortar launches a shell toward German positions in Normandy, 26 July 1944. Due to their high trajectory, mortars were often the weapon of choice in the confined spaces of the *bocage*. (U.S. Army Signal Corps photo)

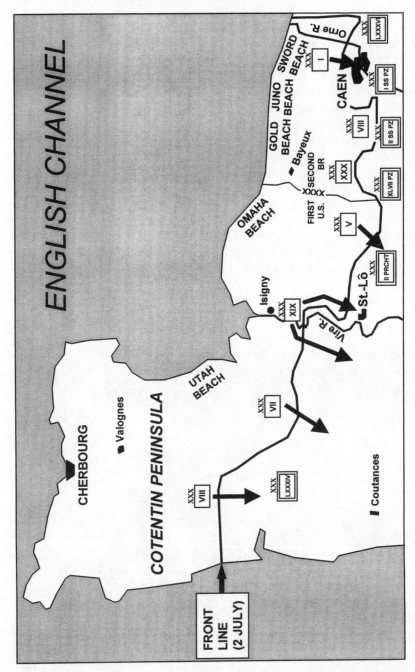

The Battle of the Hedgerows, 3–18 July 1944

assault by the 30th Infantry Division across the Taute-Vire Canal. XIX Corps' objective was St.-Lô, the most decisive piece of terrain in the American zone due to the eight roads and one railroad that converged there. With St.-Lô in American hands, the German army would be hard-pressed to reinforce the LXXXIV Corps that defended the ground between St.-Lô and the western coast of Normandy, thus paving the way for a decisive breakthrough in that area.[71]

One could hardly conceive of a more difficult mission for a division new to combat than a deliberate river crossing, but that is what the 30th Infantry Division faced in its attack across the Taute-Vire Canal. The division had entered combat on 15 June but had spent the ensuing three weeks defending in place.[72] This period allowed some limited contact with enemy forces and helped to season the green soldiers. Nevertheless, the attack on 7 July was the first large-scale combat action for most of the soldiers. "The shock of that first fight is something they just can't understand until they have been in it," General William K. Harrison Jr., the assistant division commander, stated later.[73] To ensure that the soldiers understood their roles in the upcoming attack, units conducted intensive rehearsals, to include sand table drills and actual practice river crossings.[74]

Due to its gradual exposure to combat and intensive preparations, the 30th Infantry Division conducted the assault crossing smoothly. The division performed well for its initial operation, but it still had much to learn about combat in the hedgerows, a conclusion acknowledged by contemporary U.S. Army historians:

> In general, attacking units were finding what every division learned the hard way in its opening battle in Normandy: that hedgerow terrain demanded tactical skill and know-how which green units—and even those experienced in African or Sicilian fighting—did not initially possess. The 30th Division was no exception. Coming into Normandy in mid-June, the division had had plenty of warning of trouble, and had trained to meet it. But there was no substitute for battle experience to bring out the concrete difficulties of action or test the methods for meeting them. . . . All this took time to learn and more time to digest; most units in the July battle were training as they fought.[75]

Indeed, most American infantry divisions quickly learned the methods of hedgerow fighting necessary to attack in Normandy with little assistance from higher headquarters.[76]

Although AGF sent observation teams overseas, the American army in World War II never fully centralized nor formally institutionalized a system for gathering lessons from the field, digesting them, and then disseminating them back down to lower levels.[77] The lessons-learning "system" therefore left much discretion in the hands of local commanders. This initiative reinforced the critical importance of organizational leadership in collecting and distilling lessons learned. The key leadership in this regard was at the division level. Commanders at the regimental level and below were too focused on the current battle, and corps commanders and above were too removed from the small units that did the actual fighting. If units were to alter their tactics quickly, division commanders and their staffs would have to precipitate the change.

The ability of division commanders to adapt to the situation on the ground in Normandy was the key difference that allowed some divisions to succeed in hedgerow fighting while others initially failed. All divisions sooner or later overcame the disadvantages of the terrain, but the slow learners paid a higher price in casualties and time lost. Often division commanders or operations officers would append a list of "lessons learned" to their monthly after-action report. The 1st, 3d, 9th, and 29th Infantry Divisions, among others, began this practice early and continued it throughout the war.[78] More important, successful divisions ensured that subordinate units understood and used these lessons in combat.

The success of the 30th Infantry Division allowed General Corlett to expand the attack. The First U.S. Army assigned the 9th Infantry Division, fresh from its victory at Cherbourg, to XIX Corps; the division went into the line to the west of the 30th Infantry Division. To the east, the 29th Infantry Division began

Infantry and tanks advance through a French town, 8 July 1944. Combined-arms training prior to D-Day was inadequate, forcing American soldiers to improvise solutions to tank-infantry coordination in the hedgerows of Normandy. (U.S. Army Signal Corps photo)

its attack south toward St.-Lô on 11 July. The 35th Infantry Division would also soon join in the attack.

The Germans identified XIX Corps as the American main effort and counterattacked on the night of 10 July with the elite Panzer Lehr Division to the west of the Vire River. The Germans now received a lesson in the difficulty of attacking in the hedgerows. General Fritz Bayerlein, who commanded the Panzer Lehr Division, did not know that the 9th Infantry Division had recently been moved south of the canal and was now in the line. As a result, the German counterattack fell upon a seasoned, battle-tested unit near peak efficiency. Although the 901st Panzer Grenadier Regiment, supported by Panther and Mark IV tanks, succeeded in penetrating the boundary between the 39th and 47th Infantry Regiments to a depth of up to two thousand yards, the Americans refused to panic. Instead, General Eddy ordered the 39th and 47th Infantry Regiments to seal the breach, while the 899th Tank Destroyer Battalion, division artillery, and aircraft systematically destroyed the German armor and infantry that had broken through the line. By 2100 hours on 11 July, the 9th Infantry Division had eliminated the attacking German units and had regained the ground lost early in the morning.[79]

The 30th Infantry Division likewise succeeded in halting the counterattack of the 902d Panzer Grenadier Regiment in its zone of operations. The historian of the operation concludes, "Panzer Lehr had been severely mauled by the combined onslaughts of the U.S. 9th and 30th Divisions, and was now crippled to an extent that removed the possibility of further large-scale counterattack west of the Vire."[80] The German counterattack convincingly demonstrated that well-trained and well-led American infantry divisions were as good as or better than their German counterparts in Normandy. Historians who have tried to prove otherwise have seriously underestimated the advantages conferred on the defender by the hedgerow terrain. Furthermore, the American army was the only force in Normandy that learned how to attack successfully in the *bocage*.

The 29th Infantry Division began its attack to seize St.-Lô on 11 July. Before the attack, the division had practiced combined-arms techniques designed to break through the tough hedgerows. The division's main effort, the 116th Infantry, the "Stonewall Brigade" of Civil War fame, was reinforced with tanks from the 747th Tank Battalion and the engineers of the 121st Engineer Combat Battalion. The Sherman tanks supporting the division had steel prongs welded to their final drive assemblies; these prongs would dig into embankments and either allow the tank to break through the hedgerow with the power of its engine or dig holes into which the engineers would place demolitions to blow the hedgerow apart.[81]

The 2d Infantry Division in the U.S. V Corps zone attacked on 11 July to take Hill 192, a tactically important piece of high ground east of St.-Lô. The 2d Infantry Division had also developed a tank-infantry-engineer combined-arms solution for dealing with the hedgerows.[82] The training paid off, as the division took Hill 192 from the German 3d Parachute Division in one day, an objective that had eluded the 2d Infantry Division for weeks after D-Day.

From 12 to 14 July, the German defense in front of XIX Corps stiffened; American units ground out advances measured in yards, at high cost to both attacker and defender. Between 11 and 13 July, the German 3d Parachute Division lost 4,064 men killed, wounded, and missing.[83] The Americans could replace their losses; the Germans could not. Few experiences were as terrifying as that of an infantry replacement fed directly into combat. One American officer in the 29th Infantry Division later wrote:

> On occasion, new men were fed into units actively locked in battle. Sent in by night and placed in among dark forms who occupied gravelike holes scooped out behind hedgerows, they could hardly have known where they were. . . . Sometimes, a new man did die before dawn, and none around knew him by sight or name. . . . without the sustaining strength of unit pride or comradeship, he had started battle reduced to the final resource with which every man ends it: himself, alone.[84]

General Gerhardt understood the problems associated with feeding replacements directly into units in contact. After the battle for St.-Lô, he adjusted division policy to ensure that only battalions in reserve positions received replacements.[85]

Medics administer blood plasma to a wounded American soldier in Normandy, 11 July 1944. Medical advances and forward treatment of casualties saved hundreds of thousands of lives during World War II. (U.S. Army Signal Corps photo)

A tank destroyer supports the advance of the 29th Infantry Division on the outskirts of St.-Lô, 20 July 1944. The use of tank destroyers for close support of infantry was not a doctrinal role; it grew out of battlefield experiences and innovation on the front lines. (U.S. Army Signal Corps photo)

General Corlett had XIX Corps execute an all-out attack on 15 July, just as the German defensive lines had been stretched to the limit. The 9th and 30th Infantry Divisions in what was now part of the VII Corps zone attacked to seize positions along the St.-Lô–Périers road. The pressure forced the German Seventh Army to commit units of the 5th Parachute Division into the front as soon as they arrived from Brittany. The 30th Infantry Division severely mauled the 14th Parachute Regiment. The German Seventh Army report stated that the battle "confirms our experience that newly committed troops which have not yet developed teamwork and are thrown into heavy battle without having been broken in, suffer disproportionately heavy losses."[86] American commanders would undoubtedly have agreed with this statement, but the fact remains that the German Seventh Army had the same troubles with its inexperienced units as the First U.S. Army was having with its inexperienced divisions.

Farther east, the 29th Infantry Division took the crucial town of St.-Lô on 18 July. Task Force C (named after its commander, General Cota) and the 1st Battalion, 115th Infantry, entered St.-Lô in the afternoon, forty-three days after D-Day. The 1st Battalion, 115th Infantry, was down to 450 men when it seized St.-Lô on 18 July, approximately at 50 percent strength; the three rifle companies resembled reinforced platoons more than anything else. Later its commander, Colonel Glover S. Johns Jr., remarked, "The town was being held by the artillery, really, as the infantrymen were little more than guards for the observation posts."[87] Repeatedly, the artillery broke up German counterattacks that threatened to overwhelm the battered, but indestructible, "Clay Pigeons of St.-Lô." The doctrine of immediate counterattack was costly to German forces when facing American units with strong artillery support. "Even the best and most proven tactics still require judgement and the force to do the job," Colonel Johns noted. He added, "The Germans rarely had enough of either."[88]

On 20 July a battalion from the 134th Infantry Regiment, 35th Infantry Division, relieved the 1st Battalion, 115th Infantry. St.-Lô was finally secure, and General Bradley could begin final preparations for COBRA, the operation designed to allow the First U.S. Army to break out of Normandy.

The Battle of the Hedgerows had lasted two weeks, but its result determined the outcome of the Normandy campaign. The advance was a slow, painstaking crawl through the worst of the *bocage.* Losses on both sides were heavy. Battle casualties during July 1944 totaled 4,773 men in the 9th Infantry Division, 4,718 men in the 29th Infantry Division, and 4,421 men in the 30th Infantry Division.[89] Since most of these losses were infantrymen, the infantry regiments in these divisions lost between 50 and 75 percent of their strength during this month. The American historians relate the impact of these losses on their units:

> For most of the American soldiers, it had been a thankless, miserable, disheartening battle. It was, perhaps, particularly hard on fresh divisions, coming into their first action with the zest and high morale born of long training and of confidence in their unit. Many units were—or felt they were—wrecked by the losses that hit them in the course of a few days' fighting, wiping out key men. . . . The close ties within a unit, built up by long association, were broken irreparably; new officers and new men had to be assimilated in the midst of battle, sometimes on a wholesale scale. Yet the shock was met and surmounted; units that lost 30 percent of strength or more in a week, were kept in line and went on fighting.[90]

American infantry divisions proved their worth in the Normandy campaign and vindicated the faith that General George C. Marshall and Lieutenant General Lesley J. McNair placed in them.

In turn, American infantry divisions decimated some of the best units in the German armed forces, to include the 2d SS Panzer Division *(Das Reich)*, the 17th SS Panzer Grenadier Division, the Panzer Lehr Division, and the 3d and 5th Parachute Divisions. American infantry divisions attacked these units until they could no longer hold their front without reinforcements, but no reinforcements came. The unintended strategy of attrition was every bit as effective as Grant's 1864 campaign in Virginia and more successful than the Meuse-Argonne offensive in World War I. The use of combat formations to bludgeon an enemy to death is historically part of the American way of war. American divisions in World War II were more than just blunt instruments of destruction, however. In their next battle, those same divisions that hammered their way through the hedgerows would slice across France like a rapier.

Far from being the incompetent organizations that some historians portray, American infantry divisions were tough, resilient, and capable of accomplishing their missions under the worst of battlefield conditions. The American army in Normandy found itself locked in combat against a determined enemy entrenched on some of the worst terrain imaginable for an attacking force. Hedgerow combat was a soldiers' battle, and the American soldier displayed his competence by devising new tactics, techniques, and procedures to overcome the obstacles in his path. Operational maneuver by corps and army commanders was not possible until the procedures were in place to break the tactical stalemate. The division was the key level at which these new procedures were codified, refined, and disseminated. The resulting Battle of the Hedgerows and seizure of St.-Lô were crucial to the final success of the American army in Normandy. The Battle of the Hedgerows was bloody and bitter, but the First U.S. Army finally had the battlespace necessary to mass forces to attempt a penetration of enemy lines, leaving the marshes and rivers of the Normandy coast behind. As important, the German Seventh Army had used its last reserves in the front line, while the prolonged American attack had shattered many enemy formations beyond repair. Operation COBRA would first stretch the enemy front, then break it wide open.

7

Breakout and Pursuit: Maneuver Versus Firepower

The Army of the United States was the most mobile army in the world in 1944, but American commanders had yet to prove whether they could translate the inherent ability of American units to move into effective maneuver on the battlefield. Current proponents of "maneuver warfare" cast doubt on whether the U.S. Army has ever maneuvered effectively in its history.[1] Although the Allies failed to complete their great victory in Normandy with a classic *kesselschlact* (battle of encirclement), American operations in Normandy were devastatingly effective in reducing the vaunted Wehrmacht to a shambles in a little over two months of fighting. For an army that supposedly could not maneuver well, the breakout from Normandy, the exploitation to the Seine River, and the pursuit across France were exceptional operations. Senior leaders may have lost an opportunity to end the war in 1944 by failing to close the Falaise Gap when they had the opportunity to do so, but their mistakes were predominantly operational, not tactical. Allied firepower and the tactical abilities of Allied divisions created the conditions for subsequent mobile operations. American units proved their capability to move fast and strike hard in the exploitation of Operation COBRA, the Battle of the Mons Pocket, and the invasion of southern France.

Maneuver warfare enthusiasts talk about "surfaces," areas where the enemy is present in strength, and "gaps," areas where he is not. A military force would obviously prefer to strike through gaps and avoid surfaces. In Normandy there were no gaps; the First U.S. Army had to create one through the use of mass and firepower. As the Germans later found out at Mortain and in the Battle of the Bulge, however, the ability to maneuver does not automatically translate into victory. In both cases, German maneuver foundered on the rocks of American firepower. Combat effectiveness is much more than the ability to maneuver well. German failures in intelligence, logistics, airpower, and fire support resulted in their defeat on the battlefield on numerous occasions. The Allied

160

breakout from Normandy was a convincing victory. So was the destruction of Army Group Center by the Red Army in Operation BAGRATION, which took place concurrently. Taken together, these operations show on a grand scale the limited combat effectiveness of the Wehrmacht in 1944, despite its tactical prowess and ability to maneuver.

Except for the attack across the Cotentin Peninsula by the 9th Infantry Division and the 82d Airborne Division, American operations in Normandy prior to Operation COBRA were unimaginative frontal attacks. These attacks were born of necessity, for until the 29th Infantry Division seized St.-Lô, the First U.S. Army lacked the maneuver space and road networks necessary to mass its forces. With St.-Lô in American hands, Lieutenant General Omar N. Bradley could concentrate his forces in an attempt to penetrate the German lines on a narrow front. To do this, he assigned three of his most effective divisions—the 4th, 9th, and 30th Infantry Divisions—to his best corps commander, Major General J. Lawton Collins of U.S. VII Corps. The First U.S. Army ensured that VII Corps massed its forces by giving it a narrow zone for its attack, less than five miles across at the line of departure. To open a hole in the German front, General Bradley requested the use of the heavy bombers of the American Eighth Air Force. The concept was for the bombers to "carpet bomb" the German front lines, through which the infantry divisions could then penetrate. Once the infantry divisions created a gap, the 2d Armored Division, 3d Armored Division, and 1st Infantry Division, fully motorized for the operation, would exploit the penetration to the south and west.[2]

By the commencement of Operation COBRA, the divisions of the First U.S. Army had largely solved the problems of attacking through the hedgerows. Small, combined-arms formations constituted the basis for the new assault organization.[3] To operate effectively together, infantry, armor, and engineer units had to train together during lulls in combat. Such training should have taken place in the United States and Great Britain prior to D-Day, but infantry-tank training was almost uniformly abysmal prior to the Normandy invasion.[4] Regardless of the doctrinal strictures of FM 17-36, *Employment of Tanks with Infantry,* many infantrymen were simply ignorant of the capabilities and limitations of tanks. Part of the problem was a shortage of independent tank battalions. There were not enough to assign one to each infantry division on a habitual basis for training. Formation of GHQ tank battalions had taken second priority behind formation of tank battalions in armored divisions, so most independent tank battalions arrived overseas too late to form habitual training relationships with infantry divisions. Not until 14 June 1944 did AGF direct that tank and tank destroyer battalions be attached to infantry divisions for two months of combined training prior to overseas deployment, much too late to affect the Normandy campaign.[5] Tanks were critical to the success of the infantry in fighting through the tough hedgerows of Normandy, but the infantry and tanks had to form cohesive teams before they could operate effectively together.

In combat, tanks suppressed enemy infantry with high explosive and ma-

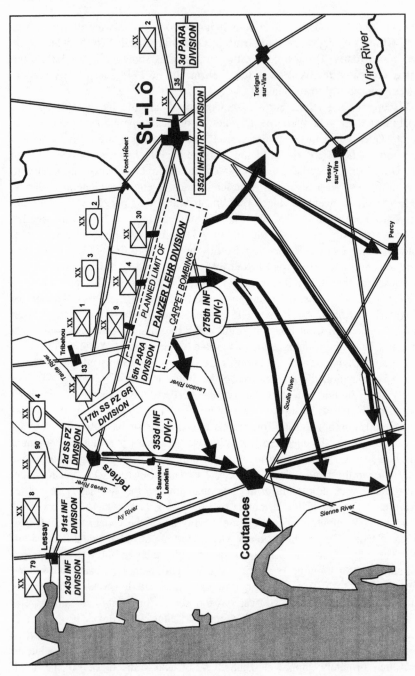

Operation COBRA, 25–29 July 1944

chine gun fire, while the infantry protected the tanks from enemy antitank guns and other antitank weapons such as *panzerfausts*. Progress through the *bocage* was slow, units fought engagements at short range, and the use of massed armor formations in accordance with doctrine was impractical. Infantrymen and tankers paid the price in blood while the divisions of the First U.S. Army adjusted their tactics and training to fit the situation on the battlefield. By the end of July 1944, infantry-tank cooperation had improved as a result of new training and experience gained in combat.[6]

Another problem with combined-arms cooperation was the lack of good tactical communications. Radios in armor, infantry, engineer, artillery, and tank destroyer units were not identical and only rarely were compatible. Combat in the *bocage* worsened this situation, since it required the formation of small teams, such as a platoon of infantry supported by a squad of engineers and a section of tanks. The infantry platoon leader could not talk to the tanks on his SCR-300 radio, and if the tanks were equipped with only SCR-538 receivers, the tankers could not talk with anyone. To overcome this situation, the troops in the field improvised. Armor units borrowed SCR-300 radios and operated

GIs from the 3d Battalion, 47th Infantry Regiment, 9th Infantry Division, move through a breach created in a hedgerow by a tank bulldozer, 5 August 1944. The ability of infantry to team up with engineer and tank support was the key to American tactical success in Normandy. (U.S. Army Signal Corps photo)

them with the antenna sticking out of the tank hatch. Some tank battalions sent radios to the supported infantry unit that could communicate with the SCR-508 and SCR-528 radios used by command tanks. The most common solution was to establish wire communications to the outside of the tank through an externally mounted handset connected to the intercom system.[7] In the long term, the army developed the AN/VRC-3 radio for installation in American tanks; this radio was a vehicular version of the SCR-300 radio carried by the infantry. The AN/VRC-3 became available in September 1944, and by mid-December the army had equipped all M4 Sherman tanks in separate tank battalions with the new radio.[8]

Terrain posed another problem for Sherman crewmen. Tanks could not negotiate the walls of hedgerows without exposing the vulnerable underside of their hulls as they climbed the embankments. The Germans covered gaps in the hedges with mines and antitank weapons. American tankers devised several means to break through the hedges. One method was for engineers to blast a hole in the hedge; a tank fitted with a dozer blade could then clear the dirt and vegetation out of the way and drive through the resulting gap.[9] Due to the large amount of explosives required and a shortage of dozer tanks in the First U.S. Army, however, this technique had limited value.

The 29th Infantry Division improvised by fitting twin prongs to the front of its supporting tanks to drive holes into hedgerows. Engineers could then plant demolition charges in the holes, a method that required far fewer explosives than externally placed charges. Experiments with these tanks soon uncovered their ability to create gaps in hedgerows under their own power and without the use of explosives. The prongs would dig into the center of a hedgerow and lift off the top of the bank with relative ease. This chance discovery proved effective in combat.[10]

Sergeant Curtis G. Culin and his crew, members of the 102d Cavalry Reconnaissance Squadron, developed a similar and more widely applicable solution. They had steel teeth welded to the front of their tank, an improvisation similar to that devised by the 747th Tank Battalion, which supported the 29th Infantry Division.[11] When the teeth dug into an embankment, the power of the engine would force the tank through and create a gap in the hedgerow. General Bradley had over five hundred of these devices installed on American tanks for use during Operation COBRA. The "Rhinoceros" attachment, as the device became known, was successful in combat, and the army decorated Sergeant Culin with the Legion of Merit for his crew's innovation.[12]

The greatest advantage the Allies possessed over the Wehrmacht in the West was air superiority. American divisions developed close bonds with their tactical air support in France, due in large measure to the efforts of Major General Elwood R. "Pete" Quesada, commander of the IX Tactical Air Command.[13] Air-ground cooperation was a key to the success of the spearheads during Operation COBRA. A flight of four fighter-bombers flew ahead of each column. A qualified pilot rode with the column in a Sherman tank modified with SCR-522 VHF radios for ground-air communications. The planes gave excellent reconnaissance information and immediate close air support.[14] With this support, the column could move farther and faster. By fall 1944 the ground forces received close air support almost as quickly and efficiently as artillery fire. Units used this support to destroy difficult targets, such as enemy tanks. The American army in France came to rely on tactical airpower to the point that the lack of support during poor weather severely curtailed the pace of the advance.[15]

The close cooperation between the First U.S. Army and its tactical air support did not carry over to its relations with the heavy bombers. COBRA was to begin with a massive bombardment by over fifteen hundred B-17 Flying Fortresses and B-24 Liberators, but misunderstandings caused problems from the very beginning of the operation. General Bradley wanted the bombers to fly parallel to the line of departure along the St.-Lô–Périers road to increase the accuracy of the bombing, but the air planners decided on a perpendicular approach, which would allow for a quicker bombing but increased the likelihood of bombs being dropped short of the target on the heads of friendly troops. The air planners failed to convey their decision to the First U.S. Army. When the attack commenced and the bombers came in perpendicular to the front line, Bradley was furious, but there was nothing he could do to change the plan short of postponing the entire operation.[16]

VII Corps scheduled COBRA to begin at 1300 hours on 24 July, but poor weather forced a twenty-four-hour postponement at the last minute. Word of the delay did not reach all of the aircraft then streaming toward the target area. Over three hundred bombers released their loads before the recall message reached them, and some of the bombs fell short of the target.[17] Even though commanders had pulled their soldiers back twelve hundred yards to the north of the St.-Lô–Périers road to prevent casualties, many bombs fell among units of the 30th Infantry Division, which suffered 24 killed and 128 wounded in the bombing.[18]

The next day brought better weather, if not better accuracy. When the aircraft returned at 1100 hours on 25 July, they hit not only the 30th Infantry Division again but also the 4th and 9th Infantry Divisions. The bombing killed Lieutenant General Lesley J. McNair, commander of AGF, who was observing the operation as commander of the fictitious 1st U.S. Army Group. Total casualties reached 111 killed and 490 wounded.[19] General William K. Harrison Jr., assistant division commander of the 30th Infantry Division, recalls, "I went back to regimental headquarters in order to get hold of a radio and tell them to send the Air Force home, we could win the war without their help—I was so mad."[20] The 30th Infantry Division developed the unenviable reputation as the most-bombed division in the American army; soldiers of the division not so jokingly referred to the Eighth and Ninth Air Forces as the "Eighth and Ninth Luftwaffe."[21]

The short bombing caused casualties, confusion, and delay among American units taking part in the assault. In the 3d Battalion, 47th Infantry Regiment, 9th Infantry Division, bombs killed the entire command group with the exception of the battalion commander and executive officer. This caused Major General Manton S. Eddy to delay the attack of the 47th Infantry Regiment while he replaced its 3d Battalion with the 1st Battalion, 39th Infantry Regiment. Bombs fell on the 8th Infantry Regiment of the 4th Infantry Division and caused numerous casualties in the 119th and 120th Infantry Regiments of the 30th Infantry Division. The bombing also demoralized the soldiers, who took little comfort from the fact that the Germans had suffered far worse than their buddies.[22]

In addition to the use of heavy bombers, the First U.S. Army massed its firepower in support of the attack by giving control of nine heavy battalions (8-inch guns), five medium battalions (155mm howitzers), and seven light battalions (105mm howitzers) of artillery to VII Corps. In addition, VII Corps also controlled the artillery of the 1st Infantry Division and the 2d and 3d Armored Divisions waiting in reserve to exploit the penetration.[23] Added to the howitzers of the assault divisions, the total fire support in VII Corps numbered an impressive forty-three battalions of artillery amounting to over five hundred tubes. Ammunition shortages had restricted the use of artillery in Normandy up to this point, but VII Corps received nearly 140,000 rounds of artillery ammunition for the operation.[24]

The bombing and artillery fires devastated large portions of the Panzer Lehr Division positioned in the path of COBRA. Bombs and shells destroyed tanks and guns, turned the area into a lunar landscape, and decimated the defenders in the bombardment zone.[25] Major General Fritz Bayerlein, commander of Panzer Lehr, had no way of controlling the battle; the bombardment cut wires leading to the front and demolished three battalion command posts. The ground attack broke through the remnants of the division. Two days later, Bayerlein walked away from the battlefield, alone. Behind him, his division had virtually ceased to exist.[26]

The ground attack by the 4th, 9th, and 30th Infantry Divisions ran into scattered resistance from the dazed survivors of the air bombardment and artillery preparation fires. To the credit of the German soldiers, they kept fighting and put up stiff resistance in spots. Nevertheless, the mass and firepower arrayed against them were more than they could handle. The 9th Infantry Division advanced two miles to the south of the St.-Lô–Périers road by nightfall and linked up with the 8th Infantry Regiment of the 4th Infantry Division near la Chapelle-en-Juger.[27] The 30th Infantry Division made steady progress toward Hébécrevon and seized the town at midnight. Although the divisions did not reach all of their assigned objectives, they had pierced the German main line of resistance.

Even though he lacked solid evidence that this was the case, General Collins, with an intuitive feel for the battlefield, sensed the time had come to release his reserves and exploit the penetration. As discussed earlier, German doctrine mandated immediate counterattacks against attacking enemy forces. When the Germans failed to do so on 25 July, Collins correctly surmised that the bombardment had disrupted their command and control network.[28] The next day, the armor rolled.

The infantry divisions did their part to further the penetration in the next two days. The 30th Infantry Division advanced eight miles and seized positions along the Vire River to protect the eastern flank of the penetration.[29] The 9th Infantry Division assisted the passage of the 1st Infantry Division and Combat Command B of the 3d Armored Division in its zone, then attacked to seize objectives that sealed off the western flank of the penetration.[30] The 4th Infantry Division drove straight south to deepen the penetration. The German reaction was too little and too late. "This thing has busted wide open," exclaimed Major General Leland Hobbs, commander of the 30th Infantry Division.[31]

The Normandy campaign had entered a new phase of mobile warfare for which the American army was particularly well suited. After the war *Generalmajor* von Buttlar, chief of army operations on the *Oberkommando der Wehrmacht* (OKW) Operations Staff, wrote:

> The WFSt [OKW Operations Staff] entirely agreed with OB WEST *[Oberkommando der West]* that [mobile] operations are generally preferable to a rigid defense. In order to be able to conduct [mobile] operations, however, the following are required: (1) troops whose organization, arms, equipment, and training fit them for mobile combat, and (2) an air force capable of giving troop movements—which are, of course, the essential element of [a mobile] operation—sufficient protection to ensure their successful execution even by daylight.
>
> Both prerequisites existed on the enemy side, but not with us. . . .
>
> In the light of the unalterable composition of the forces in the West, the WFSt feared that any attempt to carry out [mobile] operations with these forces, in the face of the enemy superiority in mobility and in the air, could only lead, at best, to an organized flight which the greatest efforts of the command would be able to stem only with difficulty.[32]

After the success of COBRA, the German army's great mistake—caused in large measure by the interference of Adolf Hitler in the battle—was to attempt to restore the situation in Normandy through maneuver instead of falling back to a more defensible position along the Seine. The result of this decision was the ill-fated counterattack at Mortain.

The success of COBRA and the subsequent exploitation of the breakthrough created the conditions for the activation of Lieutenant General George S. Patton's Third U.S. Army on 1 August. As U.S. VIII Corps advanced into Brittany in accordance with the OVERLORD plan, its movement hinged on the city of Avranches on the coast. The entire Third U.S. Army and its logistics had to move through a corridor at Avranches less than twenty miles in width, protected on the east by VII Corps. The German plan was to use the XLVII

Sergeant Wyman P. Williams, an assistant squad leader in the 12th Infantry Regiment, 4th Infantry Division, rests near Villedieu, France, 3 August 1944. He is armed with a M-1 Garand rifle and hand grenades. (U.S. Army Signal Corps photo)

Panzer Corps (2d and 116th Panzer Divisions) and the I SS Panzer Corps (1st SS and 2d SS Panzer Divisions) to penetrate the American line and seize Avranches, thereby cutting off the Third U.S. Army in Brittany.[33] In reality, superior Allied intelligence and a determined stand by the 30th Infantry Division ensured the German plan had no hope of success.

The British code-breaking success, code-named ULTRA, allowed the Allies access to nearly all German radio traffic encrypted through the Enigma machine by 1944.[34] The information gained from ULTRA was so sensitive that it never traveled lower than army level. General Bradley, the 12th Army Group commander, and Major General Courtney Hodges, the First U.S. Army commander, had access to ULTRA information, but General Collins, whose VII Corps was in the path of the attack, did not. To protect ULTRA, Bradley and Hodges had to counter the German moves without making their response too obvious. The easiest way to meet these twin goals was to mass tactical airpower at the point of the attack. In addition, Bradley ensured that VII Corps would not lack ground troops. Although the initial attack warning came too late (at midnight on 6 August) to reinforce VII Corps immediately, within twenty-four hours Collins had five infantry and two armored divisions under his command. These forces did not "materialize out of thin air," as the official historian, without knowledge of ULTRA, surmised.[35] The information provided by ULTRA in August was "of unsurpassable quality," enabling Allied commanders to anticipate or counter German moves on the battlefield.[36]

Even without ULTRA, the German counterattack would have failed. American commanders had other means of intelligence gathering at their disposal, such as air reconnaissance and radio intercept and direction finding. During the course of the war, the Ninth Air Force flew approximately thirty-one thousand reconnaissance sorties that generated nearly thirteen million photographs.[37] Reports from these means and from the front line itself quickly picked up the German armored divisions as they left their concealed assembly areas.[38] Allied tactical air support was flexible enough at this stage of the war to react to any German moves quickly, with or without prior warning.

The three outstanding units in the path of the advance, the 4th, 9th, and 30th Infantry Divisions—ironically, the same units that had created the breakthrough during Operation COBRA—fought stubbornly against the attacking panzers. The 9th Infantry Division stopped the 116th Panzer Division in its tracks.[39] The 4th Infantry Division, in VII Corps reserve, placed units in blocking positions to contain the enemy breakthroughs that did occur and engaged enemy units with heavy artillery strikes.[40] The German main effort, however, hit the 30th Infantry Division in its sector astride Mortain.

Outstanding small-unit actions by infantry and tank destroyer units at numerous roadblocks delayed the initial strong thrusts of the enemy attack. The 2d SS Panzer Division overran elements of the 120th Infantry Regiment in Mortain on 7 August, but the 2d Battalion held the decisive terrain of Hill 317 east of the city until relieved by the 35th Infantry Division five days later. Although the Germans captured the battalion command group in Mortain, the battalion fought on under the command of Captain Reynold C. Erichson. In its defense of Hill 317, the 2d Battalion lost three hundred of the nearly seven hundred men in the battalion, but forward observers on the hill called in devastating artillery strikes on the enemy tank columns arrayed below them. For its defense of Hill 317, the battalion earned a well-deserved Distinguished Unit

Citation, and each of its company commanders received the Distinguished Service Cross. General Collins called the defense of Hill 317 "one of the outstanding small-unit actions of World War II."[41]

When daylight came on 7 August, ten squadrons of rocket-firing Typhoons from the Royal Air Force converged on Mortain to attack the already stalled enemy spearheads while American fighters kept the Luftwaffe off the battlefield.[42] American artillery units fired numerous missions on enemy formations, without regard to ammunition expenditures.[43] The 2d and 3d Armored Divisions arrived on the battlefield; Combat Command B of the 3d Armored Division attacked the farthest penetration of the German 2d Panzer Division. Although the battle raged for several days, the outcome was never in doubt.

The dogged determination of the American infantry divisions in the path of the German counterattack gave the Allies an opportunity to surround and destroy two German armies in Normandy. The opportunity was, according to Bradley, one that "comes to a commander not more than once in a century."[44] American armor and infantry divisions, with their superb mobility and firepower, were well suited to the wide envelopment necessary to accomplish the encirclement of the German forces. The question remained whether the operational abilities of the senior American commanders could match the tactical performance of their units in the campaign.

Sadly, they could not. In his revisionist account of the Normandy campaign, Martin Blumenson castigates General Bradley, along with General Dwight D. Eisenhower and General Bernard L. Montgomery, for throwing away the opportunity to destroy the German forces opposing them and instead focusing their efforts on gaining ground. As a result, the bulk of the German forces in Normandy escaped the Allied trap, retreated in good order across the Seine, and were able to patch together another defensive front as the Allied pursuit died out due to logistical overstretch. "The miracle of the West," as the Germans called it, should never have happened.[45]

The OVERLORD plan was in essence a logistical document. Once ashore, the Allies floundered to devise a sound maneuver plan to execute the campaign. Even after the success of Operation COBRA, Bradley felt compelled to disperse his combat power by sending VIII Corps into Brittany to seize ports there, ports that were strongly held by German fortress troops and would take weeks, if not months, to make usable again. The emphasis on gaining and holding the OVERLORD lodgement area resulted in a lack of combat power at the decisive place and time—to close the Falaise Gap before the German army could escape. The poor performance of the Canadian and British armies in closing the gap from the north only exacerbated the problem. Over 50,000 German soldiers escaped the jaws of the trap at Falaise, and 240,000 Germans escaped the potential trap across the Seine. By any accounting, Allied operational performance was sorely lacking.[46]

Tactically, however, most American divisions performed well. The accomplishment of the 9th Infantry Division in the Battle of the Falaise Gap highlights the mobility and firepower of the American infantry division in 1944. While the 39th Infantry Regiment defended its positions near Mortain on 7 August against attacks by the 116th Panzer Division, the remainder of the division continued to attack east to widen the Avranches corridor until the 28th Infantry Division passed to its front on 12 August. The next day, the 9th Infantry Division moved fifty miles by truck to new positions on the southern face of the German pocket. On 14 August the division attacked to the north in conjunction with the 3d Armored Division, and for the next four days it pounded German positions with concentrated firepower. On 17 August the division reported, "Numerous targets of all descriptions were available. . . . 5829 rounds [of artillery ammunition expended]. . . . Considerable destruction of enemy equipment. . . . Streams of fighter-bombers attacked retreating enemy columns from 0500 until dark. Numerous fires from burning vehicles and tanks were observed in the target area."[47] The flexibility and firepower of the American infantry division made such reports possible.

The German Seventh Army, Fifth Panzer Army, and Panzer Group Eberbach suffered heavily from Allied firepower in their escape from Normandy. "Never in history had artillery enjoyed such a field day," wrote the historians of the 90th Infantry Division.[48] As many as ten thousand German soldiers perished in the Falaise Gap, and the Allies took up to fifty thousand prisoner.[49] Nevertheless, substantial numbers escaped the Allied trap. Although Bradley put much of the blame on Montgomery's inability to close the gap from the north,[50] he must share responsibility for the mistake. Bradley was slow to concentrate sufficient force to close the Falaise Gap from the south when he had the opportunity to do so. When U.S. V Corps finally attacked to close the gap on 18 August, its forces consisted of the French 2d Armored Division (more interested in Paris than Falaise), the 80th Infantry Division (in combat for the first time), and the 90th Infantry Division. This effort was hardly on the scale of Operation COBRA; Bradley had diluted his combat power near Argentan by acceding to Patton's wishes for an immediate drive to the Seine.[51]

The result was predictable. The 80th Infantry Division experienced the fate of many new divisions and barely got across its line of departure before the Germans halted it.[52] The French 2d Armored Division was more interested in achieving French political goals than in closing the gap.[53] The burden of the attack therefore fell on the revitalized 90th Infantry Division, now in the capable hands of Major General Raymond S. McLain.

The Battle of the Falaise Gap was ironic justice for the "Tough 'Ombres." Their first battle in Normandy began with calls for the division's dissolution, but at the end of the campaign they exacted a bloody revenge on their enemies. The 90th Infantry Division fought to join with Polish soldiers at Chambois and close the pocket on 19 August. As the German forces attempted to escape encirclement, the devastating effectiveness of the American infantry-artillery team once again became evident. General William E. Depuy later stated, "The artillery was good. It was just technically very sound, better than the Germans.

It could mass quicker, and we had good communications. I think the technique, the command and control of fire direction ... of the American Army were superior to the German Army."[54] With eleven battalions of artillery at their disposal and an abundance of targets at hand, the forward observers of the division implored the fire direction centers to "stop computin', and start shooting."[55]

In four days the 90th Infantry Division caused eight thousand enemy casualties and took thirteen thousand prisoners at a cost of six hundred casualties. In the "valley of death" below the division's positions lay destroyed 220 enemy tanks, 160 self-propelled guns, 700 artillery pieces, 130 antiaircraft guns, 130 half-track vehicles, 2,000 wagons, and 5,000 motor vehicles.[56] Lamentably, General McLain concluded, "If the Division had not been held back for over 24 hours in the attack on Chambois the results would have undoubtedly been greater."[57]

Despite this impressive tally, thousands of German soldiers withdrew through the porous trap. The Germans lost much of their equipment in the escape but were able to save over fifty thousand soldiers to fight again another day.[58] Although this accomplishment prolonged the war, after Normandy the decision in the West was never in doubt. The Wehrmacht lost three hundred thousand men defending Normandy, and the Allies had rendered forty German divisions combat ineffective, an achievement in many ways comparable to the Soviet victory at Stalingrad a year and a half earlier.[59] Eisenhower later called the Falaise Gap "one of the greatest killing grounds of any of the war areas," filled with scenes "that could be described only by Dante. It was literally possible to walk for hundreds of yards at a time, stepping on nothing but dead and decaying flesh."[60]

Hitler sacrificed another two hundred thousand men in defending self-proclaimed "fortresses" along the Biscayan and Channel coasts. General Bradley learned the cost of taking these ports when he committed VIII Corps and the 2d, 8th, and 29th Infantry Divisions to a bloody battle for Brest from 25 August to 18 September. These three divisions adjusted their tactics and techniques to wrest the heavily fortified city from German control. Ammunition shortages limited artillery support, and air support was less effective than expected. The three divisions fought a continual battle of small-unit actions to probe weak points in the defense, isolate enemy strongpoints, and then reduce them at close range with a combined-arms assault from large-caliber howitzers (sometimes used in direct fire mode), infantry, engineers using demolitions and flamethrowers, tanks, and tank destroyers. In the streets of Brest, small units learned to advance by blasting through the walls of buildings rather than advance along the deadly, open avenues. These tactics eventually took their toll on enemy forces. VIII Corps took the city along with 38,000 prisoners at a cost of 9,831 casualties.[61] It was a Pyrrhic victory; the Germans had so thoroughly demolished the port facilities that the Americans never made any attempt to use them.

Freed from the battle for Normandy and with little organized resistance to the east, the U.S. First and Third Armies pursued the fleeing enemy like a windswept tide. This was the campaign of large-scale, sweeping maneuver for which the army had trained its divisions in massive army-level exercises back in the United States. The highly mechanized American divisions excelled in fighting this war of movement. Excluding the airborne divisions, the only units of the American army without organic transportation were the infantry regiments of the standard infantry divisions. While the armored divisions raced across France, the infantry divisions kept pace through various means. Army commanders could completely motorize a standard infantry division through the attachment of six quartermaster truck companies with a total of 288 trucks.[62] Since the armies needed most of their truck companies to haul gasoline and other supplies during the pursuit, however, infantry divisions had to use other methods. Most divisions shuttled their infantry regiments forward using organic supply vehicles or trucks belonging to division artillery units. Some divisions put their infantrymen on tanks and tank destroyers to speed the advance. When no transportation was available, the infantry continued to march forward on foot.

By this stage of the campaign, combined-arms coordination, especially between tanks and infantry, was much improved. The 1st Infantry Division used battalion task forces in the pursuit, each force being a self-contained combat unit capable of overcoming light enemy resistance. A typical battalion task force might consist of an infantry battalion, a platoon of medium tanks, a platoon of light tanks, a platoon of tank destroyers, a platoon of towed antitank guns, an assault gun platoon, and a company of heavy mortars. Techniques of bounding overwatch, with infantry leading in close country and tanks leading in more open terrain, became routine. "The success of such operations," noted Lieutenant Colonel Clarence E. Beck, the division operations officer, "depends upon the attachment of tanks to the infantry units with which they are to fight in sufficient time to allow the tank crews and the infantry to arrive at solutions to their joint liaison and tactical problems and to develop mutual understanding and confidence."[63] Not until after the war did the army make tank battalions an organic part of the infantry division, thus eliminating the problem.

As long as fuel supplies lasted, the speed of the pursuit was nothing short of spectacular. The report of the 9th Infantry Division on 28 August stated, "Enemy disorganized and apparently wondering what it is all about."[64] Indeed, the American army moved at a rate the bulk of the Wehrmacht, with its horse-drawn artillery and logistics, could only dream of matching. Only German panzer and panzer grenadier units could move as fast as American divisions, but by 1944 these organizations were a shadow of their former selves. Lack of fuel and Allied air interdiction hampered the movement of even the most mobile German units. Hans Speidel, chief of staff of Army Group B, recalls, "The events of the last weeks of August were like a raging torrent that nothing could stem. . . . an orderly retreat had become impossible. The Allied motorized armies surrounded the slow and exhausted German divisions marching in separate groups, and smashed them. There was a jam of retreating German formations at Mons and considerable numbers were destroyed by the Allied armored units which overtook them."[65] The First U.S. Army took twenty-five thousand prisoners in the Mons Pocket, the remnants of twenty Germany divisions.[66]

The invasion of southern France by the Seventh U.S. Army on 15 August 1944 hastened the German collapse in the West. U.S. VI Corps, which made the initial landings under the capable leadership of Major General Lucian K. Truscott, was an experienced combat organization. This was the fourth amphibious invasion for the veteran 3d Infantry Division, the third for the seasoned 45th Infantry Division, and the second for the 36th Infantry Division. Hard training and attention to lessons learned in previous operations contributed to the success of the landing. After the Fifth U.S. Army withdrew VI Corps from combat in Italy in June, the 3d, 36th, and 45th Infantry Divisions had two months to integrate replacements and train for the upcoming invasion. The 3d Infantry Division stressed physical conditioning (especially speed marching), attack of fortifications, obstacle breaching, weapons firing, and infantry-tank cooperation. The training culminated in several landing exercises on beaches north of Naples.[67]

Troops of the 3d Infantry Division load onto transports near Formia, Italy, for amphibious training prior to the invasion of southern France, 31 July 1944. Intensive training, veteran units, and excellent planning made Operation DRAGOON one of the most successful amphibious invasions during World War II. (U.S. Army Signal Corps photo)

VI Corps put lessons from previous operations to good use. The invasion plan included the use of smoke to obscure the initial wave from enemy observation and the use of bulk-loaded landing craft and combat-loaded amphibious trucks to ensure quick resupply.[68] Since VI Corps landed in daylight, planners decided to rely on firepower rather than surprise to achieve their objectives. Naval forces supported the 3d Infantry Division alone with one battleship, six light cruisers, and five destroyers, along with smaller craft carrying guns or rockets. The warships executed a prearranged bombardment of known artillery positions for ninety minutes prior to H-hour, after which they took calls-for-fire from spotter planes and the nine shore fire control parties that landed in the first wave. The naval liaison officer at the division artillery headquarters had communications with all spotters and shore parties, which in effect created a naval fire direction center with the capability of massing the fire of all ships on a single target. The air forces, based mainly on Corsica or on escort carriers, attacked targets in southern France for ten days prior to the invasion and gained air superiority over the area.[69]

As a result of the thorough preparations, good communications, and pinpoint targeting, air and naval gunfire support were more effective than on 6 June, and VI Corps put more infantry battalions ashore at H-hour than in the Normandy landing. The excellent plan, well-trained and combat-experienced troops, and the low quality of German opposition combined to make Operation ANVIL/DRAGOON one of the most successful amphibious invasions in history. VI Corps casualties on 15 August totaled only 95 killed and 385 wounded, while the corps carved out a solid beachhead east of Toulon.[70]

The VI Corps breakout from its beachhead and pursuit of the German Nineteenth Army up the Rhone Valley was as spectacular in terms of ground gained as the Allied breakout and pursuit from Normandy. Once again American artillery had a field day. Major Walter T. Kerwin Jr., the 3d Infantry Division Artillery S-3, described the scene: "They [the Germans] had the [Rhone] river on their left, and the mountain line and us on the right, so that it was a turkey shoot. . . . It was like at Fort Sill sitting up there in all your great glory, with nobody shooting at you, and looking out there on just masses and masses of people and being able to pick your target."[71] As at Falaise, however, the American forces were not able to seal the trap. The German Nineteenth Army largely escaped to fight again in Alsace, despite losing one-fifth of its strength in the bitterly contested Battle of Montélimar as it withdrew north.[72]

Part of the reason for the failure to destroy the German forces was the emphasis that Lieutenant General Alexander M. Patch, the Seventh U.S. Army commander, put on seizing the ports of Toulon and Marseille before conducting more aggressive operations against the German forces in the Rhone Valley.[73] The French II Corps, under the command of General Jean de Lattre de Tassigny, attacked and seized both cities by 28 August, four weeks earlier than expected. As Eisenhower believed when he argued with Prime Minister Winston Churchill over whether to launch ANVIL, these ports turned out to be crucial to maintaining Allied logistics in France. During the critical months of September through December 1944, over one-third of all supplies shipped to France landed at Toulon or Marseille; not until March 1945 did Antwerp overtake the two southern ports in terms of tonnage unloaded.[74]

In the pursuit across France, logistics was clearly the limiting factor. In the planning for OVERLORD, Supreme Headquarters Allied Expeditionary Forces (SHAEF) used phase lines to estimate the advance of Allied forces across France. The staff estimated the establishment of the lodgement area along the Seine by D+90 (ninety days after D-Day) and closure on the Rhine by D+350. The operations staff was not as tied to the dates as the logisticians, who used the timed phase lines to pace the progress of an orderly supply buildup on the Continent.[75] Once the Allies secured the lodgement area, the logisticians assumed the armies would halt while the Communications Zone (COMZ) established a logistics base for a renewed advance across the Seine.[76] Since the operations staff assumed that the Germans would defend the Seine, thereby forcing the Allies into a deliberate river-crossing operation, they accepted the assumption of an operational pause at the river to build up forces.[77]

The OVERLORD logistics plan assumed steady progress. The Allies were to reach Avranches by D+20, Le Mans by D+40, and the entire lodgement area to the Seine by D+90. In the actual event the Allies reached the Seine at D+79, but the pace of the advance was hardly uniform. Between D+49 and D+79, the Allies occupied ground they had planned on taking between D+15 and D+90. Between 25 August and 12 September, Allied forces advanced from the D+90 to the D+350 phase line.[78] The engineers could not restore the railroads or build gas pipelines at the pace of the divisions rolling eastward. The Allies captured Paris on 25 August (fifty-five days ahead of schedule), burdening the overloaded supply system with an additional requirement of fifteen hundred tons per day for civil relief. Eisenhower's decision on 23 August to carry the pursuit across the Seine stretched the logistical tail even farther.

Until the Allies seized and repaired more ports, most supplies landed at either Cherbourg or across the beaches in Normandy. The Communications Zone moved the supplies from these points across France to the advancing armies. Allied air forces had destroyed much of the French rail system to prevent German reinforcements from reaching Normandy, but now the Allies had to repair the damage before using the railroads to move supplies forward. Lack of forward airfields and diversion of transport aircraft for airborne operations limited the use of aerial resupply. Motor transport, therefore, carried the bulk of the supplies forward. There were a finite number of trucks on the Continent, however, and they simply could not carry the 22,200 tons of supplies required daily by the thirty-seven Allied divisions on the Continent at the end of August. Eisenhower concluded that the logistics base as organized at the end of August 1944 could not support an Allied advance deep into Germany.[79]

Through a number of expedients, COMZ was able to cope with the in-

American troops and equipment arrive in Normandy. The Allied failure to open a deepwater port forced the majority of reinforcements, supplies, and equipment to enter France via the invasion beaches throughout the summer and fall of 1944. (U.S. Army Signal Corps photo)

creased needs of the armies through the third week of August. Eisenhower's decision to pursue the retreating Germans across the Seine, however, forced logisticians to improvise on a greater scale. To move supplies forward into the Chartres–La Loupe–Dreux triangle, COMZ organized the Red Ball Express, a series of one-way, loop highways along which convoys would travel twenty-four hours per day.[80] The system began operation on 25 August with 118 companies hauling supplies between the beaches and Chartres. On 6 September COMZ expanded the system. The routes diverged at Versailles, one branching northeast to support the First U.S. Army at Soissons and another branching east to support the Third U.S. Army at Sommesous. Although the plan for the Red Ball Express was a good one, execution fell short of expectations for several reasons: the shortage of military police to control the routes, the slow loading time for convoys, lack of vehicle maintenance, the "hijacking" of convoys by the armies to move supplies farther forward to divisional dump sites, and the lack of a uniform system of traffic regulation.[81]

Allied forces used other expedients as well. The Communications Zone formed sixty-eight truck companies by immobilizing the 26th, 95th, and 104th Infantry Divisions, and diverting two engineer service regiments, a chemical smoke-generating battalion, and assorted antiaircraft units into transportation duty. The armies also used their internal transport for line-of-communication hauling. On 22 August General Bradley ordered his armies to leave their heavy artillery west of the Seine and to use their trucks for cargo movement. The armies also diverted engineer, artillery, antiaircraft, ordnance, and chemical units to transport duties.[82]

Air supply averaged 600 tons per day from 19 to 25 August, but the needs of Paris and the proposed Tournai airborne operation reduced the amount of air supply to 12th Army Group. From 27 August to 2 September, air supply averaged only 250 tons per day. Although air deliveries increased to 1,000 tons per day from 3 to 16 September, Operation MARKET-GARDEN seriously reduced aerial resupply to 12th Army Group from 17 to 29 September.[83]

The Red Ball Express and other expedient measures allowed the American armies to continue the pursuit into the middle of September, but at a high cost to both equipment and the COMZ infrastructure. Near-continuous use of equipment resulted in its rapid deterioration.[84] Major repairs of trucks rose from 2,500 in mid-September to 5,750 by the end of the month. The replacement figure for the eight-ply 750 × 20 tire rose from an average of 29,142 per month from June through August to 55,059 in September, resulting in a shortfall of 40,000 tires by midmonth.[85] Stockage of spare parts, tires, and tools neared exhaustion. Extreme fatigue of drivers sent accident rates soaring. Many of the drivers were not trained as such but had been pressed into service anyway. Some untrained units neglected maintenance on their vehicles to the point that they were derisively labeled "truck destroyer battalions."[86] By the end of August, 90 to 95 percent of all Allied supplies in France were still located near the beaches in Normandy.[87]

In the situation existing in France in August, September, and October 1944, Lieutenant General Lesley J. McNair's concept of having regiments use their organic supply vehicles to pick up supplies directly from army dumps—a distance that doctrinally should have been no more than thirty miles—was unworkable. A year earlier General McNair had personally drafted a directive that stated, "Division and corps are not in the channel of supply except in emergencies."[88] If General McNair's dictum were taken literally, then American infantry divisions in France and Germany operated in emergency conditions as the norm, not the exception. In the ETO the quartermaster company of the infantry division was a key link in the chain of supply, drawing food and fuel at army truckheads—during pursuit operations often one hundred miles or more behind the advancing divisions—and distributing the supplies to regiments and separate battalions at a divisional distribution point, which was manned by the service platoon, a unit that AGF had tried unsuccessfully to disband in the summer of 1943.[89]

Division commanders understood the critical priority of the quartermaster company. During the pursuit across France, augmentation of the company by one hundred additional personnel from various sources was not uncommon to ensure it could accomplish its vital missions. The 4th Infantry Division, for instance, augmented its quartermaster company with soldiers returning from hospitals (those who were only fit for limited duty) and with soldiers recovering from battle fatigue.[90] These augmentees beefed up the service platoon and gave the truck platoons two drivers per vehicle, enough to ensure around-the-clock operations. The 3d Infantry Division after-action report of September 1944 stated:

> Tables of Organization and Equipment based on "normal operations" lack sufficient unit transportation and personnel. This Division has never been in a "normal operation" other than the stalemate below Cassino and at Anzio. Army dumps are always far behind. Army transportation is never available for troop movements. Since Divisions are always in abnormal situations they must be capable of taking care of themselves.[91]

As in nearly every other area critical to the combat effectiveness of the American army in World War II, the division proved to be a critical source of logistical assets necessary, indeed essential, to the accomplishment of missions on the battlefield.

Given the almost complete collapse of the German army in France in August 1944, Eisenhower's decision to pursue as far as possible was worth the resulting cost to the logistical system. By the middle of September, however, the supply system had deteriorated to the point that the pursuit had to end. After the first few days of intense fighting at the Moselle River, Aachen, and in Holland in mid-September, the Allied armies quickly exhausted their ammunition stocks. They could hardly launch a major offensive on the basis of receiving ammunition on the same day they fired it. The Allies now faced the "real meaning of the tyranny of logistics" and could no longer afford to neglect the development of a viable administrative structure.[92] The Allies could not have supported an advance into Germany in September 1944 with their jerry-rigged supply system based primarily on the beaches in Normandy.[93] Friction would have thwarted the attempt.

The failure of Operation MARKET-GARDEN, the Allied ground-airborne operation designed to seize a bridgehead over the Rhine at Arnhem, and the resurgence of German strength in the West brought the Allied pursuit to an end in September. German strength increased everywhere on the Western Front by the end of the month. German staffs and headquarters that escaped the debacle in Normandy collected the remnants of broken formations, new replacements, and assorted reinforcements, and molded them into *kampfgruppen* capable of effective resistance. Hitler transferred two panzer grenadier divisions from Italy to the Moselle, where they opposed Patton's advance. Shortened lines of communication eased the task of replenishing supplies and moving replacements and reinforcements forward. The first volks grenadier divisions began to appear on the front. By early September, ten new panzer brigades, rehabilitated fragments of units from the Eastern Front combined with newly established tank battalions, were ready for deployment. More of the tanks coming out of German factories were Panthers and Tigers, giving German armored forces a qualitative edge in the upcoming battles. The Germans labeled the resurrection of their army in the Netherlands, Belgium, and France in September 1944 "the miracle of the West," an apt description for what must have been a chaotic phenomenon.[94]

The Allied logistical apparatus and the transportation assets of the combat forces endured enormous strain during the breakout and pursuit operations in August and September 1944. When the armies came into contact with the refurbished German forces on the Moselle, West Wall, and in Holland, the Allies quickly exhausted their ammunition supplies. Until Field Marshal Montgomery's 21st Army Group could open the Scheldt Estuary to allow ships to dock at Antwerp, Allied divisions would lead a hand-to-mouth existence. Montgomery's failure to open Antwerp earlier was the second most crucial mistake of the campaign, ranking right behind the Allies' failure to close the Falaise Gap sooner. Without Antwerp, the Allies lacked the ports necessary to off-load the supplies that were available but floating useless on Liberty ships in the English Channel. Without Antwerp in Allied hands, Operation MARKET-GARDEN was doomed to failure, even had British XXX Corps been successful in linking up with the 1st British Airborne Division at Arnhem. Instead, Allied armies found themselves locked in a battle of attrition on the periphery of Germany in the fall and winter of 1944–1945. In this situation the combination of supply shortages and the worsening fall weather, which often grounded air support, did not bode well for the use of firepower upon which Allied divisions depended for support.

By the late summer of 1944, the combat effectiveness of American divisions was equal to or superior to that of their German adversaries. American generals had demonstrated their tactical competence, although their ability to craft tactical engagements into a larger operational strategy to close with and destroy the enemy remained questionable. American infantry divisions solved the problem of attacking in the difficult hedgerow terrain of Normandy and dramatically improved combined-arms and joint coordination. Commanders melded tanks, infantry, field artillery, engineers, tactical airpower, and other elements into a cohesive team that consistently overwhelmed the enemy forces before it. Innovations such as the "Rhinoceros" device for penetrating hedgerows and placing forward air controllers in tanks near the front of exploiting columns played their role in the success of American forces during and after Operation COBRA. Mass and firepower paved the way for the breakout of Allied forces from Normandy. Superior intelligence and logistics systems sustained those forces during exploitation and pursuit. In the Normandy campaign and the pursuit to the German border, the American army had proved its effectiveness in battle against one of the most tactically competent military forces ever to exist.

8

Sustaining the Force: The Siegfried Line, Lorraine, and Vosges Campaigns

As the Allied offensive reached its culminating point in the fall of 1944, American infantry divisions found themselves embroiled in bitter battles for Aachen, the Huertgen Forest, Alsace, and Lorraine. By the end of September 1944, there were twenty-three American infantry divisions in the ETO, fifteen of which had gained significant combat experience in Italy, Normandy, or southern France.[1] By the end of the year, twelve more infantry divisions had arrived in France.[2] The challenge for the inexperienced divisions was to adapt to the battlefield against combat-experienced enemy forces that occupied strong defensive positions near their homeland. The vast majority of American infantry divisions met this challenge. The divisions that had been in combat since the early summer had to find ways to maintain their effectiveness during long periods of combat even while sustaining high casualties. Constant employment at the front caused an increase in combat stress and nonbattle casualties, especially when the weather turned rainy and cold. Bad weather also negated the huge Allied advantage of air supremacy, while supply shortages caused by the failure to open Antwerp in a timely manner reduced the availability of artillery ammunition on which American divisions relied so heavily. In the fall and winter of 1944, American infantry divisions improvised to accomplish their missions while personnel managers and logisticians worked to sustain the force. Both efforts were crucial to ultimate victory.

The Battle of Aachen and the Battle of the Huertgen Forest typify both the successes and the failures of American infantry divisions to adapt to combat and sustain their effectiveness during the fall of 1944. Aachen, birthplace of Charlemagne and for many centuries the capital of the Holy Roman Empire, held a prominent place in National Socialist ideology and therefore was an important objective for the First U.S. Army as it crossed the German border.[3] The mission of seizing Aachen would fall to Major General J. Lawton Collins's U.S. VII Corps, which would attack the city from the south and west. Major

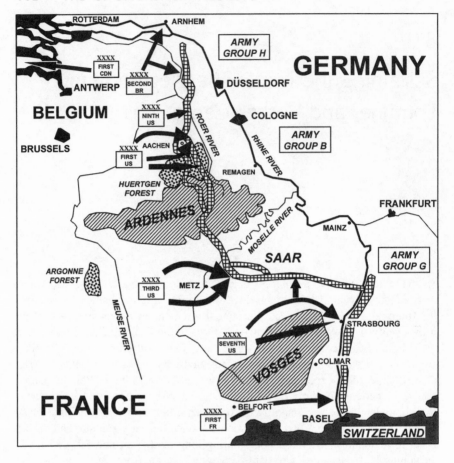

Breaching the West Wall, Fall 1944

General Charles H. Corlett's U.S. XIX Corps would assist in the operation by encircling Aachen from the north and linking up with VII Corps east of the city.

Collins and Corlett tasked their most experienced divisions—the 1st and 30th Infantry Divisions—with the encirclement of Aachen. The initial attempt by VII Corps to take Aachen in September failed due to shortages of gasoline and artillery ammunition, poor weather that grounded close air support, exhaustion of American forces that had just finished a long pursuit, and defensive advantages the Germans gained from the West Wall fortifications.[4] The West Wall, or Siegfried Line as many Allied soldiers called it, was a belt of fortifications that stretched from Switzerland to a point north of Aachen. The fortifications averaged a depth of three miles and included hundreds of pillboxes, observation and command posts, and thousands of obstacles to include barbed wire, minefields, and "dragon's teeth" antitank obstacles.[5] What the German army in the fall of 1944 lacked in the way of quantity and quality of its troops, it made up for by the strength of its defensive positions.

A two-week hiatus in the battle ensued as the American divisions prepared for another effort. The crisis in ammunition supply was the overriding factor behind the lull in combat, which cast a pall over all Allied planning during the late fall. The tactical pause was not without its benefits, however. Divisions were able to take advantage of the time to train replacements and prepare their forces for upcoming operations. The 30th Infantry Division made elaborate preparations for its attack. Battalions rotated out of the line to train on sand tables and mock-ups of the assault area. Infantry units practiced combined-arms techniques for breaching obstacles and assaulting pillboxes, much as they had retrained to assault the hedgerows of Normandy three months earlier. Twenty-six artillery battalions formed the basis of an impressive fire support plan for the attack. Planners also requested the use of heavy and medium bombers to pummel German fortified positions in the West Wall prior to the infantry assault, although in the event only 360 medium bombers and 72 fighter-bombers were available for the bombardment.[6]

On 2 October the offensive resumed with a deliberate attack on a narrow front by the 30th Infantry Division. The results of the air bombardment were poor, so Corlett decided to release the corps' contingency stocks of artillery ammunition to support the attack. Within twelve hours the artillery had fired over eighteen thousand rounds.[7] The fires did not destroy the West Wall fortifications but did suppress the defenders long enough to allow the infantry to close with the enemy manning them. Although the 117th and 119th Infantry Regiments did not penetrate far into German lines, the dent was large enough for Corlett to commit the 2d Armored Division to the battle the next day. Enemy artillery slowed the commitment of the armor and took its toll of the attackers; one American artillery commander "hazarded a guess that the Germans had finally found a copy of the American field artillery manual telling how to mass their fires."[8] After beating off several counterattacks in the next few days, the 30th Infantry Division made good progress to the south. By 7 October Major General Leland Hobbs could report that his division was through the West Wall. "We have a hole in this thing big enough to drive two divisions through," Hobbs told Corlett.[9]

Now the critical task was to encircle Aachen through a linkup of XIX Corps and VII Corps east of the city. On 8 October Major General Clarence Huebner's 1st Infantry Division joined the offensive by attacking from its positions in the Stolberg Corridor south and east of Aachen. Like the units of the 30th Infantry Division, the Big Red One conducted training in pillbox-reduction techniques prior to the attack. The 18th Infantry Regiment, which would form the main effort, also gained surprise by attacking under cover of darkness. Within forty-eight hours, the 18th Infantry had taken its three objectives with only light casualties.[10]

Although the initial attacks had gone well, much hard fighting remained before the American divisions could isolate Aachen. The Germans launched several strong counterattacks, which the 1st Infantry Division repulsed with some difficulty.[11] The First U.S. Army commander, Lieutenant General Court-ney H. Hodges, encouraged Corlett to relieve Hobbs of his command if he could not get the 30th Infantry Division to close the gap soon.[12] Hodges need not have worried. One day after his conversation with Corlett, the 30th and 1st Infantry Divisions linked up east of Aachen. Five days later, on 21 October 1944, the Germans in the city surrendered to the 1st Infantry Division.

Hodges had unfairly jumped to conclusions about the performance of the 30th Infantry Division in the Siegfried Line campaign. After the war the War Department would award the division a Distinguished Unit Citation for its performance in the breaching of the Siegfried Line. In his endorsement of the unit citation recommendation, the ETO historian, Colonel S. L. A. Marshall, rated the 30th Infantry Division as one of the best in the European theater:

> In its tactical planning and execution as well as in its ability to meet and combat unforeseen contingencies, superior initiative, courage and tenacity were displayed at all levels of the Division. . . . at every stage of operation this division performed with any who were associated with it either in equal or superior manner. . . . [The 30th Infantry Division displayed] al-ways steady and not infrequently brilliant performance, conservative of its own force and fully hurtful to the enemy.[13]

The 1st Infantry Division also received a Distinguished Unit Citation for its performance at Aachen. Together, these two veteran infantry divisions formed a formidable team.

During the Battle of Aachen the Wehrmacht recognized the salient charac-teristics of Allied offensive operations at the tactical level as careful planning and massed use of fire support. A report by the Intelligence Section of Army Group B dated 23 October 1944 detailed the German impression of American and British tactics:

> Strong use of equipment, preservation of manpower. Attacks begin on a narrow front.
> Exceptionally strong massing of artillery, lavish expenditures of muni-tions. Before attacks begin, systematic, lengthy artillery preparations. In-fantry and tanks advance behind a heavy curtain of mortar and machine gun fire. The artillery is divided into three groups. The first supports the attack with a rolling barrage; the second fires in support of individual calls-for-fire from the infantry in the main battle area; the third conducts coun-terbattery fire (with effective use of aerial observers). Multiple smoke screens obscure the attack zone in order to obscure defensive weapons and obser-vation posts; in some cases a smoke screen is placed immediately forward of the front at the beginning of the attack.
> Little massing of infantry; mostly battalion or regimental strength. Units broken down into small assault groups to exploit the terrain.
> Tanks attack in support of the infantry, but remain beyond the range of

dug-in anti-tank weapons. They fire from camouflaged positions on strong-points. Occasional use of flamethrower and bulldozer tanks to burn or collapse strongpoints.

The infantry advances only after the strongpoints have been neutralized.

The enemy immediately prepares captured terrain against counterat-tacks. Reserves are then aggressively pushed forward to seize subsequent objectives.

The attack goes according to a well-timed and organized plan. Piece after piece of the defensive line is broken. Less value is placed on initiative than on coordinated fire support.

If the attack plan is disturbed, the attack is broken off and renewed only after reinforcement by greater material assets.[14]

This report details the respect that Army Group B held for its adversaries in the battles on the periphery of Germany during the fall of 1944. In the eyes of the enemy, Allied material superiority enabled American and British forces to ex-ecute devastating attacks while remaining cautious with their soldiers' lives. Given the shortage of munitions at the front in the fall of 1944, however, material superiority alone is an insufficient explanation for the success of Al-lied forces in breaching the fortifications of the West Wall.

The capture of Aachen was a significant victory for the First U.S. Army. Together, the 1st and 30th Infantry Divisions took nearly twelve thousand prisoners during the battle.[15] German commanders committed valuable forces to futile counterattacks to relieve the city; their destruction weakened the German defense along the next major obstacle, the Roer River. American tactical commanders showed the ability to maneuver to avoid the strength of the German defenses. The Germans had expected an attack from the west or south; instead, the attacking American divisions enveloped the defenders and attacked them from the north and east.[16] Ironically, the First U.S. Army would ignore this lesson in its very next battle—the struggle for the Huert-gen Forest.

The Battle of the Huertgen Forest was a miserable blunder. Lieutenant General James M. Gavin, whose 82d Airborne Division occupied the area well after the fighting there was over, compared the battle to the disastrous British offensive in Flanders in 1917 by calling it "our Passchendaele."[17] Ernest Hem-ingway went one step further by dubbing it "Passchendaele with tree bursts."[18] To the north of the Huertgen Forest lay the Stolberg Corridor and Aachen. The Roer River framed its eastern and southern boundaries. Inside these limits lay an area of dense pine forest, steep hills, and deep gorges. The terrain had no intrinsic value except for the dams along the Roer that lay beyond it. Posses-sion of these dams was necessary to prevent the Germans from flooding the areas downstream (to the north) as the Allied forces advanced farther into Germany. Incredibly, neither the Germans nor the Americans understood the critical na-ture of the dams until well into the battle.[19] As units of VII Corps neared the

Soldiers of the 39th Infantry Regiment, 9th Infantry Division, pass through a breach in the West Wall near Roetgen, Germany, 15 September 1944. (U.S. Army Signal Corps photo)

German border in September 1944, possession of the west bank of the Roer seemed reason enough to attack through the Huertgen Forest.[20]

The 9th Infantry Division, under the command of Major General Louis A. Craig, was the first major American combat unit to enter the forest.[21] After the pursuit across France, the 9th Infantry Division ran into the fortifications of the West Wall on 14 September in the vicinity of Lammersdorf and Monschau. The 39th Infantry Regiment penetrated the first belt of German fortifications near Lammersdorf after a difficult, three-day battle but could advance no farther.[22] The VII Corps commander, General J. Lawton Collins, redirected the 9th Infantry Division farther north to attack through the Huertgen Forest and seize Huertgen and Kleinhau, six miles east of Zweifall.[23] While the 47th Infantry Regiment guarded the southern flank of the 3d Armored Division in the Stolberg Corridor, the 39th and 60th Infantry Regiments attacked through the difficult forest terrain studded with enemy mines, barbed wire, antitank obstacles, and pillboxes.

Craig faced the impossible task of sweeping back the enemy along a nineteen-mile front in difficult, compartmentalized terrain. The only justification for such a mission was that the enemy lacked strength in the forest.[24] The assumption was incorrect. The 9th Infantry Division ground out gains slowly when it gained any ground at all. The weather turned wet and cold, thereby increasing the incidence of trench foot and other diseases. Artillery shells exploded in the trees and sent thousands of lethal metal and wood splinters flying through the air. Land navigation in the dark forest was difficult, if not impossible. Charles B. MacDonald, who commanded two companies in the 2d Infantry Division and after the war became a respected military historian and author, writes of the battle: "It was a wearying and frustrating experience: counterattack following every attack; Germans infiltrating in the night into defensive perimeters; enemy patrols ambushing supply parties; mortar and artillery shells snapping branches and tops from the thick furs as if they were toothpicks and killing or maiming the men underneath."[25]

The 9th Infantry Division had to improvise to destroy the heavily fortified pillboxes of the West Wall. The 15th Engineer Battalion learned that the concept of engineer assault teams using ten-pound pole charges or flamethrowers to destroy enemy pillboxes did not work. German pillboxes were of different types, but all were strongly constructed. A typical pillbox had eight to ten inches of steel covered by anywhere from one to eight feet of reinforced concrete and dirt. The division developed a six-step procedure for reducing pillboxes:

1. Approach as close as possible with an infantry platoon and engineer section.
2. Use a tank, tank destroyer, antitank gun, or bazooka for supporting fire.
3. Suppress the pillbox with artillery or mortars.
4. Use direct fire weapons to suppress apertures and entrances.
5. Close in with infantry and engineers.
6. Destroy the pillbox by using demolitions on the roof or by using the point-blank fire of supporting weapons.

Engineers found that the only sure way to penetrate enemy pillboxes was to attack through the roof with consecutive blasts of sixteen to twenty-four beehive charges, followed by placing a two-hundred-pound block of TNT in the resulting hole. The concussion was normally great enough to induce the enemy to surrender if the pillbox was not destroyed outright.[26] The procedure was effective, but progress was measured pillbox by pillbox, in meters rather than miles.

On 6 October the 9th Infantry Division made one final attack in an attempt to take Schmidt and clear the Huertgen Forest, but it could not do so after a brutal, ten-day battle in the dense foliage.[27] The battle was an unnecessary waste of manpower. At this stage of the war, too many American corps and army commanders had still not learned a fundamental lesson of modern warfare: that the best way through a difficult enemy position is to go around it. By ordering the 9th Infantry Division to make a frontal attack through the Huertgen Forest, the First U.S. Army commander, General Courtney Hodges, and the VII Corps commander, General Collins, nearly succeeded in destroying the 9th Infantry Division as a fighting organization. When the 28th Division relieved the 39th and 60th Infantry Regiments in the Huertgen Forest on 25 October, the

A portion of the Huertgen Forest, blasted by artillery fire. One look at this photograph shows why American forces had so many problems attacking through this terrain in the fall of 1944. (U.S. Army Signal Corps photo)

9th Infantry Division was a shell of its former self and badly needed an extended period of rehabilitation. The division moved to Camp Elsenborn to integrate replacements, train, conduct maintenance on men and equipment, and rest.

By the end of October, Hodges should have realized that a lone infantry division could not clear the Huertgen Forest. By fighting in the forest, the Americans gave up most of their advantages in terms of close air support, tank and tank destroyer support, and artillery firepower. The forest fighting was an infantry-against-infantry slugfest—the type of combat in which the tactically competent German forces, fighting on the defensive in prepared positions, excelled. Any renewed offensive would take at least a corps; better yet, the First U.S. Army could use economy of force measures in the forest to mass forces elsewhere and bypass the difficult area. Instead, Hodges committed the 28th Infantry Division, operating under Major General Leonard Gerow's U.S. V Corps, to the Huertgen in an attempt to seize the key terrain in the forest: the village of Schmidt and the high ground in its vicinity that dominated the approaches to the Roer River and its critical dams.

The 28th Infantry Division, the "Keystone Division," was a National Guard unit from Pennsylvania. After the War Department activated the division in

February 1941, it moved to Indiantown Gap to receive fillers and conduct training. The division participated in the Carolina maneuvers in the fall of 1941. Major General Edward Martin, the division's overage commander (he had enlisted in the National Guard in 1897), was relieved after Pearl Harbor. Army Ground Forces believed that the division needed a solid commander to transform it into an effective team. Marshall and McNair chose Major General Omar N. Bradley for the position.[28]

Like most National Guard divisions, the 28th Infantry Division experienced a high turnover of its personnel during its training. Bradley also had problems with hometown cliques in units that prevented the formation of cohesive teams among the National Guard soldiers and the new arrivals in the division. To combat these problems, he transferred every officer and most noncommissioned officers out of their hometown units to different companies. By the fall of 1942, the 28th Infantry Division was beginning to show progress, and Bradley soon received orders assigning him to Eisenhower's headquarters in Tunisia.[29] In October 1943 the 28th Infantry Division deployed overseas to England in preparation for the Normandy invasion.

The 28th Infantry Division engaged in its first combat in Normandy near the town of Percy and participated in early attempts to penetrate the West Wall with V Corps. The soldiers of the division gained valuable combat experience in these actions.[30] In October the division received a period of rest and was at full strength by the end of the month. The division's new commander, Major General Norman D. Cota, was a combat veteran who had waded ashore with the 29th Infantry Division on D-Day and had distinguished himself in the heavy fighting afterward.[31] Together, these factors augured well for the division's upcoming attack in the Huertgen Forest. The attack would fail disastrously due not to the quality of the units involved but to abysmally poor planning by senior-level commanders and their staffs.

General Hodges intended the attack of the 28th Infantry Division in the Huertgen Forest to be a supporting attack for the main effort by VII Corps farther to the north. The V Corps commander, General Gerow, ordered the division to use two of its infantry regiments to guard its northern and southern flanks, however, which left only the 112th Infantry Regiment for the main attack to seize the high ground near Schmidt. The only supply route for this force was a steep cart path, unsuitable for heavy armored vehicles, that traversed the Kall River gorge. General Hodges concurred in Gerow's plan of attack. The dictates by army and corps commanders and staffs had left almost no initiative to General Cota and his division staff.[32] Worse still, although bad weather and the slow arrival of divisions forced General Bradley to postpone VII Corps' attack for two weeks, no senior commander, from Bradley to Hodges to Gerow to Cota, suggested a postponement of the attack of the 28th Infantry Division in the Huertgen Forest. The Pennsylvanians would attack alone, "thrown to the wolves," in the words of the U.S. Army historian of the operation.[33]

As a result of poor planning by army, corps, and division staffs, the 28th

Infantry Division met disaster in the Huertgen Forest. The division attacked as scheduled on 2 November, and the 112th Infantry Regiment even succeeded in seizing Schmidt the next day.[34] For the next two weeks, however, the lack of action elsewhere allowed the Germans to recover and decimate the three American infantry regiments in the Huertgen Forest. The 109th Infantry Regiment took only half its objectives, and the 110th Infantry Regiment went nowhere. German counterattacks drove the 112th Infantry Regiment from Schmidt and eventually forced it back across the Kall River. German artillery hammered constantly at the exposed American troops. Poor weather grounded air support and worsened the physical condition of the men. Many leaders collapsed under the prolonged strain of the intense battle. Morale in the Keystone Division finally vanished, replaced by apathy.[35]

Within a week the combination of too many casualties leaving and too many untrained replacements arriving rendered the regiments of the 28th Infantry Division combat ineffective.[36] On 9 November the G-1 warned:

> Upon learning that it was contemplated to commit the 2d Battalion, 112th Infantry Regiment, to an attack on the morning of the 10th, a report was made to the G-3 that this battalion, while up to strength, could not be considered more than 20 percent effective for combat, 515 replacements having been placed in the battalion the day previous.[37]

By the time the 28th Infantry Division left the battlefield on 19 November, it had sustained well over five thousand casualties; soldiers began referring to the red keystone-shaped patch of the division as the "bloody bucket."[38] The division required extensive reconstitution to regenerate its combat power.[39] The First U.S. Army staff decided the best place to accomplish this task was in a quiet part of the front—in the Ardennes Forest directly east of the Belgian town of Bastogne.

Three more divisions were to enter the crucible of the Huertgen Forest before the battle ended. The 1st, 4th, and 8th Infantry Divisions—all battle-tested units—fared little better than the 9th and 28th Infantry Divisions in combat there. The employment of these divisions followed the earlier pattern. Each participated in single-division attacks, suffered horrendous casualties, became combat ineffective for offensive operations, and was only then relieved by a fresh division. One can trace the failure of American infantry divisions in the Huertgen Forest to the enemy, terrain, and weather, but the real culprit was the failure of the First U.S. Army commander and his staff to maneuver their forces effectively at the operational level of war. No single division could have succeeded alone in the Huertgen Forest, yet Hodges allowed division after division to be sucked into the quagmire in piecemeal fashion. Hodges could have used a corps to attack through the Monschau Corridor and Losheim Gap to seize Schmidt and the Roer River dams from the south. Instead, in the best tradition of the American Expeditionary Forces in the Battles of the Meuse River and the Argonne Forest in World War I (in which Hodges participated), he used an unimaginative frontal attack directly through the worst terrain in his zone of operations. After the failure of the 9th Infantry Division to seize its objectives in September and October, even a casual observer should have recognized that the best way to get behind the forest was to go around it. Instead, over thirty-three thousand American troops paid the price in blood to seize a piece of worthless terrain.[40]

Losses on the scale experienced by the 12th Army Group in the fall of 1944 required herculean efforts by personnel managers to reconstitute divisions and keep them in the fight. An examination of casualty statistics in the 9th Infantry Division between 1 July and 31 October highlights the problem (Table 8.1). The 9th Infantry Division lost 17,974 men in just four months. Of these men, 3,235 returned to duty within thirty days. The net loss for the division was therefore 14,739 men, or over 100 percent of its organic strength. The situation in the three infantry regiments was even bleaker. In these four months the infantry regiments, which accounted for only half of the division's strength, sustained over 85 percent of the division's casualties. Not even counting nonbattle casualties, the three regiments had 1,651 men killed and 7,072 men wounded, more than the total organic strength of the twenty-seven infantry companies in the division.[41] Constant battle and continuous casualties had depleted the stock of trained and experienced men with which the 9th Infantry Division had entered the continent of Europe.

Officer casualties were particularly severe. Between 10 June and 30 September, the 47th Infantry Regiment lost 163 officers in combat. Every infantry company had lost at least six officers, with an average loss per company of eleven; one company had lost eighteen officers.[42] Since the authorized officer strength of an infantry company was six, the impact of these losses on the leadership of the unit is not hard to imagine. As the campaign progressed, the average experience level of the company-grade officers declined.

The impact of continuous combat on the soldiers took a tremendous toll. "No one was enamored of constantly being in the line," one veteran wrote. "There was no out except KIA [killed in action], WIA [wounded in action], captured, or war over."[43] The 60th Infantry Regiment's history explained the burden of the infantryman in combat: "You were generally tired. Fighting and moving on foot for weeks on end—sleeping out on the ground, wet most of the time, always tense, eating cold rations, seeing buddies die—you just never

Table 8.1   9th Infantry Division Casualties, 1 July–31 October 1944

Month	Killed	Wounded	Exhaustion	Nonbattle	Total
July	712	2,989	520	1,315	5,536
August	376	1,809	280	1,540	4,005
September	218	1,551	161	1,457	3,387
October	384	2,224	280	2,158	5,046
Total	1,690	8,573	1,241	5,155	17,974

Source: HQ, 9th Infantry Division, Report of Operations, July–October 1944, 309-0.3, Box 7326, Record Group 407, National Archives II.

seemed able to really rest. You seldom had your raincoat, and it never failed to rain—rain until there wasn't a dry stitch on your body."[44] The infantryman had to wage a war against two enemies: the Germans and nature. If the enemy did not kill, wound, or capture him, there was a good chance that the infantry soldier would succumb to trench foot, hypothermia, illness, or disease.

As the First U.S. Army sent in more and more individual replacements to fill the depleted ranks of the infantry companies, the character of the 9th Infantry Division changed. Many of these men became casualties within a week of arrival. The 60th Infantry Regiment warned:

> Never send replacements to a company in the heat of battle. It has been found from experience that new men arriving during a fight are bewildered by lack of knowledge of the situation and not knowing their leaders they are in many cases more hindrance than help. We have had several new men become casualties almost immediately after being assigned because of this. We have found it a good policy to wait for a slight lull in the battle so the replacements have a chance to get oriented.[45]

General Dwight D. Eisenhower, supreme Allied commander, and Lieutenant General Omar N. Bradley, commander of the 12th Army Group, talk with Major General Louis A. Craig, commander of the 9th Infantry Division, in Butgenbach, Belgium, 8 November 1944. The 9th Infantry Division was recovering from its bloodletting in the Huertgen Forest the previous month. (U.S. Army Signal Corps photo)

To integrate new men into their units, most companies teamed up replacements with veteran soldiers to teach the new men how to stay alive in combat. As time progressed, however, veterans became an endangered breed. "At one point [in the] Huertgen Forest," one soldier stated, "a vet was 2 weeks old."[46] If a replacement survived a week or two in combat, he usually became a capable part of the team. Many did not live that long. Like most infantry divisions in Europe, the 9th Infantry Division suffered during its extended periods in the line and paid the price of the ninety-division gamble in blood.

The U.S. Army had not always used a system of individual replacements. During the Civil War the Union army raised regiments, which then fought without replacements until they were completely destroyed, disbanded, or amalgamated with other units. This policy changed in World War I, during which the United States fielded fifty-eight divisions and shipped forty-two of them overseas. Twelve of the divisions sent to France were disbanded to provide replacements for the twenty-nine divisions committed to the Battles of St.-Mihiel and the Meuse–Argonne Forest.[47] By contrast, in World War II the War Department was able to maintain all of the divisions it raised at close to full strength by providing enough individual replacements to restore losses without completely disbanding other units to provide them. Since infantry divisions committed to combat in the ETO tended to remain engaged for extended periods without relief, they had to integrate thousands of individual replacements on or near the front line.[48]

Training these replacements once they arrived in their unit became a major concern to commanders. One battalion commander in the 80th Infantry Division outlined the basic problem:

The most important factor in improving the combat effectiveness of my unit was training. For instance, it was not unusual to have a company reduced to a handful of men during a particularly vicious attack or defense. That night the unit was filled by replacements who came up in the dark, were placed into a foxhole in the dark, never knew what their squad leader looked like, and did not know their platoon or company commander. The cohesiveness of such a squad, platoon, company was not good and the biggest problem was to get these people together in one place so that they knew each other and began to get some sense of each other's capabilities. This process was ongoing because units (such as my battalion) stayed in the line for as long as three or four months without rest or the ability to form in one place so we could see what we each looked like. At every opportunity I put a different company in reserve and then had it train until it was needed. The veterans were invaluable in teaching the new replacements the vagaries of the battlefield and the new replacements learned quickly or they became casualties.[49]

Battalion commanders, however, could do only so much to ease the integration of replacements into their organizations. Division commanders, on the other hand, had more resources at their disposal to help fix the problem.

Many divisions developed mechanisms to cope with the problem of integrating individual replacements into the organization during extended operations. Major General Charles Gerhardt of the 29th Infantry Division, for example, formed a training center from combat-experienced officers and noncommissioned officers. The purpose of the center was to train new junior officers, noncommissioned officers, and replacements to prepare them for their future duties. Rather than move replacements and soldiers returning from hospitals directly to their new units, the division held them at the training center for two days to issue them new clothing and equipment, give them a chance to fire their weapons and throw a hand grenade, have them participate in standard battle drills, let them have a hot meal and a shower, sew the division patch on their helmets and clothes, and orient them to the division's past achievements and its current situation. During November 1944 the replacement battalion retrained 250 artillery soldiers as infantrymen to combat the growing shortage of infantry replacements at the front.

Gerhardt also used the training center to rehabilitate soldiers who performed poorly in combat, men who had performed criminal acts, and combat exhaustion cases. Soldiers reacted positively to their experiences in the training center. One soldier remarked, "The 29th Training Center is the best that I have been through. Since I have been wounded, the other replacement depots treated us like a bunch of bastards."[50] Lamentably, the care and concern shown for the replacements assigned to the Blue and Gray Division were not reflected uniformly throughout the rest of the ETO.

Care of combat exhaustion cases became an increasingly serious problem as the campaign lengthened. Between 12 June and 2 October 1944, the 29th Infantry Division sustained 1,827 combat exhaustion cases (12.5 percent of all battle casualties), but the training center was able to return 1,053 men to duty (enough to man over five infantry companies at full strength). The psychiatrist of the 29th Infantry Division resided at the training center with fifteen medical assistants. His purpose was to screen combat exhaustion cases and to rehabilitate those considered "salvageable." The division routed all combat exhaustion cases directly from clearing stations to the division training center. The casualties received two days of rest along with a chance to eat, shower, and change into clean clothes. On the third day, the division psychiatrist interviewed each man to determine whether to return him to duty, enroll him in the program at the training center, or evacuate him out of the division. The training process consisted of five to ten days of weapons firing and battle drills designed to give the soldier self-confidence in his ability to handle combat situations.[51]

The division psychiatrist of the 29th Infantry Division, Major David I. Weintrob, found that the majority of combat exhaustion cases stemmed from either poor precombat training or excessive physical fatigue stemming from extended periods of combat. Another problem was that many replacements who originated from divisions training in the United States found themselves suddenly thrust into combat with leaders and soldiers with whom they had neither trained nor come to trust. A significant number of combat exhaustion cases stemmed from replacements who were in combat for the first time. "I believe that the practice of breaking up a trained division, and parceling its troops out to various combat divisions as replacements, negates a fundamental and very important principle of military philosophy," Major Weintrob stated. "The unit morale, long association with one's 'buddies,' is immediately lost, and the man goes into combat a total stranger to his outfit."[52] He was a perceptive observer.

The personnel replacement system used by the Army of the United States was impersonal, but it effectively kept America's combat divisions in the fight. The following is one officer's recollection of his return to his old battalion after six months in the hospital:

> My return was received casually enough; after nine months of constant turnover, there was little notice of coming and going; some men had been wounded, evacuated, and returned twice and three times. The corps personnel officer who had stirred my ire at Vire by speaking of the battalion as a machine with replaceable parts was right. There were a few veterans who had come all the way, and their faces and movements showed it. Apologetically, they had to ask when it was I had left; one thought I had been killed.[53]

Sooner or later, most soldiers employed too long at the front reached a breaking point or succumbed to fear and fatigue by reaching a somnambulist state dubbed "combat numbness" by one observer.[54] The key to their recovery, as the 29th Infantry Division discovered, was early treatment close to the front lines.[55] The key to the prevention of combat exhaustion was to rotate troops out of the front line at frequent intervals, a course of action not available to American commanders due to the lack of divisions in France in the fall of 1944. Perhaps what is remarkable about American infantrymen in the campaign for France and Germany is not the fact that they succumbed to battle fatigue, but that they could recover their morale so quickly despite the lack of prospects for immediate relief from combat.

General George C. Marshall and the War Department understood the need to give American forces in the European theater a rest and offered to speed up the delivery of divisions to the Continent. They assured the theater that transport ships were available and the sailing dates of new divisions could be stepped up provided the theater was willing to forgo some of the training exercises that normally capped a new division's training. SHAEF and European theater planners pointed to two problems with the plan: lack of port discharge capacity (Cherbourg was still the only port in northern France open at the time) and lack of the logistical infrastructure necessary to support the divisions in combat.[56] What was lost on SHAEF and theater planners was that the additional divisions would not generate an excessive logistical strain if they were used to replace

Infantrymen of the 79th Infantry Division await transport to a rest camp, 25 October 1944. The division had been fighting since 12 June 1944 with little pause for rest. (U.S. Army Signal Corps photo)

divisions on the front line, which could then rest and train behind the front with minimal support. Despite the warnings of his staff, Eisenhower accepted the War Department plan to accelerate troop shipments.

General Marshall suggested another method to relieve troops on the front. If the War Department shipped the infantry regiments of a division early, these units could replace regiments currently carrying the burden of combat in France. The organic combat service and combat service support elements of their parent division could arrive later. By then, the infantry regiments would have been seasoned in combat under an experienced division command and control structure, and at least some infantry regiments would have had time to rest and recuperate away from the front.[57] The European theater approved the scheme for the infantry regiments of the 42d, 63d, 66th, 69th, 70th, 75th, 76th, 87th, and 106th Infantry Divisions. Two of these divisions managed to enter combat as complete entities; others went into their first battles piecemeal. The shortage of troops in France in 1944 was so great that army and corps commanders sometimes gave the infantry regiments of these divisions hastily assembled combat service and combat service support assets from army and corps pools and put them into the line alongside existing divisions.

Severe losses in battle may have strained the fabric of American infantry divisions, but the Wehrmacht was clearly impressed with the ability of the Army of the United States to replace its losses and keep on fighting at a high level of effectiveness. The Intelligence Division of Army Group B prepared a lengthy report dated 23 November 1944 detailing the Germans' view of the Allied combat divisions they faced on the Army Group B front. The following excerpts are taken from that report:[58]

1st American Inf. Div.: Exceptionally good, good source of officers and men, temporarily weakened through losses.

2d American Inf. Div.: Appears to be good, apparently good officer corps.

4th American Inf. Div.: Until the most recent replacements good.

8th American Inf. Div.: Judged as good.

9th American Inf. Div.: Very good, according to press reports one of the best American divisions.

28th American Inf. Div.: With the exception of the newest replacements, good. Temporarily hampered due to high losses.

29th American Inf. Div.: Good, good training and fighting spirit.

30th American Inf. Div.: Battle value high before the battle for Aachen, the younger replacements are partially poor.

83rd American Inf. Div.: Battle value good.

84th, 99th, 102nd, 104th American Inf. Div.: Few details available.

The report goes on to state that although the enemy casualties sustained in the battles around Aachen "are doubtlessly very high," the ability to replace those losses has enabled the "divisions which have been fighting for extended periods to remain combat ready."[59] Army Group B recognized one of the key elements of the success of the American army in World War II—its resilience and endurance.

While veteran divisions wrestled with the problems involved in maintaining their effectiveness in the fall of 1944, other divisions underwent their first experiences in combat. Some of these divisions performed well; others took longer to develop into effective teams. An examination of the 84th and 104th Infantry Divisions in their first few weeks in combat shows the challenges faced and overcome by newly arrived divisions in their first battles despite their lack of combat experience.

The Timberwolves of the 104th Infantry Division underwent their first combat experience in Holland between 23 October and 7 November 1944 as part of British I Corps, First Canadian Army, during its operations to clear the Scheldt Estuary. After relieving the British 49th Division, the U.S. 104th Infantry Division attacked north toward Zundert along the highway from Antwerp to Breda. Characteristically, Major General Terry de la Mesa Allen ordered his units to conduct night attacks to seize their objectives.[60] His field order to the division also reflected his personality and echoed his past history with the 1st Infantry Division in North Africa as he wrote in the coordinating instructions, *"NOTHING IN HELL CAN STOP THE TIMBERWOLF DIVISION."*[61]

The 104th Infantry Division performed its first missions well by seizing Zundert and conducting a deliberate crossing of the Mark River at night.[62] The soldiers of the division proved the soundness of their training by successfully conducting difficult limited-visibility attacks night after night. Upon the division's departure from Holland to join U.S. VII Corps near Aachen, the commander of the First Canadian Army, Lieutenant General G. G. Simmonds, wrote:

> I realize that it is not easy for a division to have its introduction to battle in an Army other than its own. Nevertheless, once the "Timberwolves" got their teeth into the Boche, they showed great dash, and British and Canadian troops on their flanks expressed the greatest admiration for their courage and enthusiasm. During the time 104 US Infantry Division has served in the First Canadian Army relations have been most cordial and we have received the utmost cooperation from General Allen, his Staff and all commanders. I am sorry that they are leaving and feel sure that when they again meet the Boche "all hell cannot stop the Timberwolves."[63]

Indeed, the 104th Infantry Division had received its baptism of fire, was measured, and was not found wanting.

General Collins understood the bond between Allen and his old division, the Big Red One. Collins believed that Allen was on a quest to make his new command the equal of the 1st Infantry Division. "With a view to stimulating both divisions," Collins recalled, "I placed the 104th in the line adjacent to the 1st."[64] When VII Corps attacked on 16 November, Allen's division initially had some difficulty in clearing the Eschweiler-Weisweiler industrial area. Collins "made clear to Allen that I expected better results."[65] Four days after the assault began, the 414th Infantry Regiment finally broke the enemy resistance on the Donnerberg, the key terrain in the area, by infiltrating enemy positions under the cover of darkness.[66] Allen then unleashed his regiments in a series of night attacks that swept through German defenses and earned for the Timberwolves a reputation as the premier night-fighting division in the Army of the United States.[67] Allen told General Hobbs of the 30th Infantry Division on his northern flank that the Timberwolves "don't go to bed too early. In fact, they have insomnia."[68]

Limited-visibility attacks are tricky operations that require well-trained troops and a high degree of expertise among the tactical commanders involved. Allen had made sure through hard training in the United States that the Timberwolves were ready for night operations when their time came. General Collins also gave Allen's assistant division commander, Brigadier General Bryant E. Moore, "a large measure of credit" for the success of the 104th Infantry Division. Moore had served as a regimental commander on Guadalcanal, and according to Collins his "skill as a tactician and trainer complemented perfectly Allen's flamboyant leadership."[69] Collins later commended the Timberwolves: "I regard the operation which involved the seizure of Lamersdorf–Inden–Lucherberg as one of the finest single pieces of work accomplished by any unit of the VII Corps since D-Day. . . . We regard the Timberwolf Division as one of the finest assault divisions we have ever had in this Corps."[70] By the end of the war in Europe, Collins believed that Allen had made good on his boast to make the 104th Infantry Division the equal of the Big Red One.[71]

Like many divisions in the fall of 1944, the 84th Infantry Division—the "Railsplitters"—made a rapid transition from training to combat. An Organized Reserve division formed in October 1942 at Camp Howze, Texas, the 84th Infantry Division participated in army maneuvers in Louisiana in the fall of 1943 before being gutted for replacements. Filled with new men garnered from ASTP, the Army Air Forces, and other miscellaneous sources, the division departed from Camp Claiborne, Louisiana, for England on 20 September 1944; two months later it was positioned near the front in the northern portion of the Ninth U.S. Army's zone. Its combat history from then until V-E Day was in many ways representative of the experiences of any number of American infantry divisions in Europe during the final six months of the war.

The Railsplitters were not afforded the luxury of an easy introduction to combat. Their first mission was an attack against heavily fortified enemy positions in the West Wall near Geilenkirchen. The Germans anchored their defenses in the numerous towns and villages in the heavily fortified area, which commanded open terrain with clear fields of fire that often extended up to two thousand yards. In the early-morning darkness of 18 November, the 334th Infantry Regiment attacked to seize Prummern and the high ground east of Geilenkirchen. The Railsplitters received support from British armor, Sherman tanks of the Sherwood Rangers Yeomanry Regiment. The combined-arms attack was successful. Flail tanks cleared minefields, other tanks kept German pillboxes buttoned up with continual suppressive fire, while American infantrymen, in combat for the first time, overcame their fear and apprehension and advanced to their objectives. That night they learned even more about fighting the Germans, as they beat back a battalion-size counterattack against Prummern launched by the 9th Panzer Division.[72]

The 333d Infantry Regiment attacked the next day to clear Geilenkirchen and seize the town of Sueggerath beyond. British tanks assisted the infantry in clearing the city. The British had unusually effective tanks, too, the "funnies" that the British 79th Armoured Division had debuted on D-Day. Crocodile flamethrower tanks were especially useful in the West Wall to destroy pillboxes, if they could get close enough; Sherman flail tanks made the task of breaching minefields easier.

Despite assistance from British armor, the attack soon stalled as infantrymen came up against strong enemy defenses in the West Wall fortifications manned by the well-trained soldiers of the 15th Panzer Grenadier Division.

Tanks could not maneuver off the roads; those that tried soon became mired in deep mud. Mines disabled several vehicles. Artillery coordination was inadequate. More important, the 84th Infantry Division had not conducted the necessary small-unit, combined-arms training to deal with German fortifications. Infantry attacked pillboxes unsupported by engineers, close air support, tank destroyers, and self-propelled artillery. Casualties in the infantry companies that attacked reached 60 percent.[73] The results were predictable and, sadly, avoidable.

Why were American infantry companies ground up in futile attacks on fortifications in wet, cold conditions that produced thousands of dead and wounded and hundreds of cases of trench foot and other cold weather injuries for minimal gains? One explanation is that the ETO lacked a coherent, theater-wide system for receiving new divisions and passing onto them the lessons learned by more veteran formations in the theater. Captain John J. O'Grady of the Ninth Army Historical Section, an observer of the 333d Infantry Regiment's attack beyond Geilenkirchen, stated afterward, "The 84th Division walked into the most touted defensive line in modern warfare without so much as the benefit of a briefing by combat officers who had been fighting the problem for some months and had found workable solutions."[74] Commanders in the 84th Infantry Division would not have had to travel far to gather the advice they needed. In XIX Corps immediately south of their positions, the 30th Infantry Division had significant, recent, and successful experience with attacking German fortifications in the vicinity of Aachen.

The sad fact was that the ETO had gathered a massive amount of information on tactics, techniques, and procedures by placing combat observers with each corps. Their reports were collected by the Combat Lessons Branch, G-3 Division, ETO. The Combat Lessons Branch would extract lessons learned and disseminate them in two publications, "Battle Experiences" and "Immediate Reports." "Battle Experiences" was designed to provide a medium for rapid exchange of combat information among units in theater. Examples of observer reports include information on tank-killing methods, tank-infantry cooperation, river-crossing techniques, proper integration of replacements, use of tank destroyers as assault guns, maintenance of men and equipment in cold weather, night combat, mine warfare, and assaulting pillboxes.[75] Other than the publication of "Battle Experiences," however, there was no formal program for cross-training between divisions in the theater. The ETO G-3 Combat Lessons Branch merely established itself as a clearinghouse for information; the onus was on individual units to seek the information they needed. For newly arrived divisions, asking the right questions was harder than finding the right answers.

Contributing to this problem was the command arrangement under which the 84th Infantry Division worked. To maintain unity of command in the Geilenkirchen salient, the Ninth U.S. Army Commander, Lieutenant General William H. Simpson, had placed the newly arrived 84th Infantry Division under command of Lieutenant General Brian G. Horrocks's British XXX Corps. The

British gave extensive armor support to the Americans but were perhaps understandably reluctant to give their Allied brethren advice on how to fight. Horrocks was impressed with the Railsplitters, later writing, "The 84th was an impressive product of American training methods which turned out division after division complete, fully equipped, and trained for war."[76] He was less than enamored with senior American leadership, who he claims rarely visited the front and so lacked a grasp of the reality of life there.[77]

Learning to fight the Germans was only part of the infantryman's battle; he also had to learn how to survive in a harsh climate. "In war, there are two kinds of battles and many times it is hard to know which is worse," writes Theodore Draper, the historian of the 84th Infantry Division. "There is the battle to kill the enemy and there is the battle with yourself to live. The one is against people, the other against mud or ice or rain or vermin or boredom or homesickness or imaginary terrors. In Germany in November, it was mud. Now and then we fought the enemy, for a few hours or a few days. The mud we fought always, every miserable minute. The mud was Germany."[78] To sustain the men at the front, units in reserve formed carrying parties to transport clean socks, water, food, ammunition, and clean rifles forward. Rain filled foxholes with water, making trench foot and hypothermia a constant danger.

The 84th Infantry Division followed the attack on Geilenkirchen and Prummern a week later on 29–30 November with a successful attack on Beeck and Lindern, which the Railsplitters held against counterattacks by elements of the 9th Panzer Division and the 10th SS Panzer Division. By that date the division had learned a great deal about assaulting fortifications. Massive firepower did little damage to the well-constructed pillboxes of the West Wall. They had to be taken by combined-arms assault, with engineers using demolitions or 155mm self-propelled howitzers blasting open the entrances. Attacks had to be planned and troops trained with careful attention to detail. Combined-arms action by infantry, engineers, artillery, and armor was essential to success. Attacks by small assault groups worked as well as or better than attacks by entire companies or battalions. More men invited more enemy fire without increasing the effectiveness of the assault. The timing and coordination of artillery fires with the assault were also critical.[79]

Despite its inexperience and the mistakes it made in its first two weeks of combat, the 84th Infantry Division had destroyed 112 pillboxes, taken over fifteen hundred prisoners, penetrated parts of the most heavily fortified area in the world, and fought against and defeated elements of two panzer divisions and numerous infantry formations. Due to the workings of the replacement system, the division remained combat effective despite having sustained over twenty-one hundred casualties.[80] Like other divisions that dreary fall, the Railsplitters now worked to meld combat veterans and green replacements into effective teams. Their success in that endeavor would soon be tested in the largest battle in American history.

By 4 December the combined efforts of the 2d Armored Division and the

29th, 30th, 84th, and 102d Infantry Divisions had enabled the Ninth U.S. Army to penetrate the West Wall and close up to the western bank of the Roer River. It was a major accomplishment, especially for the 84th and 102d Infantry Divisions, new to combat. To the south, the 9th and 83d Infantry Divisions and the 3d and 5th Armored Divisions of Collins's VII Corps also fought their way to the Roer by mid-December. There the advance stalled, held in check by the threat of a flood of water from the undamaged Urft and Schwammenauel Dams farther upriver and the beginning of the great German counteroffensive in the Ardennes Forest. The Siegfried Line campaign was not without its benefits, however. Although operations by the U.S. First and Ninth Armies in closing up to the Roer did not lead to a breakthrough, they did keep German divisions engaged and continued the attrition of enemy forces while the Allies opened Antwerp as a supply conduit.[81]

To the south of the First U.S. Army, Lieutenant General George S. Patton's Third U.S. Army struggled toward the German border through Lorraine. In the fall of 1944 his divisions fought the same difficult combination of stiffening enemy resistance, rough terrain, and bad weather with which their counterparts to the north contended. The battle for Metz illustrates the problems that faced infantry divisions in the Third U.S. Army during the fall of 1944.

Patton gave the mission of seizing Metz to the U.S. XX Corps, under the command of Major General Walton Walker.[82] The corps consisted of two veteran divisions, the 5th and 90th Infantry Divisions, and two new divisions, the 95th Infantry Division and the 10th Armored Division. The attack would commence on 9 November with an attack by the 90th Infantry Division to isolate Metz from the north while the 5th Infantry Division enveloped the city from the south.

Both the 5th and the 90th Infantry Divisions had seen action during the Normandy campaign. The 5th Infantry Division, the "Red Diamond" Division, was activated in October 1939 and took part in both the Tennessee and the Louisiana maneuvers of 1941. The War Department then sent the division to garrison Iceland, where it languished until it moved to Great Britain in August 1943. The division landed on UTAH Beach on 9 July 1944 and participated in the latter stages of the Normandy campaign. For a full month between mid-September and mid-October, the 5th Infantry Division had attempted to take Metz, but it failed in the face of heavy opposition.[83] Its commander was Major General S. LeRoy Irwin, U.S. Military Academy Class of 1915, an artillery officer who had commanded the division artillery of the 9th Infantry Division during the North African campaign.[84]

The 90th Infantry Division would enter the battle for Metz under a new commander, Brigadier General James A. Van Fleet, another member of the West Point Class of 1915.[85] He had commanded a machine gun battalion during the Meuse-Argonne offensive in World War I, where he was wounded in action and earned two citations for valor. Van Fleet was an imposing man, a football player who coached at the University of Florida while on ROTC duty in 1923–

1924. He commanded the 8th Infantry Regiment in the 4th Infantry Division for three years prior to D-Day while his classmates rose to the general officer ranks. General McNair and General Marshall had confused Van Fleet with another officer who had both a drinking problem and a similar last name. The confusion kept Van Fleet from being promoted, even though every commander of the 4th Infantry Division from 1940 to 1944—Fredendall, Griswold, Wallace, and Barton—had recommended him for elevation to general officer.[86] Van Fleet's well-trained regiment spearheaded the invasion of UTAH Beach on D-Day.

After General Bradley cleared up the confusion over his identity, Van Fleet rose quickly. He was given his first star and became assistant division commander of the 2d Infantry Division during the battle for Brest and was serving as acting commander of the 4th Infantry Division (Barton was ill) when he was ordered to take over the 90th Infantry Division on 15 October.[87] William E. Depuy, who at the time was the regimental S-3 of the 357th Infantry, recalled the change of command:

> We hated to see McLain go but Van Fleet was recognized as a fine fellow and he was. Van Fleet got around and talked to people and he wasn't a command post general. He was not as articulate as McLain, he was more stolid. Indeed, he was a massive man; he was sort of awe-inspiring because of his mass. And he knew what he was doing. There wasn't a ripple when he came in. He didn't change anything.[88]

Eisenhower called Van Fleet's battle record the best "of any regimental, divisional, or corps commander we produced."[89]

As with other veteran divisions, constant commitment at the front caused a drain on the manpower of the 5th and 90th Infantry Divisions. Like their counterparts to the north, the divisions of Patton's Third U.S. Army found that the best way to integrate replacements was while in reserve. General Van Fleet recalled:

> Our strength around Metz, where we were temporarily on the defensive preparing for the capture of Metz, our units got very depleted. Replacements were slow coming, and by then we had learned not to put replacements in a front line unit, but put them in a reserve unit and get them acquainted with their buddies and a little bit of orientation before they're committed to battle. So, our units that we were not using, we broke up. . . . All those units were assigned to fill in the infantry, and we even took headquarters clerks and said they all had to do a tour of the front.[90]

Improvisations such as these kept infantry divisions in the fight, but the lack of trained replacements reduced the effectiveness of infantry units. Shortly after the battle for Metz, when the 90th Infantry Division assaulted across the Saar River, Depuy (now a battalion commander) had to put some soldiers into the boats at pistol point. "I suppose that is not an approved leadership technique," he later quipped.[91]

The 95th Infantry Division was an Organized Reserve division activated in July 1942 at Camp Swift, Texas, with cadre drawn from the 7th Infantry Division. The division participated in maneuvers in Louisiana and at the Desert Training Center in California before deploying to Great Britain in August 1944. During its existence, the division had only one commander, Major General Harry L. Twaddle, who had come from the War Department, where he had served as the G-3. Although the division entered the lines on 19 October in the Moselle River bridgehead, Metz would be its first significant combat experience.[92]

The XX Corps plan for the seizure of Metz envisioned an attack to encircle the city by the 5th and 90th Infantry Divisions, while the 95th Infantry Division contained the German salient west of the Moselle. General Walker gave the 10th Armored Division the mission of following the 90th Infantry Division until he committed it to closing the pincers east of Metz.[93]

For two months the 5th and 90th Infantry Divisions had faced the enemy positions at Metz. This interval allowed the American units to plot precise enemy locations and develop detailed plans for the attack. Commanders rotated troops out of the line, integrated replacements, and trained units in assault tactics. Prior to the attack, commanders briefed units down to the lowest level on the plan and the role of each soldier in it.[94]

The weather for the operation was miserable. Incessant rain and snow flurries grounded air support for much of the time, slowed road traffic, turned the numerous streams in the area into raging torrents, and caused the Moselle to reach flood stage.[95] Nevertheless, the attack commenced as scheduled on 9 November.

The 90th Infantry Division began the assault with a crossing of the Moselle at 0330 hours under cover of darkness. The strong current made the crossing by assault boat extremely difficult, but the lead battalions managed to cross by dawn. Despite this success, the swift current swept numerous assault boats downriver. The rapidly rising river made bridging operations nearly impossible. Engineers worked waist-deep in freezing water to complete their tasks. Meanwhile, the eight infantry battalions on the far side of the river found themselves without the support of tanks or tank destroyers. Engineers completed work on a treadway bridge at 0200 hours on 11 November, but flooding of the causeway leading to the bridge rendered it unusable for another twenty-four hours. For four days the eight infantry battalions across the river fought with only the limited supplies that could be ferried across the Moselle at night, albeit protected by substantial artillery support. Rain and cold heightened the impact of continuous combat and caused numerous exposure and trench foot casualties. Despite these obstacles, the infantry battalions continued their attack through the forts of the old Maginot Line. On the morning of 12 November, the Moselle finally receded enough to allow vehicles to cross the bridge.[96]

Armored vehicles began crossing the Moselle none too soon, for a *kampf-*

gruppe of the German 25th Panzer Grenadier Division launched a strong coun-terattack against the 359th Infantry Regiment at 0300 hours on 12 November. The enemy nearly penetrated to the bridge site before the 359th Infantry, sup-ported by the twenty battalions of artillery available to the division, held firm. Two tank destroyers that crossed the Moselle in the early morning hours soon arrived to take the enemy armor under fire. A counterattack by the 2d Battalion forced the Germans to retreat, but enemy artillery fire destroyed the bridge over the Moselle. The engineers of the 991st Engineer Treadway Bridge Company responded by putting a heavy ferry into operation while they built another bridge.[97] DUKWs soon arrived from Third U.S. Army depots to help transport supplies.[98]

By the end of the fourth day of the operation, six battalions of infantry in the 90th Infantry Division were at only 50 percent strength. While work pro-ceeded on another bridge, two sections of a smoke generator company, a chem-ical mortar battalion, and two battalions of artillery protected the area by creating a continuous smoke screen during daylight hours to prevent enemy observation of the bridge site. Enemy mines, uncovered as the Moselle receded, delayed construction. At 1740 hours on 13 November, the first vehicle finally crossed the Moselle on the completed bridge. Throughout the night, traffic rolled across the river in a steady stream. In less than twenty-four hours, the vehicles of the 90th Infantry Division, to include attachments and four additional battalions of artillery, crossed the river on a single span. The Tough 'Ombres were across the Moselle to stay.[99]

To expand the bridgehead, Walker ordered the 10th Armored Division to cross the Moselle on 14 November. The next day, the armor entered the battle alongside the 90th Infantry Division. Both divisions continued the attack to the south and east. The G-3 of the 90th Infantry Division noted,

Teamwork among the several components of the Division developed in five months of hard combat was paying off. The artillery was meeting every demand for fires and anticipating the bulk of the requests. Tanks and tank destroyers rendered close effective support at all times. The Engineers were closely integrated with the infantry in the assault team formations and had the routes open to traffic immediately behind the leading infantry elements.[100]

Despite having sustained twenty-three hundred casualties, the division advanced the final twenty-one kilometers to its objective and captured twenty-one hun-dred enemy soldiers along the way.[101] On 17 November the weather finally cleared, and planes of the XIXth Tactical Air Command joined the fight to bomb and strafe enemy forces. At 1100 hours on 19 November, the 90th Re-connaissance Troop made contact with the 735th Tank Battalion, supporting the 5th Infantry Division, thus completing the encirclement of Metz. General Pat-ton wrote to Van Fleet, "The capture and development of your bridgehead over the Moselle River ... will ever rank as one of the epic river crossings of history."[102] Fittingly, during the middle of the operation Van Fleet received his second star. For its role in the operation, the 90th Infantry Division earned a Distinguished Unit Citation, one of only a dozen awarded to American divisions in the ETO.

While the 90th Infantry Division conducted the corps' main attack, the 5th and 95th Infantry Divisions conducted supporting attacks to envelop and seize Metz. The 5th Infantry Division had the advantage of beginning the attack from a bridgehead east of the Moselle, although it still had to cross the smaller Seille River in its zone. Due to the wide zone for which his division was responsible, General Irwin committed only the 2d Infantry Regiment to the attack for the first several days. The lone regiment was able to cross both the Seille and the Nied River, aided by the advance of the 6th Armored Division to its south.[103]

Late on 13 November, General Walker gave Irwin the mission of seizing Metz from the south. The 10th and 11th Infantry Regiments swung north into the attack. By the time the 2d Infantry Regiment made contact with the 90th Infantry Division east of the city, the 10th and 11th Infantry Regiments had already secured the southern half of Metz. Meanwhile, the 95th Infantry Division joined in the assault on Metz from the west. On 19 November the 377th and 378th Infantry Regiments entered Metz after hard fighting and linked up with the 5th Infantry Division. Mopping-up operations took three days, but by the afternoon of 22 November, Metz was finally in American hands.[104]

Adjacent to Patton's Third U.S. Army, on 15 September 1944 SHAEF activated the 6th Army Group under Lieutenant General Jacob L. Devers to control the operations of the First French Army and the Seventh U.S. Army. One of the advantages this arrangement conferred was the use of an independent supply line for the 6th Army Group running through southern France from the port of Marseilles on the Mediterranean coast. Devers's mission was to destroy German forces, penetrate the West Wall fortifications in his zone, and seize crossings over the Rhine River. There were several problems with these objectives. German forces ensconced in fortifications built into the extremely rough, wooded, and mountainous terrain of Alsace would be difficult to destroy and would likely exact a high toll on the attacking forces. The best avenue of approach, moreover, was through the Belfort Gap at the extreme southern end of the Allied line. To keep the four American armies in northeastern France adjacent to each other (coalition interoperability had its limits), Eisenhower dictated that the French First Army would operate near the Swiss border, leaving the more powerful Seventh U.S. Army with the least desirable terrain astride the rugged Vosges Mountains. Most important, even if the 6th Army Group seized crossings over the Rhine in its zone, SHAEF planners believed the imposing obstacle of the Black Forest to the east negated any real operational or strategic advantage from exploiting them. As the official U.S. Army historians state, "From a theater point of view, a major effort in the south seemed pointless."[105] Eisenhower was content to let the 6th Army Group tie down German forces, a task it could accomplish without drawing on supplies intended for use by the more strategically positioned army groups to its north.[106]

In retrospect, SHAEF's viewpoint begs the question of why the 6th Army Group was allowed to attack at all. If there were no strategic objectives to be gained, then why not limit Devers's forces to an economy-of-force role and put more assets elsewhere where they would do more good? Other alternatives were not even considered, such as using the 6th Army Group, once it had crossed the Rhine, to attack north to envelop the forces defending against Patton's Third U.S. Army and seize the Saar industrial region from the south. Instead, SHAEF allowed Devers to attack into the Saverne and Belfort Gaps and through the Vosges with the vaguest of strategic objectives in mind. When the 6th Army Group's offensive turned out to be unexpectedly successful in nearly destroying the German Nineteenth Army, seizing Strasbourg, and closing to the west bank of the Rhine, SHAEF failed to capitalize on the opportunities presented. Instead of exploiting the breakthrough, Eisenhower turned the Seventh U.S. Army's energies north to attack the West Wall in yet another location, with marginal operational and strategic results.

Lieutenant General Alexander M. Patch's Seventh U.S. Army came up against German defenses anchored in the western foothills of the Vosges Mountains after pursuing enemy forces up the Rhone River Valley and across south central France. In the Vosges, German Army Group G found ideal conditions for constructing a firm defensive barrier, while lack of priority on Allied airpower, logistics, and manpower seemed to negate any advantages the Seventh U.S. Army might otherwise have held over its opponents. More often than not, the airplanes that were available to support the advance were grounded by poor flying weather in the fall and winter of 1944–1945. Given the lack of suitable terrain for its employment, Allied advantages in armor support were also negligible. The German Nineteenth Army enjoyed defending prepared positions built for its divisions by the Organisation Todt using conscripted civilian labor. The Wehrmacht also had history on its side—no army had ever successfully attacked through the Vosges Mountains. Moreover, the infantry strength of the opposing sides was roughly equivalent. As one historian of the Vosges campaign, Keith E. Bonn, has commented, "The victor, therefore, would be decided not by numbers, air power, or armor superiority, but by training and tactical proficiency."[107]

The commander of U.S. VI Corps, Major General Lucian Truscott, understood the heavy penalty that awaited his troops if they allowed the enemy time to fortify their positions in the Vosges Mountains, as the Germans had done in the Apennines in Italy. He therefore pushed his corps into the attack on 15 October with the 3d Infantry Division as the main effort. The objective of Operation DOGFACE was to secure the region prior to the onset of winter.[108] In difficult mountain warfare in cold, wet weather, the veteran 3d, 36th, and 45th Infantry Divisions and the separate 442d RCT (Nissei) succeeded in opening a gap in the German lines in the vicinity of Bruyeres–St.-Dié by early November.

In the process VI Corps virtually destroyed the 16th Volks Grenadier Division and forced the Germans to withdraw behind the Meurthe River. VI Corps sustained 6,189 casualties but took over 5,000 prisoners and inflicted thousands of losses on the enemy in killed and wounded.[109] American losses were soon made up through replacements and resupply, while German units lost men and matériel at unsustainable rates. Combat in the Vosges seemed to be turning into a war of attrition that would be won by the side that could sustain its strength and will to fight the longest.

As in other areas of the ETO that dreary fall season, the divisions of VI Corps experienced increased rates of skin disease, trench foot, combat exhaustion, and desertion as constant exposure to the cold and wet weather took its toll on the soldiers. Troops who had fought through the bitter Italian winter a year earlier had little desire to face another in the Vosges Mountains of France. Physical and mental lethargy reduced the effectiveness of the infantrymen who daily faced nature's ravages. Regular rotation of battalions to the rear for rest, hot food, and hygiene alleviated, but could not eliminate, the problems. Division commanders walked a fine line between putting enough battalions in the line to accomplish their missions and leaving sufficient numbers in reserve to rest and ensure their strength would be available for the next operation.[110]

When Operation DOGFACE ended, the 3d, 36th, and 45th Infantry Divisions, in continuous combat since 15 August, were tired and needed time to rest and integrate replacements to make up for the losses sustained in the recent attack. The effective integration of replacements was crucial to the Seventh U.S. Army's success, for operations in mountainous terrain demand solid unit cohesion. This is especially true for the force on the offensive, which must expose its soldiers to all the miseries of the terrain and weather, unlike the defender, who can exact some modicum of comfort from his fixed fortifications with overhead cover and use of man-made shelter in villages and towns. For the divisions of VI Corps, help was on the way in the form of the newly arrived 100th and 103d Infantry Divisions and the 14th Armored Division. Eisenhower's decision to divert these units from northern France, where ports were taxed beyond capacity, to Marseilles, where excess capacity was available, was a good one. The new divisions allowed Devers and Patch to rotate divisions out of the line for rest, while simultaneously increasing the combat power of the 6th Army Group in time for its general offensive designed to carry it to the banks of the Rhine. The arrival of two new infantry divisions nearly doubled the combat power of VI Corps—provided those divisions could execute a difficult attack in their combat debut. The army's Mobilization Training Program was once again about to be put to the test.

For the next offensive, Lieutenant General Patch ordered Major General Wade H. Haislip's U.S. XV Corps, consisting of the 44th and 79th Infantry Divisions and Major General Jacques Leclerc's French 2d Armored Division, to attack through the Saverne Gap while Major General Edward Brooks's VI Corps attacked into the heart of the Vosges Mountains. Haislip used his forces doctrinally, with his two infantry divisions attacking to penetrate enemy defenses and the French 2d Armored Division held in reserve to exploit success. Brooks once again assigned the main effort to the refitted 3d Infantry Division in the center of the corps zone. His plan, however, hinged on the ability of the 100th Infantry Division to seize the area in the vicinity of Raon l'Etape to secure the corps' flank and divert German attention away from the 3d Infantry Division. The veteran but tired 45th Infantry Division had earlier experienced difficulty attacking toward Raon l'Etape during Operation DOGFACE. How the men of the Century Division would fare in their first major combat operation on the same ground was anyone's guess. By assigning such a key objective to a new division, Major General Brooks was placing his faith in the system used by the Army of the United States to mobilize and train divisions to an adequate level of effectiveness prior to their movement overseas.

The 100th Infantry Division was activated on 15 November 1942 at Fort Jackson, South Carolina, where it underwent mobilization training. It participated in the Second Army maneuvers in Tennessee in November and December 1943, the first time army-level maneuvers had been held in winter. The experience was valuable for the men of the Century Division, for the terrain and weather conditions they experienced in the mountains east of Nashville were very similar to what they would find in the Vosges a year later. The division commander, Major General Withers A. Burress, was a 1914 graduate of the Virginia Military Institute who had served in World War I with the 23d Infantry Regiment at Château-Thierry, Aisne-Marne, and St.-Mihiel. He had been assigned as the assistant commandant of the Infantry School—the same position General Marshall had held during the interwar period—prior to assuming command of the division. He was the only commander the 100th Infantry Division had during the war.[111]

Eschewing a frontal assault on Raon l'Etape, Major General Burress opted to envelop the enemy defenders on the east bank of the Meurthe River from the north, using the bridgehead at Baccarat seized earlier by the French 2d Armored Division. It was an inspired plan, based on professional judgement gained through years of study and practice in the interwar period.[112] On 12 November the 397th and 399th Infantry Regiments attacked southeast toward Raon l'Etape. After probing enemy defenses for two days, the division launched a series of attacks that succeeded in penetrating German positions. As veteran divisions could have told the new arrivals, rain, mud, snow, and thick woods presented as many obstacles as the resistance of the newly arrived 708th Volks Grenadier Division. The Centurymen persevered and by 18 November were in possession of Raon l'Etape, thus placing the gates of the Vosges in the hands of VI Corps.[113] The 100th Infantry Division had accomplished its mission in difficult conditions and by doing so had yet again proved the soundness of the army's Mobilization Training Program in preparing its divisions for combat.

The day after the seizure of Raon l'Etape, the 3d Infantry Division infiltrated several platoons across the Meurthe River, which allowed division engineers to emplace two footbridges that night. By dawn five infantry battalions were across the river. After a thirty-minute artillery preparation, the 3d Infantry Division attack commenced at 0645 hours. The German commanders, focused on the threat posed by the 100th Infantry Division at Raon l'Etape, were completely surprised.[114] Enemy mines and poor weather were the major obstacles to the attack. Floods washed away or forced the removal of much of the tactical bridging across the Meurthe on 21 November, but nevertheless both the 3d and the 100th Infantry Division made progress against increasingly chaotic German defenses. Brooks ordered his division commanders to begin pursuit operations. Pursuit of withdrawing enemy units by motorized task forces was hampered by roadblocks, craters, mines, and other obstacles, but the steady advance of the infantry regiments kept the pressure on.[115] The VI Corps attack annihilated the 708th and 716th Divisions and overran the German winter defensive line in the High Vosges.[116] On 24 November the 3d and 100th Infantry Divisions began a race down the Bruche River Valley in an effort to reach Strasbourg. Two days later, the 3d Infantry Division linked up with patrols from the 45th Infantry Division assigned to XV Corps, only to hear the news that Strasbourg had already been liberated by the French 2d Armored Division exploiting the successful penetration of the Saverne Gap by XV Corps.

In the aggregate, 6th Army Group's offensive shattered six of eight divisions in the German Nineteenth Army and brought American and French units to the banks of the Rhine near Strasbourg and in the Belfort Gap. In the 6th Army Group zone, only the German positions near Colmar remained as a thorn west of the Rhine. Satisfied with 6th Army Group's progress, Eisenhower ordered Devers to shift the direction of the Seventh U.S. Army north to assist Patton's Third U.S. Army in its advance toward the Saar industrial basin. Devers heatedly objected to the change in direction, but Eisenhower held firm. The 6th Army Group was to drop immediately any plans and preparations for crossing the Rhine, despite the fact that the river was virtually undefended now that the German Nineteenth Army had been shredded. The Seventh U.S. Army was to orient north to assist Patton, while the First French Army cleaned out the Colmar pocket.[117] German commanders in World War II had a name for such a decision, opting for a safe plan over a more ambitious scheme with potentially greater operational and strategic value: the small solution. General Bradley, visiting 6th Army Group with Eisenhower at the time, fully concurred in the decision. It is ironic that a little over three months later, when faced with a similar opportunity, Eisenhower would give Bradley his full consent for sending forces across the Rhine to take advantage of an unforeseen opportunity at a small town named Remagen.

The reasons for the Seventh U.S. Army's tactical success were severalfold. Its divisions were well-trained, cohesive organizations that brought to the battlefield solid and often exceptional capabilities to conduct combat operations, even in their first battles. American commanders developed good tactical plans that were well executed by their units. Personnel and logistical systems promptly replaced losses, which kept American divisions functioning when their enemy counterparts were disintegrating. On the other hand, German defensive lines were poorly sited, their units were haphazardly organized and poorly trained, and their soldiers were kept in the fight only by brutal discipline and the threat of capital (and summary) punishment.[118]

German troops enjoyed several major advantages: fortified positions with overhead cover; extensive use of mines, felled trees, barbed wire, and blown bridges; and protected shelters that shielded soldiers from the worst of nature's ravages. Even with these advantages, German commanders lacked the capability to plug gaps in the line when they occurred.[119] The army's official historians conclude, "The German high command and control system was incapable of keeping pace with the tempo of the Allied operations and was unable to respond effectively."[120] Historian Keith Bonn's judgment is even more severe: "Although the Americans in this zone had gained overall numerical superiority, they did not need it; battalion on battalion, company on company, they were outfighting the Germans and overrunning them. Maneuvers such as these, creating such lopsided casualty ratios (greater than six to one) rapidly brought the defenders to the verge of collapse."[121] Army Group G, ordered by Hitler to hold the High Vosges until April 1945, had delayed the Seventh U.S. Army just six weeks.

After the liberation of Strasbourg, the Seventh U.S. Army directed its efforts at assisting the French First Army in reducing the Colmar pocket and penetrating the West Wall fortifications in the Low Vosges to the north. Forces of the German First Army manned strong defenses in the West Wall and fortifications of the French-built Maginot Line in the vicinity of Bitche. While the 45th and 103d Infantry Divisions attacked to penetrate the West Wall near Wissembourg, the 44th and 100th Infantry Divisions tackled the unenviable task of prying the German defenders out of the Maginot Line fortresses near Bitche. The bitter battle that ensued earned for the soldiers of the Century Division the inevitable moniker—"sons of Bitche."

German forces in the Low Vosges conducted a skillful delay in the first half of December. Nature did not help; the Americans were attacking heavily forested hills in weather that included rain, fog, ice, and snow. German forces enjoyed a certain amount of shelter defending stone farmhouses, hamlets, and towns, while attacking American troops were subject to all the hardships that a miserable, wet, cold late fall in the mountains had to offer. Nevertheless, advances by the 12th Armored Division in the western portion of the XV Corps zone and by VI Corps to the east forced the German First Army to withdraw into its fixed fortifications by 15 December, the day before the Battle of the Bulge was to begin. The Germans had achieved their objective; the Seventh U.S. Army attack did not interfere with preparations for the German counteroffensive in the Ardennes.

The assaults by the 44th and 100th Infantry Divisions on the Maginot Line fortifications played out under the backdrop of the Battle of the Bulge. Interestingly, the German 275th Infantry Division had attacked these same fortifications from the same direction in June 1940, only to be decisively repelled at the hands of the already defeated French army.[122] The forts of the Maginot Line were made of reinforced concrete and steel, with walls and overhead cover varying from three to ten feet thick and underground shelters as many as five stories deep. The fortifications in the vicinity of Bitche were the strongest in the Maginot Line. The area included four great fortresses, Simserhof, Schiesseck, Otterbiel, and Grand Wohekirkel, each consisting of six to eleven armored casemates, along with smaller pillboxes to cover the intervening gaps.[123] Despite the imposing strength of these barriers, which gave every advantage to their German defenders, the 44th and 100th Infantry Divisions succeeded in breaching the Maginot Line in less than a week of combat and at a relatively modest cost in casualties.

The 100th Infantry Division's battle for Fort Schiesseck is an excellent example of the power of the combined-arms team against fixed fortifications. After the 398th Infantry Regiment advanced to the last covered and concealed position south of the Bitche basin on 14 December, it trained in assault tactics while division and corps artillery pummeled the German positions around Fort Schiesseck for two days. The fort survived numerous direct hits from 240mm, 8-inch, 155mm, 105mm, and 4.2-inch shells that simply ricocheted harmlessly off the four-foot-thick concrete cupolas and seven-inch steel doors and disappearing gun turrets. Close air support did no better; fifty-four P-47 Thunderbolts dropping twenty-seven tons of bombs had no effect on the fort.[124]

The next day, 17 December, the Americans employed different tactics. Tank destroyers with 90mm guns and M12, 155mm "Long Tom" artillery pieces were moved into position to blast the enemy fortifications at point-blank range. The heavy direct fire support forced the German defenders to button up and remain underground. After a short artillery preparation, the 3d Battalion, 398th Infantry Regiment, advanced with attached engineers behind a rolling barrage to destroy the casemates in close combat. Engineers from the 325th Engineer Combat Battalion used demolitions to blow the door to the casemate open. Infantry would then enter the fortification to kill any enemy in the cupola. Dynamite charges of between sixty and sixteen hundred pounds were placed and detonated to destroy the stairs and elevators leading to the lower levels. A tank dozer would then bury the casemate with tons of earth, interring anyone left inside. The enemy below remained there indefinitely. The procedure was repeated on the next fort. By 20 December all eleven of Fort Schiesseck's casemates had been systematically neutralized. For their performance in this operation, the 3d Battalion, 398th Infantry, and Company B, 325th Engineer Combat Battalion, received the Distinguished Unit Citation.[125]

These were extraordinary accomplishments for a division that had been in combat for only one month and had never before trained for such an operation. The 398th Infantry Regiment had penetrated the most heavily fortified region of the Maginot Line at a cost of fourteen killed, eighty wounded, and sixteen missing.[126] "At the cost of the same number of killed and 57 more wounded, a regiment that was a product of the U.S. Army Mobilization Training Plan, without special training or experience, accomplished what a regiment of the vaunted 1940 German army had utterly failed to do: penetrate the Ensemble de Bitche," writes historian Keith Bonn. "Moreover, they accomplished it without the months of training and minute intelligence that had been available to the Germans in 1940."[127] To the west, the 44th Infantry Division had been equally successful in seizing Fort Simserhof. To the east the VI Corps offensive was even more successful, completely rupturing German positions, decimating the 245th and 256th Volks Grenadier Divisions, and forcing German forces back to the West Wall. Despite these successes, the Battle of the Bulge finally forced a halt to the XV Corps offensive on 21 December 1944. The men of the Century Division would eventually seize Bitche three months later.

The Siegfried Line, Lorraine, and Vosges campaigns demonstrated the ability of American divisions to perform well during their initial entry into combat. The official historian of the Siegfried Line campaign observes, "In Normandy

Soldiers of the 71st Infantry Regiment, 44th Infantry Division, investigate battle-scarred Simserhof Fortress, part of the Maginot Line near Bitche, France, 19 December 1944. Despite the imposing strength of barriers such as this, which gave every advantage to their German defenders, the 44th and 100th Infantry Divisions succeeded in breaching the Maginot Line in less than a week of combat and at a relatively modest cost in casualties. (U.S. Army Signal Corps photo)

it had become almost routine for a division in its first action to incur severe losses and display disturbing organizational, command, and communications deficiencies for at least the first week of combat indoctrination. Yet in no case was this tendency present to a similar degree among those divisions receiving their baptism of fire during the Siegfried Line Campaign."[128] Perhaps, as the official historian felt, the reason for the success of these divisions was better training based on actual combat experience and the high percentage of ASTP candidates these divisions possessed. Perhaps the Wehrmacht at this stage of the war was losing some of the effectiveness that characterized its earlier campaigns. Another likely reason is that the German high command was holding the bulk of its reinforcements and many of its best units for the impending winter counteroffensive in the west. In that battle among the hills, forests, and river valleys of the Ardennes Forest, German and American divisions would clash in a titanic struggle that would determine the ultimate fate of the Third Reich.

The battles on the periphery of Germany in the fall of 1944 demonstrated the strengths and weaknesses of the Army of the United States at the time. The tactical prowess of American divisions produced victories at Aachen, Metz, and in the Vosges, while the poor operational capabilities of senior commanders doomed numerous divisions to a futile campaign in the murky darkness of the Huertgen Forest and threw away potential opportunities in Alsace. Tactical innovations such as the use of night attacks by Terry Allen's Timberwolf Division and innovative combined-arms assaults on the fortifications of the Maginot Line and West Wall helped American forces accomplish their missions. The ultimate triumph, however, belonged to the American foot soldier, who persevered in the cruelest of conditions and despite severe hardship. He fought for the men around him and, more generally, because he knew the shortest way home lay along the road to Berlin. The American soldier was impressed by German technology but not by the Nazi military machine. Backed by superior artillery and airpower and bolstered by adequate logistical, personnel, intelligence, engineer, and signal support, GIs rarely lost a tactical engagement in the fall of 1944. If their accomplishments during this time seem few in number, the blame lay elsewhere, either in the inevitable necessity of an operational pause to gather supplies and upgrade the lines of communication or in the poorly conceived operational concepts of their senior commanders.

The broad-front strategy executed by the Western Allies may have been an exercise in political expediency, but it was effective in preventing German forces from recovering their full combat potential after the breakout from Normandy. For German commanders in France, operations progressed from crisis to crisis, with little time for rest, refitting, or the training essential to successful reconstitution of shattered formations or the orderly introduction to combat of newly formed units. Continuous pressure generated by the multiple offensives necessary to execute the broad-front strategy not only gained ground but also chewed up German units at an unsustainable rate. Infusions of untrained replacements led to heavy casualties among the badly battered German formations, especially the recently mobilized volks grenadier divisions.

American divisions, on the other hand, were on the whole better trained for their missions, were kept at a higher state of readiness due to superior personnel and logistical systems, and were more cohesive than their enemy counterparts. The ability of infantry divisions to accomplish their missions was central to the success of the broad-front strategy. Armored divisions, spread across the front, could exploit local successes but were so dispersed they could not achieve gains of operational significance. The heavy demands of attrition warfare often meant that armored divisions were used in a nondoctrinal role on the front, just like infantry divisions. In the final analysis, the battles on the periphery of Germany in the fall of 1944 were primarily an infantryman's war.

The American army's ability to regenerate combat power on a continuous basis was essential to the successful execution of the broad-front strategy and the war of attrition it provoked. The replacement of huge numbers of casualties required an efficient personnel management system. Although the American replacement system more or less met its numerical goals, it did so by all but ignoring the needs and plight of replacement soldiers. Division commanders recognized this problem and stepped in to fill the void by expedients such as the division training center created by Major General Gerhardt in the 29th Infantry Division. Perhaps the highest compliment paid to the American replacement system was given by the German Army Group B, which recognized the ability of the American army to restore the combat effectiveness of its divisions after only a short time. By keeping its combat formations intact and infusing them with individual replacement soldiers, the Army of the United States was never forced to resort to the creation of ad hoc battle groups *(kampfgruppen)* that came to dominate the German order of battle as the war progressed. Historians who praise the ability of the Wehrmacht to fight with such improvised formations should never forget that because of the existence of the much-beleaguered individual replacement system, the American army was never forced to do so.

9

The Battle of the Bulge

The Normandy campaign and the Battle of the Bulge were the two most critical tests of the Army of the United States in World War II. One was a great offensive victory, the other a defensive triumph. Both displayed the strengths and weaknesses of American infantry divisions in combat: their great staying power, the effectiveness of the infantry–tank–artillery team, the ability of veteran units to accomplish their missions despite heavy casualties, and the problems associated with inexperienced divisions committed to heavy fighting upon their initial entry into combat. There were some important differences, too. In Normandy the Allies enjoyed consistent close support from their air forces. During the first week of the Battle of the Bulge, poor weather grounded most aircraft. Although the Wehrmacht experienced supply shortages (particularly fuel) in the Ardennes, their lines of communication were shorter than in Normandy and not as vulnerable to Allied air interdiction. In short, the strength of the opposing forces was much more equal during the German counteroffensive in the Ardennes, at least during the first critical week. More than any other event in World War II, the Battle of the Bulge would test the combat effectiveness of the ground divisions of the Army of the United States against a capable opponent on nearly equal terms.

The German counteroffensive in the Ardennes, code-named *WACHT AM RHEIN* (Watch on the Rhine), hit the weakest part of the Allied front. The U.S. VIII Corps in the Ardennes Forest, commanded by Major General Troy Middleton, was composed of both veteran divisions in need of rest and green divisions in need of combat experience. The 4th and 28th Infantry Divisions had both undergone severe combat in the Huertgen Forest, had taken huge losses, and needed time to integrate replacements into the ranks. The 106th Infantry Division and 9th Armored Division were both new to combat, the former only entering the front line on 10 December. The Ardennes, 12th Army Group commander, Lieutenant General Omar N. Bradley, and First U.S.

Army commander, Lieutenant General Courtney Hodges, believed, was the perfect place for these divisions. It was a quiet part of the front where nothing much ever happened. For that reason, VIII Corps was the economy-of-force effort for the Allies in the West. Middleton's forces were stretched along an eighty-five-mile front, three times the doctrinal distance for a corps in the defense.[1]

The terrain of the Ardennes was hardly conducive to mobile armored warfare, which was both the appeal and the drawback of the area. The Germans had mounted major military operations through the Ardennes in both 1914 and 1940, but those campaigns were fought in the good weather of spring and summer. The Ardennes in the winter is a forbidding place. Only one major avenue of approach, the Losheim Gap in the north, runs east to west. To the south of the Losheim Gap, an area of rugged, wooded hills called the Schnee Eifel ("Snow Mountains") rises at the German border. Running to the rear of the Schnee Eifel south to Luxembourg, the Our River presents an obstacle to vehicular traffic. To the rear of the Our River in the center of the VIII Corps sector, a dominant ridgeline (dubbed "Skyline Drive" by American troops) blocks any easy egress from the river below. The restricted road network in the Ardennes follows along numerous streams and valleys, and two towns, St.-Vith and Bastogne, form critical communications hubs in the region. Rugged hills, deep valleys, and the cold and snowy weather in December 1944 made movement difficult, to say the least. Surprise, Adolf Hitler believed, would make up for the drawbacks of the terrain and weather.[2]

The 28th Infantry Division defended Skyline Drive and the Our River in the center of the VIII Corps sector. During the previous three months, the division had sustained 8,959 enlisted and 365 officer casualties, most of them during the abortive attack on Schmidt in the Huertgen Forest in November.[3] The division had also lost a great deal of equipment in the Battle of Schmidt. The strength of the American logistical system is evident in the fact that by 16 December the 28th Division had a full complement of authorized equipment and a basic load of ammunition on hand.[4] By comparison, the weakness of the personnel system is shown by the fact that many of the replacements who joined the division were antiaircraft or other combat support soldiers who had been retrained and reassigned to the infantry. "A morale problem confronted us from the beginning of the reorganization," recalls William F. Train, who served as the executive officer of the 112th Infantry Regiment.[5] Major General Norman Cota used the time available to rehabilitate and train his division as it defended a quiet sector in widely dispersed strongpoints along the Our River.

The 106th Infantry Division, the "Golden Lions," took over the positions of the 2d Infantry Division only a week before the German attack commenced in order to release the "Indian Head" Division for an attack on the Roer River dams to the north. Major General Alan Jones did not like the exposed positions of two of his regiments on the Schnee Eifel, but Eisenhower, Bradley, and Hodges wanted the salient into Germany held.[6] Americans had paid for that part of the Siegfried Line with their blood, and unless there was a compelling reason to give it back, the Golden Lions would stay. As a division commander in combat for the first time, Jones was not in a good position to argue his case. By the time the Wehrmacht made the case for him, the regiments on the Schnee Eifel would be in danger of encirclement.

To make matters worse, the 106th Infantry Division was not ready for combat. The 12th Army Group had placed the division in the Ardennes Forest to give it some battle experience in a "quiet" sector before using it in offensive operations. The division had not yet recovered from the raids on its trained personnel back in the United States. "I hardly got to know the men in my platoon before we were in combat," states James B. Giles Jr., a member of the West Point Class of 1944 who was assigned as a rifle platoon leader in Company K, 422d Infantry Regiment. "I did not really know the non-coms I had to count on very well. We were a bunch of strangers—not just in my company— but all over the 106th Division. It sure didn't help us any."[7] Had the Germans not launched their counteroffensive in the Ardennes Forest, the 106th Infantry Division probably would have developed along the same lines as most other American infantry divisions in World War II: a rough introduction to combat, but steady improvement as combat weeded out the incompetent and gave experience to those who remained. Unfortunately, the Golden Lions had only six days in the line before the German juggernaut hit them.

At 0530 on 16 December 1944, the VIII Corps front erupted in flame as an artillery barrage marked the start of the German winter counteroffensive. Six divisions—two panzer, three volks grenadier (infantry), and one parachute— slammed into the Keystone Division in the center of the VIII Corps sector at odds of roughly five to one.[8] Because of the extreme width of its twenty-five-mile sector, the 28th Infantry Division fought with three regiments on line and had only one infantry battalion in reserve. German artillery fire disrupted the division's communications network early in the battle. With few reserves at his disposal, there was little General Cota could do to influence the battle anyway.

On the division left, the 112th Infantry Regiment delayed the advance of the LVIII Panzer Corps by thirty-six hours before the 116th Panzer Division gained a bridgehead across the Our River. The regiment inflicted heavy losses on attacking enemy forces and remained intact as a fighting organization. Cota wanted the regiment to fall back on Bastogne, but enemy advances soon made this impossible. Instead, the 112th Infantry joined the 106th Infantry Division to its north on 19 December and soon became an integral part of the defense of the key communications nexus of St.-Vith.[9]

On the division right, the 109th Infantry Regiment defended behind the Sauer and Our Rivers from 16 to 20 December against the supporting attacks of the 352d Volks Grenadier Division and the 5th Parachute Division. On 20 December German pressure finally forced the 109th Infantry Regiment to withdraw south to maintain its link with the 9th Armored Division. By this date the regiment had lost over a quarter of its strength in personnel and most of its heavy equipment. Ammunition expenditures show the intensity of the fighting; in three days the regiment expended 280,000 rounds of small-arms ammunition, 5,000 mortar rounds, 3,000 grenades, and 300 bazooka rounds.[10] Most important, the regiment had disrupted the attack timetable of the German Seventh Army by four crucial days. American forces on the southern flank of the Bulge—the 4th Infantry Division, the 109th Infantry Regiment, Combat Command A of the 9th Armored Division, and the 10th Armored Division (less Combat Command B, which was in Bastogne with the 101st Airborne Division)—firmly jammed the southern shoulder of the Bulge for the remainder of the battle.

In the center of the division, the 110th Infantry Regiment defended with two battalions abreast (the 2d Battalion was in division reserve). The fifteen-mile sector and rough terrain mandated the separation of units, with the gaps between covered only by nightly patrols. As a result, the regiment fought for its existence from a series of company strongpoints centered on Skyline Drive to the west of the Our River.[11] Despite the overwhelming combat power of the enemy 2d Panzer and 26th Volks Grenadier Divisions, American infantry companies fought from their strongpoints with dogged determination.

After a day of battle, Cota finally released the 2d Battalion from reserve, but the reinforcement could only delay the inevitable. By the evening of 17 December, German tanks finally overran the regimental command post in Clervaux, but the headquarters company turned the medieval château in the center of town into another Alamo, defending it for eighteen hours before surrendering.[12] By 18 December the 110th Infantry Regiment ceased to operate as a cohesive unit, having been reduced from 3,117 officers and men to 587 in just two days.[13] "When men in foxholes refuse to admit overwhelming odds," writes historian Charles B. MacDonald, "advance through or past them may be inevitable, but it is seldom easy or swift."[14] Ordered to hold at all costs, the 110th Infantry Regiment was destroyed in battle but gained the crucial hours needed for the Allied command to move the 101st Airborne Division to Bastogne before the Germans arrived.

The determined stand of the 28th Infantry Division helped to give the Allied commanders the time they needed to move reinforcements to the Ardennes to stem the German tide. For a division that had been nearly annihilated a month earlier in the Huertgen Forest and occupied the widest sector on the Western Front, the feat was remarkable. Nowhere had American soldiers fled the battlefield as they had at Schmidt. Despite heavy losses, the division would reconstitute once again after the Ardennes fighting. Between 4 and 16 January 1945, the 110th Infantry received twenty-five hundred replacements and once again began the training process to integrate them and form cohesive teams.[15] The 28th Infantry Division then moved south to fight another tough battle in the Colmar pocket. Filled with replacements and given time to rest and train, the Keystone Division displayed the resilience of the infantry divisions of the

Army of the United States by reconstituting major subordinate elements from scratch—not once but twice.

In the northern portion of VIII Corps, the 106th Infantry Division had the misfortune of occupying a twenty-seven-mile sector that included some of the most exposed positions along the American front. The German 18th Volks Grenadier Division took advantage of this situation by attacking the northern flank of the 422d Infantry Regiment in the Losheim Gap, a position defended by the relatively weak 14th Cavalry Group. The 293th Infantry Regiment of the 18th Volks Grenadier Division attacked the southern flank of the 423d Infantry Regiment on the southern edge of the Schnee Eifel, a position defended by only a provisional battalion of relatively weak antitank, reconnaissance, and fire support assets. Within twenty-four hours the two pincers of the enemy attack had joined at the town of Schoenberg behind the two American infantry regiments, which were now trapped.[16]

A quick decision by General Jones to withdraw the two exposed infantry regiments from the Schnee Eifel on 16 or early 17 December could have saved them from encirclement. Jones did what he could to halt the German attack by committing his reserve (two infantry battalions) on 16 December, but the lack of an attached tank battalion (a serious deficiency) doomed this weak effort to failure.[17] To bolster Jones's position, General Middleton attached Combat Command B of the 9th Armored Division, commanded by Brigadier General William H. Hoge, to the 106th Infantry Division on the evening of 16 December. Middleton also informed Jones that the 7th Armored Division was on its way south and that its first combat command would arrive at St.-Vith the next morning.[18]

Buoyed at first, Jones had increasing doubts as the evening progressed. Late that night, he placed another call to General Middleton in Bastogne and recommended the withdrawal of the two regiments from the Schnee Eifel. "You know how things are up there better than I do," Middleton responded, "but I agree it would be wise to withdraw them."[19] By a quirk of fate, Jones received only the first half of the message, and he put down the phone convinced that Middleton wanted him to hold in place.[20] "Well, that's it. Middleton says we should leave them in," Jones told a member of his staff. In Bastogne, Middleton set down the phone and stated, "I just talked to Jones. I told him to pull his regiments off the Schnee Eifel."[21] The lack of understanding between Jones and his corps commander sealed the fate of the 422d and 423d Infantry Regiments.

Only a strong counterattack by the armored commands on their way to St.-Vith could remedy the predicament of the Golden Lions. Because Middleton and Jones misjudged the arrival time of the 7th Armored Division, however, Jones ordered the first unit to arrive, Combat Command B of the 9th Armored Division, to counterattack toward Winterspelt to relieve the strain on the hard-pressed 424th Infantry Regiment.[22] The lead elements of the 7th Armored Division, delayed by massive traffic jams, did not reach St.-Vith until the afternoon of 17 December, by which time the German pincers had closed around the Schnee Eifel at Schoenberg.

Confusion reigned in the headquarters of the 106th Infantry Division. Instead of orchestrating the various assets available to the division, the staff panicked and proved incapable of even controlling the traffic clogging St.-Vith, much less coordinating a counterattack to relieve the regiments encircled on the Schnee Eifel.[23] On the crucial day of 17 December, the division staff packed up and moved from St.-Vith to Vielsalm, thereby throwing the entire organization into mass confusion. No one on the staff had a clear picture of the positions of either enemy or friendly forces in the division's sector. The most powerful asset at the Americans' disposal was the big guns of the numerous corps artillery battalions in the area, but lack of central coordination by the division artillery prevented the massing of fires on critical targets.[24] Only a gallant stand by the 81st Engineer Battalion and part of the 168th Engineer Battalion fighting as infantry prevented the Germans from taking St.-Vith on 17 December.[25]

To Brigadier General Bruce C. Clarke, whose Combat Command B was the first unit of the 7th Armored Division to arrive at St.-Vith, General Jones's behavior seemed odd. Jones repeatedly expressed concern over the fate of his son, a staff officer in the 423d Infantry Regiment, trapped on the Schnee Eifel.[26] Finally, Jones told Clarke, "I've thrown in my last chips. I haven't got much, but your command is the one that will defend this position. You take over command of St. Vith right now."[27] Jones outranked Clarke by one star yet was relinquishing command to him.[28] Furthermore, Clarke was junior to every other general officer in the St.-Vith area, which included not only the 106th Infantry Division but also Combat Command B of the 9th Armored Division, Combat Command B of the 7th Armored Division, and the 112th Infantry Regiment from the 28th Infantry Division. In the ensuing days, Clarke's leadership would be tested as never before. St.-Vith would be the finest hour in his distinguished career.

For the 422d and 423d Infantry Regiments in the Schnee Eifel, the end came rapidly. Although the regiments held strong positions and had adjusted them for all-around defense, they had only a limited amount of ammunition and other supplies. Bad weather and poor staff coordination eliminated any chance of large-scale aerial resupply. If the American units holding St.-Vith could not attack to open a corridor to the trapped units, Jones concluded early on 18 December, then the infantry regiments would have to try to break out on their own. Colonel Charles C. Cavender and Colonel George L. Descheneaux complied with their division commander's order and attacked at 1000 hours. For units that had just entered combat and included a large number of poorly trained replacements, the mission was too challenging and the opposition too powerful. Nearly out of ammunition and food, both regiments surrendered to the enemy on 19 December, the largest mass surrender of American forces in World War II.[29] Altogether, over sixty-eight hundred soldiers in the 106th Infantry Division either surrendered or were captured during the battle.[30] The devastation was so complete that American leaders decided not to reconstitute the division after the battle—the only American division destroyed as a unit by the German army in World War II.

The historian of the 106th Infantry Division blames the division's fate on the stripping of the unit for replacements prior to its entry into combat.[31] This explanation is appealing but incomplete. When the Germans attacked the division on 16 December, those units engaged fought as well as one could expect given their state of training and lack of combat experience. The 424th Infantry Regiment, which escaped encirclement and fought in the subsequent defense of St.-Vith, developed into a solid unit by the end of the Battle of the Bulge.[32] A quick decision to withdraw the 422d and 423d Infantry Regiments from the Schnee Eifel on 16 or early 17 December would have saved them from their eventual fate and allowed them to develop their combat potential in subsequent battles.

The inability of General Jones and his division staff to make timely decisions and orchestrate the combat power at their disposal caused the defeat of the 106th Infantry Division. One cannot ascribe this problem to the stripping of the division for replacements, for the division staff remained intact throughout the unit's precombat training in the United States. Jones was not mentally prepared to lead his division in combat. He did not control his staff in the heat of battle, he failed to make timely decisions, and he constantly vacillated in his positions when discussing matters with his corps commander. Even after the encirclement of two of his regiments in the Schnee Eifel, Jones had an entire division's worth of combat power at his disposal (424th Infantry Regiment, Combat Command B of the 9th Armored Division, 112th Infantry Regiment from the 28th Infantry Division, plus his divisional artillery), but he failed to coordinate it and instead turned the battle over to Clarke, the most junior general officer (but also the most experienced combat commander) in St.-Vith.[33]

Ultimately, Jones's decision to relinquish command was his greatest contribution to the battle, for Clarke fought an outstanding mobile defense that held the Germans in the St.-Vith area for several crucial days while the Allied high command rushed reinforcements to the Ardennes. Jones was not present to witness the triumph of American forces in the subsequent fighting. On 22 December Major General Matthew B. Ridgway, commander of the U.S. XVIII Airborne Corps, relieved him of his command. Soon afterward, Jones collapsed from a heart attack and was evacuated off the battlefield.[34] Perhaps had the Ardennes remained the quiet front it was prior to 16 December, Jones would have had time to acclimate himself and his division to combat operations. Instead, the cruel hand of fate determined that after twenty-seven years of service and promotion to one of the premier positions in his profession, Jones would survive less than two weeks in combat.

To the north of St.-Vith, the German Sixth Panzer Army conducted the enemy's main attack toward the Meuse River. The 1st SS Panzer Corps attacked on 16 December with the 3d Parachute Division, the 12th and 277th Volks

Grenadier Divisions, and the 1st and 12th SS Panzer Divisions. In their path stood the 99th Infantry Division, commanded by Major General Walter E. Lauer, which had only arrived on the Continent the previous month. Like the 106th Infantry Division to its south, the 99th Infantry Division was put in the Ardennes to gain experience.[35] The enemy plan was to use the three infantry divisions to penetrate the American lines to create a hole through which the panzer divisions would exploit.[36]

The initial German attack struck hard at the 99th Infantry Division, which for the most part held up well against the enemy onslaught.[37] Only on the division's southern flank, which was loosely tied in with the 14th Cavalry Group in the Losheim Gap, did the enemy penetrate the division's lines in great strength. A *kampfgruppe* composed primarily of the 1st SS Panzer Regiment of the 1st SS Panzer Division, led by *Obersturmbannfuehrer* Joachim Peiper, exploited through this gap on 17 December, accompanied by dismounted infantry from the 3d Parachute Division.[38]

As Peiper's column headed west toward its assigned objectives on the Meuse River, the 99th and 2d Infantry Divisions fought stubbornly to ensure that other enemy columns would not be able to duplicate Peiper's feat. The 2d Infantry Division, in particular, found itself in quite a predicament. The division had begun an attack toward the Roer River dams on 13 December along a narrow axis to the north of the 99th Infantry Division. The Indian Head Division's line of communication ran down a single road parallel to enemy lines and through the 99th Infantry Division's sector. Only quick action by the veteran commander of the 2d Infantry Division, Major General Walter M. Robertson, saved the division from disaster. On the first day of the German counteroffensive, Robertson suspended his division's attack and ordered his units to prepare for withdrawal from their exposed positions.[39]

On the morning of 17 December, General Hodges, finally convinced that the German counteroffensive was more than just a local riposte, belatedly gave his permission for Robertson to conduct a withdrawal. The call almost came too late. The lone withdrawal route ran through the twin villages of Rocherath and Krinkelt, which were also the key objectives for the 277th Volks Grenadier Division and the newly committed 12th SS Panzer Division. The survival of the Indian Head Division depended on the ability of American troops to hold these two villages until the division could withdraw through them to more defensible positions along Elsenborn Ridge to the west. The task fell to the embattled 393d Infantry Regiment of the 99th Infantry Division and the 3d Battalion, 23d Infantry Regiment, of the 2d Infantry Division.[40]

Late in the morning on 17 December, General Lauer gave his permission for the 393d Infantry to withdraw from its positions to the east of the 3d Battalion, 23d Infantry. For four hours, this lone infantry battalion, under orders to hold at all costs, held its ground to allow the bulk of the 2d Infantry Division to pass to its rear.[41] For this feat the valiant defenders earned a Distinguished Unit Citation and two Medals of Honor. General Robertson spent the entire day pushing his troops along the road to safety and fashioning another defensive line to the east of the twin villages with troops from the 1st Battalion, 9th Infantry Regiment, and Company K, 3d Battalion, 9th Infantry. To bolster this line, General Robertson gave it priority of fires. Backed up by the support of three battalions of 105mm howitzers and four battalions of heavy 155mm howitzers, the 1st Battalion, 9th Infantry, held its position long enough for the remainder of the 2d Division to escape the German trap.[42]

After the withdrawal of the 2d Infantry Division to Rocherath and Krinkelt, the immediate danger of another breakthrough in the U.S. V Corps sector passed. On 20 December a relieved General Hodges wrote to General Robertson, "What the 2d Infantry Division has done in the last four days will live forever in the history of the United States Army."[43] Indeed, the difference between the quick actions of General Robertson to save his division and the inaction of General Jones of the 106th Infantry Division is striking. Ironically, the 2d Infantry Division had occupied the Schnee Eifel until the Golden Lions assumed control of the sector to release the Indian Head Division for its offensive mission. One is left to ponder whether Robertson would have withdrawn from the Schnee Eifel in time to save the regiments positioned there. Certainly, the presence of a veteran division under the command of a seasoned leader would have caused the battle around St.-Vith to develop in a much different manner than it did.

To ensure the northern flank held, the veteran 1st and 9th Infantry Divisions quickly moved south to take up positions on the flanks of the 2d and 99th Infantry Divisions. By daylight on 20 December, they were firmly ensconced on Elsenborn Ridge, the high ground to the west of the twin villages. Each of these divisions occupied a narrow sector, which allowed them to prepare defenses in depth. As important, three of the best infantry divisions in the ETO were now firmly planted in the path of the German main effort.

The next day the 12th SS Panzer Division launched one of the strongest attacks yet against the American forces on the northern shoulder. The 25th Panzer Grenadier Regiment and a tank battalion from the 12th SS Panzer Regiment, supported by artillery and rocket launchers, attacked the positions of 2d Battalion, 26th Infantry Regiment, of the 1st Infantry Division near Dom Butgenbach. The battalion commander, Lieutenant Colonel Derrill M. Daniel, called for indirect fires in front of his positions. As usual, American artillerymen responded by massing the fires of all battalions within range: eight battalions from the 1st and 2d Infantry Divisions, one battalion from the 99th Infantry Division, three battalions from V Corps, and a battalion of 4.2-inch mortars.[44] The artillery fired more than ten thousand rounds in support of Daniel's battalion.[45]

The result was devastating. Coupled with the valiant actions of infantry, tanks, and tank destroyers, the massed artillery fire enabled Daniel's battalion to repel the German assault. The enemy forces left nearly 800 dead soldiers and forty-seven tanks and tank destroyers on the battlefield, while American losses amounted to 250 men, five antitank guns, and four tanks and tank destroyers.[46]

The courageous stand by Daniel's men is even more remarkable in light of the fact that the two units most heavily engaged, Companies E and F, "had been virtually wiped out" three weeks earlier in fighting in the Huertgen Forest.[47] This battle once again illustrates the ability of American infantry divisions to reconstitute quickly even after suffering devastating losses in combat. Backed by the tremendous firepower of massed artillery, the four divisions on the northern flank of the Bulge held the German forces facing them in check for the duration of the battle.

The German Sixth Panzer Army had missed a great opportunity during the first days of the fight. Had the 1st SS Panzer Division attacked north after its breakthrough in the Losheim Gap, it most likely would have surrounded the 2d and 99th Infantry Divisions in their exposed positions to the east of Elsenborn Ridge. Another option would have been to move the 12th SS Panzer Division south to follow the 1st SS Panzer Division through the Losheim Gap and expand the breakthrough. By adhering inflexibly to their original plan of attack, the Germans allowed American commanders the time they needed to move reinforcements to the Ardennes and restore the continuity of their defensive positions. The only unit in the Sixth SS Panzer Army to break through American lines was *Kampfgruppe Peiper.* The German main effort had clearly failed, a fact confirmed when the German High Command shifted the *schwerpunkt* (main effort) of the offensive south to the Fifth Panzer Army on 20 December.

The task of destroying *Kampfgruppe Peiper* fell to the 30th Infantry Division, the 82d Airborne Division, and Combat Command B of the 3d Armored Division. An improvised defense by combat engineers, who blew the bridges Peiper needed to exit the Amblève River Valley, trapped the *kampfgruppe* on 18 December. Observation aircraft from First U.S. Army pinpointed Peiper's positions by evening.[48] General Hodges directed the commander of the 30th Infantry Division, Major General Leland Hobbs, to move his division south to engage Peiper's forces and secure the northern flank of the Bulge from Malmédy west to Stoumont. Hobbs's division was fully combat effective, since it had just finished several weeks in a narrow defensive sector that allowed the rotation of units for rehabilitation, maintenance, and small-unit training. Additionally, the division was at 97 percent of its authorized personnel strength.[49] The 82d Airborne Division also arrived on the battlefield on 19 December and established a firm blocking position to the west of Peiper's column. With the help of Combat Command B of the 3d Armored Division, the 30th Infantry Division and the 82d Airborne Division would destroy *Kampfgruppe Peiper* in the next few days.

The first task faced by the Americans was to cut Peiper's line of communication. The 1st Battalion, 117th Infantry Regiment, of the 30th Infantry Division achieved this objective by attacking and seizing the town of Stavelot on 18–19 December. Cut off from both reinforcements and supplies (especially fuel), *Kampfgruppe Peiper* could not maneuver out of the trap in which it found itself. American units closed in for the kill. Task Force Lovelady cut the German line of communication in another place near Trois Ponts, the 82d Airborne Division erased a German bridgehead over the Amblève at Cheneux, and the 119th Infantry Regiment fought a bitter battle against the spearhead of Peiper's force at Stoumont. Constricted terrain made concentration of forces difficult, but American artillery fire was enhanced by the use of new, highly secret proximity fuses, which caused shells to explode above their targets (artificially creating the dreaded "airbursts" that made artillery fire so deadly in the Huertgen Forest).[50] On the night of 23–24 December, Peiper and eight hundred of his men left their vehicles and wounded behind and withdrew from the shrinking pocket on foot. Although Peiper and his men were soon back in action with the remainder of their division, American units had effectively destroyed the 1st SS Panzer Regiment.[51]

With the main attack by the Sixth Panzer Army contained on Elsenborn Ridge in the north, the fate of the battle now rested with the Fifth Panzer Army and the American forces in the southern and western portions of the Bulge. Once the crisis in the Ardennes became apparent, American commanders wasted no time in moving reinforcements to the area. The mobility of the American army was as useful in defense as it was on offense. The Germans took two months to build up forces for the Ardennes counteroffensive; what Americans accomplished in moving divisions to stem the German advance they did in two weeks. For example, the 84th Infantry Division was fighting with the Ninth U.S. Army in Germany on 19 December; two days later it was positioned seventy-five miles away near Marche in the direct path of the German advance toward the Meuse River. Hitler and his commanders had not counted on such a swift reaction to their winter counteroffensive.

With its flanks in the air for three days, the 84th Infantry Division was an island in the midst of attacking forces from the 2d and 116th Panzer Divisions. Its orders were to hold south of the Hotton-Marche highway "at all costs."[52] This was a tall order for an infantry division extended over a twelve-mile front. The first thing Major General Alexander Bolling and the Railsplitters encountered were rumors: Germans in American uniforms and vehicles were roaming behind friendly lines, German paratroopers were in the rear, American supply dumps had been captured. The veracity of these rumors was in question, but Bolling did know two things: strong German forces had pushed the First U.S. Army line back forty miles, and the Germans were headed in his direction.

When the 84th Infantry Division arrived in the Ardennes, Bolling had little intelligence on which to base his deployment. The 84th Reconnaissance Troop and the Intelligence and Reconnaissance Platoons of the 334th and 335th Infantry Regiments deployed south to look for the enemy. Orders from XVIII Airborne Corps, under which Bolling's division operated, also sent two infantry battalion task forces on a counterreconnaissance screen ten miles to the southwest in the vicinity of Rochefort. On 23 December, as the 2d Armored Division assembled and other elements of U.S. VII Corps raced down from the north, the

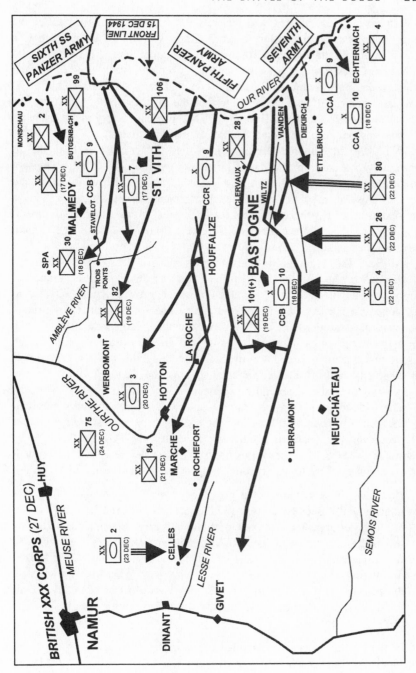

The Battle of the Bulge, December 1944

3d Battalion, 335th Infantry, and attached elements engaged the van of the Panzer Lehr Division in an effort to delay its approach to the Meuse River. This lone reinforced battalion held Rochefort for eighteen hours, long enough to enable the 2d Armored Division to prepare a counterattack near Ciney and Celles. *Generalleutnant* Fritz Bayerlein, commander of the Panzer Lehr Division, later compared both the courage and the significance of the American defense of Rochefort to that at Bastogne.[53] The American victory in the Ardennes was forged from such small-unit actions against great odds.

While the 2d Armored Division and Allied fighter-bombers dealt the 2d Panzer Division a severe blow on Christmas Day, the 84th Infantry Division fought the 116th Panzer Division near Verdenne, midway between Hotton and Marche. This was a soldier's battle, with companies and platoons enduring a semi-independent existence in a confused and dangerous situation. Temperatures hovered around zero degrees Fahrenheit, turning the earth into cement and providing an added measure of misery to the situation.

Artillery was crucial to the Railsplitters' defensive victory. The 84th Infantry Division could call on 150 guns from its own division artillery and the reinforcing guns of VII Corps. Besides fire in support of forces in direct contact, American artillery also interdicted enemy lines of communication, likely command post locations, and logistical installations. Targets identified during the day by map reconnaissance, by aerial and ground observers, and through prisoner interrogations were hit at irregular intervals throughout the long nights with time-on-target (TOT) fire. For the Germans, the nightly artillery fire was a nerve-racking and disheartening experience.[54]

The 84th Infantry Division learned—as did all American units eventually—the value of massed artillery fire. The counterattack against German forces near Verdenne was ineffective until the division used TOT fires to destroy enemy forces laagered in the woods north of the town. The effect was tremendous, as witnessed by the men from Company K, 333d Infantry Regiment:

> How long it lasted, we could only guess—probably no more than five minutes, but it seemed endless. Whole trees were tossed into the air, and the forest disappeared in clouds of white and gray smoke, ripped apart by red explosions which merged into a continuous roar. Rocks and clods of frozen earth pelted K Company's perimeter. . . . It was the heaviest, most devastating bombardment we had ever witnessed. When the fire stopped, the cries for help from wounded and dying Germans carried clearly to our lines. We admitted to ourselves that we were sorry for the poor bastards up there in the pocket.[55]

By the night of 26 December, German forces in the Ardennes were no longer attacking. They had reached their high-water mark short of the Meuse River, due in large measure to the rapid deployment of American forces into the path of the German spearhead.

While American forces in the west (the 2d, 3d, and 7th Armored Divisions and the 75th and 84th Infantry Divisions) blunted the spearhead of the German attack, Lieutenant General George S. Patton's Third U.S. Army wheeled ninety degrees to counterattack the enemy salient from the south and relieve the encircled 101st Airborne Division at Bastogne. The value of Allied air superiority and American mobility now made itself felt as the divisions of the Third Army moved north along clogged roads. "And them roads were jammed," one truck driver in the 26th Infantry Division later recalled. "Us and the Fourth Armored and God only knows how many other divisions. We were bumper to bumper all the way."[56]

The U.S. III Corps (4th Armored Division and 26th and 80th Infantry Divisions) began the counterattack on 22 December. All three divisions were combat experienced and were in quiet sectors or reserve positions when called upon to move north.[57] The 4th Armored Division conducted the main attack from Arlon north toward Bastogne, while the 26th and 80th Infantry Divisions conducted supporting attacks to clear the ground to the east of the main effort. While the 4th Armored Division ran into stubborn defenses manned by the German 5th Parachute Division, the two infantry divisions advanced unopposed until they hit the 352d Volks Grenadier Division in the flank. The Germans reacted quickly by moving the Fuehrer Grenadier Brigade and the 79th Volks Grenadier Division into the fight. In a brutal slugging match in extremely rough terrain, the 26th and 80th Infantry Divisions managed to reach the southern bank of the Sure River by 26 December, the same day that the Reserve Command of the 4th Armored Division relieved Bastogne.[58]

By 26 December the crisis in the Bulge had passed. Clear weather brought out Allied fighter-bombers in droves to pummel German motorized columns from the air. Allied commanders had massed enough combat power in the Ardennes not only to stop the German drive but also to attack German forces in the salient to regain lost ground and destroy the bulk of the enemy's mobile reserve forces. That Allied forces did not accomplish more one can attribute to the lack of creativity among the senior Allied commanders in crafting an operational design to reduce the Bulge.

Stopping the German drive was one thing; eliminating the Bulge was something altogether different. While the Third U.S. Army attacked north from Bastogne, Major General J. Lawton Collins's VII Corps attacked south toward Houffalize with the 83d and 84th Infantry Divisions and the 2d and 3d Armored Divisions. The terrain and weather placed the onus of the counterattack on the infantry. The terrain was vintage Ardennes: hilly, wooded, with a poor road network connecting isolated villages. The weather was some of the worst Europe had to offer in over half a century. Snow, sleet, and rain pelted the soldiers. Roads turned into ice rinks, and tanks and vehicles constantly slid off them to block columns. Infantry trudged to their objectives through knee-deep snow. Starting on 3 January 1945, when the counterattack began, it snowed every day for a week. Two of these snowstorms were bona fide blizzards. Temperatures hovered near zero degrees Fahrenheit.[59]

Like other outfits, the soldiers of the 84th Infantry Division faced an enormous challenge in coping with the weather. Half of the division's casualties in the Bulge were due to sickness and trench foot. To keep the division operating, it was necessary to return a substantial portion of these men to their units after a short recovery period. The division clearing station became a bottleneck, since by doctrine it was organized to move patients to the rear, not care for them in its small, twenty-five-bed recovery facility. Like other divisions, the 84th Infantry Division improvised to meet its needs. Division medical personnel commandeered a large castle in Durbuy, Belgium; filled it with cots, blankets, and equipment borrowed from the Ninth U.S. Army and Military Government sources; and trained members of the division band to administer to patients while they convalesced. The center could hold three hundred patients, 40 percent of whom were returned to duty after a short stay.[60]

The intense cold weather made living conditions brutal for the average infantryman. The cold affected everything: weapons froze and became inoperable, vehicles often failed to start, food cooked in company kitchens was cold by the time it was delivered to the front, men's resistance to disease faded. All too many senior leaders, moreover, failed to visit their soldiers at the front or understood the challenges they faced. Digging a foxhole was often impossible in soil turned hard as concrete by subzero temperatures. Sleep was elusive, which was just as well. Often the reward for getting to sleep was to awaken with frostbitten limbs. Water froze in canteens. Soldiers learned how to adapt where possible. They refrained from lubricating their weapons, for the oil would freeze the moving parts together. Units used man-made shelter (cellars were preferred) whenever possible to thaw out, eat, and rest. If outside, men kept moving to keep from freezing and to stay awake. They dressed in numerous layers of clothing.[61]

The clothing worn by GIs in the ETO during the fall and winter of 1944–1945 was unsuitable to the conditions they faced. Winter clothing developed by the U.S. Army was of adequate quality, but the specialized versions were nearly absent at the front lines. The standard GI overcoat, when caked with mud or soaked with moisture, was too heavy to wear in offensive operations. Particularly crucial was proper foot care to avoid trench foot, caused by prolonged exposure to water. Attacking units, unprotected from the elements, suffered the most, and the lack of consistent unit rotation into reserve for rest exacerbated their problems. Supply of dry socks and felt-lined rubber boots (called "shoe-pacs") received command attention, but in the end it was up to the individual soldiers and their leaders to improvise solutions to keep warm and dry. Experienced infantrymen carried an extra pair of socks close to their body to dry them out and exchanged wet socks for a dry pair at frequent intervals. Infantrymen piled on layers of standard-issue clothing to compensate for their lack of specialized winter gear. The after-action report of the 334th Infantry Regiment, 84th Infantry Division, noted ruefully on 31 January 1945, "Plans were being made to equip our front line troops with complete arctic uniforms which our

Infantrymen of the 9th Infantry Regiment, 2d Infantry Division, pass a .30-caliber machine gun position and a dead German as they advance along a road in the Monschau Forest, 3 February 1945. The shattered trees are silent witnesses to the destructive fire of the artillery that blew them apart. (U.S. Army Signal Corps photo)

experiences in recent operations indicated as being sorely needed."[62] It was an understatement, to say the least. When the frontline soldiers finally received their cold weather uniforms, the worst of the winter weather was over.

When the Battle of the Bulge began, the Seventh U.S. Army in Alsace was attacking north to penetrate German positions in the West Wall on the southern flank of Patton's Third U.S. Army. When Patton's forces wheeled ninety degrees north to counterattack toward Bastogne, Lieutenant General Alexander Patch's forces were ordered to extend their lines to the north to fill the void and assume a defensive posture. The 44th and 100th Infantry Divisions in U.S. XV Corps suddenly found themselves on the defensive, each responsible for more than ten miles of the front. These divisions were reinforced on 31 December by the newly arrived 253d and 255th Infantry Regiments, integral components of the 63d Infantry Division, which had preceded the shipment of the divisional combat support and combat service support troops to Marseilles. Although continually stripped for replacements and new to combat, these regiments gave the commanders of the 44th and 100th Infantry Divisions the luxury of placing all three of their organic infantry regiments on line while still retaining a regiment in reserve.

The counterpart to *WACHT AM RHEIN* in Alsace was Operation *NORD-WIND*, which was designed to relieve pressure on German forces attacking in the Ardennes and to destroy American forces in northern Alsace. H-hour was 2300 hours, 31 December 1944. The German plan was to attack in two groups to encircle the 100th Infantry Division near Bitche and then drive south to retake the Saverne Gap. XIII SS Corps in the west included the 17th SS Panzer Grenadier Division and the 19th and 36th Volks Grenadier Divisions. The eastern prong consisted of the LXXXIV and XC Corps, with the 256th, 257th, 361st, and 559th Volks Grenadier Divisions and the 6th SS Mountain Division, the latter an elite formation that had spent much of the war fighting Russians in northern Finland. Waiting in reserve to exploit success on either wing was the XXXIX Panzer Corps, with the 21st Panzer Division and the 25th Panzer Grenadier Division.[63]

The Germans launched Operation *NORDWIND* without benefit of an artillery preparation in order to take advantage of what German leaders felt would be a great surprise due to the secrecy of the attack plans. They only fooled themselves. Relying on accurate photo reconnaissance and ULTRA intercepts, the Seventh U.S. Army was able to issue its units an intelligence estimate on 29 December that warned of a pending enemy counteroffensive in Alsace.[64] The ongoing German attack in the Ardennes lent credence to the warning and sent defensive preparations in XV and U.S. VI Corps into high gear. The Seventh U.S. Army's intelligence estimate, in fact, was written before most German officers and soldiers below regimental level even were aware of the impending offensive.

The attack commenced on schedule on 31 December, but it achieved no surprise. The poor training and preparation of the assault troops led to their slaughter in droves. Tenacious defense by the 71st Infantry Regiment, 44th Infantry Division, and the 3d Battalion, 397th Infantry Regiment, 100th Infantry Division, completely stymied the attacks of the XIII SS Corps on the first day of battle. In the east, the 399th Infantry Regiment, 100th Infantry Division, held the advance of the 559th Volks Grenadier Division short of Lemberg, a gain of a few kilometers at high cost. To the east of the Century Division, however, the 257th Volks Grenadier Division ruptured the thinly held screen of the 117th Cavalry Squadron and pushed ten kilometers to the south, threatening to envelop the right flank of the 399th Infantry Regiment. The 361st Volks Grenadier Division likewise made good progress after muscling aside the 94th Cavalry Squadron.[65]

The XIII SS Corps continued its attack on 2 January, but commitment of regimental and division reserves by the 100th Infantry Division succeeded in holding the key terrain in the vicinity of Rimling and stopping the momentum of the enemy advance. The determined stand forced Army Group G to abandon its planned encirclement of the 100th Infantry Division and instead seek to widen and deepen the penetration made in the east. The abandonment of the supporting attack in the west enabled Major General Haislip of XV Corps and

Major General Brooks of VI Corps to focus their efforts on the German main effort. Reinforcements were quickly moved in that direction; by 4 January eight American infantry regiments had been moved into the path of the enemy forces to seal the exits from the Vosges Mountains.[66] While German volks grenadiers wore out from the strain of attacking in the mountains of the Low Vosges, American regiments moved to the sound of the guns, plugged the gap, and sealed the fate of Operation *NORDWIND*. Although the offensive ground on until the end of January, it was a dismal failure.

The battles of January 1945 validated the abilities of the divisions of the Seventh U.S. Army in the defense. The 100th Infantry Division held firm in the center of the enemy advance, withstood attacks on Rimling and Bitche, and gave no ground to the vastly superior enemy forces attacking on each of its flanks. American tactical commanders proved up to the challenge of sorting out the confusion caused by the numerous shifts of units to stem the German advance. American regiments fought well and were supported by good intelligence, unlike their counterparts in the Ardennes fighting. American corps and army commanders—Patch, Brooks, and Haislip—displayed tactical competence in shifting forces that blocked every German move with effective defensive deployments. American divisions, like their counterparts to the north in the Ardennes, proved tenacious in the defense. As in the Ardennes, too, the ultimate triumph belonged to the American soldier. "If the actions of the American generals were critical in halting *NORDWIND*," write the official U.S. Army historians, "credit for the victory in the Vosges must go to the American and French small-unit commanders and their unheralded infantrymen."[67]

The Battle of the Bulge and its counterpart in Alsace marked the last manpower crisis for the Army of the United States. Of the two infantry divisions en route to the Continent in December, SHAEF immediately sent the 75th Infantry Division to the front and would have sent the 66th Infantry Division to the Ardennes also had it not lost over eight hundred soldiers when a German submarine torpedoed the troop transport *Leopoldville* in the English Channel on Christmas Eve.[68] On 20 December SHAEF ordered two thousand privates stripped from the 42d, 63d, and 70th Infantry Divisions in the 6th Army Group for use as replacements for the Third U.S. Army.[69] The infantry regiments of these divisions had been shipped earlier from the United States without the other divisional components in order to compensate for the shortage of infantry in the ETO. On Christmas Day SHAEF stripped 25 percent of the enlisted strength from the three infantry regiments of the 69th Infantry Division (newly arrived from the United States) for use as replacements for the First and Ninth U.S. Armies.[70] These emergency measures clearly could not continue without endangering the combat effectiveness of the infantry divisions in the ETO.

General Eisenhower became extremely concerned over his lack of reserves and took steps to resolve the situation. He asked the U.S. Army chief of staff, General George C. Marshall, to send more forces to the ETO. The JCS complied by accelerating the departure of the 71st, 86th, and 97th Infantry Divi-

Two soldiers of the 142d Infantry Regiment, 36th Infantry Division, stand guard behind a machine gun near Bischwiller, France, 24 January 1945. (U.S. Army Signal Corps photo)

sions, the 13th Airborne Division, and the 16th and 20th Armored Divisions to Europe.[71] The 42d, 63d, and 70th Infantry Divisions had not yet completed their training in the United States but sent their infantry regiments to France with the remainder of the division elements to follow later. All were sent to the Seventh U.S. Army, then located in the Vosges Mountains and other parts of Alsace. The Seventh U.S. Army's front had widened considerably to relieve Third U.S. Army divisions for use near Bastogne. When the Wehrmacht launched Operation *NORDWIND*, the Seventh U.S. Army was forced to use these infantry regiments on the front, augmented with corps artillery units and odd assortments of signal and quartermaster units. The Seventh U.S. Army G-3, Brigadier General John S. Guthrie, noted, "In some cases it was a harrowing and expensive experiment. *Not recommended for future use!!!*"[72]

The ETO needed huge numbers of replacements to fill shortages, especially in infantry divisions. Marshall had earlier ordered the Zone of the Interior in the United States to strip its training installations for replacements. Eisenhower now forced COMZ in the ETO to do likewise through the creation of a U.S. Theater Manpower Section, responsible directly to the supreme Allied commander, empowered to supervise and control the conversion of support soldiers to infantrymen.[73] Up until this time, COMZ, by virtue of its dual hat as the U.S.

European theater headquarters, had been in charge of allocating manpower among the various competing entities in the ETO. No wonder the attempt to convert combat service support soldiers to infantry replacements had failed so miserably, given COMZ's vested interest in the matter. Too late, manpower issues in the ETO were consolidated under the Theater Manpower Section, which reported to Lieutenant General Ben Lear in his capacity as the deputy theater commander.

In late December 1944 the ETO ordered the use of the term "replacement" discontinued, since it denoted a sense of expendability on the part of those to whom it referred. Instead, the term "reinforcement" was substituted on the grounds that these soldiers should be considered a combat reserve.[74] The new term was apt, since individual replacements did in fact constitute the ground reserve for the combat divisions in the ETO. There were simply too few divisions available to hold large numbers out of the line for the purpose of creating a theater reserve.

The treatment of replacements also improved. In March 1945 General Joseph W. Stilwell, the new commander of AGF, proposed that replacements be grouped in squad- or platoon-size units and shipped together overseas.[75] Upon arrival at their final unit of assignment, these groupings would be broken up, but the idea was for soldiers to travel through the replacement system with others who shared a common background and experiences. The war ended before the results of this new idea could be fully evaluated, but it was a step in the right direction.

The manpower crisis brought on by the Battle of the Bulge also finally caused SHAEF to change its policy regarding "casuals" (hospital discharges). A soldier recovered from wounds usually wanted to return to the same unit with which he had previously served. Theater policy, however, was to return casuals only to units for which personnel managers had valid requisitions. Since units engaged in combat were often filled with new replacements by the time a soldier recovered from his wounds, there were not always valid requisitions on hand when casuals were ready to return to duty. This policy was based on the grounds that if the theater automatically returned casuals to their units of origin, some organizations would become overstrength while others would remain understrength. Field commanders argued vehemently against this policy, and casuals complained bitterly about their journey back to the front in another succession of replacement depots. In January 1945 SHAEF relented, finally authorizing the return of casuals back to their units of origin regardless of end strength.[76] Belatedly, field commanders had won their argument with personnel managers over the relationship among strength management, the morale of the soldier, and combat effectiveness.

Eisenhower also called for volunteers from segregated black combat service support units to fill the need for more infantrymen. The response was so great that by February 1945, 4,462 African-American soldiers had volunteered, to include many noncommissioned officers who accepted reductions in rank to do so.[77] By the end of the war, black infantry platoons served honorably and competently side by side with white soldiers in nearly fifty American infantry companies in Europe.[78] By the time the 12th Army Group had erased the bulge in its lines at the end of January 1945, the solution to the manpower crisis in Europe was not far off.

By that date, the ETO had also finally overcome its logistical crisis. The opening of Antwerp to traffic, the restoration of rail and road links in France, and the relative stability of the front line had finally allowed the COMZ to organize logistical support of the American armies on a more permanent basis. The final offensive into Germany would be sustained by "a highly complex, technical, and skilled logistical apparatus" that more than fulfilled the needs of the combat forces as they overran the ashes of the Third Reich.[79] The logistical tail of the Army of the United States sustained combat effectiveness by funneling the abundance of American industrial might into America's combat forces. One must agree with the view of the official U.S. Army historian who wrote that the final offensive into Germany was "a logistical *tour de force* by the most highly motorized and mechanized armies the world had ever known."[80]

After the American triumph in the Battle of the Bulge, final Allied victory became inevitable within a matter of months—a victory made possible in large measure by the valor and sacrifice of a relative handful of American divisions positioned as an economy-of-force measure in a supposedly "quiet" part of the Western Front in December 1944. These divisions bought the time the Allied high command needed to move reinforcements to the Ardennes to stem the German tide. The American First and Third Armies then capitalized on their strengths—massed firepower, air superiority, tactical mobility, steadfast infantry, superior tank strength, and inexhaustible logistics—to defeat German forces in the Bulge and regain lost territory. Most American divisions had not defended against a major enemy attack when the Germans launched their winter counteroffensive in the Ardennes Forest. Extremely cold and wet weather presented yet another set of obstacles to the ground combat soldier. American commanders and soldiers rose to the challenge. Actions on Elsenborn Ridge, Skyline Drive, and around Bastogne proved the ability of American commanders to coordinate a combined-arms defense, while small-unit actions across the battlefield showed the American soldier at his best when the conditions in which he fought were at their worst. American divisions had taken on the best of the Wehrmacht in appalling conditions and had emerged victorious.

10

The American Blitzkrieg

By the winter of 1945, the Army of the United States was nearing the height of its combat effectiveness. Equipment and supplies were plentiful, personnel shortages were abating, and combat experience had produced seasoned veterans by the hundreds of thousands in its combat divisions. American leaders had adjusted to the hard realities of combat. Senior commanders displayed skill both tactically and operationally in devising and executing the last major offensives of the war in Germany and Italy. The attacks that encircled the Ruhr and led Allied forces into the Po River Valley led to the destruction of hundreds of enemy divisions and the capture of hundreds of thousands of prisoners, bringing Allied forces into the very heart of the Third Reich. These campaigns led to few new innovations in tactics, techniques, and procedures, for the American army had learned its lessons well over the past months and years. The final triumph in Europe was its ultimate and well-deserved reward.

The major obstacles that stood in the path of the Allied advance into the heart of the Third Reich in February 1945 were the great barriers of the Roer and Rhine Rivers in Germany and the Apennines in northern Italy. The German forces that defended the Reich were a shell of their former selves. Although enemy factories still produced ammunition and equipment in quantity, German manpower reserves were dwindling. The Wehrmacht could neither reconstitute the mobile reserves wasted in the ill-fated Ardennes counteroffensive nor adequately sustain existing forces with replacements and fuel. What reserves there were went east to fight the advancing Red Army, which opened its winter offensive on 12 January 1945. Nevertheless, German soldiers continued to fight, held together by the remaining corps of noncommissioned officers, spurred on by ideology and ruthless discipline, and driven by the fact that they were defending their own soil.

Before the Ninth U.S. Army could cross the Roer, American forces would have to control the Urft and Schwammenauel Dams upriver. Should Allied forces cross the Roer with these dams still in enemy hands, they risked being cut off in the event that the Germans destroyed the dams, thus releasing a flood of water that would destroy the bridges used for supplies and reinforcements. These dams were the ultimate objectives during the bloody fighting in the Huertgen Forest in the fall of 1944. At the end of the Battle of the Bulge in January 1945, they were still under German control.

The mission of seizing the Schwammenauel Dam would fall to the 78th Infantry Division. Instead of attacking the dam directly through the Huertgen Forest, the division would advance along the plateau from Monschau northeast toward Schmidt, then turn south to seize the objective. The division had attacked along this same avenue from 13 to 16 December 1944, but the German counteroffensive forced a halt to operations.[1] Seven weeks later, the division resumed its attack against the same foe, the 272d Volks Grenadier Division.

The operation against the Roer dams began auspiciously when the 9th Infantry Division seized the Urft Dam intact on 4 February. The 78th Infantry Division attacked the next day and also made good progress. The 309th Infantry Regiment caught the enemy by surprise and opened a penetration in the defensive belt. Regrettably, conflicting orders of the division commander, Major General Edwin P. Parker Jr., and U.S. V Corps commander, Major General Clarence R. Huebner, caused confusion among the attacking regiments and delayed exploitation.[2] The next day the 310th Infantry Regiment entered the fight. It encountered many of the same problems of attacking in deep woods that other American units had experienced earlier in the Huertgen Forest and suffered similar consequences. On 7 February General Parker committed all three of his regiments to the attack, which made good progress. Supported by the 744th Tank Battalion, the 311th Infantry Regiment entered Schmidt, which it finally cleared of enemy the next day.[3]

Despite the progress made so far, General Hodges at the First U.S. Army was unhappy with the pace of the advance. At V Corps Huebner felt the problem might be the inexperience of the 78th Infantry Division headquarters. On 8 February he ordered Major General Louis A. Craig to move the 9th Infantry Division headquarters and two infantry regiments to Schmidt and to take control of the battle. Huebner then attached the 309th and 311th Infantry Regiments to Craig's division. The veteran staff of the 9th Infantry Division reacted quickly, and by midnight the forces were in place and prepared to continue the attack. The attack the next day made slow progress, but it reached the Schwammenauel Dam at midnight. Although the Germans did not destroy the dam, they damaged the discharge valves and thus released a steady flow of water, which forestalled an Allied offensive across the Roer River for two weeks.[4] With the objective in hand, Huebner could look on the actions of the 78th Infantry Division with more objectivity. Operating under difficult circumstances, the inexperienced division had accomplished a tough mission that had thwarted several other divisions over a period of months. Happy at last, Huebner remarked to Hodges that he had "made him another good division."[5]

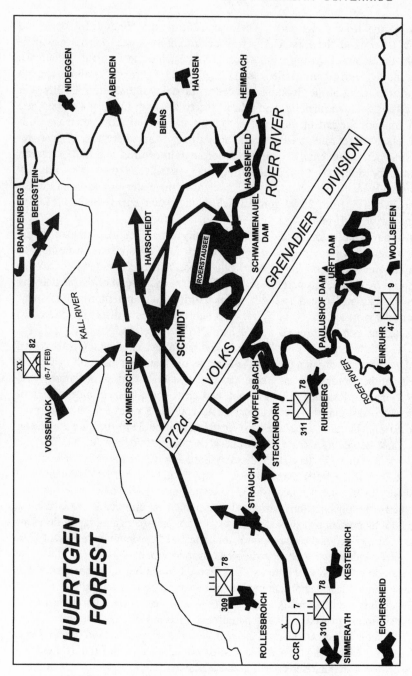

The Seizure of the Roer River Dams, 5–9 February 1944

With the Roer dams under American control, the Ninth U.S. Army and U.S. VII Corps of the First U.S. Army could finally launch Operation GRENADE, the assault crossing of the Roer River. Lieutenant General William H. Simpson, the army commander, set D-day for 23 February to allow enough time for the worst of the flooding to recede. The delay in executing GRENADE allowed for detailed planning and rehearsals. In the 84th Infantry Division, the 334th Infantry Regiment, designated to lead the assault, conducted six full-dress rehearsals at sites on the Wurm River near Marienberg and Suggerath.[6] Planning focused on engineer support, coordination of fires, and traffic control. Six infantry divisions (8th, 29th, 30th, 84th, 102d, and the 104th Infantry Divisions) were to assault across the river at night under the cover of smoke and artillery fire from 2,000 guns, which would batter enemy defenses for 45 minutes prior to H-hour.[7]

Although the crossing did not go entirely according to plan due to the rapid current and preregistered enemy artillery fire, all divisions were able to reach the far bank and carve out bridgeheads. Enemy counterattacks were broken up by small arms and massed artillery fire. By the end of the second day of the attack, bridgehead strength equaled thirty-eight battalions of infantry, supported by armor and artillery.[8] By 26 February enemy disorganization was complete and a breakthrough was at hand.

The 84th Infantry Division had the serendipity to attack along a German corps boundary. After the division crossed the Roer, its orientation to the north rather than the east further confused enemy commanders. To take advantage of the situation, Major General Alexander Bolling established Task Force Church under the command of his assistant division commander to conduct a rapid exploitation to the Rhine River. This task force consisted of the motorized 334th Infantry Regiment, 771st Tank Battalion, 326th Field Artillery Battalion, Company A(+)/637th Tank Destroyer Battalion, Battery D/557th AAA Battalion, Company B/309th Engineer Combat Battalion, 84th Reconnaissance Troop(–), and Company B/309th Medical Battalion.[9] Task Force Church was a powerful, mobile, flexible, self-contained, combined-arms organization that closely resembled an armored division combat command. Its operations exhibit the power of standard American infantry divisions in the final months of the war—power that compared favorably with that of German panzer and panzer grenadier divisions in their prime.

At 0700 hours on 27 February, Task Force Church began its advance to the Rhine. It moved fast, leaving numerous prisoners to be mopped up by the 333d and 335th Infantry Regiments trailing in its wake. Task Force Church destroyed supply columns, overran artillery battalions, smashed through the enemy rear echelon, and ushered prisoners to the rear with the wave of a hand. Krefeld was reached on 2 March, and the Rhine two days later. The 84th Infantry Division had executed a major river crossing and advanced forty-five miles in ten days, took 5,445 prisoners, and destroyed eighty-two enemy large-caliber guns, eighteen tanks and assault guns, 159 vehicles, and thirteen supply dumps.[10] During the two weeks of Operation GRENADE, the Ninth U.S. Army as a whole

Soldiers of the 16th Infantry Regiment, 1st Infantry Division, cross a footbridge over the Roer River near Kreuzau, Germany, 25 February 1945. (U.S. Army Signal Corps photo)

advanced fifty-three miles from the Roer to the Rhine, while capturing approximately 30,000 German soldiers in the process.[11] The first great river barrier had fallen.

The Rhine River was the last place the battered Wehrmacht could gain a major defensive advantage against the advancing Allied armies. While Field Marshal Bernard Montgomery's 21st Army Group planned an elaborate delib-

Field artillery observers of the 4th Infantry Division man an observation post in the Prum Valley, Germany, 3 March 1945. The combination of radio-equipped forward observers, centralized fire direction centers, and flexible gun batteries enabled the American army to mass firepower on an imposing scale in World War II. (U.S. Army Signal Corps photo)

erate attack to assault the river barrier, General Bradley ordered the 12th Army Group to launch Operation LUMBERJACK to bring the First and Third U.S. Armies to the river's edge. During the course of this operation, American forces would show their flexibility by crossing the Rhine in several places before the Germans could establish an effective defense along the eastern bank.

On 7 March 1945 troops from Combat Command B of the 9th Armored Division, under the command of William M. Hoge, seized intact the Ludendorff railway bridge over the Rhine at Remagen. Bradley and Hodges immediately decided to reinforce the 9th Armored Division, and Major General John Milliken of the U.S. III Corps sent the 9th Infantry Division and 78th Infantry Division to Remagen to hold and expand the bridgehead there.[12] The Remagen bridgehead was the supreme test for the 9th Infantry Division, the culmination of all its training and combat experiences during the war.

On 9 March the 9th Infantry Division assumed control over the entire bridgehead east of the Rhine, and for several days the division staff in effect acted as a corps headquarters to control the operations of the three divisions in the bridgehead.[13] The division G-4 became the coordinating agency for the movement of supplies across the Rhine. The G-4 traffic section controlled all movement within the bridgehead and established traffic control points on the western approaches to Remagen. The military police platoon earned a rare Distinguished Unit Citation for its actions in keeping traffic moving over the Ludendorff bridge under fire. Likewise, the 9th Signal Company earned a Distinguished Unit Citation for its efforts in keeping communications lines across the bridge intact, despite the intense enemy artillery fire and bombing that constantly cut them. The division artillery controlled all indirect fires in the area. At one point Brigadier General Reese M. Howell, the artillery commander, had seventeen battalions of artillery firing under his command. Only an experienced division staff could handle these assignments. The staff of the "Old Reliables" stood up to the test.[14]

Technical innovations helped defend the Remagen bridge from German attempts to destroy it. One such innovation was "artificial moonlight," created by bouncing searchlight beams off overhead clouds. This technique created enough ambient light to allow defending American forces to see at night. Artificial moonlight was used not just at Remagen but at many places along the front in the fall of 1944 and winter of 1945.[15] It was one more example of just how far the Army of the United States had come in its tactical and technical procedures since the first battles of the war in North Africa only two short years before.

In bitter fighting, the 9th Infantry Division attacked to expand the bridgehead to the east, while the 78th Infantry Division attacked to the north and the 99th Infantry Division and the armored infantry of the 9th Armored Division attacked to the south. In the center of the bridgehead, the 47th Infantry Regiment of the 9th Infantry Division fought one of the bloodiest actions in its history when it held off counterattacks by the 9th and 11th Panzer Divisions. The 9th Infantry Division chief of staff, Colonel William C. Westmoreland, called the 47th Infantry the "keystone in the arch" that kept the Remagen bridgehead from collapsing, words later included in the Distinguished Unit Citation awarded to the regiment for its actions.[16] Casualties again rose to the levels of Normandy and the Huertgen Forest:

> The losses of the 47th [Infantry Regiment] in the Remagen Bridgehead were appalling, and none but a veteran organization could have taken them and gone on fighting. Platoon leaders saw entire platoons annihilated in pushing up to the high, commanding ground on the east bank. Company commanders saw entire companies dissolve right before their eyes. Battalion commanders began to consider themselves lucky if they could muster one good company out of an entire battalion.
>
> After the first couple of days in this almost suicidal-type battle, the sight of an officer in a rifle company was rare, because most of them were gone.[17]

The Germans suffered more than the Americans, however, and they eventually ran out of reserves to throw into the fight. When the First U.S. Army attacked to break out of the Remagen bridgehead on 25 March, it had three corps, six infantry divisions, and three armored divisions across the Rhine River.[18]

Patton's Third U.S. Army also crossed the Rhine without elaborate attack preparations. After overrunning the Saar-Palatinate region, Patton sought to breach the Rhine in stride to maintain the momentum of his attack. The unit chosen to cross first was the 5th Infantry Division. River crossings had become something of a specialty for the Red Diamond Division; the Rhine would be its twenty-third river crossing since landing in France.[19] Division commander Major General S. LeRoy Irwin received his orders only hours before execution. If the timing caught him by surprise, the Germans were even more befuddled.

At 2230 hours on 22 March 1945, the first assault boats started across the Rhine River at Oppenheim and Nierstein. To maintain surprise, no artillery preparation heralded the assault, although thirteen artillery battalions were ready to fire on call. At Nierstein surprise was total, while at Oppenheim the 1st Battalion of the 11th Infantry Regiment overcame enemy resistance after a short, sharp fight. By midnight the entire regiment had crossed the vaunted obstacle of the Rhine at the cost of twenty casualties.[20] By the afternoon of 23 March, three infantry regiments supported by tanks and tank destroyers were across the river, and a class 40 treadway bridge had been installed.[21] The crossing was so successful that Major General Manton S. Eddy, commander of U.S. XII Corps, ordered the 4th Armored Division to cross into the bridgehead the next day. German weakness is evidenced by the fact that the only unit the enemy could muster to counterattack the bridgehead was a regiment formed from students of an officer candidate school in Wiesbaden.[22] They attacked with great élan and were destroyed with even greater firepower.

On 25 March the First and Third U.S. Armies exploded out of their bridgeheads across the Rhine, while farther south the 3d and 45th Infantry Divisions of the Seventh U.S. Army crossed the Rhine at Worms the next morning. In the north, Montgomery's 21st Army Group had crossed the Rhine a day earlier with a massive deliberate attack that easily overcame enemy resistance. Compared with the Roer River crossing, the fight for the Rhine was a walkover.

Troops of the 89th Infantry Division keep as low as possible as they cross the Rhine River near Oberwesel, Germany, 26 March 1945. (U.S. Army Signal Corps photo)

Stunned German forces could do nothing to halt the onslaught, which soon encircled over three hundred thousand enemy soldiers in the Ruhr industrial region and sent Allied forces deep into the heart of Germany to meet the advancing Red Army along the Elbe River. With a substantial logistical network in place, the advance of Allied forces across Germany was nowhere near as complicated as the pursuit across France had been.

Allied forces in Italy met with similar success in their final offensive of the war. The Fifth U.S. Army had been largely stalemated in the northern Apennines since the onset of heavy rains in the fall of 1944. In the center of the Italian peninsula, vertical escarpments and deep, narrow gorges, supplemented by ever-present minefields, enabled the enemy to defend his positions with a minimum of forces. In the Fifth U.S. Army, battle-weary and understrength divisions established winterized defensive positions that included shelters with overhead cover for forward infantry units. Rain kept artillery, tanks, and tank destroyers confined to a few trafficable roads. To renew the strength and morale of the army, divisions rotated from the front at intervals to rear areas, and individual soldiers were sent for brief periods to rest centers located in major cities such as Rome and Florence.

In the winter of 1945, the Fifth U.S. Army received new divisions and replacements, which gave it roughly a two-to-one superiority over the German forces to its front.[23] By the start of the spring offensive on 9 April, Lieutenant General Lucian Truscott's forces consisted of the 34th, 85th, 88th, 91st, and 92d U.S. Infantry Divisions, the U.S. 10th Mountain Division, the U.S. 1st Armored Division, the 6th South African Armoured Division, and the Brazilian Expeditionary Force. In April 1945 these forces would decisively rupture the German line in Italy and pursue retreating enemy forces through the Po River Valley to the Alps.

By this point in the war in Italy, technical improvements to air-ground coordination made by the XXII Tactical Air Command supporting the Fifth U.S. Army had finally made close air support "close enough." Flights of fighter-bombers ("Rover Joe" and "Rover Pete" missions) would circle the battlefield. Ground observers used SCR-193 VHF radios to coordinate with an L-5 Piper Cub overhead, which then talked the fighter-bombers onto target.[24] Airpower also assisted divisions by suppressing enemy artillery and mortar fire. Often the mere appearance of a small, unarmed liaison plane overhead would force German gunners to cease fire for fear of detection, which would inevitably lead to counterfire on their positions. When Rover Joe was unavailable, artillery concentrations using the new VT fuse, which created deadly airbursts of high explosive and shrapnel, were available on call. During the first week of Operation CRAFTSMAN, the Fifth U.S. Army spring offensive, Allied planes would fly 11,902 sorties in support of the Fifth U.S. and British Eighth Armies, the greatest aerial effort for any week of the entire 602-day Italian campaign.[25]

The Fifth U.S. Army's final offensive of the war began on 14 April. Massed firepower of heavy bombers, fighter-bombers, and a thirty-five-minute preparation by over two thousand artillery pieces preceded the attack by the 10th Mountain Division, the spearhead of Major General Willis D. Crittenberger's U.S. IV Corps.[26] The mountaineers attacked from their positions on Monte Della Spe at 0945 hours. Attacks by the 85th and 87th Mountain Infantry Regiments gained some ground, but the enemy defense took its toll on the attackers. Artillery concentrations and mines slowed the advance and prevented tanks and tank destroyers from accompanying the lead units. The next day the 87th Mountain Infantry Regiment took to the ridges to infiltrate past the heavily defended enemy positions on the valley floor. The positions of the German 94th Infantry Division, understrength to begin with, began to crumble. On 16 April the 87th Mountain Infantry completed the breakthrough of enemy positions by seizing Monte Croce against strong resistance, while the 86th Mountain Infantry Regiment seized the hills in the vicinity of Monte Monosco. The Brazilian Expeditionary Force on the left and the 1st Armored Division on the right kept pace with the mountaineers. The lack of enemy counterattacks signaled their disorganization.[27]

To the east of IV Corps, the U.S. II Corps attack on 15 April met with stiff resistance along Highway 65, the direct and therefore most heavily defended route to Bologna. Progress was slow and costly, but by the third day of the attack the German defenses astride Highway 65 began to waver. Truscott, sensing that a breakthrough was imminent, shifted II Corps west to take advantage of the progress created by the 10th Mountain Division.[28]

Major General Geoffrey Keyes moved the 88th Infantry Division to the western flank of his corps. The 1st Armored Division moved behind the 10th Mountain Division to assume a zone on its western flank. Truscott released the 85th Infantry Division from the Fifth U.S. Army reserve to join IV Corps. Crittenberger placed the 85th Infantry Division on the eastern flank of the 10th Mountain Division adjacent to the 88th Infantry Division. With this shuffling of forces complete, the Fifth U.S. Army began the exploitation of its breakthrough, which by 19 April had carried it to the edge of the Po River Valley.[29]

The next day IV Corps exploded into the Lombard Plain, followed soon thereafter by II Corps. The enemy withdrawal turned into a rout. The Germans attempted to stem the tide by throwing in the 90th Panzer Grenadier Division on the western flank, but the 1st Armored Division easily fended off its blows. Infantrymen and mountaineers hitched rides aboard tanks and tank destroyers to pursue the fleeing enemy. On 21 April a battalion of soldiers from the 133d Infantry Regiment, 34th Infantry Division, riding aboard the tanks of the 752d Tank Battalion, entered Bologna. Other units collected an odd assortment of organic and captured transportation to shuttle troops forward. On 23 April the 10th Mountain Division conducted an assault crossing over the Po River, the first time the division had attempted a river crossing either in training or in combat.[30] By noon the next day, all three mountain infantry regiments were across the river, and the engineers began construction of a treadway and a pontoon bridge.

The pursuit north began on 25 April, spearheaded by Task Force Darby of the 10th Mountain Division. The remainder of the 10th Mountain Division moved behind Task Force Darby to clear out pockets of resistance. Task Force Darby advanced rapidly, moving past Verona on the morning of 26 April and then attacking up the eastern shore of Lake Garda toward the Brenner Pass.[31] The 85th and 88th Infantry Divisions attacked toward Verona, troops of the latter division clearing the city on the evening of 25 April. The 88th and 91st Infantry Divisions, with the 6th South African Armoured Division screening their right flank, then forced a crossing over the Adige River and sped on toward Vicenza and Treviso in northeast Italy abreast of the British Eighth Army, while the 1st Armored Division, 34th Infantry Division, and Brazilian Expeditionary Force mopped up resistance in northwest Italy. Major General Ned Almond's 92d Infantry Division seized Genoa on 29 April. Nearly a hundred thousand prisoners graced Fifth U.S. Army POW cages.[32] On 2 May enemy resistance in Italy ended with the unconditional surrender of German forces there, an appropriate conclusion to a victory won decisively in the previous three weeks by Allied forces on the battlefield.

Crushed by the superiority of Allied power, the Third Reich succumbed to the inevitable on 8 May 1945. Only eleven months had elapsed since the great invasion of Normandy, but in that short space of time the Army of the United

States had matured into a veteran military organization. The final offensive that swept Allied forces into the heart of Germany produced few new insights in American doctrine, tactics, techniques, and procedures; what the campaign did display was the ultimate effectiveness of the American fighting machine in its prime. Indeed, American divisions displayed a great capacity to learn from their early mistakes and an enormous resilience that kept them combat effective despite the sacrifices they endured. In the spring of 1945, the Army of the United States reached the zenith of its power and effectiveness as it helped to destroy the last remnants of the once-vaunted Wehrmacht, a fitting tribute to the vision of General George C. Marshall and the other senior leaders who had worked to realize it. America's army had come of age.

11

The Combat Effectiveness of Infantry Divisions in the Army of the United States

Given the resource and time constraints under which it operated, the Army of the United States did a credible job in developing the large number of combat formations required to fight a global war. The most important limitation by far was time. The United States—the last major combatant to enter World War II— began at a relatively low level of mobilization and readiness. Production of equipment for lend-lease competed with the needs of combat divisions and air groups. Construction of training facilities took place simultaneously with the activation of numerous new military formations. Personnel needs of the services competed with each other and with the needs of war industries. As a result of this turmoil, new divisions took a longer time to organize and train than was called for by the Mobilization Training Plan, and the army eventually had to scale back the number of divisions it activated to eighty-nine. Despite these drawbacks, the process of creating new divisions was sound. When the system worked properly, divisions were able to progress through their training relatively unmolested by personnel turbulence, received adequate time to train small units at their home stations, and then deployed to take part in army-level maneuvers or in the excellent program established at the Desert Training Center in the Arizona-California Maneuver Area. When the mobilization plan fell short of its stated goals, the problem usually rested in constant personnel turnover as the War Department called upon divisions in training to provide large numbers of replacement soldiers, officer candidate and air cadet drafts, and cadres to form new units.

Army Ground Forces under Lieutenant General Lesley J. McNair attempted to create each combat division from the same "mold" to ensure that they were equally combat effective. In an attempt to economize manpower, however, General McNair centralized many assets—such as independent tank and tank destroyer battalions—at army level under the assumption that every division did not need these assets all the time. What General McNair failed to see was the need for the combat division to be as self-contained as possible to foster the teamwork and cohesiveness necessary for successful functioning on the battle-field. The results of this centralization were inadequate numbers of tank battal-ions to support infantry divisions and a bloated, centralized supply system that lacked the flexibility the combat divisions required of their own organic logis-tical organizations. American infantry divisions successfully improvised to meet the demands of the battlefield with the organic and attached assets at their disposal, although often these assets were less robust than division commanders felt they needed. After the war, army leaders recognized the shortfall in divi-sional assets by making tank battalions an organic part of the infantry division structure.

On the whole, AGF succeeded in developing divisions that could attain a high degree of effectiveness after their initial battles, but few divisions were fully effective upon their entry into combat. Nor were all divisions created equal; some were clearly more combat effective than others. These differences were a function primarily of the leadership exercised by the division com-mander and combat experience, but experience alone could not make a division effective. The 90th Infantry Division had plenty of experience in Normandy by the end of July 1944, but only after Major General Raymond McLain took command did it finally become a combat-effective organization. Too much combat could also lower the effectiveness of divisions by creating large-scale losses and demoralization.

The combat divisions of the Army of the United States were not static organizations. Divisions changed over time as leaders changed, casualties left and replacements arrived, combat taught new lessons, and units trained to new standards. The experience of the 9th Infantry Division illustrates this point. The division arrived in North Africa as an untested organization and showed its weaknesses in its first battles. Under Major General Manton Eddy's leadership, the division learned from its mistakes and became a veteran outfit. The division reached a peak of effectiveness during the campaign in the Cotentin Peninsula, before the huge losses of the hedgerow fighting and the Huertgen Forest de-pleted its ranks. After integrating replacements in November 1944, the division spent three months on relatively quiet sectors of the front, which kept losses low. By the time it underwent its next crisis at the Remagen bridge, the division was once again at a peak of effectiveness.

The cyclical nature of combat effectiveness in the 9th Infantry Division was common to most of the divisions that fought in Europe. Without a system of unit rotation, divisions spent too much time in combat. The primary problem was the lack of divisions, which forced commanders to keep units in the line long after they should have been withdrawn and reconstituted. Instead, theater commanders funneled hundreds of thousands of individual replacements to divisions in contact with the enemy to keep them operating. Commanders la-bored mightily to integrate these soldiers into their units before they became casualties, with mixed results. The dips in combat effectiveness were unavoidable, and the cost of the system of individual replacements was high. Between June 1944 and May 1945, the 9th Infantry Division sustained over thirty-three thousand battle and nonbattle casualties, nearly two and one-half times the division's authorized strength.[1] Many of these casualties returned to the division after a stay in the hospital; many did not. The soldiers of the 9th Infantry Division earned their place in the Great Crusade through a great deal of effort and an enormous expenditure of blood.

Not all branches suffered equally on the battlefield. One of the reasons American artillery units were so effective was that they took very few casualties (except for their forward observers). By the end of the war, therefore, artillery battalions that had been together for several months or years were extremely proficient. The same holds true for most combat support and combat service support units. Staff work also improved as officers learned the business of coordinating operations. No matter how good planning was, however, the plans had to be executed by the combat soldiers at the front. More often than not, these soldiers were far less experienced than the soldiers who supported them.

A closer look at some statistics on combat usage and casualties shows why replacements were so crucial to the success of American infantry divisions in World War II. Between 8 November 1942 and 8 May 1945, the 1st Infantry Division spent 442 days in combat. During the campaigns in North Africa and Sicily, this combat was punctuated by periods of rest and training. Additionally, the division received a long period of rest and training in Great Britain prior to the Normandy invasion. Between D-Day and V-E Day, the division spent 317 days in combat with almost no rest. Nearly every month the Big Red One sustained 2,000 to 3,000 battle and nonbattle casualties; in November 1944 the casualty totals exceeded 5,500 men.[2] During the campaign for France and Germany, the 1st Infantry Division sustained 29,630 battle and nonbattle casualties, yet it ended the war at nearly full strength. Other divisions endured similar fates; Table 11.1 details the losses sustained by American infantry divisions in France and Germany in 1944–1945. Clearly, once an infantry division of the Army of the United States entered combat in Europe and sustained losses, it could never maintain a high level of combat effectiveness unless it integrated its replacements in a suitable manner.

Most of these replacements, regardless of their initial training, went to infantry regiments. A look at the casualties in a typical infantry division shows why this was so. Of the 22,858 battle casualties suffered by the 9th Infantry Division in World War II, over 96 percent were sustained by the three infantry regiments.[3] Army Ground Forces was not initially prepared to replace losses to infantry regiments on this scale. Until early 1944, the replacement training centers geared the rate at which they produced soldiers with different skills to the needs of mobilization, not losses in combat. Since losses overwhelmingly involved combat soldiers, the result of this system was an oversupply of technical specialists and an undersupply of infantrymen. By late 1943 the lack of

Table 11.1   Total Battle and Nonbattle Casualties, Infantry Divisions, 1944–1945

Division	Casualties	% Loss	Division	Casualties	% Loss
4th ID	35,545	252%	100th ID	12,215	87%
9th ID	33,864	240%	99th ID	11,987	85%
1st ID	29,630	206%	87th ID	11,587	82%
29th ID	28,776	204%	94th ID	10,810	77%
3d ID	28,400	202%	106th ID	10,671	76%
90th ID	27,617	196%	95th ID	10,204	72%
45th ID	26,449	188%	84th ID	9,811	70%
36th ID	26,157	186%	103d ID	9,369	67%
30th ID	26,038	185%	102d ID	8,825	63%
2d ID	25,884	184%	70th ID	8,201	58%
35th ID	25,488	181%	63d ID	8,019	57%
80th ID	25,472	181%	75th ID	8,016	57%
28th ID	24,840	176%	42d ID	5,949	42%
83d ID	23,980	170%	76th ID	5,556	39%
5th ID	23,487	167%	69th ID	3,347	24%
79th ID	23,457	167%	65th ID	2,302	16%
8th ID	21,056	149%	89th ID	2,080	15%
26th ID	16,851	120%	66th ID	1,947	14%
44th ID	13,748	98%	71st ID	1,869	13%
104th ID	13,407	95%	97th ID	1,318	9%
78th ID	12,257	87%	86th ID	1,282	9%

Source: *Order of Battle, United States Army in World War II: European Theater of Operations* (Office of the Theater Historian, December 1945).

infantry replacements created a crisis overseas, which the AGF temporarily solved by stripping 35,249 men from combat divisions still training in the United States.[4] This action disrupted the divisions in training. The situation got worse before it got better. Between April and September 1944, the War Department stripped 91,747 men from twenty-two combat divisions still in the United States, an average of 4,170 men per division (or nearly two-thirds of the infantry in each division).[5]

After the pursuit across France ended in the fall of 1944, casualties rose, and the American army groups soon used up the available pool of in-theater replacements. Eisenhower's staff pleaded with the War Department to increase the rate of infantry replacements. The War Department responded by culling men from the Zone of the Interior in the United States, eliminating the ban on the use of eighteen-year-old soldiers in combat, and urging the ETO to cull personnel from its COMZ for retraining as infantrymen. The ETO also converted some antiaircraft artillery units to infantry as the need for antiaircraft defense dwindled.[6]

The replacement system slowly adjusted to the need to produce more infantrymen (Table 11.2). As the war progressed, the authorized percentage of infantry replacement capacity in replacement training centers rose from 46 percent in October 1940 to a high of 86.7 percent in January 1945. The figures for replacement capacity by the latter date took into account the results of combat experience in Europe and were a rough indication of how casualties were distributed among the various arms during the war.

Although replacement soldiers were treated poorly by the system through which they traveled to their final destination, divisions adopted various expedients to integrate them more smoothly. As discussed earlier, some divisions formed training centers to indoctrinate and train replacements, rehabilitate combat exhaustion cases, and train junior officers and noncommissioned officers before they assumed leadership positions. By treating soldiers arriving in the division fairly and with respect, the division training center went a long way to ensuring that replacements would integrate smoothly into their new units. Not all divisions formed training centers at division level, but over time most learned to integrate replacements into units while they were in reserve positions and not at the front.

In *Eisenhower's Lieutenants,* historian Russell Weigley contends that American infantry divisions in World War II were victims of the heritage of the U.S. Army.[7] Torn between the mobility of the frontier army and the power of the large divisions sent to France in World War I, the Army of the United States in World War II formed divisions with too little staying power for the battles of attrition in France and Germany in 1944 and 1945.

Weigley's argument is attractive but superficial. American infantry divisions in World War II routinely operated with numerous attachments in combat—to include artillery, tank, tank destroyer, engineer, and antiaircraft units—which gave them much greater power than one would surmise from a look at their tables of organization. Additionally, the conversion to the triangular infantry division did not cause the replacement problems overseas in World War II. In his comments on the 1940 maneuvers, General McNair stated:

> Both square and triangular divisions embody a high degree of strategic and tactical mobility; great fire power; and when employed properly, adequate ability to sustain combat. The triangular division has the advantage of being controlled and maneuvered more easily than the square division. The impression that the triangular division is weak is erroneous. While the triangular division is the smaller, a given man power permits correspondingly more triangular divisions than square divisions. Thus a given front

Table 11.2   Percentage Trainee Capacity of Replacement Training Centers, 1940–1945

Date	AAA	ARMOR	CAV	FA	INF	TD	Immaterial
OCT 40	21.1	6.4	4.9	21.6	46.0	—	—
AUG 42	16.0	9.6	2.1	14.6	37.5	7.0	13.2
SEP 43	8.6	6.1	2.3	11.9	67.4	3.7	—
FEB 44	6.6	4.6	2.5	9.6	74.2	2.5	—
AUG 44	5.5	4.9	2.4	9.0	76.1	2.1	—
OCT 44	2.5	6.3	3.1	6.8	80.0	1.3	—
JAN 45	1.0	5.1	2.1	4.3	86.7	.8	—

Source: William R. Keast, Robert R. Palmer, and Bell I. Wiley, *The Procurement and Training of Ground Combat Troops* (Washington, D.C.: Office of the Chief of Military History, 1948), 172.

can be held equally strongly by both types with the same total number of men. Fewer square divisions, each occupying a larger front, give the same strength as more triangular divisions, each occupying a smaller front.[8]

Weigley's argument would only hold true had the army substituted square for triangular divisions on a one-for-one basis. The extra infantry strength of the square division would then have allowed an internal unit replacement system at the division level.

A smaller number of square divisions in France in 1944, however, would have forced commanders to employ all four infantry regiments on the front line. In a conference held in June 1945 with representatives from U.S. VII, VIII, and XIX Corps and the 30th, 69th, 76th, 78th, 87th, and 102d Infantry Divisions, Colonel Gilbert E. Parker of AGF inquired regarding the advisability of adding a fourth infantry regiment to the triangular division to allow rotation of regiments to rest areas. The VIII Corps G-3 believed the idea was a good one provided the old brigade structure was not also revived. All other officers responded negatively to the idea. Although they considered the goal of rotating units in combat an admirable one, "they would not take the idea seriously because they were unanimous in the belief that higher commanders would be unable to resist the temptation to use the extra regiment tactically instead of restricting it to its intended role."[9] Given the constraints of the ninety-division gamble, the Army of the United States simply lacked enough divisions in 1944 and 1945 to operate a unit replacement system in Europe. Individual replacements were the only other recourse.

Many historians have criticized the manner in which the Army of the United States integrated its replacements during World War II. Stephen Ambrose, one of the great champions of the American army in Europe, goes so far as to write, "Had the Germans been given a free hand to devise a replacement system for ETO, one that would do the Americans the most harm and least good, they could not have done a better job."[10] On a strictly human level these arguments have merit, but they ignore the learning process that occurred at the division level as the war progressed. Initially, divisions treated replacements poorly and paid the price. As time went on, however, most divisions came to realize that they had to treat incoming replacements well and ensure their smooth integration into combat units behind the front. Failure to do so meant an increase in casualties and a drop in combat effectiveness, for once engaged in combat, divisions were only as good as the replacements they received to keep them up to strength. The alternative was to leave units in the line without giving them replacements, as the Wehrmacht did. The Germans often withdrew units from combat only when they took so many losses that they required complete rebuilding. One wonders whether this policy was any more humane than that employed by the American army in the ETO.

The German penchant for employing numerous *kampfgruppen*, small units formed from the fragments of divisions or regiments that had once been at full strength, was a vastly inferior method to the American system of keeping every combat division effective through the infusion of individual replacements. Not only did the American replacement system function better in maintaining divisions at an adequate strength level; the uniform organization of American units was superior to the numerous ad hoc organizations employed by Germany as the war progressed. The employment of *kampfgruppen* as an emergency measure may be a justified necessity, but one should not view crisis management of combat forces as a superior method to the careful administration of individual replacements on a continual basis.

The United States was the only nation able to maintain its fighting forces near full strength throughout the war, a fact that greatly impressed German commanders. The individual replacement system had its flaws, but these flaws stemmed from poor administration of the system rather than an inherent flaw in the concept. Given the determination to limit the number of divisions mobilized, the decision to keep them at full strength through the infusion of individual replacements was the correct one. The task for division commanders was to take these replacements and integrate them in such a manner as to maintain the combat effectiveness of their organizations. By doing so, American commanders were able to maintain the combat effectiveness of their organizations even as the Wehrmacht slowly disintegrated.

While American divisions had a uniform organization and a baseline level of proficiency, the same was not true of the German army. The polyglot collection of units the Wehrmacht fielded in 1944 consisted of more than a dozen types of divisions with widely varying organizational structures and degrees of effectiveness. Constant reshuffling of units among corps, armies, and army groups led to confusion and diminished command and control. Other than the handful of airborne divisions and the one mountain division formed by the Army of the United States, American divisions fell into one of two categories—infantry and armored—with consistent tables of organization and equipment. Unlike their German counterparts, American corps, army, and army group commanders basically knew what to expect from the divisions under their command. The Army of the United States fielded robust, balanced, and capable divisions that proved highly effective in combat after their initial encounters.

Few American commanders of the World War II era would agree with authors such as Martin van Creveld that the German army was more effective. While the cream of the Wehrmacht, the panzer and panzer grenadier divisions, were combat-effective organizations and a match for the divisions of the Army of the United States, the bulk of the German army was not composed of these units. The average German infantry division could not defeat an American infantry division in battle, while American infantry divisions consistently proved their ability to accomplish their missions against the enemy divisions to their front. In terms of mechanization and their ability to conduct mobile warfare, American infantry divisions were in a class by themselves. Nor could the German army consistently sustain its fighting power. The Wehrmacht could field superb formations equipped with technologically advanced weapons, but its failure to provide adequate means for support and sustainment led to their undoing. Historians may criticize the American emphasis on logistics, but that emphasis helped lead the Army of the United States to victory in Europe.

The experience of senior American commanders was also an important element in the development of combat effectiveness in the Army of the United States. The American army mobilized in a very short time and lacked combat experience. Senior American leaders lacked experience in commanding large formations due to the scarcity of resources in the interwar army. They had learned their profession mostly through intensive study in the army's professional school system. How they would perform in battle was anybody's guess.

Russell Weigley claims that the "unimaginative caution" of competent but inexperienced American generals resulted in a battle of attrition when a bolder use of resources could have shortened the war.[11] More recently, Michael Doubler has modified this claim by stating that "American commanders were adept at operational maneuver and in concentrating firepower."[12] The latter assertion by Doubler is valid; his former assertion is questionable. In the campaigns in North Africa and Europe, American commanders performed much better tactically than they did operationally. This study has shown that at the division level, American commanders learned how to use both maneuver and firepower to defeat enemy forces and seize terrain. Above the corps level, however, American commanders often lacked a clear concept of operations. Lieutenant General Mark Clark's failure to allow Major General Lucian Truscott's VI Corps to block the Valmontone Gap during the breakout from the Anzio beachhead in May 1944, Lieutenant General Omar Bradley's failure to close the Falaise Gap in August 1944, and the failure of Lieutenant General Courtney Hodges to find a way around the Huertgen Forest in October 1944 are but three examples of the lack of expertise shown by senior American commanders in executing operational maneuver during the course of the war. With experience, the operational abilities of senior leaders improved. In the final battles to encircle the Ruhr Basin and exploit into the Po River Valley, senior American leaders displayed operational excellence. This speaks highly of their ability to learn from past mistakes.

At the division level, American commanders displayed the ability to learn from their experiences and change tactics and techniques, sometimes even in the midst of combat, such as during the bitter fighting in the hedgerows during the Normandy campaign. Without a doubt, one of the strong suits of the Army of the United States in World War II was its ability to improvise solutions to tactical problems on the battlefield.[13] American infantry divisions adapted to combat in a variety of environments and innovated extensively to get their missions accomplished. American commanders learned how to combine the efforts of the various arms and services to defeat the enemy and accomplish their missions. These efforts to learn and adapt usually took place at the division level. Commanders at the regimental level and below had to focus their efforts on the current battle; commanders at the corps level and above were too far removed from combat to develop new operating methods. In the Army of the United States in World War II, uniform and widespread changes in tactics, techniques, and procedures were usually instituted at the division level.

One enormous advantage that American divisions had in combat was their vastly superior fire support, made possible by the advances in fire support coordination and technique during the interwar period. American artillery was the best in the world by the time the army entered into combat overseas. Tooled with new, more powerful, more mobile weapons, and directed through a combination of radio-equipped forward observers and fire direction centers, American artillery had the ability to mass fire on the enemy that impressed both friend and foe alike. Was the Army of the United States too firepower oriented in World War II? Perhaps. This emphasis on firepower, however, took advantage of the strongest arm in the army and largely negated the superior ability of German units to maneuver at the small-unit level. Most American commanders, however, eventually learned that they must strike a balance between maneuver and firepower or risk failure in combat.

In *Men against Fire,* a groundbreaking study of command and control in World War II published in 1947, S. L. A. Marshall asserted that American infantrymen often displayed a lack of ability to maneuver under fire.[14] *Men against Fire* shattered many commonly held beliefs about the motivations and actions of soldiers on the field of battle. Marshall contended that fewer than 25 percent of infantrymen fired their weapons in any given battle; therefore, a special few carried the combat burden for the majority of units. He also stated that men in combat are motivated out of fear of letting their comrades down in battle, rather than by abstract notions of patriotism or freedom. The primary problem of American commanders in World War II was to get their men to advance under fire (thus the title of the book). Good maneuver alone could not solve the problem; American units had to gain fire superiority over their adversaries before they could dominate the battlefield. Many factors contributed to the problem of men against fire: combat isolation, poor use of weapons in combat, unrealistic training, inadequate communications, and the lack of recognition of small-unit cohesion as a necessary component of combat effectiveness.

Marshall believed that fewer than 25 percent of riflemen fired their weapons in any given battle, even though the situation should have allowed at least 80 percent to do so.[15] Members of crew-served weapons did not have the same problem. They routinely fired their weapons, as did soldiers who were armed with automatic weapons.[16] The ratio of firers to nonfirers did not change with the terrain, the tactical situation, the nature of the enemy, or the amount of combat experience.[17] A few men (the "killers") did most of the firing for the unit in combat. Marshall stated that routine marksmanship training did not do enough to instill in soldiers the need to use their weapons against the enemy in combat.[18]

Marshall believed that many American commanders did not understand the use of fire in battle. Maneuver alone is not sufficient to achieve victory. "The essence of success in tactics comes of what you do with fire after you get there. In his realistic restatement of Forrest's principle, Major General Charles W. O'Daniel put it this way: 'In battle, it is a matter of getting there first, regardless, and then having the ability to stay put.' "[19] To S. L. A. Marshall, the modern battlefield necessitated the movement of fire to overwhelm the enemy in combat. If American riflemen would not fire their weapons in combat, American infantry units could not establish fire superiority over their enemy. Part of the problem, Marshall believed, stemmed from American culture, which taught American soldiers to believe that aggression and killing are bad.[20]

Why, then, did American soldiers fight? Marshall believed that men remained in combat due to the presence of their comrades. Soldiers do not want to appear as cowards to their peers.[21] Patriotism and moral ideas cannot sustain the soldier in combat. Small-unit cohesion is therefore key to combat effectiveness. "In battle," Marshall states, "you may draw a small circle around a soldier, including within it only those persons and objects which he sees or which he believes will influence his immediate fortunes. These primarily will determine whether he rallies or fails, advances or falls back."[22]

Marshall's emphasis on small-unit cohesion as the key to battle was an important part of his thesis. His goal was to change the individual replacement system, which he felt worked so poorly in the Army of the United States in World War II. The War Department had not taken small-unit cohesion into account when designing replacement policies. Marshall decried the result:

> While giving lip service to the humanitarian values and while making occasional spectacular and extravagant gestures of sentimentality, those whose task it was to shape personnel policy have tended to deal with man power as if it were motor lubricants or sacks of potatoes.... They have moved men around as if they were pegs and nothing counted but a specialist classification number. They have become fillers-of-holes rather than architects of the human spirit.[23]

Through his writings, Marshall aimed to force the army to recognize the value of the human spirit on the modern battlefield.

Marshall wanted his readers to know that men, not machines, ensured Allied victory in World War II. Though Americans believe that war is best fought with machines in order to conserve the lives of its soldiers, there are limits to the ability of technology to replace soldiers in combat. The industrial productivity of the United States made Allied victory possible, but did not ensure it. Marshall reiterated this point when he wrote that

> The great victories of the United States have pivoted on the acts of courage and intelligence of a very few individuals.... Victory is never achieved prior to that point; it can be won only after the battle has been delivered into the hands of men who move in imminent danger of death. I think that

we in the United States need to consider well that point, for we have made a habit of believing that national security lies at the end of a production line.[24]

Unfortunately, future generations of army officers and historians would latch onto Marshall's contention that most American riflemen did not fire their weapons in combat as the most important part of his book. As the army worked to increase the "fire ratio" and historians cited Marshall's "evidence" of the lack of aggressiveness of American infantry in combat, other tenets of Marshall's work—small-unit cohesion and the importance of the soldier on the battle-field—were minimized or forgotten.

Until the mid-1980s, historians took Marshall's word for his statistics. Influential works of military history, to include John Keegan's *Face of Battle,* Russell Weigley's *Eisenhower's Lieutenants,* and Max Hastings's *Overlord,* quoted Marshall's statistics as historical truth.[25] In the past decade, however, several writers and historians have examined Marshall's evidence and found it wanting. The first assault came from Harold P. Leinbaugh and John D. Campbell, who coauthored *The Men of Company K.*[26] Leinbaugh and Campbell examined the experience of their infantry company in World War II, part of the 333d Infantry Regiment, 84th Infantry Division, and discovered no basis for Marshall's claims. Furthermore, they believed that their experience was not significantly different from that of the other twelve hundred or so rifle companies that fought in Europe.[27] Leinbaugh checked into Marshall's other writings and found more inconsistencies, to include the fact that Marshall lied about his own experience in the 90th Division during World War I.[28] Was it possible that Marshall had also fabricated his statistics?

Marshall claimed that the data he used to write *Men against Fire* came from over four hundred company-level after-action interviews, a technique he pioneered while assigned as a theater historian in the Pacific in 1943. Yet when Roger J. Spiller, deputy director of the Combat Studies Institute at the U.S. Army Command and General Staff College at Fort Leavenworth, sought out Marshall's evidence, he found none. John Westover, Marshall's assistant in Europe, does not recall Marshall ever asking about "fire ratios" in his interviews or discussing the issue in conversation. Marshall's own surviving papers and notebooks bear no evidence that he was collecting statistics. Spiller concludes, "The 'systematic collection of data' that made Marshall's ratio of fire so authoritative appears to have been an invention."[29]

The records of the theater historian, ETO, located in the National Archives, bear no traces of Marshall's quest for firing ratio statistics in Europe. Nor can one locate any material on the subject in the S. L. A. Marshall Military History Collection located at the University of Texas at El Paso. This lack of data is not surprising when one considers that infantry companies in Europe spent most of their time either in the line or preparing to return to the line. Combat in Europe did not facilitate the lengthy group interview methods that Marshall had used so effectively on Makin Island in the Pacific.[30] Even if Marshall had inter-viewed one company every day from D-Day to V-E Day (which, given his other duties as deputy theater historian, is a doubtful proposition), he would have reached only 330 to 340 companies.

No other theater historian has written or spoken of helping Marshall with his quest for statistics. Quite to the contrary, at least one army historian firmly rejected Marshall's emphasis on the company as the primary level for historical interviews. In a memo written to Marshall on 9 December 1944, Major Hugh M. Cole (the Third U.S. Army historian and later one of the principal architects of the U.S. Army history of World War II) described the difficulties his team was having in interviewing units, since most were employed constantly on the front line. The report goes on to state Cole's belief that the most appropriate level for historical coverage is at the RCT or Combat Command level, with some participation by battalion commanders, battalion staff, and company and platoon leaders. "I do not believe it is possible to go lower than that and trace the activities of the individual soldier or his squad unless we are prepared to accept a hit and miss story of the Third Army," Major Cole wrote.[31] Yet if Cole's team did not go lower than platoon leader level, there is no way they could have determined the percentage of soldiers who fired their rifles in a given engagement. Sadly, one must agree with the conclusion of one of Mar-shall's critics: "It is strange that a reputation he [Marshall] would come to deserve was founded on his most irresponsible work."[32]

Men against Fire was authoritative because it offered hard statistics in place of anecdotal observations. Marshall's critics have attacked his evidence, but what about the argument? Even if Marshall fabricated his statistics, he must have had some intuitive basis for his observations. Marshall's training was as a journalist, not as a historian.[33] Marshall the reporter might have sensed some-thing about infantry combat in Europe that he could not prove empirically. The question the historian must try to answer, then, is whether Marshall's intuition was correct.

In a questionnaire sent to several hundred West Point graduates who served in Europe between 1942 and 1945, officers were asked the following question:

> In his book *Men against Fire,* historian S. L. A. Marshall contends that American riflemen had difficulty engaging the enemy in combat; indeed, that fewer than 25 percent of them fired their weapons at the enemy in any given battle, even when offered the opportunity to do so. Despite the fact that Marshall's evidence has been attacked in recent years, do you agree with Marshall's contention? If so, what caused this problem? If not, why not?

Of the 144 officers who expressed an opinion, 36 agreed with Marshall, 24 partly agreed, and 84 disagreed. Yet when one analyzes the written responses, many similarities emerge among both those who agree and those who disagree with Marshall's ratio-of-fire statistics.

Respondents who agreed or partially agreed pointed out many factors, but the most frequent one was that troops often had nothing to shoot at. Army Ground Forces trained American troops to fire at point, not area, targets. Soldiers rarely saw their enemies on the battlefield in World War II, especially in places such as the hedgerows of Normandy. Units often needed to direct fire at areas, not individual targets. Artillery, mortar fire, and automatic weapons (light machine guns and Browning automatic rifles) were better for suppressive fire on area targets; the M-1 rifle was better suited for point targets and close-range engagements. Some soldiers feared that firing their weapon would expose their position and draw return fire. They preferred to let the artillery do the work— and American infantry units usually enjoyed excellent artillery support. Some respondents stated that after heavy casualties in a unit, leaders would rely on the few remaining experienced soldiers to do most of the fighting. Only a few officers believed that the moral beliefs of American soldiers made them reluctant to kill enemy soldiers.

Some officers stated that although they agreed with Marshall, the lack of rifle fire did not adversely affect most battles, since artillery and crew-served weapons provided most of the firepower for the army. One former rifle company commander wrote:

> Generally, infantry fighting in Europe did not consist of companies of infantrymen getting up and advancing in a line firing rifles as you moved across open terrain. It usually consisted of small groups making a penetration under fire and the rest exploiting those gains. While you might have supporting fire from others as some advanced it was not a situation where everyone was firing at the same time. In addition we generally had a platoon of tanks or TDs attached to the attacking rifle companies. The supporting fire from these tanks as a group advanced was much more awesome than a number of riflemen firing. Even if 2/3 of the soldiers at any one time did not fire their weapons their mere presence created fear in the enemy. Also when it came to a counterattack the added firepower helped. I think there is a misconception of infantry fighting as being one continuous rain of bullets. It was more spurts and small group penetrations and others taking advantage of a small breakthrough to overrun a position.[34]

Combat in Europe was not the uniform laboratory environment that would make Marshall's statistics meaningful, even if they were true.

Some respondents believed that soldiers had trouble only in their first few firefights. After gaining experience and learning that the rule of the battlefield was "kill or be killed," soldiers had no difficulty firing their weapons at anything that moved. One company commander described the GI's motivation in this way: "As a rule, American infantrymen were eminently practical so, when it came down to 'him or me,' there was no question about his choice. Once he understood 'me' meant firing his rifle, he would ... especially if led properly."[35] Indeed, the common sense of the American infantryman emerges in many of the respondents' comments. In his fight for survival, the rifleman was nothing if not practical.

Those respondents who disagreed with Marshall's fire ratio believed that training and leadership were the keys to ensuring that riflemen engaged the enemy on the battlefield. They believed their units fired when they had to. Many of these respondents also stated that riflemen rarely had an opportunity to engage in a firefight with a visible enemy. They also pointed out that if riflemen were not firing their weapons, why was so much small-arms ammunition used in the war? Ammunition resupply was a constant concern for infantry units. If the soldiers were not shooting at the enemy, why were they firing their weapons? Unit records support this claim. Between 8 June 1944 and 8 May 1945, the 90th Infantry Division expended 5,612,455 rounds of M-1 rifle ammunition, or roughly 900 rounds per weapon in the division.[36] Statistics from other divisions are similar. Apparently, the soldiers fired their weapons more often than S. L. A. Marshall gave them credit for.

American infantrymen in World War II fired their weapons as necessary to accomplish their mission and survive on the battlefield. The fact is, however, that small-arms fire from the M-1 rifle was not the determining factor in whether American units achieved "fire superiority" on the battlefield. Firepower for infantry units came from many sources, most of them external to the infantry battalion itself, and chief among which was the excellent artillery support that American units enjoyed throughout the war. Reflecting on his experience as an infantry battalion commander in World War II, General William E. Depuy concluded that what he really accomplished "was that I moved the forward observers of the artillery across France and Germany."[37] The artillery massed firepower that the infantry lacked, and although the infantryman was essential to take and hold ground, he was not the primary killing instrument of the American army in the ETO. The percentage of soldiers who fired their rifles in any given engagement is, to a certain extent, irrelevant. The Army of the United States achieved its dominance in firepower over the German army through the skillful use of all the combat resources at its disposal. The victory belonged to the combined-arms team—not to any one part of it.

American divisions had other advantages in battle, advantages that sometimes are overlooked by historians who focus too narrowly on the tactical maneuvers of armor and infantry units in battle. The Allies had an outstanding intelligence system, although noticeable failures in 1944 at Arnhem and in the Ardennes tarnished its reputation somewhat. The information provided by ULTRA was of tremendous value to those commanders who possessed knowledge of it. At corps level and below, a steady stream of enemy prisoners, patrol reports, and superior aerial reconnaissance also provided a great deal of information to American commanders. American logistics and transportation assets surpassed those of any other nation. Although certain American weapons, such as tanks and machine guns, were not as effective as their German counterparts, American soldiers successfully used the weapons at their disposal to close with and destroy the enemy. The American armed forces also proved their ability to operate in a joint environment with air and naval forces, although this took longer than it should have in the case of the development of an effective close air support system for ground units. Looked at in its totality, the combat effectiveness of the Army of the United States in 1944 and 1945 was impressive.

This study has analyzed the process used in developing combat-effective divisions in the American army during World War II. Did German leaders believe that American divisions were as good as their counterparts in the Wehrmacht? At the end of 1944, *Oberkommando des Heeres* (High Command of the Army) published a series entitled "Battle Experiences," which outlined the German view of American soldiers, tactics, and weapons.[38] Although the documents are heavily laden with Nazi propaganda and officially maintain the superiority of the German infantryman, the German army recognized the improvement in American soldiers since the Normandy invasion. "Battle Experiences" praises the coordination of American infantry, tanks, and planes. The High Command recognized the vast superiority of American artillery due to its rapid communications, accuracy, volume of fire, greater range, and its organic aerial observers. Interestingly, the manuscripts rate the American replacement system as being very effective. The Germans also evaluated highly American tactical leadership, which they recognized as being very adaptive and quick to learn from mistakes on the battlefield.[39]

Despite these admissions, the German High Command believed the American soldier relied too heavily on massive material support, avoided close combat, disliked night fighting, and surrendered too easily. The German High Command also believed that American planning was too cautious and American attack methods too rigid. The official U.S. Army historian of the Lorraine campaign concludes: "To what extent the above observations are valid and valuable can best be determined by the trained soldier who has made an unbiased and critical study of the operations in Lorraine and in other areas of the Western Front during the autumn and early winter of 1944."[40]

This study verifies some of the German claims, such as the reliance of American divisions on heavy fire support. On the other hand, if an army has an effective fire support system, why not use it to overwhelm the enemy and reduce casualties? American planning was also cautious, especially in Normandy until the breakout during Operation COBRA. Even after the pursuit across France, American planning was often methodical at best, as the Battle of the Huertgen Forest shows. As the campaign for France and Germany progressed, however, American tactical commanders learned from their mistakes and adapted their tactics to fit the situation on the battlefield. Contrary to the German High Command's beliefs, the American soldier did not avoid close combat, nor was he a poor night fighter. The assertion that the American soldier surrendered too easily is surprising given the massive disparity between the large number of Germans taken prisoner and the relatively small number of Americans who surrendered.

What the German leaders did not see in their analysis was the progression of American divisions since the beginning of mobilization in mid-1940. Army leaders turned the potential of industrial and manpower resources into the capabilities of combat power as expressed in the infantry, armored, airborne, and mountain divisions of the Army of the United States. Over time, the Army of the United States developed into a more combat-effective force than the Wehrmacht because of the ability of the United States to sustain its forces at a relatively high degree of combat effectiveness over an extended period of time. The American army in Europe never had enough divisions at its disposal simply to overwhelm its adversaries with mountains of men and matériel. The Army of the United States accomplished its mission of assisting in the destruction of Axis forces through the superior effectiveness of its ground combat divisions, backed by powerful naval and air forces that ruled the seas and skies of Europe. American industrial capability did not assure victory; rather, material abundance enabled the United States to maintain the combat effectiveness of its divisions overseas in extended and grueling campaigns fought thousands of miles from the homeland.

General of the Army Dwight D. Eisenhower belatedly came to the realization that the combat soldier identified with his division more than any other unit of which he was a part. In recommending several divisions for Distinguished Unit Citations[41] after the war, Eisenhower wrote to General of the Army George C. Marshall that "the Army esprit de corps centers around a division much more than it does any other echelon. Consequently, the citation of particular battalions within a division does not mean as much to the soldier as a commendation to the division itself."[42] Marshall replied that the 3d Infantry Division's "performance was so outstanding as to warrant beyond question the Presidential Citation," and he recommended that Eisenhower carefully screen other divisions for similar awards and forward them to the War Department in a group.[43]

To assist him in making his decision, Eisenhower asked the ETO chief historian, Colonel S. L. A. Marshall, to evaluate the combat records of the divisions that fought in the European campaign. The theater historians placed the divisions that distinguished themselves into two categories. In the first category were those divisions whose "performance has been consistently strong and meritorious and in particular operations has been outstanding."[44] This group included (in order) the 30th, 1st, and 5th Infantry Divisions. The second category included "those divisions which have given long, arduous and workmanlike service but have either lacked the luster of those named in the first category or at one stage or another have performed somewhat less well." This group included (in order) the 9th, 29th, 4th, and 45th Infantry Divisions. In addition, the historians recommended the 2d Armored Division for a unit citation because the 3d and 4th Armored Divisions had already been recommended for awards.

Before he left Europe to return to the United States in November 1945,

Eisenhower approved recommendations for unit citations for eight divisions.[45] His list, in order of priority, read as follows:

1st Infantry Division:	Capture of Aachen
2d Armored Division:	St.-Lô Breakthrough [COBRA]
3d Armored Division:	Exploitation of the Remagen Bridgehead and Encirclement of the Ruhr Pocket
5th Infantry Division:	Drive from Luxembourg across the Rhine River
30th Infantry Division:	Breaching the Siegfried Line during the Aachen Campaign
2d Infantry Division:	Defensive Stand at Elsenborn Ridge
90th Infantry Division:	Reduction of Metz
29th Infantry Division:	Drive from the Siegfried Line to the Roer River

With the acceptance of these recommendations, the War Department would have cited eleven divisions that fought in the ETO: one of four airborne divisions (the 101st Airborne Division for its stand at Bastogne); three of thirteen armored divisions (the 2d, 3d, and 4th Armored Divisions); and seven of forty-three infantry divisions (the 1st, 2d, 3d, 5th, 29th, 30th, and 90th Infantry Divisions). In making his recommendations, Eisenhower rejected recommendations for unit citations for numerous divisions, to include the 5th, 6th, 9th, and 10th Armored Divisions and the 4th, 9th, 26th, 36th, 45th, 79th, 80th, and 99th Infantry Divisions.[46]

What made outstanding divisions so good? First and foremost, they had good senior leadership and capable staff officers at the division level. Early combat experience provided the 1st, 3d, 9th, and 45th Infantry Divisions with a marked advantage over other divisions that faced their first test of battle on or after D-Day. Similarly, those divisions that fought in Normandy were much more effective than those that arrived in the fall of 1944. Combat experience alone was insufficient to make a unit effective, however. Only after commanders had digested lessons learned and had initiated programs to train units on their weaknesses did divisions improve. The best divisions wrote the most critical and complete after-action reports. They also developed an early appreciation for the combined-arms team. Good divisions also placed a great deal of emphasis on instilling in their soldiers organizational pride and a belief in unit heritage. None of these units could have functioned effectively over an extended period, however, without the ability to take losses and continue on with their missions. All good divisions developed effective replacement integration systems.

One day the United States of America may yet again have to mobilize an army for war. To succeed, the army of the future must field highly effective combat organizations, for our past and recent history suggests that it is the quality of units rather than their quantity that will determine the difference between victory and defeat. The experiences of the Army of the United States in preparing its forces for combat have many lessons to offer in this regard. Its commanders successfully took the raw materials of war provided by American society and industry and fashioned them into units capable of closing with and destroying the enemy in a variety of combat environments. The experiences of American divisions in World War II also counsel that an army's basic building blocks must be as self-contained as possible. Pooling of assets at higher levels garners false economies of scale that will come back to haunt an army in sustained combat operations. The American experience in World War II also teaches that the endurance of a military force—its ability to sustain and regenerate combat power—is an integral component of combat effectiveness. Military forces ignore the importance of combat service support at their peril. Additionally, the entry-level training received by new soldiers must be lengthy, thorough, and rigorous enough to prepare them for combat upon integration into their gaining units. To do less is to consign some of these soldiers to unnecessary wounds or death in battle, as happened with too many poorly trained replacements in the American army in World War II.

The great achievement of the Army of the United States in World War II was to mold a large army of citizen-soldiers into an effective fighting force in a short time. The process did not work smoothly, and perhaps the end result was not what army leaders had intended when they began the mobilization process in 1940. Nevertheless, American divisions, led by a small slice of Regular Army and National Guard cadre and filled with draftees and the products of officer candidate schools, performed competently on the battlefield once they overcame the initial shock of combat. The first battles were for the most part traumatic affairs, but American divisions displayed the ability to learn from their mistakes and improve their performance in future battles. Lieutenant General Lucian K. Truscott Jr., who fought in operational command of American soldiers from the invasion of North Africa to V-E Day, recognized this progression. "When American soldiers first came in contact with the German soldier," Truscott wrote,

> the latter was already a veteran with a long military tradition, the product of long and thorough military training, led by experienced and capable officers, and equipped with the most modern weapons. The German was then better trained especially for operations in small units, and the quality of his leadership was superior. German soldiers displayed an ingenuity and resourcefulness more American than British. The American quickly adapted himself and learned much from the German. Sicily and southern Italy proved that he had mastered his lessons well. From Anzio on there was never a question of the superiority of American soldiers.[47]

There was never a question, that is, in the minds of American commanders. It remained for the defeated German army and its apologists to perpetuate a flawed theory that the Army of the United States had blundered its way to victory by throwing mountains of matériel at the superior but hopelessly out-numbered forces of the Wehrmacht.

The Army of the United States succeeded in World War II due to its development of combat-effective organizations that could not only fight and win battles but also sustain that effort over years of combat. Logistical superi-ority helped to give American ground combat divisions endurance, but it did not assure victory on the battlefield. With only forty-two infantry divisions, sixteen armored divisions, and three airborne divisions in the ETO, American commanders had to ensure that the combat effectiveness of their units matched or exceeded that of their enemies. The key to this development was the trans-formation of the standard American infantry division from untested organiza-tion to a fighting unit capable of closing with and destroying the enemy in a variety of combat environments. Throughout the battles for North Africa, Italy, France, and Germany in 1943, 1944, and 1945, the infantry divisions of the Army of the United States were the building blocks upon which American commanders crafted their operations to destroy the Wehrmacht and achieve ultimate victory in the largest and most destructive war in human history.

Glossary

Allied Forces Headquarters (AFHQ)—The controlling headquarters for Allied operations in North Africa and Italy.

ANVIL—The code name for the Allied invasion of southern France in August 1944, later changed to DRAGOON.

Army Air Forces—The air components of the Army of the United States, which were not formed into a separate service until 1947.

Army General Classification Test (AGCT)—The test given to all inductees to classify them for service. The test grouped inductees into five categories, with I as the highest rating and V as the lowest.

Army Ground Forces (AGF)—The headquarters created in 1942 to coordinate the mobilization and training of all combat and combat support forces in the United States. AGF was commanded by Lieutenant General Lesley J. McNair until his death in Normandy in July 1944.

Army maneuvers—Large-scale training exercises conducted between 1940 and 1945 in five massive maneuver areas located in Louisiana, the Carolinas, Tennessee, Arizona-California, and Oregon.

Army of the United States (AUS)—The temporary organization of the ground and air forces of the United States in time of war. Created by the National Defense Act of 1920, the AUS consisted of the Regular U.S. Army, the National Guard, and the Organized Reserves.

Army Service Forces (ASF)—The successor to the Services of Supply, ASF was responsible for the mobilization and training of all combat service support units in the United States.

Army Specialized Training Program (ASTP)—A program designed to keep some servicemen in college by deferring their assignment to tactical units.

Artificial moonlight—The effect created by bouncing searchlight beams off clouds to create an artificial illumination to improve visibility at night.

AVALANCHE—The code name for the Allied invasion of Italy in September 1943.

Battle of the Hedgerows—The name given by U.S. Army historians to the American offensive in Normandy that began on 3 July 1944 and ended with the seizure of St.-Lô by the 29th Infantry Division two weeks later.

Bazooka—Nickname for the 2.36-inch antitank rocket launcher used by American forces.

Bocage—The terrain in Normandy characterized by a mass of small, irregularly shaped fields separated by hedgerows.

Broad-front strategy—The strategy championed by General Dwight D. Eisenhower and used by the Western Allies in France during World War II. This strategy entailed simultaneous offensives by all Allied armies across the front in France. It ensured that all American, British, and Canadian armies were significantly involved in the campaign to enter the heart of Germany and complete the destruction of the Wehrmacht.

Browning Automatic Rifle (BAR)—A .30-caliber, magazine-fed assault rifle used by American infantrymen.

BUFFALO—The code name for the Allied operation to break out from the Anzio beachhead in May 1944.

Carpet bombing—The massed use of heavy bombers to destroy enemy forces in a confined area.

Close air support—The use of airplanes to destroy targets within artillery range of friendly ground forces.

COBRA—The code name for the American offensive that began on 25 July 1944 and resulted in a decisive breakthrough of the German front in Normandy.

Combat exhaustion—A term used by the American army to denote a soldier incapacitated by psychological trauma suffered as a result of intense or prolonged exposure to battle. The term used during World War I was "shell shock."

Combat service support—Those units involved in administration, finance, logistics, maintenance, medical care, transportation, and other housekeeping functions in support of ground forces.

Combat support—Those units that operate in direct support of combat units, but whose primary mission does not involve combat with enemy forces. Combat support units include chemical, military intelligence, military police, and signal organizations.

Command and General Staff School—A professional development school for midcareer army officers located at Fort Leavenworth, Kansas. The school taught army doctrine and the basics of division, corps, and army operations.

Communications Zone (COMZ)—Responsible for the organization of lines of communication and logistics for a theater of operations.

CRAFTSMAN—The code name for the Fifth U.S. Army offensive into northern Italy in April 1945.

Desert Training Center—A training center located in California and Arizona designed to prepare men and units to fight in desert conditions. Renamed the California-Arizona Maneuver Area on 20 October 1943.

DIADEM—The code name for the Allied offensive in southern Italy in May 1944.

Distinguished Unit Citation—An award given to a unit whose collective heroism in battle would merit the award of a Distinguished Service Cross, the second-highest decoration for valor, to an individual. Units awarded the citation distinguished themselves in battle by extraordinary heroism, gallantry, determination, and esprit de corps in overcoming unusually difficult and hazardous conditions that set them apart from other units participating in the same engagement.

DOGFACE—Operation by U.S. VI Corps in the Vosges Mountains that began on 15 October 1944 and ended in early November with the seizure of St.-Dié.

Draftee divisions—A nickname for the divisions of the Organized Reserve, created upon the entry of the United States into World War II.

DRAGOON—The code name for the Allied invasion of southern France in August 1944.

DUKW—A six-wheel, 2.5-ton amphibious truck, designed to carry supplies from cargo vessels to the beachhead and beyond. The "D" was a code for the first year of production (1942), the "U" stood for utility, the "K" denoted front-wheel drive, and the "W" meant the vehicle had two rear driving axles. The troops affectionately nicknamed the vehicle the "Duck."

European theater of operations (ETO)—The area of responsibility comprising Great Britain, Norway, France, the Netherlands, Belgium, Luxembourg, Denmark, and Germany. Headquarters, ETO, was the national controlling headquarters for American forces in Europe during World War II.

FORTITUDE—The code name for the Allied deception plan to make the Germans believe the Allied invasion of France would take place in the Pas-de-Calais.

General Headquarters (GHQ), United States Army—Created on 26 July 1940 to control the four armies in the continental United States, GHQ Aviation, harbor defense troops, and the newly created Armored Force. GHQ was responsible for training field forces for combat.

Germany first strategy—The strategy of the United States and Great Britain in World War II, which envisioned the sequential defeat of Germany/Italy and Japan. In reality, the United States allocated its resources in such a manner that the Allies defeated all the Axis powers nearly simultaneously.

GRENADE—The code name for the Ninth U.S. Army offensive in February 1945 that succeeded in crossing the Roer River and resulted in the seizure of the west bank of the Rhine River.

HUSKY—The code name for the Allied invasion of Sicily in July 1943.

Invasion Training Center—An area located in southwest England dedicated to the training of units for the invasion of the European Continent.

Joint Chiefs of Staff (JCS)—The collective leadership of the armed forces of the United States, consisting of the U.S. Army chief of staff (General George C. Marshall); the chief of naval operations (Admiral Ernest J. King); the deputy U.S. Army chief of staff for air and commander of the Army Air Forces (General Henry H. "Hap" Arnold); and the president's personal chief of staff, who also acted as the informal head of the JCS (Admiral William D. Leahy).

Joint Planning Staff (JPS)—A multiservice staff located in Washington, D.C., that provided reports and recommendations to the Joint Chiefs of Staff.

Kampfgruppe—An ad hoc battle group of German forces.

Kasserine Pass—The location of the first major battle of American forces in Tunisia in February 1943. The battle ended with the withdrawal of German forces to their initial positions, but only after the disastrous defeat of several American units in their initial combat.

Kesselschlact—A German military term meaning "battle of encirclement."

Landing craft, tank (LCT)—The basic vehicle-carrying landing craft used by Allied forces in World War II. It was designed to carry up to six medium tanks weighing roughly forty tons each.

Landing ship, tank (LST)—A large, oceangoing vessel designed to carry men and equipment in amphibious operations from port to shore.

Maginot Line—The system of French fortifications along the Franco-German border built in the interwar period in an effort to halt another German invasion of France.

MARKET-GARDEN—The combined airborne-ground offensive by the 21st Army Group in the Netherlands in September 1944, designed to penetrate across the Rhine River and envelop the German defenses along the West Wall from the north.

Mediterranean theater of operations (MTO)—The area of responsibility comprising the Mediterranean Sea, Turkey, Greece, the Balkans, Sicily, and Italy. Headquarters, MTO, was the national controlling headquarters for American forces in Sicily and Italy during World War II.

MG 42—A machine gun used by German forces, one of the best of its kind produced during World War II.

Mobilization Training Program—A guide to the mobilization and training of units produced by the Army Ground Forces.

NEPTUNE—The code name for the amphibious portion of Operation OVER-LORD.

NORDWIND—The German code name for the winter counteroffensive in Alsace that began on 31 December 1944.

North African theater of operations (NATO)—The area of responsibility comprising Morocco, Algeria, Tunisia, Libya, and Egypt. Headquarters, NATO, was the national controlling headquarters for American forces in North Africa during World War II.

Organized Reserves—One of the components of the Army of the United States created by the National Defense Act of 1920. In theory Organized Reserve divisions were kept in cadre status and activated upon mobilization. In reality they existed largely on paper.

OVERLORD—The code name for the Allied invasion of Normandy that took place in June 1944.

Panzer—The German word for "tank."

Panzerfaust—A handheld antitank weapon widely used by German forces in 1944 and 1945.

Panzer Grenadier—Literally, "tank grenadier," an infantry soldier assigned to an armored or mechanized division.

POINTBLANK—The code name for the Allied Combined Bomber Offensive against Germany begun in 1943.

Preparation for Overseas Movement (POM)—The army program designed to bring units to a final state of combat readiness, move them to a port, and load them on transports for shipment overseas.

Red Ball Express—A series of one-way, loop highways initiated by COMZ on 25 August 1944, along which convoys would travel twenty-four hours per day carrying supplies from the invasion beaches to depots inland.

Reconstitution—The process of rejuvenating the combat power of an organization through rest, reorganization, repair of broken equipment, and infusion of fresh replacements, supplies, and weapons.

Regimental Combat Team (RCT)—A task-organized unit formed by attaching various combat support and combat service support units to an infantry regiment.

Reichswehr—The German army of the Weimar Republic from 1919 to 1933.

Remagen bridge—The Ludendorff railroad bridge spanning the Rhine River at Remagen, Germany. It was seized by elements of the 9th Armored Division on 7 March 1945 and immediately led to a massive movement of American divisions across the Rhine in an effort to expand the bridgehead on the east bank.

Rhinoceros—An attachment to the front of a Sherman tank created by welding steel teeth to the hull, which allowed the tank to break through hedgerows without exposing its weak underside armor to the enemy.

ROUNDUP—The code name for the Allied plan to invade the Continent in 1943.

Rover Joe—The code name used by the Fifth U.S. Army for a flight of fighter-bombers that would circle the battlefield awaiting targets of opportunity called by ground or air observers.

Selective Service Act—The legislation that authorized the drafting of young men into the service of the United States. The Selective Service Act of 1940 was the first peacetime draft in American history.

SHINGLE—The code name for the Allied invasion of Anzio, Italy, in January 1944.

Siegfried Line—The nickname given to the West Wall, an extensive series of fortifications on the western frontier of Germany.

Signal Corps Radio (SCR)—A family of tactical radios used by American ground forces in World War II.

SLEDGEHAMMER—The code name for the Allied plan to invade the Continent in 1942.

Square division—The organization of infantry divisions prior to 1940. These divisions consisted of two infantry brigades with two regiments in each brigade, in addition to combat support and combat service support units.

Supreme Headquarters Allied Expeditionary Forces (SHAEF)—The controlling headquarters for the operations of all Western Allied Forces in northwest Europe in 1944 and 1945.

Table of organization—A compilation of authorized personnel and equipment for a specific type of unit.

Time-on-target (TOT)—A technique used to mass indirect fires from multiple artillery batteries on a single target so that the shells land nearly simultaneously.

TORCH—The code name for the Allied invasion of North Africa in November 1942.

Trench foot—A disease affecting extremities exposed for too long to moisture, causing massive swelling, destruction of skin cells, and, if left untreated, infection and gangrene.

Triangular division—The organization of U.S. infantry divisions during World War II. These divisions consisted of three infantry regiments along with combat support and combat service support units.

ULTRA—The code name for the supersecret Allied program to decode the supposedly undecipherable radio traffic encrypted by the German Enigma machine.

Victory Program—The War Department plan drafted in fall 1941 for the wartime force structure of the Army of the United States. The program projected an army of 215 divisions and 8,795,658 men at full strength under the assumption that the United States and Great Britain would have to defeat Germany without the help of the Soviet Union, which was on the verge of collapse at the time.

Volks Grenadier—Literally, "people's grenadier," the name given by Hitler to newly created infantry divisions of the Wehrmacht in 1944.

WACHT AM RHEIN—Code name for the German counteroffensive in the Ardennes Forest beginning on 16 December 1944.

Wehrmacht—The German armed forces during World War II.

West Wall—The system of fortifications along the western German border used extensively by German forces in the fall and winter of 1944–1945. Also called the "Siegfried Line" by Allied troops.

Notes

CHAPTER 1. INTRODUCTION

1. Charles B. MacDonald, *The Siegfried Line Campaign* (Washington, D.C.: Office of the Chief of Military History, 1963), 25.

2. Trevor N. Dupuy, Curt Johnson, and Grace P. Hayes, *Dictionary of Military Terms* (New York: H. W. Wilson, 1986), 52.

3. Chester Wilmot, *The Struggle for Europe* (New York: Harper, 1952); Omar N. Bradley, *A Soldier's Story* (New York: Rand McNally, 1951); Sir Bernard L. Montgomery, *Normandy to the Baltic* (Boston: Houghton Mifflin, 1948); Dwight D. Eisenhower, *Crusade in Europe* (Garden City, N.Y.: Doubleday, 1948); Charles B. MacDonald, *The Mighty Endeavor: The American War in Europe* (New York: Quill, 1969).

4. S. L. A. Marshall, *Men against Fire: The Problem of Battle Command in Future War* (New York: Quill, 1947).

5. Trevor N. Dupuy, *Numbers, Predictions, and War: Using History to Evaluate Combat Factors and Predict the Outcome of Battles* (Indianapolis, Ind.: Bobbs-Merrill, 1979).

6. Ibid., 62.

7. Ibid., 63.

8. Russell F. Weigley, *Eisenhower's Lieutenants: The Campaign of France and Germany, 1944–1945* (Bloomington: Indiana University Press, 1981).

9. Ibid., 729–730.

10. Martin van Creveld, *Fighting Power: German and U.S. Army Performance, 1939–1945* (Westport, Conn.: Greenwood Press, 1982).

11. Ibid., 4.

12. Ibid., 33.

13. Ibid., 79.

14. Ibid., 170.

15. Ibid., 168.

16. John Keegan, *The Second World War* (New York: Penguin Books, 1990); Max Hastings, *Overlord: D-Day, June 6, 1944* (New York: Simon and Schuster, 1984); John

Ellis, *Brute Force: Allied Strategy and Tactics in the Second World War* (New York: Viking, 1990).

17. John Sloan Brown, *Draftee Division: The 88th Infantry Division in World War II* (Lexington: University Press of Kentucky, 1986).

18. Ibid., 169.

19. Ibid., 174.

20. Allan R. Millett, "The United States Armed Forces in the Second World War," in *Military Effectiveness,* vol. 3, *The Second World War,* ed. Allan R. Millett and Williamson Murray (Boston: Unwin Hyman, 1988), 45–89.

21. Ibid., 84.

22. Keith E. Bonn, *When the Odds Were Even: The Vosges Mountains Campaign, October 1944–January 1945* (Novato, Calif.: Presidio Press, 1994).

23. Ibid., 228–231.

24. Michael D. Doubler, *Closing with the Enemy: How GIs Fought the War in Europe, 1944–1945* (Lawrence: University Press of Kansas, 1994).

25. Ibid., 1–9.

26. Richard Overy, *Why the Allies Won* (New York: W. W. Norton, 1996).

27. Ibid., xiv.

28. Ibid., 318.

29. Stephen E. Ambrose, *D-Day, June 6, 1944: The Climactic Battle of World War II* (New York: Simon and Schuster, 1994); idem, *Citizen Soldiers: The U.S. Army from the Normandy Beaches to the Bulge to the Surrender of Germany* (New York: Simon and Schuster, 1997).

30. Maurice Matloff, "The 90-Division Gamble," in *Command Decisions,* ed. Kent Roberts Greenfield (Washington, D.C.: Office of the Chief of Military History, 1960; repr., Washington, D.C.: Center of Military History, 1983), 381.

31. William R. Keast, Robert R. Palmer, and Bell I. Wiley, *The Procurement and Training of Ground Combat Troops* (Washington, D.C.: Office of the Chief of Military History, 1948), 3.

32. Weigley, *Eisenhower's Lieutenants,* 571.

33. Keast, Palmer, and Wiley, *The Procurement and Training of Ground Combat Troops,* 177.

34. Ibid., 230.

35. Williamson Murray, *The Change in the European Balance of Power, 1938–1939: The Path to Ruin* (Princeton, N.J.: Princeton University Press, 1984), 219.

36. Ibid., 222.

37. Manfred Messerschmidt, "German Military Effectiveness between 1919 and 1939," in *Military Effectiveness,* vol. 2, *The Interwar Period,* ed. Allan R. Millett and Williamson Murray (Boston: Unwin Hyman, 1988), 219.

38. Christopher R. Gabel, *Seek, Strike, and Destroy: U.S. Army Tank Destroyer Doctrine in World War II* (Fort Leavenworth, Kans.: Combat Studies Institute, 1985), 49.

39. See John Desch, "The 1941 German Army/The 1944–45 U.S. Army: A Comparative Analysis of Two Forces in Their Primes," *Command Magazine* 18 (September–October 1992): 54–63, for a brief comparison. Desch gives the edge to the American army of 1944–1945.

40. For the impact of ideology on the German army in World War II, see Omer Bartov, *The Eastern Front, 1941–1945: German Troops and the Barbarisation of Warfare* (Basingstoke, Hampshire: Macmillan in association with St. Antony's College,

Oxford), 1985); idem, *Hitler's Army: Soldiers, Nazis, and War in the Third Reich* (New York: Oxford University Press, 1991). For the ideological basis of the elite Waffen SS divisions and its effect on the performance of German soldiers, see Charles W. Sydnor Jr., *Soldiers of Destruction: The SS Death's Head Division, 1933–1945* (Princeton, N.J.: Princeton University Press, 1977).

CHAPTER 2. THE MOBILIZATION OF THE ARMY OF THE UNITED STATES

1. Kent Roberts Greenfield, Robert R. Palmer, and Bell I. Wiley, *The Organization of Ground Combat Troops* (Washington, D.C.: Historical Division, United States Army, 1947), 9.

2. Ibid., 6–7.

3. Material extracted from E. J. Kahn Jr., *McNair: Educator of an Army* (Washington, D.C.: Infantry Journal Press, 1945).

4. Ibid. Lieutenant General McNair was one of the two most senior American officers killed in World War II. His only son, the chief of staff of the 77th Infantry Division, was killed in the same month as his father in fighting on Guam.

5. Greenfield, Palmer, and Wiley, *The Organization of Ground Combat Troops,* 10.

6. Christopher R. Gabel, *The U.S. Army GHQ Maneuvers of 1941* (Washington, D.C.: Center of Military History, 1991).

7. Greenfield, Palmer, and Wiley, *The Organization of Ground Combat Troops,* 11.

8. Kahn, *McNair,* 22–23.

9. Ibid., 28.

10. Greenfield, Palmer, and Wiley, *The Organization of Ground Combat Troops,* 12.

11. Gabel, *The U.S. Army GHQ Maneuvers of 1941,* 172–174.

12. For a good, concise account of the first battles of the United States Army in World War II, see Charles E. Heller and William A. Stofft, eds., *America's First Battles, 1776–1965* (Lawrence: University Press of Kansas, 1986), chaps. 7 and 8.

13. Greenfield, Palmer, and Wiley, *The Organization of Ground Combat Troops,* 31.

14. Ibid., 52–54.

15. Mark W. Clark, Oral History, Mark W. Clark Papers, USAMHI, 120–123.

16. Martin Blumenson, "America's World War II Leaders in Europe: Some Thoughts," *Parameters* 19, no. 4 (December 1989): 3.

17. Ibid., 9.

18. The following statistics are taken from Lieutenant Colonel Gary Wade, Combat Studies Institute Report No. 7, "World War II Division Commanders," U.S. Army Command and General Staff College, Fort Leavenworth, Kansas.

19. Among the division commanders in this sample were Terry de la Mesa Allen (1st and 104th Infantry Divisions); Paul W. Baade (35th Infantry Division); Raymond O. Barton (4th Infantry Division); Alexander R. Bolling (84th Infantry Division); Withers N. Burress (100th Infantry Division); Norman D. Cota (28th Infantry Division); Louis A. Craig (9th Infantry Division); Charles H. Gerhardt (29th Infantry Division); Leland S. Hobbs (30th Infantry Division); S. Leroy Irwin (5th Infantry Division); Walter E. Lauer (99th Infantry Division); John W. O'Daniel (3d Infantry Division); Walter M. Robertson (2d Infantry Division); Charles W. Ryder (34th Infantry Division); Donald A. Stroh (8th Infantry Division); and Ira T. Wyche (79th Infantry Division).

20. Charles E. Kirkpatrick, "The Very Model of a Modern Major General: Back-

ground of World War II American Generals in V Corps" (paper delivered at the Army Historian's Conference, Washington, D.C., June 1992).

21. For the most recent assertion of this argument, see Alan Gropman, ed., *The Big L: American Logistics in World War II* (Washington, D.C.: National Defense University Press, 1997).

22. William R. Keast, Robert R. Palmer, and Bell I. Wiley, *The Procurement and Training of Ground Combat Troops* (Washington, D.C.: Office of the Chief of Military History, 1948), 434.

23. Ibid., 435–436.

24. HQ, AGF, 16 February 1942, Subject: Training of Newly Activated Infantry Divisions, 353/21, Record Group 337; GNTRG 353/1043, 23 April 1942, Subject: Training Directive for the Period: June 1–October 31, 1942, Record Group 337, National Archives.

25. Bell I. Wiley, *Training in the Ground Army, 1942–1945*, AGF Study No. 11 (Fort Monroe, Va.: Historical Section, Army Ground Forces, 1948), 48.

26. Omar N. Bradley and Clay Blair, *A General's Life* (New York: Simon and Schuster, 1983), 172.

27. Wiley, *Training in the Ground Army*, 44.

28. Ibid., 2–3.

29. Greenfield, Palmer, and Wiley, *The Organization of Ground Combat Troops*, 200–201.

30. Letter, Lieutenant Colonel Bryce F. Denno to Chief of the Infantry Branch, Training Division, G-3, Army Ground Forces, 15 April 1945; reprinted in a letter from Colonel Bryce F. Denno to author, 7 April 1993.

31. Maurice Matloff and Edwin M. Snell, *Strategic Planning for Coalition Warfare, 1941–1942* (Washington, D.C.: Office of the Chief of Military History, 1953), 49.

32. Wiley, *Training in the Ground Army*, 24.

33. Memo, HQ, Second Army, 17 February 1943, Subject: Special Battle Courses, 330-0.3.0, Box 8727, Record Group 407, National Archives II; Wiley, *Training in the Ground Army*, 40.

34. Kahn, *McNair*, 32.

35. Wiley, *Training in the Ground Army*, 14.

36. Ibid., 5–9.

37. Ibid., 12.

38. Sidney L. Meller, *The Desert Training Center and the C-AMA*, AGF Study No. 15 (Washington, D.C.: Historical Section, Army Ground Forces, 1946).

39. Wiley, *Training in the Ground Army*, 65.

40. Keast, Palmer, and Wiley, *The Procurement and Training of Ground Combat Troops*, 471.

41. Wiley, *Training in the Ground Army*, 72.

42. Keast, Palmer, and Wiley, *The Procurement and Training of Ground Combat Troops*, 482.

43. Ibid., 565.

44. Lucian K. Truscott Jr., *Command Missions: A Personal Story* (New York: E. P. Dutton, 1954; repr., Novato, Calif.: Presidio, 1990), 100.

45. Keast, Palmer, and Wiley, *The Procurement and Training of Ground Combat Troops*, 574.

46. Ibid., 582–593; GNGCT 370.5/171, 19 February 1943, Subject: Preparation

and Movement of Units for Overseas Shipment, 330-0.3.0, Box 8727, Record Group 407, National Archives II.

47. Keast, Palmer, and Wiley, *The Procurement and Training of Ground Combat Troops,* 596–597.

48. Charles E. Kirkpatrick, *An Unknown Future and a Doubtful Present: Writing the Victory Plan of 1941* (Washington, D.C.: Center of Military History, 1990), 100–101.

49. Maurice Matloff, "The 90-Division Gamble," in *Command Decisions,* ed. Kent Roberts Greenfield (Washington, D.C.: Office of the Chief of Military History, 1960; repr., Washington, D.C.: Center of Military History, 1983), 373.

50. Gen. George C. Marshall to JCS, 24 August 1942, ABC 370.01 (7-25-42), Record Group 165, National Archives.

51. Paul V. McNutt to JCS, 16 September 1942, ABC 370.01 (7-25-42), Record Group 165, National Archives. For an examination of the impact of the size of the army on the labor force, see Bryon Fairchild and Jonathan Grossman, *The Army and Industrial Manpower* (Washington, D.C.: Office of the Chief of Military History, 1959), 45–56.

52. Notes on JPS 36th Meeting, 23 September 1942, ABC 370.01 (7-25-42), Record Group 165, National Archives.

53. Ibid.

54. Ibid.

55. JCS to President, 30 September 1943, Indorsement signed by F.D.R., ABC 370.01 (7-25-42), Record Group 165, National Archives.

56. JCS Memorandum for Information No. 33, 5 November 1942, ABC 370.01 (7-25-42), Record Group 165, National Archives.

57. Ernest K. Lindley, "So Large an Army," *Washington Post,* 18 December 1942; "Big Enough for Victory," *Kansas City Star,* 30 December 1942; Ernest K. Lindley, "Size of the Army," *Washington Post,* 6 January 1943; Frank R. Kent, "The Great Game of Politics," *Washington Evening Star,* 8 January 1943; U.S. Congress, Senate, Subcommittee of the Senate Committee on Appropriations, *Manpower Hearings,* 78th Cong., March 1943.

58. General Marshall gave the speech in New York. WDCSA 320.2 (12-15-42), 15 December 1942, Record Group 165, National Archives.

59. JPS 57/8, 26 April 1943, Troop Bases for All Services for 1944 and Beyond, ABC 370.01 (7-25-42), Record Group 165, National Archives.

60. Notes on JPS 72d Meeting, 5 May 1943, ABC 370.01 (7-25-42), Record Group 165, National Archives.

61. Memorandum for Deputy Chief of Staff, 5 June 1943, Subject: Troop Bases for All Services for 1944 and Beyond," ABC 400 (2-20-43), Record Group 165, National Archives.

62. WDCSA 320.2 (5-24-43), Subject: Revision of Current Military Program, ABC 400 (2-20-43), Record Group 165, National Archives.

63. "Revision of Current Military Program, Interim Report by Special Army Committee," 1 June 1943, ABC 400 (2-20-43), Record Group 165, National Archives.

64. Matloff, "The 90-Division Gamble," 375.

65. Ibid., 376.

66. Ibid., 381.

67. Russell F. Weigley, *Eisenhower's Lieutenants: The Campaign of France and Germany, 1944–1945* (Bloomington: Indiana University Press, 1981), 13–14.

68. Greenfield, Palmer, and Wiley, *The Organization of Ground Combat Troops,* 170.

69. Ibid., 203.

70. Ibid., 170.

71. Ibid., 176.

72. Ibid., 175.

73. AGF 320.2/31 (Troop Basis 1943), 22 June 1943, 320.2, Record Group 165, National Archives.

74. Greenfield, Palmer, and Wiley, *The Organization of Ground Combat Troops,* 235–236.

75. Ibid., 241–242.

76. Ibid., 273.

77. Ibid., 278.

78. Ibid., 297–299.

79. Ibid., 311.

80. Ibid., 308.

81. GNTRG 353, 20 May 1942, Subject: Combined Infantry-Tank Unit Training, Record Group 337, National Archives.

82. For an examination of the problems in combined arms training in the First U.S. Army in Normandy and the solutions to them, see Michael D. Doubler, *Busting the Bocage: American Combined Arms Operations in France, 6 June–31 July 1944* (Fort Leavenworth, Kans.: Combat Studies Institute, 1988).

83. Keast, Palmer, and Wiley, *The Procurement and Training of Ground Combat Troops,* 4–5.

84. Ibid., 10–11; HQ, AGF, 2 September 1942, "The Problem of Classification and Assignment Relative to the Activation of an Infantry Division," Entry 24, Box 3, Record Group 337, National Archives.

85. WDGAP 320.2, 21 November 1942, Subject: Report of the Inspector General on Military Manpower, Record Group 165, National Archives.

86. Keast, Palmer, and Wiley, *The Procurement and Training of Ground Combat Troops,* 14.

87. Ibid., 20.

88. Ibid., 19.

89. Ibid., 74.

90. Ibid., 72–74.

91. Ibid., 38–39.

92. Ibid., 77–78.

93. Ibid., 84.

94. The experiences of ASTP soldiers varied from division to division, but many noncommissioned officers felt resentment toward the "smart-ass college boys" who had suddenly appeared in their units. See Louis E. Keefer, *Scholars in Foxholes: The Story of the Army Specialized Training Program in World War II* (Jefferson, N.C.: McFarland, 1988), 219.

95. HQ, European Theater of Operations, War Department Observers Board, AGF Report No. 1044, 25 June 1945, 4-3.1044/45, Box 24459, Record Group 407, National Archives II.

96. Roland G. Ruppenthal, *Logistical Support of the Armies,* vol. 2, *September 1944–May 1945* (Washington, D.C.: Office of the Chief of Military History, 1959), 338.

97. Keast, Palmer, and Wiley, *The Procurement and Training of Ground Combat Troops,* 188.

98. Elbridge Colby, "Replacements for a Field Army in Combat," *Infantry Journal* 60 (March 1947): 12–18.

99. HQ, AGF, "Reports on Quality of Overseas Replacements," 29 October 1943, Tab I, 322, Record Group 337, National Archives.

100. WDGCT 320.2, 13 June 1943, Subject: Loss Replacements, Record Group 337, National Archives.

101. GNGCT 320.2/562, 25 June 1943, Subject: Loss Replacements, Record Group 337, National Archives.

102. Memorandum for Deputy Chief of Staff, AGF, 26 January 1945, Subject: Data Regarding Suitability of AGF Replacements, 322, Record Group 337, National Archives.

103. Keast, Palmer, and Wiley, *The Procurement and Training of Ground Combat Troops,* 226.

104. Wiley, *Training in the Ground Army,* 60.

105. Ibid., 62.

106. Keast, Palmer, and Wiley, *The Procurement and Training of Ground Combat Troops,* 228.

107. JPS 57/8, 26 April 1943, Troop Bases for All Services for 1944 and Beyond, ABC 370.01 (7-25-42), Record Group 165, National Archives.

108. Ulysses Lee, *The Employment of Negro Troops* (Washington, D.C.: Office of the Chief of Military History, 1966), 405.

109. Ibid., 407.

110. Ibid., 408.

111. Ibid., 411.

112. Ibid., 411–412.

113. Ibid., 426–427.

114. Greenfield, Palmer, and Wiley, *The Organization of Ground Combat Troops,* 159.

115. Matloff and Snell, *Strategic Planning for Coalition Warfare, 1941–1942,* 99.

116. The 24th, 25th, 27th, and 40th Infantry Divisions in the central Pacific; the Americal, 37th, and 43d Infantry Divisions in the South Pacific; and the 32d and 41st Infantry Divisions in the southwest Pacific. Maurice Matloff, *Strategic Planning for Coalition Warfare, 1943–1944* (Washington, D.C.: Office of the Chief of Military History, 1959), 396.

117. Using only the nine army divisions in the Pacific at the end of 1942 in a limited offensive would have freed the 6th, 7th, 31st, 33d, 38th, 77th, 81st, 93d, 96th, and 98th Infantry Divisions, the 1st Cavalry Division, and the 11th Airborne Division for use in Europe. Matloff, *Strategic Planning for Coalition Warfare, 1943–1944,* 396, 520.

118. On 31 December 1942 the army had 463,868 soldiers, 9 divisions, and 23 air groups in the Pacific theaters. By September 1944 these numbers had grown to 1,314,931 soldiers, 21 divisions, and 57 air groups. The personnel cost of stationing 12 more divisions and 34 more air groups in the Pacific between these two dates was thus over 800,000 men, nearly 30 percent of the number stationed in Europe by the end of September 1944. Ibid., 392–393, 519–520.

CHAPTER 3. CITIZENS TO SOLDIERS

1. Maurice Matloff, ed., *American Military History* (Washington, D.C.: Center of Military History, 1985), 377–378.

2. See map of maneuver areas in Army Ground Forces, *Statistical Data* (Washington, D.C.: HQ, Army Ground Forces, 1945).

3. The 9th Infantry Division at Camp Bragg, North Carolina, is one example. "Activation and Reorganization Information," pp. 3–4, 309-0.19, Box 7327, Record Group 407, National Archives II.

4. Identification of Regular Army, National Guard, and Organized Reserve Divisions was done through a numbering system. Regular Army divisions were numbered 1–9, National Guard Divisions were numbered 26–59, and all other numbers were slated for divisions of the Organized Reserve. Numbers 10–22 were reserved for mountain and airborne divisions, the former receiving even numbers and the latter receiving odd numbers. The exceptions were the 82d and 101st Airborne Divisions, which were converted from standard Organized Reserve divisions already in existence. The 23d, 24th, and 25th Infantry Divisions were special cases. The 23d Infantry Division, the Americal Division, was formed on New Caledonia from various elements brought together on site to defend the island. The 24th and 25th Infantry Divisions were formed in Hawaii from elements of the old Regular Army Hawaiian Territorial Division after Pearl Harbor.

5. Department of the Army, *Combat Chronicle: An Outline History of U.S. Army Divisions* (Washington, D.C.: Army Historical Division, 1948), 4.

6. War Department, "Reports from Triangular Divisions," 18 December 1939, p. 1, 301-0.3.0, Box 5663, Record Group 407, National Archives II.

7. Ibid., 5.

8. HQ, 1st Infantry Division, "Triangular Division," 25 May 1940, p. 1, 301-0.3.0, Box 5663, Record Group 407, National Archives II.

9. HQ, 1st Infantry Division, "Partial Final Report—Third Army Maneuvers," 22 May 1940, p. 7, 301-0.3.0, Box 5663, Record Group 407, National Archives II.

10. HQ, 1st Infantry Division, "Triangular Division," 5.

11. HQ, 1st Infantry Division, "Final Report—Army and Navy Joint Exercise No. 7," 1941, 2:1, 301-0.3.0, Box 5663, Record Group 407, National Archives II.

12. 1st Infantry Division, "Final Report—Army and Navy Joint Exercise No. 7—1st Div. Task Force," 1941, 301-0.3, Box 5662, Record Group 407, National Archives II.

13. For a thorough analysis of the Louisiana and Carolina maneuvers of 1941, see Christopher R. Gabel, *The U.S. Army GHQ Maneuvers of 1941* (Washington, D.C.: Center of Military History, 1991).

14. HQ, 1st Infantry Division, "Report on First Army Maneuvers, 1941," 1 December 1941, 301-0.3.0, Box 5663, Record Group 407, National Archives II.

15. Ibid., 3.

16. Ibid., 10.

17. Christopher R. Gabel, *The U.S. Army GHQ Maneuvers of 1941* (Washington, D.C.: Center of Military History, 1991), 172–174.

18. HQ, 1st Infantry Division, "Report of G-3 Section," 17 January 1942, 301-0.3, Box 5662, Record Group 407, National Archives II.

19. Except where noted, the following biographical information is taken from the biographical sketch of General Allen located in the Terry de la Mesa Allen Papers, USAMHI.

20. Major General (Ret.) Terry Allen to Major Fred Dunham, undated memo, Terry de la Mesa Allen Papers, USAMHI.

21. Letter, Quentin Reynolds to Mrs. Terry Allen, 20 June 1944, Terry de la Mesa Allen Papers, USAMHI.

22. The cadres came from a variety of old army posts: Camp Custer, Michigan; Fort Thomas, Kentucky; Fort Benjamin Harrison, Indiana; Fort Sam Houston, Texas; Fort Warren, Wyoming; Fort Snelling, Minnesota; Fort DuPont, Delaware; Fort Moultrie, South Carolina; Fort Devens, Massachusetts; Madison Barracks, New York; and Fort D. A. Russell, Texas, to name a few. "Activation and Reorganization Information," pp. 1–2, 309-0.19, Box 7327, Record Group 407, National Archives II.

23. Ibid., 3–4.

24. The 60th Infantry Regiment, for example, trained 1,800 volunteer recruits and 1,807 draftees. "Regimental History, Sixtieth Infantry, 1940–1942," pp. 1–2, 309-INF(60)-0.1, Box 7535, Record Group 407, National Archives II.

25. Information and Education Division, ETOUSA, *Hitler's Nemesis: The 9th Infantry Division* (Paris: Desfosses-Neogravute, 1944), 5.

26. W. F. Damon and Claud P. Brownley, "9th Reconnaissance Troop on Maneuvers," *Cavalry Journal* 50, no. 5 (September–October 1941): 86–88. The recon troop trained with only four of sixteen authorized radios, and no .50-caliber machine guns were available to the unit for the first year of its existence.

27. Major General Rene E. DeRussey Hoyle was a member of the United States Military Academy Class of 1906. His father and grandfather were both graduates of West Point, in 1875 and 1812, respectively.

28. Gabel, *The U.S. Army GHQ Maneuvers of 1941*, 133.

29. Information and Education Division, ETOUSA, *Hitler's Nemesis*, 6.

30. Gabel, *The U.S. Army GHQ Maneuvers of 1941*, 133–150.

31. Ibid., 161.

32. Ibid., 174.

33. "Regimental History, Sixtieth Infantry, 1940–1942," p. 2, 309-INF(60)-0.1, Box 7535, Record Group 407, National Archives II.

34. 9th Infantry Division, "General Order 31," 3 December 1941, 309-1.13, Box 7329, Record Group 407, National Archives II.

35. Kent Roberts Greenfield, Robert R. Palmer, and Bell I. Wiley, *The Organization of Ground Combat Troops* (Washington, D.C.: Historical Division, United States Army, 1947), 89.

36. Ninth Medical Battalion, "Battalion History," 1942, p. 3, 309-MED-0.1, Box 7544, Record Group 407, National Archives II.

37. John Sloan Brown, *Draftee Division: The 88th Infantry Division in World War II* (Lexington: University Press of Kentucky, 1986), 18.

38. Maurice Matloff and Edwin M. Snell, *Strategic Planning for Coalition Warfare, 1941–1942* (Washington, D.C.: Office of the Chief of Military History, 1953), 317–318.

39. Major General R. E. D. Hoyle went on to finish his career in command of a field artillery replacement training center.

40. Greenfield, Palmer, and Wiley, *The Organization of Ground Combat Troops*, 10. During the Great Depression the National Guard was treated as another element of the New Deal, its primary role being to give people employment. See John K. Mahon, *History of the Militia and National Guard* (New York: Macmillan, 1983), 177.

41. Greenfield, Palmer, and Wiley, *The Organization of Ground Combat Troops*, 11.

42. Gabel, *The U.S. Army GHQ Maneuvers of 1941*, 116–118.

43. Bruce Jacobs, "Tensions between the Army National Guard and the Regular Army," *Military Review* 73 (October 1993): 12–13.

44. This excerpt from the memorandum from Lieutenant General McNair to General Marshall is contained in a memorandum from Major Bell I. Wiley, War Department Historical Section, to Colonel Rogers, G-2, SUBJECT: Training of National Guard Units, 21 April 1945, AGF 314.7, Entry 16, Box 4, Record Group 337, National Archives.

45. Ibid.

46. This excerpt from the memorandum from General Marshall to Under Secretary of War Patterson is contained in a memorandum from Major Bell I. Wiley, War Department Historical Section, to Colonel Rogers, G-2, SUBJECT: Training of National Guard Units, 21 April 1945, AGF 314.7, Entry 16, Box 4, Record Group 337, National Archives.

47. Gabel, *The U.S. Army GHQ Maneuvers of 1941,* 117.

48. World War II Combat Effectiveness Questionnaire, Col. (Ret.) Robert C. Works, USMA 1938. Colonel Works went on to serve as G-2 (intelligence officer) and infantry battalion commander in the 10th Mountain Division in the United States and Italy, where he earned two Silver Stars.

49. 29th Infantry Division, "Division History," 1943, p. 1, 329-0.1, Box 8623, Record Group 407, National Archives II.

50. The divisional history reads, "Vital training was obtained on these maneuvers but they were child's play compared with what was to come next." Ibid., 2.

51. Ibid., 4.

52. Ibid. General Reckord had commanded the 115th Infantry Regiment of the 29th Division in World War I.

53. Ibid., 5.

54. Ibid., 8.

55. Ibid., 9. See also Joseph Binkoski and Arthur Plaut, *The 115th Infantry Regiment in World War II* (Washington, D.C.: Infantry Journal Press, 1948), 1.

56. "Confidential Notes on the 29th Division," written by an officer in the 3d Battalion, 115th Infantry Regiment, Fall 1943, 329-0.1, Box 8623, Record Group 407, National Archives II; Joseph Balkoski, *Beyond the Beachhead: The 29th Infantry Division in Normandy* (Harrisburg, Pa.: Stackpole, 1989; repr., New York: Dell, 1992), 27–28.

57. Charles R. Cawthon, *Other Clay: A Remembrance of the World War II Infantry* (Niwot: University Press of Colorado, 1990), 8–9.

58. Balkoski, *Beyond the Beachhead,* 36.

59. 29th Infantry Division, "Division History," 11–17.

60. Ibid., 50–51.

61. Ibid., 20.

62. Ibid., 22.

63. Binkoski and Plaut, *The 115th Infantry Regiment,* 2.

64. 29th Infantry Division, "Division History," 24.

65. Ibid., 25.

66. HQ, 29th Infantry Division, "Division Diary," entry for 5 January 1943, 329-0.3.0, Box 8626, Record Group 407, National Archives II.

67. 29th Infantry Division, "Division History," 33.

68. Ibid., 42.

69. Binkoski and Plaut, *The 115th Infantry Regiment,* 4.

70. The following biographical information is taken from the unpublished memoirs of Charles H. Gerhardt located in the Charles H. Gerhardt Papers, USAMHI.

71. Ibid., 39.

72. Balkoski, *Beyond the Beachhead,* 61.

73. Gerhardt, "Memoirs," 36; HQ, 29th Infantry Division, Training Circular No. 115, 13 November 1943, 329-3.0, Box 8641, Record Group 407, National Archives II.

74. Letter, Colonel (Ret.) Glover S. Johns Jr. to Mr. Robert Hawk, 23 March 1970, Charles H. Gerhardt Papers, USAMHI.

75. Cawthon, *Other Clay,* 27.

76. Balkoski, *Beyond the Beachhead,* 63.

77. The following two paragraphs are based on "Confidential Notes on the 29th Division."

78. Ibid.

79. Ibid.

80. Balkoski, *Beyond the Beachhead,* 54–56.

81. "Division Diary," entry for 2 November 1943.

82. HQ, V Corps, "Report of Exercise 'DUCK,' " 10 January 1944, 329-3.0, Box 8641, Record Group 407, National Archives II.

83. Ibid., 3.

84. HQ, V Corps, "CRITIQUE," 28 January 1944, p. 17, 329-3.01, Box 8642, Record Group 407, National Archives II.

85. Ibid., 18.

86. HQ, 29th Infantry Division, "Exercise DUCK 2," 17 February 1944, 329-3.01, Chief Umpire report, Box 8642, Record Group 407, National Archives II.

87. Ibid.

88. Ibid., Annex XII.

89. HQ, 29th Infantry Division, "Critique—Exercise 'FOX,' " 15 March 44, p. 1, 329-3.01, Box 8642, Record Group 407, National Archives II.

90. Ibid., 6.

91. Ibid., 8.

92. Ibid., 10.

93. Cawthon, *Other Clay,* 38.

94. Letter, Colonel S. L. A. Marshall to General Leland S. Hobbs, 16 March 1946; copy reproduced in *History of the 117th Infantry, 1944–1945* (Baton Rouge, La.: Army and Navy Publishing, 1946), 152.

95. William K. Harrison Jr., Oral History, Section I:22–23, William K. Harrison Jr. Papers, USAMHI.

96. HQ, 30th Infantry Division, "Record of Events," 3 March 1944, p. 1, 330-0.1, Box 8723, Record Group 407, National Archives II.

97. HQ, Second Army, "Comments by the Army Commander on Second Army Field Training," 28 June 1941, p. 3, 330-0.3.0, Box 8724, Record Group 407, National Archives II.

98. Ibid., 4.

99. Harrison, Oral History, 25.

100. General Headquarters, U.S. Army, "Complaints from Soldiers," 8 September 1941, 330-0.3.0, Box 8724, Record Group 407, National Archives II.

101. HQ, I Army Corps, "Condition of the 30th Infantry Division," 26 March 1942, File 16A, Box 60, Record Group 337, National Archives.

102. 20th Infantry Division, "Record of Events," 2; HQ, 119th Infantry Regiment, "History," 1943, 330-INF(119)-0.1, Box 8908; HQ, 30th Infantry Division, "Resume of

State of Training of 30th Division," 11 September 1942, p. 1, 330-0.3.0, Box 8727, Record Group 407, National Archives II.

103. 30th Infantry Division, "Resume of State of Training of 30th Division," 1; "Regimental History of the 120th Infantry," 1944, p. 3, 330-INF(120)-0.1, Box 8917, Record Group 407, National Archives II; *History of the 117th Infantry,* 22.

104. The following biographical information located in 330-0.1, Box 8723, Record Group 407, National Archives II.

105. Harrison, Oral History, 22.

106. Ibid., 230.

107. Ibid., 26–27.

108. Ibid., 28–29.

109. HQ, VII Corps, "Infantry Battalion Field Exercise Tests, 30th Infantry Division," 29 June 1943, 330-0.3.0, Box 8727, Record Group 407, National Archives II.

110. Harrison, Oral History, 231.

111. 30th Infantry Division, "Record of Events," 2–3.

112. *History of the 117th Infantry,* 22.

113. Charles E. Kirkpatrick, *An Unknown Future and a Doubtful Present: Writing the Victory Plan of 1941* (Washington, D.C.: Center of Military History, 1990), 100.

114. HQ, 42d Infantry Division, Unit History, File 342-0, Box 10653, Record Group 407, National Archives II.

115. John Colby, *War from the Ground Up: The 90th Division in WWII* (Austin, Tex.: Nortex Press, 1991).

116. Ibid., 25–26.

117. Ibid., 148.

118. Ibid., 2.

119. Ibid.

120. HQ, 90th Infantry Division, "Brief History of the 90th Division since Reactivation," 27 April 1944, p. 1, 390-0.1, Box 13278, Record Group 407, National Archives II.

121. Ibid., 1–2.

122. War Department, "Designation of Parent Units," 1 May 1942, 390-0.19, Box 13285, Record Group 407, National Archives II.

123. HQ, Army Ground Forces, "Armored and Motorized Divisions," 7 August 1942, 390-0.19, Box 13285, Record Group 407, National Archives II.

124. William E. Depuy, Oral History, William E. Depuy Papers, USAMHI, 9.

125. Ibid., 12.

126. HQ, VIII Corps, "Additional Comments on 90th Division D-1 Maneuvers," 20–31 December 1942, p. 2, 390-3.0, Box 13300, Record Group 407, National Archives II.

127. HQ, VIII Corps, "Notes on Attack Phase of 90th Division Problem," 29–30 December 1942, p. 3, 390-3.0, Box 13300, Record Group 407, National Archives II.

128. Ibid.

129. HQ, VIII Corps, "D-3 Problem 90th Division," 7–9 January 1943, pp. 2–3, 390-3.0, Box 13300, Record Group 407, National Archives II.

130. HQ, VIII Corps, "D-4 Problem with 90th Division," 10–12 January 1943, p. 4, 390-3.0, Box 13300, Record Group 407, National Archives II.

131. Ibid.

132. HQ, VIII Corps, "Notes on Attack Phase of 90th Division Problem," 2.

133. Depuy, Oral History, 9.

134. HQ, 90th Infantry Division, "Brief History of the 90th Division," 4.

135. *345th Field Artillery Battalion, 90th Infantry Division* (Munich: F. Bruckmann, 1946), 10.

136. Ibid., 4–5.

137. HQ, 90th Infantry Division, "Historical Sketches," 27 April 1944, 390-0.1, Box 13278, Record Group 407, National Archives II.

138. Depuy, Oral History, 11.

139. Colby, *War from the Ground Up*, 475–476.

140. HQ, 104th Infantry Division, "History of the 104th Infantry Division, 1921–1943," p. 1, 3104-0.1, Box 14615, Record Group 407, National Archives II.

141. Ibid., 12.

142. Copies of these pamphlets are located in the Terry de la Mesa Allen Papers, USAMHI.

143. Memo, Major General (Ret.) Terry Allen to Major Fred Dunham, Command and General Staff College, Fort Leavenworth, Kansas, undated, copy located in the Terry de la Mesa Allen Papers, USAMHI.

144. HQ, 104th Infantry Division, "Night Attacks," 5.

145. Ibid.

146. HQ, 104th Infantry Division, "Directive for Offensive Combat," 26.

147. Ibid., 28.

148. HQ, 104th Infantry Division, "Combat Leadership."

149. 104th Infantry Division, *Trail of the Timberwolves* (San Luis Obispo, Calif.: 1945), 12–13.

150. Letter, Major General Terry de la Mesa Allen to Mr. Quentin Reynolds, 13 June 1944, Terry de la Mesa Allen Papers, USAMHI.

151. Letter, Major General (Ret.) Terry Allen to Mr. Paul Miller, 23 July 1947, Terry de la Mesa Allen Papers, USAMHI.

152. "Welcome New Timberwolves as Training Program Starts," *The Timberwolf*, 13 April 1944.

153. Leo A. Hoegh and Howard J. Doyle, *Timberwolf Tracks: The History of the 104th Infantry Division, 1942–1945* (Washington, D.C.: Infantry Journal Press, 1946), 39.

154. Biographical material extracted from the Alan W. Jones Papers, USAMHI.

155. Martin Blumenson, "America's World War II Leaders in Europe: Some Thoughts," *Parameters* 19, no. 4 (December 1989): 5.

156. HQ, 106th Infantry Division, "Summary of Activation and Training," 3106-0.1, Box 14717, Record Group 407, National Archives II; R. Ernest Dupuy, *St. Vith—Lion in the Way: The 106th Infantry Division in World War II* (Washington, D.C.: Infantry Journal Press, 1949), 5–6.

157. Bell I. Wiley, *Training in the Ground Army, 1942–1945*, AGF Study No. 11 (Fort Monroe, Va.: Historical Section, Army Ground Forces, 1948), 62.

158. Dupuy, *Lion in the Way*, 7.

159. "Notes of General Lear's Conference with 106th Infantry Division, Camp Atterbury, Indiana," 8 September 1944, AGF 333.1, Entry 16, Box 12, Record Group 337, National Archives.

160. HQ, 100th Infantry Division, "100th Inf Div History: Post Maneuver Period, Second Phase," File 3100-0.1, Box 14216, Record Group 407, National Archives II.

161. Ibid.

CHAPTER 4. FIRST BATTLES

1. Maurice Matloff and Edwin M. Snell, *Strategic Planning for Coalition Warfare, 1941–1942* (Washington, D.C.: Office of the Chief of Military History, 1953), 272–284.

2. HQ, 1st Infantry Division, "TORCH Operation, G-3 Report," 24 November 1942, 301-3, Box 5759, Record Group 407, National Archives II.

3. George F. Howe, *Northwest Africa: Seizing the Initiative in the West* (Washington, D.C.: Office of the Chief of Military History, 1957), 126.

4. 9th Infantry Division, "Standard Operating Procedure," 1941, p. 2, 309-0.24, Box 7327, Record Group 407, National Archives II.

5. Combat Team 39, "After Action Report, 7–9 November 1942," 22 November 1942, 309-INF(39)-0.3, Box 7500, Record Group 407, National Archives II.

6. Ibid.

7. 26th Field Artillery Battalion, "Report of Operations, 7–10 November 1942," 16 November 1942, 309-FA(26)-0.3, Box 7456, Record Group 407, National Archives II.

8. Combat Team 39, "After Action Report, 7–9 November 1942," 22 November 1942.

9. Lucian K. Truscott Jr., *Command Missions: A Personal Story* (New York: E. P. Dutton, 1954; repr., Novato, Calif.: Presidio, 1990), 85–88.

10. HQ, 47th RCT, "Final Report on Operation of 47CT at SAFI for period 2400Z 7 Nov. '42 to 0730Z 11 Nov. '42," 2 Dec. 1942, 309-IN(47)-0.3, Box 7515, Record Group 407, National Archives II.

11. HQ, 60th Infantry, "Operations, 8–11 November 1942," 15 November 1942, 309-INF(60)-3.0, Box 7535, Record Group 407, National Archives II.

12. Truscott provides a good account of this operation, and his problems as the commander, in *Command Missions,* 108–123.

13. HQ, 60th Combat Team, "Comments upon the Operations in the Vicinity of Port Lyautey, Africa," 15 November 1942, 309-INF(60)-3.0, Box 7535, Record Group 407, National Archives II.

14. HQ, Sub–Task Force GOALPOST, "Operations Report—Invasion of French Morocco, 11 October–30 November 1942," 309-INF(60)-3.0, Box 7535, Record Group 407, National Archives II.

15. HQ, 1st Infantry Division, "Report after Action against Enemy," 5 December 1942, p. 3, 301-0.3, Box 5662, Record Group 407, National Archives II.

16. Ibid., 4.

17. HQ, 1st Infantry Division, "Lessons from Operation TORCH," 25 December 1942, p. 7, 301-3.01, Box 5771, Record Group 407, National Archives II.

18. Martin Blumenson, "Kasserine Pass, 30 January–22 February 1943," in *America's First Battles, 1776–1965,* ed. Charles E. Heller and William A. Stofft (Lawrence: University Press of Kansas, 1986), 240.

19. Richard W. Stewart, "The 'Red Bull' Division: The Training and Initial Engagements of the 34th Infantry Division, 1941–1943," *Army History* 25 (winter 1993): 1–10.

20. Ibid., 7.

21. Howe, *Northwest Africa,* 490–492.

22. Ibid., 560–562.

23. HQ, 1st Infantry Division, "Report of Operations, 15 January to 8 April,

1943," 17 April 1943, p. 11, 301-3, Box 5759, Record Group 407, National Archives II.

24. HQ, 9th Infantry Division Artillery, "Narrative of Events, Thala Engagement, 21–24 February 1943," 309-ART-0.3, Box 7424, Record Group 407, National Archives II.

25. Howe, *Northwest Africa*, 574–577.

26. HQ, 9th Infantry Division, "Report of Operations, 26 March–8 April 1943," 25 August 1943, 309-0.3, Box 7326, Record Group 407, National Archives II.

27. Ibid.

28. Ibid.

29. Ibid., 10–11. The medics treated cases of combat fatigue with heavy sedation, a practice contrary to modern techniques of treating combat exhaustion. This probably accounts for the low return-to-duty rate.

30. Ibid., 14–15.

31. HQ, 1st Infantry Division, "Report of Operations, 15 January to 8 April, 1943," 17.

32. Ibid.

33. Information and Education Section, MTOUSA, "The Story of the 34th Infantry Division," pp. 14–20, 334-0, Box 9416, Record Group 407, National Archives II.

34. Howe, *Northwest Africa*, 614.

35. McNair recovered from his wounds but was killed a little over a year later in Normandy by friendly fire while observing the attack of the U.S. VII Corps in Operation COBRA.

36. Howe, *Northwest Africa*, 625.

37. Ibid., 632.

38. HQ, 34th Infantry Division, "Historical Record of 34th Division in the Tunisian Campaign," 13 Dec. 1943, 334-0.3, Box 9417, Record Group 407, National Archives II.

39. Howe, *Northwest Africa*, 638.

40. HQ, 9th Infantry Division, "Report of Operations, 11 April–8 May 1943," 10 September 1943, p. 4, 309-0.3, Box 7326, Record Group 407, National Archives II.

41. Ibid., 4–12.

42. Ibid., 12–16.

43. Ibid., 17.

44. Ibid., 18–23.

45. Omar N. Bradley, *A Soldier's Story* (New York: Rand McNally, 1951), 100–101.

46. Carlo D'Este, *Bitter Victory: The Battle for Sicily, 1943* (New York: E. P. Dutton, 1988), 267 n.

47. "Allen and His Men," *Time,* 9 August 1943.

48. U.S. War Department, *Lessons from the Tunisian Campaign* (Washington, D.C.: Government Printing Office, 15 October 1943), 1–2.

49. Christopher R. Gabel, *Seek, Strike, and Destroy: U.S. Army Tank Destroyer Doctrine in World War II* (Fort Leavenworth, Kans.: Combat Studies Institute, 1985), 39.

50. U.S. War Department, *Lessons from the Tunisian Campaign,* 3–16.

51. HQ, 9th Infantry Division, "Report on Combat Experience and Battle Lessons for Training Purposes," 21 June 1943, 309-0.3, Box 7326, Record Group 407, National Archives II.

52. U.S. War Department, *Lessons from the Tunisian Campaign,* sect. III.

53. HQ, 9th Infantry Division, "Report on Combat Experience and Battle Lessons for Training Purposes," 7.

54. William F. Ross and Charles F. Romanus, *The Quartermaster Corps: Operations in the War against Germany* (Washington, D.C.: Office of the Chief of Military History, 1965), 62.

55. Kent Roberts Greenfield, Robert R. Palmer, and Bell I. Wiley, *The Organization of Ground Combat Troops* (Washington, D.C.: Historical Division, United States Army, 1947), 311.

56. B. H. Liddell Hart, ed., *The Rommel Papers* (London: Collins, 1953), 523.

57. HQ, 34th Infantry Division, "Historical Record of the 34th Division in the Tunisian Campaign," sect. XIII, pt. 5.

58. Maurice Matloff, *Strategic Planning for Coalition Warfare, 1943–1944* (Washington, D.C.: Office of the Chief of Military History, 1959), 24–26.

59. HQ, 3d Infantry Division, "Report of Operations, 10–18 July 1943," 10 September 1943, Section I (Training), 303-0.3, Box 6098, Record Group 407, National Archives II.

60. Albert N. Garland and Howard McGaw Smyth, *Sicily and the Surrender of Italy* (Washington, D.C.: Office of the Chief of Military History, 1965); Charles B. MacDonald, *The Mighty Endeavor: The American War in Europe* (New York: Quill, 1986), chap. 10; D'Este, *Bitter Victory.*

61. Frank J. Price, *Troy H. Middleton* (Baton Rouge: Louisiana State University Press, 1974), 144.

62. HQ, 45th Infantry Division, "Comments and Recommendation, 45th Division, Task Force," 31 July 1943, 345-0.3.0, Box 10861, Record Group 407, National Archives II.

63. Ibid.

64. Truscott relates his experiences as a wartime leader in *Command Missions,* one of the best personal narratives to emerge from World War II.

65. Ibid., 175–176.

66. John A. Heintges, Oral History, John A. Heintges Papers, USAMHI, 145–146.

67. Heintges, Oral History, 416.

68. Garland and Smythe, *Sicily and the Surrender of Italy,* 165–174.

69. D'Este, *Bitter Victory,* 304–305.

70. Patton describes the method he used to initiate offensive operations without specific orders as "rock soup." George S. Patton Jr., *War As I Knew It* (Boston: Houghton Mifflin, 1947), 125.

71. William B. Rosson, Oral History, William B. Rosson Papers, USAMHI, 56.

72. D'Este, *Bitter Victory,* 422–423.

73. Garland and Smythe, *Sicily and the Surrender of Italy,* 309.

74. D'Este, *Bitter Victory,* 458.

75. HQ, 1st Infantry Division, "Report of Operations, 1 August 1943 to 31 August 1943," 3 September 1943, 301-3, Box 5759, Record Group 407, National Archives II.

76. A full accounting of Allen's relief is given by D'Este, *Bitter Victory,* 468–475. The following paragraph is taken from his account.

77. Bradley, *A Soldier's Story,* 154–156.

78. "Terry Allen and the First Division in North Africa and Sicily" (undated manuscript located in the Terry de la Mesa Allen Papers, USAMHI), p. 55. Bradley believed that Allen's men lacked discipline under his leadership. This belief stemmed from the conduct of the soldiers of the Big Red One after the Tunisian campaign. While

Allen felt his men deserved the opportunity to blow off some steam after their battles, Bradley saw things differently: "The Big Red One literally ran amok along the entire coast of North Africa from Bizerte to Oran. In Algiers, cocky veterans of the fighting hunted down and assaulted the rear area troops, touching off widespread rioting. . . . this incident (and others too numerous and trivial to mention) convinced me that Terry Allen was not fit to command, and I was determined to remove him and Teddy Roosevelt from the division as soon as circumstances on Sicily permitted." Omar N. Bradley and Clay Blair, *A General's Life* (New York: Simon and Schuster, 1983), 172–173.

79. Roosevelt wrote a very poignant letter to the officers and men of the 1st Infantry Division upon his departure. It read in part: "I do not have to tell you what I think of you, for you know. You will always be in my heart. I have been ordered away. It is a great grief to me, and my hope is that sometime I may return, for it is with you that I feel I belong. . . . May luck go with your battle worn colors as glory always has." Letter, Brig. Gen. Theodore Roosevelt to the Officers and Men of the 1st Division, 6 August 1943, 301-FA(33)-0.1, Box 5898, Record Group 407, National Archives II.

80. "Terry Allen and the First Division in North Africa and Sicily," 57.

81. Department of the Army, FM 22-103, *Leadership and Command at Senior Levels* (Washington, D.C.: Government Printing Office, 1987), 71–73.

82. The 9th Infantry Division came over from North Africa to replace the 45th Infantry Division, which withdrew from operations to prepare for the upcoming invasion of the Italian mainland. The 9th Infantry Division was not slated for the Italian campaign. After the end of the Sicilian campaign, the 1st and 9th Infantry Divisions deployed to Great Britain in preparation for OVERLORD.

83. HQ, 9th Infantry Division, "Report of Operations, 5–14 August 1943," 15 August 1943, p. 4, 309-0.3, Box 7326, National Archives II.

84. Tom Henry, "March of the Silent Men," *Washington Evening Star,* 30 September 1943.

85. HQ, 9th Infantry Division, "Report of Operations, 5–14 August 1943," 20.

86. Donald G. Taggart, ed., *History of the Third Infantry Division in World War II* (Washington, D.C.: Infantry Journal Press, 1947), 64–74.

87. Ibid., 76.

88. Garland and Smythe, *Sicily and the Surrender of Italy,* 552–553.

89. HQ, 1st Infantry Division, "Report of Operation, 1 August 1943 to 31 August 1943," Section III; HQ, 3d Infantry Division, "Report of Operations, July 19–Aug 17, 1943," 13 December 1943, 303-0.3, Box 6099, Record Group 407, National Archives II; HQ, 9th Infantry Division, "Report of Operations, 5–14 August 1943," Annex 2; HQ, 45th Infantry Division, "Report of Operation of the 45th Infantry Division in the Sicilian Campaign," 1 September 1943, Section VII, 345-0.3, Box 10858, Record Group 407, National Archives II.

90. HQ, 3d Infantry Division, "Report of Operations, 10–18 July 1943," 1.

91. HQ, 1st Infantry Division, "Report of Operation, 1 August 1943 to 31 August 1943," 21.

92. Ibid.

93. "DUKW" stood for the following: D = first year of production, 1942; U = utility; K = front-wheel drive; W = two rear driving axles. The troops affectionately called the vehicle the "Duck."

94. Lida Mayo, *The Ordnance Department: On Beachhead and Battlefront* (Washington, D.C.: Office of the Chief of Military History, 1968), 162–163.

95. Ross and Romanus, *The Quartermaster Corps,* 80.

96. HQ, 9th Infantry Division, "Report of Operations, 5–14 August 1943," Annex 2, p. 5.

97. HQ, 9th Infantry Division, "Report of Operations, 14 June–1 July 1944, Cotentin Peninsula," 14 July 1944, 309-0.3, Box 7326, Record Group 407, National Archives II.

98. G-3 Training Section, Allied Force Headquarters, "Training Notes from the Sicilian Campaign," 25 October 1943, 301-0.4, Box 5665, Record Group 407, National Archives II.

CHAPTER 5. THE LONG ROAD TO GERMANY

1. Martin Blumenson, *Salerno to Cassino* (Washington, D.C.: Office of the Chief of Military History, 1969), 69.

2. Ibid., 43.

3. Dominick Graham and Shelford Bidwell, *Tug of War: The Battle for Italy, 1943–1945* (New York: St. Martin's Press, 1986), 52.

4. Blumenson, *Salerno to Cassino,* 99–112.

5. Des Hickey and Gus Smith, *Operation Avalanche: The Salerno Landings, 1943* (London: Heinemann, 1983), 226.

6. HQ, 82d Airborne Division, "The 82d Airborne Division in Sicily and Italy," pp. 49–54, 382-0.3, Box 12346, Record Group 407, National Archives II; Mark W. Clark, *Calculated Risk* (New York: Harper and Brothers, 1950), 203.

7. HQ, 82d Airborne Division, "The 82d Airborne Division in Sicily and Italy," 49.

8. Blumenson, *Salerno to Cassino,* 127.

9. Geoffrey Perret, *There's a War to Be Won: The United States Army in World War II* (New York: Random House, 1991), 197.

10. GNGCS 320.2, 7 February 1944, Subject: Replacement Situation, Record Group 337, National Archives.

11. Memorandum for Deputy Chief of Staff, AGF, 26 January 1945, Subject: Data Regarding Suitability of AGF Replacements, Tab C, 322, Record Group 337, National Archives.

12. HQ, U.S. Fifth Army, "Proceedings of a Board of Officers Re: Replacements Received by Fifth Army," 31 December 1943, Item 16A, Box 53, Record Group 337, National Archives.

13. Ibid., 5.

14. Ibid., 7–10.

15. HQ, 3d Infantry Division, "Casualties and Replacements," 17 December 1943, p. 1, 303-1.16, Box 6144, Record Group 407, National Archives II.

16. Ibid., 2.

17. Ibid.

18. Ibid., 4.

19. Ibid., 5.

20. HQ, 45th Infantry Division, "Operation of the Forty Fifth Infantry Division in Italy, November 1–November 30, 1943," 345-0.3, Box 10858, Record Group 407, National Archives II.

21. William B. Rosson, Oral History, William B. Rosson Papers, USAMHI, 61.

22. William F. Ross and Charles F. Romanus, *The Quartermaster Corps: Operations in the War against Germany* (Washington, D.C.: Office of the Chief of Military History, 1965), 105, 241.

23. Lida Mayo, *The Ordnance Department: On Beachhead and Battlefront* (Washington, D.C.: Office of the Chief of Military History), 216.

24. Ross and Romanus, *The Quartermaster Corps,* 105.

25. Ibid., 107.

26. Graham and Bidwell, *Tug of War,* 104–106.

27. Although Churchill avidly supported the operation, he did not develop the plan. Carlo D'Este, *Fatal Decision: Anzio and the Battle for Rome* (New York: HarperCollins, 1991), 72.

28. Ibid., 77.

29. Ibid., 79.

30. Robert L. Wagner, *The Texas Army: A History of the 36th Division in the Italian Campaign* (Austin, Tex.: 1972), 96.

31. Graham and Bidwell, *Tug of War,* 147.

32. Wagner, *The Texas Army,* 100–104.

33. Blumenson, *Salerno to Cassino,* 333–338.

34. Wagner, *The Texas Army,* 112–116.

35. Ibid., 121.

36. HQ, 34th Infantry Division, "Operations Report, 1–31 January 1944," 28 February 1944, 334-0.3, Box 9417, Record Group 407, National Archives II; Information and Education Section, MTOUSA, "The Story of the 34th Infantry Division," pp. 56–60, 334-0, Box 9416, Record Group 407, National Archives II.

37. Walter T. Kerwin Jr., Oral History, Walter T. Kerwin Papers, USAMHI, 144.

38. HQ, 3d Infantry Division, "Organization and Training for Operation 'SHINGLE,' " 18 January 1944, 303-3.13, Box 6247, Record Group 407, National Archives II.

39. D'Este, *Fatal Decision,* 123.

40. Ibid., 264. Churchill's remark referred to the poorly conducted amphibious invasion of Sulva Bay during the Gallipoli campaign in Turkey during World War I.

41. Graham and Bidwell, *Tug of War,* 139.

42. D'Este, *Fatal Decision,* 184.

43. Lucian K. Truscott Jr., *Command Missions: A Personal Story* (New York: E. P. Dutton, 1954; repr., Novato, Calif.: Presidio, 1990), 328; for Truscott's reforms in VI Corps, see pp. 329–340.

44. Andrew G. Ellis, "On Time—On Target: The Birth of Modern American Artillery," *Field Artillery* (August 1988): 26–30.

45. Ibid.; Allan R. Millett, "Cantigny, 28–31 May 1918," in *America's First Battles, 1776–1965,* ed. Charles E. Heller and William A. Stofft (Lawrence: University Press of Kansas, 1986), 185; Harry Lemley, Oral History, Harry Lemley Papers, USAMHI, Section I: 30.

46. Lemley, Oral History, Section II: 52.

47. Truscott, *Command Missions,* 325–326.

48. Lemley, Oral History, Section II: 54.

49. Letter, Major General (Ret.) Ralph C. Cooper to author, 27 May 1993. Major General Cooper (then a colonel) was the commander of the 36th Field Artillery Group in Italy and France.

50. Truscott, *Command Missions,* 345.

51. Lemley, Oral History, Section II: 44.

52. Truscott, *Command Missions,* 347.

53. Lemley, Oral History, Section II: 62.

54. John Bowditch III, *Anzio Beachhead* (Washington, D.C.: Historical Division, War Department, 1948), 74.

55. Ibid., 72.

56. HQ, 45th Infantry Division, "Operation of the Forty Fifth Infantry Division in Italy, Anzio Beachhead, February 1–29, 1944," 345-0.3, Box 10858, Record Group 407, National Archives II.

57. Mayo, *The Ordnance Department,* 192.

58. Bowditch, *Anzio Beachhead,* 105.

59. HQ, 30th Infantry Regiment, "Report of Operations, 1–31 March 1944, p. 6, 303-0.3, Box 6102, Record Group 407, National Archives II.

60. HQ, 3d Infantry Division, "Casualties and Replacements for the Anzio Operation," 17 April 1944, 303-1.16, Box 6144, Record Group 407, National Archives II.

61. Ibid., 3.

62. Ibid., 2.

63. HQ, 34th Infantry Division, "Report of Operations, 1–31 May 1944," 20 June 1944, 334-0.3, Box 9417, Record Group 407, National Archives II.

64. John Sloan Brown, *Draftee Division: The 88th Infantry Division in World War II* (Lexington: University Press of Kentucky, 1986), 105.

65. Ibid., 22–23.

66. Ibid., 31.

67. Ibid., 12.

68. John A. Heintges, Oral History, John A. Heintges Papers, USAMHI, 259.

69. Ibid., 416.

70. Headquarters, 3d Infantry Division, "Report of Operations, 1–31 March 1944," 17 April 1944, pp. 4–5, 303-0.3, Box 6102, Record Group 407, National Archives II.

71. HQ, 30th Infantry Regiment, "Report of Operations, 1–31 May 1944," 14 June 1944, p. 9, 303-0.3, Box 6104, Record Group 407, National Archives II.

72. Ibid.

73. HQ, 7th Infantry Regiment, "Report of Operations, 1–30 June 1944," 4 July 1944, 303-0.3, Box 6105, Record Group 407, National Archives II.

74. Ernest F. Fisher Jr., *Cassino to the Alps* (Washington, D.C.: Center of Military History, 1977), 68.

75. Ibid., 66.

76. Ibid., 77.

77. Brown, *Draftee Division,* 139.

78. Donald G. Taggart, ed., *History of the Third Infantry Division in World War II* (Washington, D.C.: Infantry Journal Press, 1947), 155–156.

79. Ibid., 157–171.

80. Ibid., 171.

81. For an excellent discussion of Lieutenant General Clark's motives in shifting the axis of the VI Corps attack, see D'Este, *Fatal Decision,* 366–373.

82. Truscott, *Command Missions,* 375.

83. Ibid., 375–376.

84. Fisher, *Cassino to the Alps,* 165.

85. Ibid., 175.

86. Ibid., 184.

87. Ibid., 189.

CHAPTER 6. NORMANDY

1. Gordon A. Harrison, *Cross-Channel Attack* (Washington, D.C.: Office of the Chief of Military History, 1951), 300–301.

2. Ibid., 302.

3. Henry I. Shaw Jr., Bernard C. Nalty, and Edwin T. Turnbladh, *History of U.S. Marine Corps Operations in World War II: Central Pacific Drive*, vol. 3 (Washington, D.C.: Historical Branch, G-3 Division, HQ, U.S. Marine Corps, 1966), 110–111.

4. Geoffrey Perret, *There's a War to Be Won* (New York: Random House, 1991), 299.

5. In a typical comment regarding the air and naval fire support on OMAHA Beach, Lieutenant Colonel Herbert C. Hicks Jr., commander of the 2/16th Infantry, stated, "It is felt that too much confidence and weight was put on what the supporting fires were going to do. Supporting fires were of absolute[ly] no consequence on Omaha Red Beach. The Air Corps might just as well have stayed home in bed for all the good that their bombing concentration did. There were no indications of any bombs hitting closer than fifteen hundred yards to any of the strongpoints, and there were indications of the greater quantity of them falling four thousand yards inland. It is not understood why the naval support plan could not have been more effective." HQ, 2/16th Infantry, "Comments and Criticisms on Operation Neptune," 29 June 1944, pp. 3–4, 301-INF(16)-3.01, Box 5927, Record Group 407, National Archives II.

6. Charles H. Gerhardt, unpublished memoirs, Charles H. Gerhardt Papers, US-AMHI, Annex 1.

7. HQ, CT 16, "Comments and Criticisms of Operations 'FOX,' 'FABIUS I,' and 'NEPTUNE,' " 30 June 1944, p. 3, 301-INF(16)-3.01, Box 5927, Record Group 407, National Archives II.

8. Charles H. Taylor, *Omaha Beachhead* (Washington, D.C.: Historical Division, War Department, 1945), 39.

9. 29th Infantry Division, "Battle Lessons and Conclusions," After Action Report, June 1944, p. 1, 329-0.3, Box 8623, Record Group 407, National Archives II.

10. Harrison, *Cross-Channel Attack*, 313.

11. Taylor, *Omaha Beachhead*, 44.

12. Ibid., 58; Charles R. Cawthon, *Other Clay: A Remembrance of the World War II Infantry* (Niwot: University Press of Colorado, 1990), 58–63.

13. Stephen E. Ambrose, *D-Day, June 6, 1944: The Climactic Battle of World War II* (New York: Simon and Schuster, 1994), chap. 20.

14. HQ, CT 16, "Invasion of France," 1944, p. 20, 301-INF(16)-0, Box 5907, Record Group 407, National Archives II.

15. "16-E on D Day," Combat Interviews (CI-1), Box 24011, Record Group 407, National Archives II. Both Lieutenant Spaulding and Technical Sergeant Streczyk received the Distinguished Service Cross for their exploits.

16. Society of the First Division, *Danger Forward: The Story of the First Division in World War II* (Atlanta, Ga.: A. Love, 1947; repr., Nashville, Tenn.: Battery Press, 1980), 213.

17. Stephen Ambrose, "Why We Won the War: The Politics of World War II,"

Army, June 1994, 17. This action is depicted in the opening scenes of Steven Spielberg's 1998 movie *Saving Private Ryan.*

18. Joseph Balkoski, *Beyond the Beachhead: The 29th Infantry Division in Normandy* (Harrisburg, Pa.: Stackpole, 1989; repr., New York: Dell, 1992), 154.

19. Ibid., 156–157.

20. Taylor, *Omaha Beachhead,* 106–109.

21. Roland G. Ruppenthal, *Utah Beach to Cherbourg* (Washington, D.C.: Historical Division, Department of the Army, 1947), 45–47.

22. Ibid., 55.

23. James A. Van Fleet, Oral History, James A. Van Fleet Papers, USAMHI, 53–57.

24. Roosevelt died of a heart attack in his sleep on 12 July 1944. Bradley and Eisenhower had decided to make him a division commander shortly before his death but had not informed Roosevelt of their decision before he died. The army later awarded Roosevelt a posthumous Medal of Honor for exceptional gallantry on D-Day.

25. Taylor, *Omaha Beachhead,* 138.

26. Ibid., 145.

27. Ibid., 149.

28. Omar N. Bradley, *A Soldier's Story* (New York: Rand McNally, 1951), 295.

29. Ruppenthal, *Utah Beach to Cherbourg,* 129–130; Taylor, *Omaha Beachhead,* 19.

30. Paul Kennedy, "Military Effectiveness in the First World War," in *Military Effectiveness,* vol. 1, *The First World War,* ed. Allan R. Millett and Williamson Murray (Boston: Unwin Hyman, 1988), 331.

31. Ruppenthal, *Utah Beach to Cherbourg,* 131; Taylor, *Omaha Beachhead,* 19.

32. Michael D. Doubler, *Busting the Bocage: American Combined Arms Operations in France, 6 June–31 July 1944* (Fort Leavenworth, Kans.: Combat Studies Institute, 1988), 21.

33. HQ, 9th Infantry Division, "Report of Operations, 14 June–1 July 1944, Cotentin Peninsula," 14 July 1944, Annex 2, p. 1, 309-0.3, Box 7326, Record Group 407, National Archives II.

34. Ruppenthal, *Utah Beach to Cherbourg,* 126–127.

35. Teddy H. Sanford, Oral History, Teddy H. Sanford Papers, USAMHI, 93.

36. Harrison, *Cross-Channel Attack,* 403.

37. Ruppenthal, *Utah Beach to Cherbourg,* 141–143.

38. HQ, 9th Infantry Division, "Report of Operations, 14 June–1 July 1944, Cotentin Peninsula," 8.

39. Ibid., 9–18.

40. Ibid., Annex 2, p. 1.

41. Quoted in Joseph B. Mittelman, *Hold Fast!* (Munich: F. Bruckmann, 1946), 44.

42. Bradley, *A Soldier's Story,* 297.

43. General William E. Depuy, Oral History, William E. Depuy Papers, USAMHI, Section I: 26–27.

44. John Colby, *War from the Ground Up: The 90th Division in WWII* (Austin, Tex.: Nortex Press, 1991), 148.

45. Ibid., 148–149.

46. Ibid., 149.

47. Depuy, Oral History, Section I: 22.

48. Ibid., Section I: 32.

49. Colby, *War from the Ground Up,* 152.

50. Depuy, Oral History, Section II: 6.

51. Colby, *War from the Ground Up,* 159.

52. Timothy T. Lupfer, *The Dynamics of Doctrine: The Changes in German Tactical Doctrine during the First World War,* Leavenworth Papers, no. 4 (Fort Leavenworth, Kans.: U.S. Army Command and General Staff College, 1981), 12–20.

53. U.S. War Department, *Handbook on German Military Forces* (Washington, D.C.: Government Printing Office, 1945), IV-21 to IV-23.

54. Ibid., IV-25.

55. Ibid., II-8.

56. Ibid., II-10.

57. Kent Roberts Greenfield, Robert R. Palmer, and Bell I Wiley, *The Organization of Ground Combat Troops* (Washington, D.C.: Historical Division, U.S. Army, 1947), 275.

58. U.S. War Department, *Handbook on German Military Forces,* VII-8; Balkoski, *Beyond the Beachhead,* 99.

59. Balkoski, *Beyond the Beachhead,* 102.

60. Greenfield, Palmer, and Wiley, *The Organization of Ground Combat Troops,* 275.

61. John A. English, *On Infantry* (New York: Praeger, 1981), 134.

62. Depuy, Oral History, Section III: 11–14.

63. Steve R. Waddell, "The Communications Zone (COMZ): American Logistics in France, 1944" (Ph.D. diss., Texas A&M University, 1992), 161.

64. James Lucas and James Barker, *The Battle of Normandy* (New York: Holmes and Meier, 1978), 56.

65. Letter to author, 11 March 1993.

66. After the war, official U.S. Army historians named the battle that began on 3 July the "Battle of the Hedgerows," but American forces had encountered hedgerow terrain shortly after D-Day and had been fighting through hedgerows ever since.

67. David Garth and Charles H. Taylor, *St.-Lô (7 July-19 July 1944)* (Washington, D.C.: Historical Division, War Department, 1946), 4.

68. Ibid., 4–5.

69. Ibid., 8.

70. Intelligence Annex to Army Group B War Journal, 10 July 1944, p. 2, Microcopy T-311, Roll 1, Combined Arms Research Library, Fort Leavenworth, Kansas.

71. Ibid., 5.

72. HQ, 30th Infantry Division, "After Battle Report," 15 June 1944–30 June 1944 and 1 July 1944–31 July 1944, 330-3, Box 8788, National Archives II.

73. William K. Harrison Jr., Oral History, William K. Harrison Jr. Papers, USAMHI, 57.

74. HQ, 30th Infantry Division, "After Battle Report," 1 July 1944–31 July 1944; Garth and Taylor, *St.-Lô,* 9.

75. Garth and Taylor, *St.-Lô,* 16–17.

76. Dennis J. Vetock, *Lessons Learned: A History of US Army Lesson Learning* (Carlisle Barracks, Pa.: USAMHI, 1988), 68–69.

77. Ibid., 71.

78. See the respective after-action reports of each division in 301-3, 303-0.3, 309-0.3, and 329-0.3, Record Group 407, National Archives II.

79. HQ, 9th Infantry Division, "Report of Operations, 1–31 July 1944," 1 August 1944, p. 4, 309-0.3, Box 7326, Record Group 407, National Archives II.

80. Garth and Taylor, *St.-Lô,* 46.

81. Ibid., 55–57.

82. Ibid., 59.

83. Ibid., 80.

84. Cawthon, *Other Clay,* 82.

85. Gerhardt, unpublished memoirs, 49.

86. Garth and Taylor, *St.-Lô,* 100.

87. Glover S. Johns Jr., *The Clay Pigeons of St.-Lô* (Harrisburg, Pa.: Military Service Publishing, 1958), 228.

88. Ibid., 175.

89. Figures obtained from the after-action reports of the respective divisions in 309-0.3, 329-0.3, and 330-1, Record Group 407, National Archives II.

90. Garth and Taylor, *St.-Lô,* 125.

CHAPTER 7. BREAKOUT AND PURSUIT

1. Richard D. Hooker Jr., ed., *Maneuver Warfare: An Anthology* (Novato, Calif.: Presidio, 1993).

2. Martin Blumenson, *Breakout and Pursuit* (Washington, D.C.: Office of the Chief of Military History, 1961), 215–218.

3. Michael D. Doubler, *Busting the Bocage: American Combined Arms Operations in France, 6 June–31 July 1944* (Fort Leavenworth, Kans.: Combat Studies Institute, 1988), chap. 2.

4. 12th Army Group, *Report of Operations,* vol. 11, p. 34. See also U.S. First Army, *Combat Operations Data* (Governor's Island, N.Y.: 18 November 1946), p. 165; and H. L. Hillyard, "Employment of Tanks by the Infantry Division," *Military Review* 27, no. 3 (June 1947): 50.

5. Bell I. Wiley, *Training in the Ground Army, 1942–1945, AGF Study No. 11* (Fort Monroe, Va.: Historical Section, Army Ground Forces, 1948), 75.

6. G-3 Section, Supreme Headquarters Allied Expeditionary Forces, "Employment of Tanks and Infantry in Normandy," *Military Review* 24, no. 9 (December 1944): 13–17.

7. U.S. War Department, *Employment of Tanks with Infantry, FM 17-36, Supplement No. 1* (Washington, D.C.: Government Printing Office, 7 July 1944), 59–62.

8. U.S. First Army, *Report of Operations, 1 Aug 1944–22 Feb 1945,* Annex 5, p. 46.

9. G-3, SHAEF, "Employment of Tanks and Infantry in Normandy," 15.

10. Headquarters, 29th Infantry Division, After Action Report, July 1944, p. 2, 329-0.3, Box 8623, Record Group 407, National Archives II.

11. Doubler, *Busting the Bocage,* 33.

12. First U.S. Army, *Report of Operations, 20 October 1943–1 August 1944,* Annex No. 9, 200–201; Blumenson, *Breakout and Pursuit,* 206–207; James D. Sams, "Ordnance Improvisation in the Combat Zone," *Military Review* 28, no. 2 (May 1948): 33; and Omar N. Bradley, *A Soldier's Story* (New York: Rand McNally, 1951), 342.

13. Thomas Alexander Hughes, *Over Lord: General Pete Quesada and the Triumph of Tactical Air Power in World War II* (New York: Free Press, 1995).

14. First U.S. Army, *Report of Operations, 30 Oct 1943–1 Aug 1944,* 121; XIX

Tactical Air Command, "Ground-Air Teamwork in France," *Military Review* 25, no. 2 (May 1945): 43–45.

15. First U.S. Army, *Report of Operations, 1 Aug 1944–22 Feb 1945,* 169.

16. Bradley, *A Soldier's Story,* 347.

17. Blumenson, *Breakout and Pursuit,* 229.

18. Headquarters, 30th Infantry Division, After Battle Report, 1–31 July 1944, p. 19, 330-3, Box 8788, Record Group 407, National Archives II.

19. Blumenson, *Breakout and Pursuit,* 236.

20. William K. Harrison Jr., Oral History, William K. Harrison Papers, USAMHI, 326. General Harrison was awarded the Distinguished Service Cross for his role in restoring order in the 30th Infantry Division following the bombing.

21. Ibid., 329.

22. Blumenson, *Breakout and Pursuit,* 237.

23. Ibid., 219–220.

24. Ibid., 219.

25. Paul Carell, *Invasion: They're Coming!* (New York: E. P. Dutton, 1963), 233; Blumenson, *Breakout and Pursuit,* 240. Blumenson estimates German casualties in the bombardment at one thousand men.

26. Carell, *Invasion,* 236.

27. HQ, 9th Infantry Division, "Report of Operations, 1–31 July 1944," 1 August 1944, p. 12, 309-0.3, Box 7326, National Archives II.

28. J. Lawton Collins, *Lightning Joe: An Autobiography* (Baton Rouge: Louisiana State University Press, 1979), 242.

29. HQ, 30th Infantry Division, "After Battle Report, 1 July 1944–31 July 1944," p. 21, 330-3, Box 8788, National Archives II.

30. HQ, 9th Infantry Division, "Report of Operations, 1–31 July 1944," 12–13.

31. Blumenson, *Breakout and Pursuit,* 251.

32. James F. Scoggin, ed., *OB WEST: A Study in Command* (Historical Division, European Command, 1948), vol. 1: 107.

33. Hans Speidel, *Invasion 1944* (Chicago: Henry Regnery, 1950), 130.

34. Allied governments kept this information secret long after the end of the war. The first book on ULTRA was by F. W. Winterbotham, *The Ultra Secret* (London: Weidenfeld and Nicolson, 1974). Other works soon followed: Patrick Beesly, *Very Special Intelligence* (London: Hamish Hamilton, 1977); R. V. Jones, *Most Secret War* (London: Hamish Hamilton, 1978); and Ronald Lewin, *Ultra Goes to War* (London: Hutchinson, 1978). The best account of the use of ULTRA in France in 1944 is by Ralph Bennett, *Ultra in the West* (New York: Scribner's, 1980).

35. Blumenson, *Breakout and Pursuit,* 471–472.

36. Bennett, *Ultra in the West,* 119.

37. David P. Rodgers, "The Camera Was Their Weapon," *Army* 47, no. 4 (April 1997): 50–54.

38. Blumenson, *Breakout and Pursuit,* 467.

39. HQ, 9th Infantry Division, "Report of Operations, 1–31 August 1944," 1 September 1944, pp. 5–6, 309-0.3, Box 7326, Record Group 407, National Archives II.

40. Blumenson, *Breakout and Pursuit,* 471.

41. Collins, *Lightning Joe,* 255. The best work on this action is Alwyn Feather-

ston, *Saving the Breakout: The 30th Division's Heroic Stand at Mortain, August 7–12, 1944* (Novato, Calif.: Presidio, 1993).

42. L. V. Fraser and Oliver Steward, "Rocket Typhoons: Answer to German Panzers," *Armored Cavalry Journal* 53 no. 5 (September–October 1944): 8–11; Featherston, *Saving the Breakout,* 129–137.

43. Blumenson, *Breakout and Pursuit,* 474.

44. Bradley, *A Soldier's Story,* 375.

45. Martin Blumenson, *The Battle of the Generals: The Untold Story of the Falaise Pocket—The Campaign That Should Have Won World War II* (New York: William Morrow, 1993).

46. Ibid.

47. HQ, 9th Infantry Division, "Report of Operations, 1–31 August 1944," 1 September 1944, p. 10, 309-0.3, Box 7326, National Archives II.

48. 90th Infantry Division, *A History of the 90th Division in World War II, 6 June 1944 to 9 May 1945* (Baton Rouge, La.: Army and Navy Publishing, 1946), 22.

49. Blumenson, *The Battle of the Generals,* 21.

50. Bradley, *A Soldier's Story,* 377.

51. Ibid., 379.

52. William B. Breuer, *Death of a Nazi Army* (New York: Stein and Day, 1985), 286.

53. Blumenson, *The Battle of the Generals,* 232.

54. General William E. Depuy, Oral History, William E. Depuy Papers, USAMHI, Section II: 16.

55. 90th Infantry Division, *History of the 90th Division,* 23.

56. HQ, 90th Infantry Division, "Report of Operations, August 1944," 3 October 1944, p. 11, 390-0.3, Box 13279, Record Group 407, National Archives II.

57. Ibid.

58. For the estimates of various historians and participants, see Eddy Florentin, *The Battle of the Falaise Gap* (New York: Hawthorn, 1967), 334–335.

59. James Lucas and James Barker, *The Battle of Normandy* (New York: Holmes and Meier, 1978), 19, 160.

60. Dwight D. Eisenhower, *Crusade in Europe* (Garden City, N.Y.: Doubleday, 1948), 279.

61. Blumenson, *Breakout and Pursuit,* 646–653; Headquarters, 29th Infantry Division, After Action Report, September 1944, 329-0.3, Box 8624, Record Group 407, National Archives II.

62. Kent Roberts Greenfield, Robert R. Palmer, and Bell I. Wiley, *The Organization of Ground Combat Troops* (Washington, D.C.: Historical Division, U.S. Army, 1947), 338.

63. HQ, 1st Infantry Division, "G-3 Report of Operations, 1–31 August 1944," 10 September 1944, p. 65, 301-3, Box 5761, Record Group 407, National Archives II.

64. 9th Infantry Division, "Report of Operations, 1–31 August 1944," 14.

65. Speidel, *Invasion 1944,* 145–146.

66. Blumenson, *Breakout and Pursuit,* 684.

67. HQ, 3d Infantry Division, "Report of Operations, 15–31 August 1944," 19 September 1944, pp. 1–3, 303-0.3, Box 6106, Record Group 407, National Archives II.

68. Ibid., 4–5; HQ, Eighth Amphibious Force, Training Plan 1–44, 28 June 1944, 303-3.13, Box 6247, Record Group 407, National Archives II.

69. HQ, 3d Infantry Division, "Report of Operations, 15–31 August 1944," 1–3.

70. Jeffrey J. Clarke and Robert Ross Smith, *Riviera to the Rhine* (Washington, D.C.: Center of Military History, 1993), 122.

71. Lieutenant General Walter T. Kerwin Jr., Oral History, Walter T. Kerwin Jr. Papers, USAMHI, 157–158.

72. Clarke and Smith, *Riviera to the Rhine,* 168.

73. Ibid., 137.

74. Ibid., 576, Table 1.

75. Roland G. Ruppenthal, *Logistical Support of the Armies,* vol. 1 (Washington, D.C.: Office of the Chief of Military History, 1953), 188.

76. Ibid., 189.

77. Eisenhower, *Crusade in Europe,* 291.

78. Roland G. Ruppenthal, "Logistics and the Broad-Front Strategy," in *Command Decisions,* ed. Kent Roberts Greenfield (Washington, D.C.: United States Army Center of Military History, 1987), 422–423.

79. Eisenhower, *Crusade in Europe,* 290.

80. Ruppenthal, *Logistical Support of the Armies,* 558–559.

81. Ibid., 564–568.

82. Ibid., 570.

83. Ibid., 576–581.

84. Steve R. Waddell, *United States Army Logistics: The Normandy Campaign, 1944* (Westport, Conn.: Greenwood, 1994), 134–135.

85. Ruppenthal, *Logistical Support of the Armies,* 571.

86. William F. Ross and Charles F. Romanus, *The Quartermaster Corps: Operations in the War against Germany* (Washington, D.C.: Office of the Chief of Military History, 1965), 399.

87. Ruppenthal, *Logistical Support of the Armies,* 491.

88. Ross and Romanus, *The Quartermaster Corps,* 482.

89. Ibid., 471–472.

90. Ibid., 472.

91. Headquarters, 3d Infantry Division, "Report of Operations, 1–30 September 1944," 13 October 1944, Section IV, p. 3, 303-0.3, Box 6107, National Archives II.

92. Ross and Romanus, *The Quartermaster Corps,* 583.

93. Historian Martin van Creveld disagrees. His figures, based on the number of truck companies available to the Allies in September 1944, do not take into account the tremendous attrition of the trucks and the supply infrastructure during the breakout and pursuit operations. See Martin van Creveld, *Supplying War: Logistics from Wallenstein to Patton* (Cambridge: Cambridge University Press, 1977).

94. Russell F. Weigley, *Eisenhower's Lieutenants: The Campaign of France and Germany, 1944–1945* (Bloomington: Indiana University Press, 1981), 257.

CHAPTER 8. SUSTAINING THE FORCE

1. The combat-experienced divisions were the 1st, 2d, 3d, 4th, 5th, 8th, 9th, 29th, 30th, 35th, 36th, 45th, 79th, 83d, and 90th Infantry Divisions. The 26th, 28th, 44th, 80th, 94th, 95th, 102d, and 104th Infantry Divisions had seen little or no combat by the end of September 1944.

2. These were the 42d, 63d, 66th, 70th, 75th, 78th, 84th, 87th, 99th, 100th, 103d, and 106th Infantry Divisions.

3. Charles B. MacDonald, *The Siegfried Line Campaign* (Washington, D.C.: Office of the Chief of Military History, 1963), 281.

4. Ibid., 95.

5. Charles B. MacDonald, *The Battle of the Huertgen Forest* (New York: J. B. Lippincott, 1963), 15.

6. MacDonald, *The Siegfried Line Campaign,* 253–254.

7. Ibid., 261.

8. Ibid., 269.

9. Ibid., 279.

10. HQ, 1st Infantry Division, "Report of Breaching the Siegfried Line and the Capture of Aachen," 31 October 1944, pp. 7–8, 301-0.3.0, Box 5664, Record Group 407, National Archives II.

11. HQ, 1st Infantry Division, "Report of Operations, 1–31 October 1944," 5 November 1944, 301-3, Box 5762, Record Group 407, National Archives II.

12. MacDonald, *The Siegfried Line Campaign,* 303.

13. HQ, U.S. Forces, European Theater, "Distinguished Unit Citation for the 30th Infantry Division," 14 December 1945, USFET AG Section, Unit Citation Awards, Box 3, Record Group 332, National Archives II.

14. Intelligence Annex to Army Group B War Journal, 23 October 1944, pp. 1–3, Microcopy T-311, Roll 1, Combined Arms Research Library, Fort Leavenworth, Kansas.

15. MacDonald, *The Siegfried Line Campaign,* 317.

16. 1st Infantry Division, "Report of Breaching the Siegfried Line and the Capture of Aachen," 12.

17. James M. Gavin, *On to Berlin: Battles of an Airborne Commander, 1943–1946* (New York: Viking, 1978), 268.

18. MacDonald, *The Battle of the Huertgen Forest,* 4.

19. Ibid., 64.

20. For a recent examination of the battle for the Huertgen Forest, see Edward G. Miller, *A Dark and Bloody Ground: The Huertgen Forest and the Roer River Dams, 1944–1945* (College Station: Texas A&M University Press, 1995).

21. On 19 August the former commander, Major General Manton Eddy, moved to the U.S. Third Army to take command of XII Corps.

22. HQ, 9th Infantry Division, "Report of Operations, 1–30 September 1944," 1 October 1944, pp. 13–14, 309-0.3, Box 7326, Record Group 407, National Archives II.

23. MacDonald, *The Siegfried Line Campaign,* 90.

24. Ibid., 83.

25. MacDonald, *The Battle of the Huertgen Forest,* 57–58.

26. HQ, 9th Infantry Division, "Report of Operations, 1–30 September 1944," 34, and Annex 3, pp. 1–2.

27. MacDonald, *The Battle of the Huertgen Forest,* 67–86.

28. Nicholas P. Kafkalas, Oral History, Nicholas P. Kafkalas Papers, USAMHI, 11–12.

29. Omar N. Bradley, *A Soldier's Story* (New York: Rand McNally, 1951), 14–16.

30. "History of the 110th Infantry Regiment from Activation on 17 February 1941

to Inactivation on 25 October 1945," p. 39, 328-INF(110)-0.1, Box 8596, Record Group 407, National Archives II.

31. The division commander in Normandy was Major General Lloyd D. Brown, who was relieved in August 1944. His replacement, Brigadier General James E. Wharton, was killed in action on the day he took command. General Cota then assumed command of the division.

32. Harry J. Schute Jr., "Forgotten Principles: The 28th Division in the Huertgen Forest," *Armor* 102, no. 4 (July–August 1993): 41.

33. MacDonald, *The Battle of the Huertgen Forest,* 94.

34. Charles B. MacDonald and Sidney T. Mathews, *Three Battles: Arnaville, Altuzzo, and Schmidt* (Washington, D.C.: Office of the Chief of Military History, 1952), 276–281.

35. Edward J. Drea, *Unit Reconstitution: A Historical Perspective* (Fort Leavenworth, Kans.: Combat Studies Institute, 1983), 44.

36. 28th Infantry Division, *Historical and Pictorial Review of the 28th Infantry Division in World War II* (n.p., 1946; repr. Nashville, Tenn.: Battery Press, 1980), 93.

37. HQ, 28th Infantry Division, "Unit Report No. 5," 6 December 1944, p. 12, 328-0.3, Box 8479, Record Group 407, National Archives II.

38. 28th Infantry Division, *Historical and Pictorial Review of the 28th Infantry Division,* 170.

39. Drea, *Unit Reconstitution,* 29–30. Interestingly, the division's after-action report rated the combat efficiency of the division as "excellent," an indication that the division headquarters was out of touch with events in the field. HQ, 28th Infantry Division, "Unit Report No. 5," p. 6.

40. MacDonald, *The Battle of the Huertgen Forest,* 196.

41. HQ, 9th Infantry Division, "Report of Operations, 1–31 July 1944," 1 August 1944, Annex 4; "Report of Operations, 1–31 August 1944," 1 September 1944, Annex 3; "Report of Operations, 1–30 September 1944," 1 October 1944, Section VI; "Report of Operations, 1–31 October 1944," 1 November 1944, Section VI; 309-0.3, Box 7326, Record Group 407, National Archives II.

42. HQ, 47th Infantry Regiment, "Report of Operations, 10 June–30 September 1944," 9 October 1944, 309-INF(47)-0.3, Box 7515, Record Group 407, National Archives II.

43. Roy Gordon, 47th Infantry Regiment, 9th Infantry Division World War II Survey, USAMHI.

44. *60th: Follow Thru* (Stuttgart: 1945), 92.

45. HQ, 9th Infantry Division, "Report of Operations, 1–31 October 1944," Annex 3, p. 3.

46. Leo C. Williamson, K Company, 3d Battalion, 60th Infantry Regiment, 9th Infantry Division World War II Survey, USAMHI.

47. Kent Roberts Greenfield, Robert R. Palmer, and Bell I. Wiley, *The Organization of Ground Combat Troops* (Washington, D.C.: Historical Division, U.S. Army, 1947), 189.

48. Airborne units did not suffer this problem due to the sporadic nature of their combat. Airborne divisions committed to the Normandy invasion, for instance, did not integrate any replacements into their structure until after they were withdrawn from combat in July 1944. Armored divisions suffered to some extent, but they usually

received more time in reserve than infantry divisions. The best time to integrate replacements is when a unit is in reserve.

49. Colonel James H. Hayes, commander, 2/317th Infantry, letter to author, 8 March 1993.

50. HQ, 29th Division Training Center, "After Action Report," November–January 1944, 329-TC-0.3, Box 8722, Record Group 407, National Archives II.

51. HQ, 29th Infantry Division, "Combat Exhaustion Survey," 2 October 1944, CI 84, Box 24035, Record Group 407, National Archives II.

52. Ibid.

53. Charles R. Cawthon, *Other Clay: A Remembrance of the World War II Infantry* (Niwot: University Press of Colorado, 1990), 167–168.

54. Lee Kennett, *G.I.: The American Soldier in World War II* (New York: Scribner's, 1987), 144–145.

55. HQ, Army Service Forces, "Field Therapeutical Expedient Exhaustion Center for Neuro-Psychiatric Injuries," 7 December 1944, 1-16.383/44, Box 24397, Record Group 407, National Archives II.

56. Roland G. Ruppenthal, *Logistical Support of the Armies,* vol. 2, *September 1944–May 1945* (Washington, D.C.: Office of the Chief of Military History, 1959), 278–280.

57. Ibid., 283.

58. Intelligence Annex to Army Group B War Journal, 23 November 1944, pp. 2–4, Microcopy T-311, Roll 1, Combined Arms Research Library, Fort Leavenworth, Kans.

59. Ibid.

60. HQ, 104th Infantry Division, "After Action Report," 10 November 1944, p. 4, 3104-0.3, Box 14616, Record Group 407, National Archives II.

61. HQ, 104th Infantry Division, Field Order No. 5, 24 October 1944, 3104-0.3, Box 14616, Record Group 407, National Archives II.

62. HQ, 104th Infantry Division, "After Action Report," 7 December 1944, 3104-0.3, Box 14616, Record Group 407, National Archives II.

63. HQ, First Canadian Army, "Commendation—104th Infantry Division," 3104-INF(415)-0.1, Box 14707, Record Group 407, National Archives II.

64. J. Lawton Collins, *Lightning Joe: An Autobiography* (Baton Rouge: Louisiana State University Press, 1979), 275.

65. Ibid., 275.

66. HQ, 104th Infantry Division, "After Action Report," 7 December 1944, 9–12.

67. Collins, *Lightning Joe,* 277.

68. MacDonald, *The Siegfried Line Campaign,* 504.

69. Collins, *Lightning Joe,* 277.

70. Letter, Major General J. Lawton Collins to Major General Terry de la Mesa Allen, 26 December 1944, Terry de la Mesa Allen Papers, USAMHI. In another letter in the Allen papers dated 27 December 1944, Colonel H. H. York wrote to General Allen, "I thought you might be interested to know that I personally overheard Gen. Collins say that it (yours) was *the* outstanding new division in France."

71. J. Lawton Collins, Oral History, J. Lawton Collins Papers, USAMHI, 243.

72. MacDonald, *The Siegfried Line Campaign,* 550–552.

73. Harold P. Leinbaugh and John D. Campbell, *The Men of Company K: The*

Autobiography of a World War II Rifle Company (New York: William Morrow, 1985), 62.

74. Ibid., 67–68.

75. ETO, G-3 Division, Battle Lessons Branch, Observers Reports, 1944–1945, Record Group 338, National Archives II.

76. Leinbaugh and Campbell, *The Men of Company K,* 65.

77. Ibid., 66.

78. Theodore Draper, *The 84th Infantry Division in the Battle of Germany, November 1944–May 1945* (New York: Viking, 1946), 34.

79. Ibid., 75–76.

80. HQ, 84th Infantry Division, After Action Report, November 1944, 384-0.3, Box 12633, Record Group 407, National Archives II.

81. MacDonald, *The Siegfried Line Campaign,* 616–617.

82. After World War II ended, Walker continued to rise in the U.S. Army. During the Korean War he commanded the U.S. Eighth Army in the first crucial months of the conflict. His life ended in a jeep crash in December 1950.

83. Historical Division, Department of the Army, *Combat Chronicle: An Outline History of U.S. Army Divisions* (Washington, D.C.: Department of the Army, 1948), 13.

84. Hugh M. Cole, *The Lorraine Campaign* (Washington, D.C.: Office of the Chief of Military History, 1950), 17.

85. Major General Raymond McLain, the National Guard officer who had done so much to turn the division around, received command of XIX Corps on 15 October.

86. James A. Van Fleet, Oral History, James A. Van Fleet Papers, USAMHI, vol. 1, Enclosure 1, p. 3. Of Van Fleet's service in Normandy, Bradley stated: "Van Fleet was another Ridgway, an absolutely superb soldier and leader. He was earning about three Distinguished Service Crosses a day." Omar N. Bradley and Clay Blair, *A General's Life* (New York: Simon and Schuster, 1983), 263.

87. Van Fleet would go on to command both the XXIII Corps and the III Corps during World War II. During the Korean War he served as commander of the U.S. Eighth Army after General Matthew B. Ridgway assumed General Douglas MacArthur's position as supreme commander. Van Fleet was as courageous as he was competent; his decorations from World War II include the Distinguished Service Cross with two Oak Leaf Clusters, the Distinguished Service Medal with Oak Leaf Cluster, the Silver Star with two Oak Leaf Clusters, the Legion of Merit with Oak Leaf Cluster, the Bronze Star for valor with two Oak Leaf Clusters, and the Purple Heart with two Oak Leaf Clusters. James A. Van Fleet Papers, USAMHI.

88. William E. Depuy, Oral History, William E. Depuy Papers, USAMHI, Section II: 30.

89. *Time,* 23 April 1951, 36.

90. Van Fleet, Oral History, 67.

91. Romie L. Brownlee and William J. Mullen III, *Changing an Army: An Oral History of General William E. Depuy* (Washington, D.C.: Center of Military History, 1988), 57.

92. Historical Division, Department of the Army, *Combat Chronicle,* 80.

93. Cole, *The Lorraine Campaign,* 373–374.

94. HQ, 90th Infantry Division, "Operations of the 90th Infantry Division, 1 November–1 December 1944," 1 December 1944, 390-0.3, Box 13280, Record Group 407, National Archives II.

95. Cole, *The Lorraine Campaign*, 374–375.

96. HQ, 90th Infantry Division, "Operations of the 90th Infantry Division, 1 November–1 December 1944," 9–16.

97. The 991st Engineer Treadway Bridge Company was later awarded a Distinguished Unit Citation for its actions during the battle.

98. HQ, 90th Infantry Division, "Operations of the 90th Infantry Division, 1 November–1 December 1944," 16–18.

99. Ibid., 18–22.

100. Ibid., 24.

101. Ibid., 29.

102. HQ, Third United States Army, "Commendation," 12 November 1944, 390-0.3, Box 13280, Record Group 407, National Archives II.

103. Cole, *The Lorraine Campaign*, 425–428.

104. Ibid., 433–449.

105. Jeffrey J. Clarke and Robert Ross Smith, *Riviera to the Rhine* (Washington, D.C.: Center of Military History, 1993), 229.

106. Ibid., 230.

107. Keith E. Bonn, *When the Odds Were Even: The Vosges Mountains Campaign, October 1944–January 1945* (Novato, Calif.: Presidio, 1994), 87.

108. Major General Edward H. Brooks replaced Truscott in command of VI Corps on 25 October 1944. Truscott left France on leave and took command of the Fifth U.S. Army in Italy in December.

109. Bonn, *When the Odds Were Even*, 101.

110. Clarke and Smith, *Riviera to the Rhine*, 291–292.

111. HQ, AGF, "Fact Sheet on the 100th Infantry Division," 1 March 1947, 3100-0, Box 14215, Record Group 407, National Archives II.

112. Major General Burress had served as an instructor during four different assignments in the interwar period: at the Infantry School, VMI (twice) and at the Command and General Staff School.

113. HQ, 100th Infantry Division, After Action Report, November 1944, 3100-0.3, Box 14218, Record Group 407, National Archives II.

114. Clarke and Smith, *Riviera to the Rhine*, 397.

115. HQ, 100th Infantry Division, After Action Report, November 1944.

116. Clarke and Smith, *Riviera to the Rhine*, 400.

117. Ibid., 439–440.

118. Bonn, *When the Odds Were Even*, 137.

119. Memo, Colonel Pete T. Heffner Jr. to Chief, Combat Lessons Branch, G-3, ETO, SUBJECT: Lessons Learned in Vosges Mountain Operations, 12 December 1944, ETO Observer's Reports, Box 3, Record Group 338, National Archives II.

120. Clarke and Smith, *Riviera to the Rhine*, 433.

121. Bonn, *When the Odds Were Even*, 131.

122. Ibid., 168–169.

123. HQ, Headquarters, 100th Infantry Division, After-Action Report, December 1944, 3100-0.3, Box 14218, Record Group 407, National Archives II.

124. Ibid.

125. Ibid.

126. Ibid.

127. Bonn, *When the Odds Were Even*, 170.

128. Cole, *The Lorraine Campaign,* 621.

CHAPTER 9. THE BATTLE OF THE BULGE

1. Hugh M. Cole, *The Ardennes: Battle of the Bulge* (Washington, D.C.: Office of the Chief of Military History, 1965), 56.
2. John Toland, *Battle: The Story of the Bulge* (New York: Random House, 1959), 12–15.
3. HQ, 28th Infantry Division, "Operational Data, 28th Inf. Div., 6 June 1944–11 May 1945," 328-0.3.0, Box 8480, Record Group 407, National Archives II.
4. HQ, 28th Infantry Division, "Unit Report No. 6," 15 January 1945, p. 8, 328-0.3, Box 8479, Record Group 407, National Archives II.
5. William F. Train, Oral History, William F. Train Papers, USAMHI, Appendix A, 3.
6. Toland, *Battle,* 4.
7. Letter to author, 21 March 1993.
8. S. L. A. Marshall, *Bastogne: The First Eight Days* (Washington, D.C.: Infantry Journal Press, 1946; repr., Washington, D.C.: Center of Military History, 1988), 5; Charles B. MacDonald, *A Time for Trumpets: The Untold Story of the Battle of the Bulge* (New York: William Morrow, 1984), 145.
9. Cole, *The Ardennes,* 193–205.
10. Ibid., 224.
11. "History of the 110th Infantry Regiment from Activation on 17 February 1941 to Inactivation on 25 October 1945," p. 63, 328-INF(110)-0.1, Box 8596, Record Group 407, National Archives II.
12. Ibid., 41–42.
13. Ibid., 73.
14. MacDonald, *A Time for Trumpets,* 194.
15. "History of the 110th Infantry Regiment from Activation on 17 February 1941 to Inactivation on 25 October 1945," 74.
16. Cole, *The Ardennes,* 145–158, 161–164.
17. Normally, an American infantry division would have a tank battalion attached from army reserves, but there were not enough to attach one to every infantry division in the ETO. The low priority of the Ardennes meant that the infantry divisions of VIII Corps did not have this vital support on 16 December.
18. MacDonald, *A Time for Trumpets,* 126.
19. Ibid., 128–129.
20. Ibid., 128. Apparently the switchboard operator briefly disconnected the line in the middle of Middleton's sentence to put another incoming call on hold.
21. Charles Whiting, *Death of a Division* (London: Frederick Warne, 1980), 52–53.
22. MacDonald, *A Time for Trumpets,* 310–311.
23. Jerry D. Morelock, *Generals of the Ardennes: American Leadership in the Battle of the Bulge* (Washington, D.C.: National Defense University Press, 1994), 297–298.
24. MacDonald, *A Time for Trumpets,* 314.
25. HQ, 81st Engineer Combat Battalion, "81st Engineer Combat Battalion History, 16 Dec 1944–1 Feb 1945," pp. 1–16, 3106-ENG-0.1, Box 14749, Record Group 407, National Archives II.
26. Morelock, *Generals of the Ardennes,* 299.

27. MacDonald, *A Time for Trumpets,* 327.

28. The division's after-action report maintains the fiction that Jones had merely given Clarke command of a portion of the division sector, but in the ensuing days Clarke exercised command over the entire St.-Vith battlefield. HQ, 106th Infantry Division, "Action Against Enemy, Report After," 27 January 1945, p. 3, 3106-0.3, Box 14718, Record Group 407, National Archives II.

29. William J. Dunkerley, "German Breakthrough in the ARDENNES," 3 May 1945, CI-244, Box 24081, Record Group 407, National Archives II; John G. Westover, "423 Infantry Regiment in the Ardennes Battle," 17 April 1945, CI-245, Box 24081, Record Group 407, National Archives II.

30. HQ, 106th Infantry Division, "Action Against Enemy, Report After," 4.

31. R. Ernest Dupuy, *St. Vith—Lion in the Way: The 106th Infantry Division in World War II* (Washington, D.C.: Infantry Journal Press, 1949), 7.

32. HQ, 424th Infantry Regiment, "Submission of Historical Material," 3 August 1945, 3106-INF(424)-0.1, Box 14758, Record Group 407, National Archives II; Dupuy, *Lion in the Way.*

33. Morelock, *Generals of the Ardennes,* 300.

34. Ibid., 311.

35. Cole, *The Ardennes,* 78.

36. Ibid., 81.

37. Walter E. Lauer, *Battle Babies: The Story of the 99th Infantry Division in World War II* (Baton Rouge: Military Press of Louisiana, 1950), chap. 1.

38. Cole, *The Ardennes,* 90.

39. MacDonald, *A Time for Trumpets,* 180–181.

40. Ibid., 375–377.

41. For an excellent first-person account of this action, see Charles B. MacDonald, *Company Commander* (New York: Bantam, 1978), 108–135.

42. MacDonald, *A Time for Trumpets,* 380–383, 395–397. The 1st Battalion, 9th Infantry, began the battle with around six hundred men and lost nearly four hundred of them in action in approximately twenty hours of intense combat.

43. *Second Infantry Division in World War II* (n.p.; repr., Nashville, Tenn.: Battery Press, 1979), 97.

44. MacDonald, *A Time for Trumpets,* 406.

45. Ibid., 408.

46. Ibid., 407. Lieutenant Colonel Daniel received the Distinguished Service Cross for his actions during the battle.

47. Society of the First Division, *Danger Forward: The Story of the First Division in World War II* (Atlanta, Ga.: A. Love, 1947; repr., Nashville, Tenn.: Battery Press, 1980), 322.

48. Cole, *The Ardennes,* 268–269.

49. HQ, 30th Infantry Division, "After Action Report, 1 November 1944–30 November 1944," G-1 Annex, 330-1, Box 8732, Record Group 407, National Archives II; idem, "After Battle Report, 1 December 1944–31 December 1944," G-3 Annex, 330-3, Box 8788, Record Group 407, National Archives II.

50. Cole, *The Ardennes,* 375.

51. Ibid., 376–377. One witness described the aftermath of the ferocious battle between the 30th Infantry Division and *Kampfgruppe Peiper:* "The devastation, destruction and immobilization of equipment was unbelievable, for the 30th, attacking in

three columns, caught a German *panzer* division in the flank, destroying the lead elements, the reserve and the trains in three separate engagements. The towns of Stoumont, La Gleize, and Stavelot were practically demolished by the battles there." William F. Train, Oral History, 18–19, William F. Train Papers, USAMHI.

52. Theodore Draper, *The 84th Infantry Division in the Battle of Germany, November 1944–May 1945* (New York: Viking, 1946), 89.

53. Cole, *The Ardennes,* 440.

54. Draper, *The 84th Infantry Division in the Battle of Germany,* 103.

55. Harold P. Leinbaugh and John D. Campbell, *The Men of Company K: The Autobiography of a World War II Rifle Company* (New York: William Morrow, 1985), 146–147.

56. Joe McCarthy, "4th Armored Moved Suddenly and Fast," *Yank,* 21 January 1945, 26.

57. Cole, *The Ardennes,* 510.

58. MacDonald, *A Time for Trumpets,* 516–519.

59. Draper, *The 84th Infantry Division in the Battle of Germany,* 108–111.

60. Ibid., 112.

61. Ibid., 113; Leinbaugh and Campbell, *The Men of Company K,* 168.

62. HQ, 334th Infantry Regiment, 84th Infantry Division, "After Action Report, 1 Jan 45–31 Jan 45," 384-INF(334)-0.3, Box 12716, Record Group 407, National Archives II.

63. Jeffrey J. Clarke and Robert Ross Smith, *Riviera to the Rhine* (Washington, D.C.: Center of Military History, 1993), 494–495, 498.

64. Keith E. Bonn, *When the Odds Were Even: The Vosges Mountains Campaign, October 1944–January 1945* (Novato, Calif.: Presidio, 1994), 180.

65. Clarke and Smith, *Riviera to the Rhine,* 505–508.

66. Ibid., 508–509.

67. Ibid., 565.

68. Charles B. MacDonald, *The Last Offensive* (Washington, D.C.: Office of the Chief of Military History, 1973), 477.

69. Roland G. Ruppenthal, *Logistical Support of the Armies,* vol. 2, *September 1944–May 1945* (Washington, D.C.: Office of the Chief of Military History, 1959), 322.

70. Ibid.

71. Ibid., 286.

72. Letter, Major General John S. Guthrie to author, April 1993.

73. Ruppenthal, *Logistical Support of the Armies,* 326.

74. Ibid., 342.

75. Ibid., 343.

76. Ibid., 343–345.

77. Ulysses Lee, *The Employment of Negro Troops* (Washington, D.C.: Office of the Chief of Military History, 1966), 693.

78. Ibid., 695–696. In a study of the American soldier in combat, Samuel A. Stouffer and his researchers concluded: "In the companies in which Negro platoons served, the overwhelming majority of white officers and men gave approval to their performance in combat." Samuel A. Stouffer et al., eds., *The American Soldier,* vol. 1, *Adjustment During Army Life* (Princeton, N.J.: Princeton University Press, 1949), 588–589.

79. MacDonald, *The Last Offensive,* 5.

80. Ibid., 480.

CHAPTER 10. THE AMERICAN BLITZKRIEG

1. Charles B. MacDonald, *The Siegfried Line Campaign* (Washington, D.C.: Office of the Chief of Military History, 1963), 600–606.

2. Major General Leonard T. Gerow, the former V Corps commander, had been promoted to command of the Fifteenth U.S. Army.

3. Charles B. MacDonald, *The Last Offensive* (Washington, D.C.: Office of the Chief of Military History, 1973), 73–80.

4. Ibid., 81–82.

5. Ibid., 83.

6. Theodore Draper, *The 84th Infantry Division in the Battle of Germany, November 1944–May 1945* (New York: Viking, 1946), 140.

7. MacDonald, *The Last Offensive,* 142.

8. Ibid., 163.

9. Draper, *The 84th Infantry Division in the Battle of Germany,* 162.

10. Ibid., 191.

11. MacDonald, *The Last Offensive,* 183.

12. Ibid., 219–220; Omar N. Bradley, *A Soldier's Story* (New York: Rand McNally, 1951), 510–512; Dwight D. Eisenhower, *Crusade in Europe* (Garden City, N.Y.: Doubleday, 1948), 379–380.

13. Joseph B. Mittelman, *Eight Stars to Victory: A History of the Veteran Ninth U.S. Infantry Division* (Washington, D.C.: Ninth Infantry Division Association, 1948), 326.

14. HQ, 9th Infantry Division, "Report of Operations, 1–31 March 1945," 5 April 1945, 309-0.3, Box 7326, Record Group 407, National Archives II; Joseph B. Mittelman, *The Final Thrust* (Munich: F. Bruckmann, 1945), 56–57.

15. Headquarters, 9th Infantry Division, Report of Operations, 1–30 April 1945, 5 May 1945, Annex 3, 309-0.3, Box 7326, Record Group 407, National Archives II; Headquarters, 30th Infantry Regiment, 3d Infantry Division, Report of Operations, 1–28 February 1945, 5 March 1945, 303-0.3, Box 6111, Record Group 407, National Archives II.

16. Ken Hechler, *The Bridge at Remagen* (New York: Ballantine Books, 1957), 165.

17. David E. Gillespie, ed., *Raiders* (Germany, 1945).

18. MacDonald, *The Last Offensive,* 234.

19. Ibid., 267.

20. Ibid., 270.

21. Ibid.

22. Ibid., 272.

23. Ernest F. Fisher Jr., *Cassino to the Alps* (Washington, D.C.: Center of Military History, 1977), 457–458.

24. Lucian K. Truscott Jr., *Command Missions: A Personal Story* (New York: E. P. Dutton, 1954; repr., Novato, Calif.: Presidio, 1990), 482.

25. Fisher, *Cassino to the Alps,* 483.

26. Ibid., 470–471. The 10th Mountain Division was a unique organization in the Army of the United States. Activated on 15 July 1943 at Camp Hale, Colorado, the division was designed for combat on mountainous terrain and trained to fight in severe winter conditions. The division contained many men—a high percentage of whom had attended college for one or more years—who had been outdoorsmen or skiers before the war, attracted by the unique nature of the units training for Alpine warfare and spurred on by an unorthodox recruiting campaign conducted by Charles "Minnie" Dole and the National Ski Patrol. The enlisted soldiers of the division were of extremely high quality, the equals of the volunteers who made up the four airborne divisions of the Army of the United States. The division commander, Major General George P. Hays, was a Medal of Honor winner from World War I and the former division artillery commander in the 2d Infantry Division in Europe. The 10th Mountain Division arrived in Italy in January 1945 and successfully conducted a limited objective attack in February that seized positions for the upcoming spring offensive along the Monte Belvedere–Monte Della Torraccia Ridge and Riva Ridge, an area where the highest mountain peaks reached several thousand feet and entrenched enemy forces had excellent observation and fields of fire.

27. HQ, 10th Mountain Division, Narrative Report on Combat Operations, April 1945, pp. 14–40, File 310-0.3, Box 7549, Record Group 407, National Archives II.

28. Fisher, *Cassino to the Alps,* 479.

29. Truscott, *Command Missions,* 489.

30. HQ, 10th Mountain Division, Narrative Report on Combat Operations, April 1945, pp. 51–55, 310-0.3, Box 7549, Record Group 407, National Archives II.

31. The commander of the task force, Colonel William O. Darby, was killed by an artillery airburst on the evening of 30 April at the edge of Lake Garda while leading his troops in battle. Colonel Darby had been instrumental in the formation of the first American Ranger battalions and had led the Ranger Force in combat in Italy.

32. Truscott, *Command Missions,* 496.

CHAPTER 11. THE COMBAT EFFECTIVENESS OF INFANTRY DIVISIONS IN THE ARMY OF THE UNITED STATES

1. Based on casualty statistics in 9th Infantry Division reports of operation, June 1944 to May 1945, 309-0.3, Box 7326, Record Group 407, National Archives II.

2. HQ, 1st Infantry Division, After-Action Reports, July 1944–May 1945, 301-1, Box 5672, Record Group 407, National Archives II.

3. 9th Infantry Division Reports of Operation, March 1943–May 1945, 309-0.3, Record Group 407, National Archives II.

4. GNGCS 320.2, 7 February 1944, Subject: Replacement Situation, Record Group 337, National Archives.

5. William R. Keast, Robert R. Palmer, and Bell I. Wiley, *The Procurement and Training of Ground Combat Troops* (Washington, D.C.: Office of the Chief of Military History, 1948), 201.

6. Russell Weigley, *Eisenhower's Lieutenants: The Campaign of France and Germany, 1944–1945* (Bloomington: Indiana University Press, 1981), 373–374.

7. Ibid., 22–28.

8. General Headquarters, "Comments on Army Maneuvers, 1940," 7 January

1941, p. 2, 330-0.3.0, Box 8724, Record Group 407, National Archives II.

9. Colonel Gilbert E. Parker, "AGF Report No. 1088—Tactics and T/O, Infantry Division," 4 July 1945, 4-3.1088/45, Box 24459, Record Group 407, National Archives II.

10. Stephen E. Ambrose, *Citizen Soldiers: The U.S. Army from the Normandy Beaches to the Bulge to the Surrender of Germany* (New York: Simon and Schuster, 1997), 277.

11. Weigley, *Eisenhower's Lieutenants,* 729.

12. Michael D. Doubler, *Closing with the Enemy: How GIs Fought the War in Europe, 1944–1945* (Lawrence: University Press of Kansas, 1994), 3.

13. For a good examination of the American army's ability to improvise tactics and techniques in World War II, see ibid.

14. S. L. A. Marshall, *Men against Fire: The Problem of Battle Command in Future War* (New York: William Morrow, 1947).

15. Ibid., 54.

16. Ibid., 57.

17. Ibid.

18. Ibid., 60.

19. Ibid., 68.

20. Ibid., 78.

21. Ibid., 149.

22. Ibid., 154.

23. Ibid., 155–156.

24. Ibid., 208–209.

25. Fredric Smoler, "The Secret of the Soldiers Who Didn't Shoot," *American Heritage,* March 1989, 40–41.

26. Harold P. Leinbaugh and John D. Campbell, *The Men of Company K* (New York: Quill, 1985).

27. Smoler, "The Secret of the Soldiers Who Didn't Shoot," 40–41.

28. Ibid., 42.

29. Roger J. Spiller, "S. L. A. Marshall and the Ratio of Fire," *RUSI Journal* 133, no. 4 (winter 1988): 68.

30. S. L. A. Marshall, *Island Victory* (Washington, D.C.: Infantry Journal Press, 1944), details Marshall's use of the after-action interview on Makin Island. See also Spiller, "S. L. A. Marshall and the Ratio of Fire," 68.

31. Memo, Major Hugh M. Cole to Lieutenant Colonel S. L. A. Marshall, 9 December 1944, copy located in the S. L. A. Marshall Military History Collection, University of El Paso, Texas.

32. Smoler, "The Secret of the Soldiers Who Didn't Shoot," 43.

33. Spiller, "S. L. A. Marshall and the Ratio of Fire," 66.

34. Karl E. Wolf, USMA Class of 1943, who served in combat from D-Day to V-E Day as a rifle platoon leader, rifle company XO, and rifle company commander in the 3d Battalion, 16th Infantry Regiment, 1st Infantry Division.

35. James Flannery, Commander, Company A, 1st Battalion, 314th Inf., 79th Infantry Division.

36. HQ, 90th Infantry Division, "After Action Report, May 1945," IV-6, 390-0.3, Box 13282, Record Group 407, National Archives II.

37. William E. Depuy, Oral History, Section I:14, William E. Depuy Papers, USAMHI.

38. Hugh M. Cole, *The Lorraine Campaign* (Washington, D.C.: Office of the Chief of Military History, 1950), 590.

39. Ibid., 590–591.

40. Ibid., 592.

41. Under War Department Circular 333, Section IV, 22 December 1943, the following criteria had to be met for the award of a Distinguished Unit Citation: "To justify citation, it must be clearly established that the unit distinguished itself in battle by extraordinary heroism, exhibited such gallantry, determination, and esprit de corps in overcoming unusually difficult and hazardous conditions as to set it apart and above units participating in the same engagement. As a unit, it must have distinguished itself by conspicuous battle action of a character that would merit the award to an individual of the Distinguished Service Cross [the army's second-highest award for valor]."

42. Alfred D. Chandler Jr. and Louis Galambos, eds., *The Papers of Dwight David Eisenhower, Occupation, 1945,* vol. 6 (Baltimore, Md.: Johns Hopkins University Press, 1978), entry 107.

43. Ibid.

44. HQ, U.S. Forces, European Theater, "Distinguished Unit Citations for Divisions," 3 August 1946, Tab B, Awards of Unit Citations, Box 4, Record Group 332, National Archives II.

45. Ibid.

46. Ibid., Tab F.

47. Lucian K. Truscott Jr., *Command Missions: A Personal Story* (New York: E. P. Dutton, 1954; repr., Novato, Calif.: Presidio, 1990), 556.

Bibliography

A NOTE ON SOURCES

No major war in history has been better recorded than World War II. Indeed, the wealth of primary and secondary source materials covering all facets of the conflict can intimidate even the hardiest of researchers. Fortunately, the professional staff at the National Archives and the United States Military History Institute are available and willing to guide the historian through the maze of documents. I gathered most of the primary source materials for this book in these two archives. The Modern Military Reference Branch (MMRB) of the National Archives was located in Suitland, Maryland, and has since moved to National Archives II in College Park. The United States Military History Institute (USAMHI) is located at the home of the Army War College in Carlisle Barracks, Pennsylvania.

All after-action reports and other records pertaining to the forces of the Army of the United States are stored in the Modern Military Records Branch of the National Archives. Record Group 407 contains all of the materials pertaining to the ground combat divisions that fought in World War II, cataloged by the number "3" followed by the number of the division (e.g., section "301" covers the records of the 1st Infantry Division). Record Group 332 contains the records pertaining to the awarding of unit citations.

The records of the Army Ground Forces and Joint Chiefs of Staff are located in the main depository of the National Archives in Washington, D.C. Record Group 165 contains materials relating to the American–British–Canadian (ABC) discussions over the course of the war. Many of the records pertaining to the ninety-division gamble are found in this group. Record Group 337 contains the records of the Army Ground Forces. These records are invaluable in reconstructing the course of mobilization and training of combat divisions of the Army of the United States before and during World War II.

The USAMHI has emerged as the primary depository for the personal files of U.S. Army general officers. Beginning in the 1970s, the War College began an oral history program, with students interviewing retired senior officers. The transcribed conversations are stored in the archives at Carlisle Barracks. They are an essential part of the story of the Army of the United States in World War II, for many officers became much more candid and open in relating events and feelings once they were no longer serving on active duty. The USAMHI has also embarked on an extensive survey program of officers and enlisted soldiers who served in World War II, and the results of these efforts are stored in the archives there.

Captured German records were put on microfilm and stored in the National Archives. These records include the *Kriegstagebücher* (war diaries) of the various commands and forces of the Wehrmacht. The USAMHI and the Combined Arms Research Library at the U.S. Army Command and General Staff College in Fort Leavenworth, Kansas, also have copies of this microfilm collection.

Those researchers interested in the life of S. L. A. Marshall will find his personal papers and library stored in the S. L. A. Marshall Military History Collection at the University of Texas at El Paso. Marshall's own works include *Island Victory, Men against Fire,* and *The Soldier's Load,* among numerous others. Articles dealing with the ratio-of-fire controversy include Frederic Smoler, "The Secret of the Soldiers Who Didn't Shoot" *(American Heritage),* and Roger J. Spiller, "S. L. A. Marshall and the Ratio of Fire" *(RUSI Journal).*

The Army of the United States produced numerous collections of statistics, field manuals, pamphlets, and other valuable reports during and after the war. These sources may be found in many research libraries, but the most complete collection is stored in the main library at the USAMHI. These sources include the two volumes produced by Samuel A. Stouffer et al.: *The American Soldier,* the most complete survey of the attitudes of the American soldier in World War II, and the *Reports of the Army Ground Forces Observers Board,* a collection of observations made by AGF officers sent overseas by Lieutenant General Lesley J. McNair to gather material on lessons learned in combat. Professional journals also have valuable articles relating to the history of World War II. These publications include the *Cavalry Journal* (later the *Armored Cavalry Journal* and now *Armor Magazine*), *Field Artillery Journal, Infantry Journal, Military Review,* and *Army History.*

Veterans of World War II have left numerous memoirs and accounts behind for posterity. The historian must read these with care, for most authors take more time to catalog their successes than to explore their mistakes. These works include Omar N. Bradley, *A Soldier's Story* and *A General's Life* (with Clay Blair); Mark W. Clark, *Calculated Risk;* J. Lawton Collins, *Lightning Joe;* Dwight D. Eisenhower, *Crusade in Europe;* James M. Gavin, *On to Berlin;* George S. Patton, *War As I Knew It;* and Matthew Ridgway, *Soldier* (with Harold Martin). I believe Lucian Truscott wrote the most candid memoir left by an American officer in World War II. His *Command Missions* is a classic story of leadership and command during war, an account of triumph under adversity by one of the most tactically competent officers ever to wear the U.S. Army uniform.

Secondary sources on World War II are numerous and run the gamut from pulp nonfiction to serious scholarship. The most complete and scholarly group of books are the seventy-eight volumes of the magisterial series "U.S. Army in World War II," otherwise known as the "Green Books." These were written by historians of the Office of the Chief of Military History and later the Center of Military History in Washington, D.C., between 1945 and 1993. The "American Forces in Action" series, produced immediately after World War II, is also a valuable collection detailing the history of select battles. Titles in this series include *Anzio Beachhead, Omaha Beach,* and *St.-Lô.*

Every American division produced a history of its actions during World War II. Some of these are heavy on photographs and light on narrative; others are excellent accounts of divisions in combat. The best early works include Theodore Draper, *The 84th Infantry Division in the Battle of Germany: November 1944–May 1945;* Ernest N. Dupuy, *St. Vith—Lion in the Way* (106th Infantry Division); Robert L. Hewitt, *Work Horse of the Western Front* (30th Infantry Division); Joseph B. Mittelman, *Eight Stars to Victory* (9th Infantry Division); and Donald G. Taggart, *History of the Third Infantry Division.* More recently, historians and veterans have produced new accounts of many divisions. A few of these books are outstanding, destined to set the standard for division histories in years to come. These works include Joseph Balkoski, *Beyond the Beachhead* (29th Infantry Division); John Sloan Brown, *Draftee Division* (88th Infantry Division); and John Colby, *War from the Ground Up* (90th Infantry Division).

The Combat Studies Institute at the U.S. Army Command and General Staff College has produced numerous studies on American forces, doctrine, and other aspects of World War II. Some of these studies include Michael D. Doubler, *Busting the Bocage* (tactics and innovation by American forces in Normandy); Edward Drea, *Unit Reconstitution* (a history of combat power regeneration); and Christopher Gabel, *Seek, Strike, and Destroy* (tank destroyer doctrine).

The Center of Military History has published numerous pamphlets on the history of American armed forces in World War II. These pamphlets give an in-depth look at certain aspects of the army that the "Green Books" cover only in general terms. These include Christopher R. Gabel, *The U.S. Army GHQ Maneuvers of 1941,* and Charles E. Kirkpatrick, *An Unknown Future and a Doubtful Present: Writing the Victory Plan of 1941.* The USAMHI also publishes studies, to include Dennis J. Vetock's *Lessons Learned: A History of US Army Lesson Learning.*

The debate surrounding the relative combat effectiveness of American and German forces can be traced in several books, most notably Stephen E. Ambrose, *D-Day, June 6, 1944* and *Citizen Soldiers;* Keith E. Bonn, *When the Odds Were Even;* John Sloan Brown, *Draftee Division;* Michael D. Doubler,

Closing with the Enemy; Trevor N. Dupuy, *Numbers, Predictions, and War;* John Ellis, *Brute Force;* Max Hastings, *Overlord;* Allan R. Millett and Williamson Murray, *Military Effectiveness* (vol. 3); Richard Overy, *Why the Allies Won;* Martin van Creveld, *Fighting Power;* and Russell Weigley, *Eisenhower's Lieutenants.*

No history of Allied operations in World War II would be complete without some discussion of ULTRA. Since the declassification of documents relating to ULTRA in 1974, several books have detailed the impact it had on combat operations during the war. Some of the works dealing with ULTRA include Patrick Beesly, *Very Special Intelligence;* Ralph Bennett, *Ultra in the West;* R. V. Jones, *Most Secret War;* Ronald Lewin, *Ultra Goes to War;* and F. W. Winterbotham, *The Ultra Secret.* Of these, Bennett's work is the best source for the impact of ULTRA on the Normandy campaign.

Accounts of combat action at division level and below continue to surface as more veterans relate their stories. Some of the best works on American combat forces in Europe include Charles R. Cawthon, *Other Clay;* Glover S. Johns, *The Clay Pigeons of St.-Lô;* Charles B. MacDonald, *Company Commander;* Alwyn Featherston, *Saving the Breakout;* and Harold P. Leinbaugh and John D. Campbell, *The Men of Company K.*

PRIMARY SOURCES

Archival Sources

National Archives and Records Administration, Washington, D.C.:

> Record Group 165, ABC Files, 1941–1945
> Record Group 337, Army Ground Forces, 1942–1945

National Archives and Records Administration II, Modern Military Reference Branch, College Park, Maryland:

> Record Group 332: Awards of Unit Citations

> Record Group 407:

> Section 301: Records of the 1st Infantry Division, 1940–1945
> Section 302: Records of the 3d Infantry Division, 1940–1945
> Section 309: Records of the 9th Infantry Division, 1940–1945
> Section 328: Records of the 28th Infantry Division, 1941–1945
> Section 329: Records of the 29th Infantry Division, 1941–1945
> Section 330: Records of the 30th Infantry Division, 1941–1945
> Section 345: Records of the 45th Infantry Division, 1941–1945
> Section 382: Records of the 82nd Airborne Division, 1942–1945
> Section 384: Records of the 84th Infantry Division, 1942–1945
> Section 390: Records of the 90th Infantry Division, 1942–1945

Section 3100: Records of the 100th Infantry Division, 1942–1945
Section 3104: Records of the 104th Infantry Division, 1942–1945
Section 3106: Records of the 106th Infantry Division, 1942–1945

United States Army Military History Institute, Carlisle Barracks, Pennsylvania:

1st Infantry Division World War II Survey Collection
3d Infantry Division World War II Survey Collection
9th Infantry Division World War II Survey Collection
28th Infantry Division World War II Survey Collection
29th Infantry Division World War II Survey Collection
30th Infantry Division World War II Survey Collection
45th Infantry Division World War II Survey Collection
90th Infantry Division World War II Survey Collection
104th Infantry Division World War II Survey Collection
106th Infantry Division World War II Survey Collection
Terry de la Mesa Allen Papers
Omar N. Bradley Papers
Mark W. Clark Papers
Bruce Cooper Clarke Papers
J. Lawton Collins Papers
William E. Depuy Papers
Alan W. Jones Papers
James M. Gavin Papers
Charles H. Gerhardt Papers
William K. Harrison Jr. Papers
John A. Heintges Papers
Nicholas P. Kafkalas Papers
Walter T. Kerwin Papers
Harry Lemley Papers
Matthew B. Ridgway Papers
William B. Rosson Papers
Teddy H. Sanford Papers
William F. Train Papers
James A. Van Fleet Papers

S. L. A. Marshall Military History Collection, University of El Paso, Texas

Printed Government Sources

Army Ground Forces. *Statistical Data.* Washington, D.C.: HQ, Army Ground Forces, 1945.
Department of the Army. FM 22-103. *Leadership and Command at Senior Levels.* Washington, D.C.: Government Printing Office, 1987.
12th Army Group. *Report of Operations.* N.p., 1944–1945.
U.S. Congress. Senate. Subcommittee of the Senate Committee on Appropriations. *Manpower Hearings.* 78th Cong., March 1943.

U.S. First Army. *Combat Operations Data.* Governor's Island, N.Y.: 18 November 1946.
————. *Report of Operations, 1 Aug 1944–22 Feb 1945.*
U.S. War Department. *Employment of Tanks with Infantry.* FM 17-36, Supplement No. 1. Washington, D.C.: Government Printing Office, 7 July 1944.
————. *Field Service Regulations, Operations.* FM 100-5. Washington, D.C.: Government Printing Office, 22 May 1941.
————. *Handbook on German Military Forces.* Washington, D.C.: Government Printing Office, 1945.
————. *Lessons from the Tunisian Campaign.* Washington, D.C.: Government Printing Office, 15 October 1943.

Published Sources

Bradley, Omar N. *A Soldier's Story.* New York: Rand McNally, 1951.
Bradley, Omar N., and Clay Blair. *A General's Life.* New York: Simon and Schuster, 1983.
Brownlee, Romie L., and William J. Mullen III. *Changing an Army: An Oral History of General William E. Depuy.* Washington, D.C.: Center of Military History, 1988.
Cawthon, Charles R. *Other Clay: A Remembrance of the World War II Infantry.* Niwot: University Press of Colorado, 1990.
Chandler, Alfred D., Jr., and Louis Galambos, eds. *The Papers of Dwight David Eisenhower, Occupation, 1945.* Vol. 6. Baltimore, Md.: Johns Hopkins University Press, 1978.
Clark, Mark W. *Calculated Risk.* New York: Harper and Brothers, 1950.
Collins, J. Lawton. *Lightning Joe: An Autobiography.* Baton Rouge: Louisiana State University Press, 1979.
Eisenhower, Dwight D. *Crusade in Europe.* Garden City, N.Y.: Doubleday, 1948.
Gavin, James M. *On to Berlin: Battles of an Airborne Commander, 1943–1946.* New York: Viking, 1978.
Johns, Glover S., Jr. *The Clay Pigeons of St. Lo.* Harrisburg, Pa.: Military Service Publishing, 1958.
Liddell Hart, B. H., ed. *The Rommel Papers.* London: Collins, 1953.
MacDonald, Charles B. *Company Commander.* New York: Bantam, 1978.
Montgomery, Sir Bernard L. *Normandy to the Baltic.* Boston: Houghton Mifflin, 1948.
Patton, George S., Jr. *War As I Knew It.* Boston: Houghton Mifflin, 1947.
Ridgway, Matthew B., in collaboration with Harold H. Martin. *Soldier: The Memoirs of Matthew B. Ridgway.* New York: Harper, 1956. Reprint, Westport, Conn.: Greenwood Press, 1974.
Speidel, Hans. *Invasion 1944.* Chicago: Henry Regnery, 1950.
Stouffer, Samuel A., Edward A. Suchman, Leland C. DeVinney, Shirley A. Star, and Robin M. Williams Jr., eds. *The American Soldier.* Vol. 1, *Adjustment during Army Life.* Princeton, N.J.: Princeton University Press, 1949.
————. *The American Soldier.* Vol. 2, *Combat and Its Aftermath.* Princeton, N.J.: Princeton University Press, 1949.
Truscott, Lucian K., Jr. *Command Missions: A Personal Story.* New York: E. P. Dutton, 1954. Reprint, Novato, Calif.: Presidio, 1990.

SECONDARY SOURCES

Official Histories

Blumenson, Martin. *Breakout and Pursuit.* Washington, D.C.: Office of the Chief of Military History, 1961.

———. *Salerno to Cassino.* Washington, D.C.: Office of the Chief of Military History, 1969.

Bowditch, John, III. *Anzio Beachhead.* Washington, D.C.: Historical Division, War Department, 1948.

Clarke, Jeffrey J., and Robert Ross Smith. *Riviera to the Rhine.* Washington, D.C.: Center of Military History, 1993.

Cole, Hugh M. *The Ardennes: Battle of the Bulge.* Washington, D.C.: Office of the Chief of Military History, 1965.

———. *The Lorraine Campaign.* Washington, D.C.: Office of the Chief of Military History, 1950.

Department of the Army. *Combat Chronicle: An Outline History of U.S. Army Divisions.* Washington, D.C.: Army Historical Division, 1948.

Fairchild, Bryon, and Jonathan Grossman. *The Army and Industrial Manpower.* Washington, D.C.: Office of the Chief of Military History, 1959.

Fisher, Ernest F., Jr., *Cassino to the Alps.* Washington, D.C.: Center of Military History, 1977.

Garland, Albert N., and Howard McGaw Smyth. *Sicily and the Surrender of Italy.* Washington, D.C.: Office of the Chief of Military History, 1965.

Garth, David, and Charles H. Taylor. *St.-Lô (7 July–19 July 1944).* Washington, D.C.: Historical Division, War Department, 1946.

Green, Constance McLaughlin, Peter C. Roots, and Harry C. Thompson. *The Ordnance Department: Planning Munitions for War.* Washington, D.C.: Office of the Chief of Military History, 1955.

Greenfield, Kent Roberts, Robert R. Palmer, and Bell I. Wiley. *The Organization of Ground Combat Troops.* Washington, D.C.: Historical Division, United States Army, 1947.

Harrison, Gordon A. *Cross-Channel Attack.* Washington, D.C.: Office of the Chief of Military History, 1951.

Howe, George F. *Northwest Africa: Seizing the Initiative in the West.* Washington, D.C.: Office of the Chief of Military History, 1957.

Keast, William R., Robert R. Palmer, and Bell I. Wiley. *The Procurement and Training of Ground Combat Troops.* Washington, D.C.: Office of the Chief of Military History, 1948.

Lee, Ulysses. *The Employment of Negro Troops.* Washington, D.C.: Office of the Chief of Military History, 1966.

MacDonald, Charles B. *The Last Offensive.* Washington, D.C.: Office of the Chief of Military History, 1973.

———. *The Siegfried Line Campaign.* Washington, D.C.: Office of the Chief of Military History, 1963.

MacDonald, Charles B., and Sidney T. Mathews. *Three Battles: Arnaville, Altuzzo, and Schmidt.* Washington, D.C.: Office of the Chief of Military History, 1952.

Marshall, S. L. A. *Bastogne: The First Eight Days.* Washington, D.C.: Infantry Journal Press, 1946. Reprint, Washington, D.C.: Center of Military History, 1988.

Matloff, Maurice. *Strategic Planning for Coalition Warfare, 1943–1944.* Washington, D.C.: Office of the Chief of Military History, 1959.

Matloff, Maurice, and Edwin M. Snell. *Strategic Planning for Coalition Warfare, 1941–1942.* Washington, D.C.: Office of the Chief of Military History, 1953.

Mayo, Lida. *The Ordnance Department: On Beachhead and Battlefront.* Washington, D.C.: Office of the Chief of Military History, 1968.

Ross, William F., and Charles F. Romanus. *The Quartermaster Corps: Operations in the War against Germany.* Washington, D.C.: Office of the Chief of Military History, 1965.

Ruppenthal, Roland G. *Logistical Support of the Armies.* 2 vols. Washington, D.C.: Office of the Chief of Military History, 1953, 1959.

———. *Utah Beach to Cherbourg.* Washington, D.C.: Historical Division, Department of the Army, 1947.

Shaw, Henry I., Jr., Bernard C. Nalty, and Edwin T. Turnbladh. *History of U.S. Marine Corps Operations in World War II: Central Pacific Drive.* Vol. 3. Washington, D.C.: Historical Branch, G-3 Division, HQ, U.S. Marine Corps, 1966.

Taylor, Charles H. *Omaha Beachhead.* Washington, D.C.: Historical Division, War Department, 1945.

Division and Regimental Histories

Arnold, Edmund C. *The Trailblazers: The Story of the 70th Infantry Division.* Richmond, Va.: Seventieth Infantry Division Association, 1989.

Balkoski, Joseph. *Beyond the Beachhead: The 29th Infantry Division in Normandy.* Harrisburg, Pa.: Stackpole, 1989. Reprint, New York: Dell, 1992.

Bass, Michael A., ed. *The Story of the Century.* New York: Criterion, 1946.

Binkoski, Joseph, and Arthur Plaut. *The 115th Infantry Regiment in World War II.* Washington, D.C.: Infantry Journal Press, 1948.

Bishop, Leo V., Frank J. Glasgow, and George A. Fisher. *The Fighting Forty-fifth: The Combat Report of an Infantry Division.* Baton Rouge, La.: Army and Navy Publishing, 1946.

Brown, John Sloan. *Draftee Division: The 88th Infantry Division in World War II.* Lexington: University Press of Kentucky, 1986.

Burton, Hal. *The Ski Troops.* New York: Simon and Schuster, 1971.

Byrnes, Laurence G. *History of the 94th Infantry Division in World War II.* N.p., 1948. Reprint, Nashville: Battery Press, 1982.

Colby, John. *War from the Ground Up: The 90th Division in WWII.* Austin, Tex.: Nortex Press, 1991.

The Cross of Lorraine: A Combat History of the 79th Infantry Division, June 1942–December 1945. N.p. Reprint, Nashville, Tenn.: Battery Press, 1986.

Draper, Theodore. *The 84th Infantry Division in the Battle of Germany: November 1944–May 1945.* New York: Viking Press, 1946.

Dupuy, R. Ernest. *St. Vith—Lion in the Way: The 106th Infantry Division in World War II.* Washington, D.C.: Infantry Journal Press, 1949.

89th Infantry Division Historical Board. *The 89th Infantry Division, 1942–1945.* Washington, D.C.: Infantry Journal Press, 1947.

Froberg, Magnus L. *The 63rd Infantry Division Chronicles, June 1943 to September 1945.* Sycamore, Ill.: 63d Infantry Division Association, 1991.

Fuermann, George M., and F. Edward Cranz. *Ninety-fifth Infantry Division History, 1918–1946.* Nashville, Tenn.: Battery Press, 1988.

Gillespie, David E., ed. *Raiders.* Germany, 1945.

Hewitt, Robert L. *Work Horse of the Western Front: The Story of the 30th Infantry Division.* Washington, D.C.: Infantry Journal Press, 1946.

Historical Division, Department of the Army. *Combat Chronicle: An Outline History of U.S. Army Divisions.* Washington, D.C.: Department of the Army, 1948.

History of the 117th Infantry, 1944–1945. Baton Rouge, La.: Army and Navy Publishing, 1946.

Hoegh, Leo A., and Howard Doyle. *Timberwolf Tracks: The History of the 104th Infantry Division, 1942–1945.* Washington, D.C.: Infantry Journal Press, 1946.

Information and Education Division, ETOUSA. *Hitler's Nemesis: The 9th Infantry Division.* Paris: Desfosses-Neogravute, 1944.

Lauer, Walter E. *Battle Babies: The Story of the 99th Infantry Division in World War II.* Baton Rouge: Military Press of Louisiana, 1950.

Lockwood, Theodore, ed. *Mountaineers.* Denver: Artcraft Press, 1945.

Mick, Allan H. *With the 102d Infantry Division through Germany.* Washington, D.C.: Infantry Journal Press, 1947.

Mittelman, Joseph B. *Eight Stars to Victory: A History of the Veteran Ninth U.S. Infantry Division.* Washington, D.C.: Ninth Infantry Division Association, 1948.

———. *The Final Thrust.* Munich: F. Bruckmann, 1945.

———. *Hold Fast!* Munich: F. Bruckmann, 1946.

Mueller, Ralph, and Jerry Turk. *Report after Action: The Story of the 103d Infantry Division.* Innsbruck: 103d Infantry Division, 1945.

90th Infantry Division. *A History of the 90th Division in World War II, 6 June 1944 to 9 May 1945.* Baton Rouge, La.: Army and Navy Publishing, 1946.

104th Infantry Division. *Trail of the Timberwolves.* San Luis Obispo, Calif., 1945.

Second Infantry Division in World War II. N.p. Reprint, Nashville, Tenn.: Battery Press, 1979.

78th Division Historical Association. Lightning: The History of the 78th Infantry Division. Washington, D.C.: Infantry Journal Press, 1947.

60th: Follow Thru. Stuttgart, 1945.

Society of the First Division. *Danger Forward: The Story of the First Division in World War II.* Atlanta, Ga.: A. Love, 1947. Reprint, Nashville, Tenn.: Battery Press, 1980.

Taggart, Donald G., ed. *History of the Third Infantry Division in World War II.* Washington, D.C.: Infantry Journal Press, 1947.

35th Infantry Division. *Santa Fe: The 35th Infantry Division in World War II, 1941–1945.* Atlanta, Ga.: Albert Love, 1946.

345th Field Artillery Battalion, 90th Infantry Division. Munich: F. Bruckmann, 1946.

28th Infantry Division. *Historical and Pictorial Review of the 28th Infantry Division in World War II.* N.p., 1946. Reprint, Nashville, Tenn.: Battery Press, 1980.

Wagner, Robert L. *The Texas Army: A History of the 36th Division in the Italian Campaign.* Austin, Tex.: 1972.

Wessman, Siinto S. *66: A Story of World War II.* Baton Rouge, La.: Army and Navy Publishing, 1946.

Studies

Doubler, Michael D. *Busting the Bocage: American Combined Arms Operations in France, 6 June–31 July 1944.* Fort Leavenworth, Kans.: Combat Studies Institute, 1988.

Drea, Edward J. *Unit Reconstitution: A Historical Perspective.* Fort Leavenworth, Kans.: Combat Studies Institute, 1983.

European Theater of Operations, Office of the Theater Historian. *Order of Battle of the United States Army, World War II, European Theater of Operations.* Paris, 1945.

Gabel, Christopher R. *Seek, Strike, and Destroy: U.S. Army Tank Destroyer Doctrine in World War II.* Fort Leavenworth, Kans.: Combat Studies Institute, 1985.

————. *The U.S. Army GHQ Maneuvers of 1941.* Washington, D.C.: Center of Military History, 1991.

Kirkpatrick, Charles E. *An Unknown Future and a Doubtful Present: Writing the Victory Plan of 1941.* Washington, D.C.: Center of Military History, 1990.

Lupfer, Timothy T. *The Dynamics of Doctrine: The Changes in German Tactical Doctrine during the First World War.* Leavenworth Papers, no. 4. Fort Leavenworth, Kans.: U.S. Army Command and General Staff College, 1981.

Matloff, Maurice. "The 90-Division Gamble." In *Command Decisions,* ed. Kent Roberts Greenfield, 365–381. Washington, D.C.: Office of the Chief of Military History, 1960.

Meller, Sidney L. *The Desert Training Center and the C-AMA.* AGF Study No. 15. Washington, D.C.: Historical Section, Army Ground Forces, 1946.

Ruppenthal, Roland G. "Logistics and the Broad-Front Strategy." In *Command Decisions,* ed. Kent Roberts Greenfield, 419–428. Washington, D.C.: Office of the Chief of Military History, 1960.

Scoggin, James F., ed. *OB WEST: A Study in Command.* Historical Division, European Command, 1948.

Vetock, Dennis J. *Lessons Learned: A History of US Army Lesson Learning.* Carlisle Barracks, Pa.: USAMHI, 1988.

Waddell, Steve R. "The Communications Zone (COMZ): American Logistics in France, 1944." Ph.D. diss., Texas A&M University, 1992.

Wiley, Bell I. *Training in the Ground Army, 1942–1945.* AGF Study No. 11. Fort Monroe, Va.: Historical Section, Army Ground Forces, 1948.

Books

Ambrose, Stephen E. *Citizen Soldiers: The U.S. Army from the Normandy Beaches to the Bulge to the Surrender of Germany.* New York: Simon and Schuster, 1997.

————. *D-Day, June 6, 1944: The Climactic Battle of World War II.* New York: Simon and Schuster, 1994.

————. *Eisenhower: Soldier, General of the Army, President-Elect, 1890–1952.* New York: Simon and Schuster, 1983.

Bartov, Omer. *The Eastern Front, 1941–1945: German Troops and the Barbarisation of Warfare.* Basingstoke, Hampshire: Macmillan in association with St. Antony's College, Oxford, 1985.

————. *Hitler's Army: Soldiers, Nazis, and War in the Third Reich.* New York: Oxford University Press, 1991.

Beesly, Patrick. *Very Special Intelligence*. London: Hamish Hamilton, 1977.

Bennett, Ralph. *Ultra in the West*. New York: Charles Scribner's, 1980.

Blumenson, Martin. *The Battle of the Generals: The Untold Story of the Falaise Pocket— The Campaign That Should Have Won World War II*. New York: William Morrow, 1993.

Bonn, Keith E. *When the Odds Were Even: The Vosges Mountains Campaign, October 1944–January 1945*. Novato, Calif.: Presidio Press, 1994.

Breuer, William B. *Death of a Nazi Army*. New York: Stein and Day, 1985.

Carell, Paul. *Invasion: They're Coming!* New York: E. P. Dutton, 1963.

D'Este, Carlo. *Bitter Victory: The Battle for Sicily, 1943*. New York: E. P. Dutton, 1988.

———. *Fatal Decision: Anzio and the Battle for Rome*. New York: HarperCollins, 1991.

Doubler, Michael D. *Closing with the Enemy: How GIs Fought the War in Europe, 1944–1945*. Lawrence: University Press of Kansas, 1994.

Dupuy, Trevor N. *Numbers, Predictions, and War: Using History to Evaluate Combat Factors and Predict the Outcome of Battles*. Indianapolis, Ind.: Bobbs-Merrill, 1979.

Ellis, John. *Brute Force: Allied Strategy and Tactics in the Second World War*. New York: Viking, 1990.

English, John A. *On Infantry*. New York: Praeger, 1981.

Featherston, Alwyn. *Saving the Breakout: The 30th Division's Heroic Stand at Mortain, August 7–12, 1944*. Novato, Calif.: Presidio, 1993.

Florentin, Eddy. *The Battle of the Falaise Gap*. New York: Hawthorn, 1967.

Graham, Dominick, and Shelford Bidwell. *Tug of War: The Battle for Italy, 1943–1945*. New York: St. Martin's Press, 1986.

Gropman, Alan, ed. *The Big L: American Logistics in World War II*. Washington, D.C.: National Defense University Press, 1997.

Hastings, Max. *Overlord: D-Day, June 6, 1944*. New York: Simon and Schuster, 1984.

Hechler, Ken. *The Bridge at Remagen*. New York: Ballantine Books, 1957.

Heller, Charles E., and William A. Stofft, eds. *America's First Battles, 1776–1965*. Lawrence: University Press of Kansas, 1986.

Hickey, Des, and Gus Smith. *Operation Avalanche: The Salerno Landings, 1943*. London: Heinemann, 1983.

Hooker, Richard D., Jr., ed. *Maneuver Warfare: An Anthology*. Novato, Calif.: Presidio, 1993.

Hughes, Thomas Alexander. *Over Lord: General Pete Quesada and the Triumph of Tactical Air Power in World War II*. New York: Free Press, 1995.

Jones, R. V. *Most Secret War*. London: Hamish Hamilton, 1978.

Kahn, E. J., Jr. *McNair: Educator of an Army*. Washington, D.C.: Infantry Journal Press, 1945.

Keefer, Louis E. *Scholars in Foxholes: The Story of the Army Specialized Training Program in World War II*. Jefferson, N.C.: McFarland, 1988.

Keegan, John. *The Second World War*. New York: Penguin Books, 1990.

Kennett, Lee. *G.I.: The American Soldier in World War II*. New York: Scribner's, 1987.

Leinbaugh, Harold P., and John D. Campbell. *The Men of Company K: The Autobiography of a World War II Rifle Company*. New York: William Morrow, 1985.

Lewin, Ronald. *Ultra Goes to War*. London: Hutchinson, 1978.

Lucas, James, and James Barker. *The Battle of Normandy*. New York: Holmes and Meier, 1978.

MacDonald, Charles B. *The Battle of the Huertgen Forest.* New York: J. B. Lippincott, 1963.

————. *The Mighty Endeavor: The American War in Europe.* New York: Quill, 1986.

————. *A Time for Trumpets: The Untold Story of the Battle of the Bulge.* New York: William Morrow, 1984.

Mahon, John K. *History of the Militia and National Guard.* New York: Macmillan, 1983.

Marshall, S. L. A. *Island Victory.* Washington, D.C.: Infantry Journal Press, 1944.

————. *Men against Fire: The Problem of Battle Command in Future War.* New York: William Morrow, 1966.

Matloff, Maurice, ed. *American Military History.* Washington, D.C.: Center of Military History, 1985.

Miller, Edward G. *A Dark and Bloody Ground: The Huertgen Forest and the Roer River Dams, 1944–1945.* College Station: Texas A&M University Press, 1995.

Millett, Allan R., and Williamson Murray, eds. *Military Effectiveness.* 3 vols. Boston: Unwin Hyman, 1988.

Morelock, Jerry D. *Generals of the Ardennes: American Leadership in the Battle of the Bulge.* Washington, D.C.: National Defense University Press, 1994.

Murray, Williamson. *The Change in the European Balance of Power, 1938–1939: The Path to Ruin.* Princeton, N.J.: Princeton University Press, 1984.

Overy, Richard. *Why the Allies Won.* New York: W. W. Norton, 1996.

Perret, Goeffrey. *There's a War to Be Won: The United States Army in World War II.* New York: Random House, 1991.

Price, Frank J. *Troy H. Middleton.* Baton Rouge: Louisiana State University Press, 1974.

Spector, Ronald H. *Eagle against the Sun.* New York: Random House, 1985.

Sydnor, Charles W., Jr. *Soldiers of Destruction: The SS Death's Head Division, 1933–1945.* Princeton, N.J.: Princeton University Press, 1977.

Toland, John. *Battle: The Story of the Bulge.* New York: Random House, 1959.

Van Creveld, Martin. *Fighting Power: German and U.S. Army Performance, 1939–1945.* Westport, Conn.: Greenwood Press, 1982.

————. *Supplying War: Logistics from Wallenstein to Patton.* Cambridge: Cambridge University Press, 1977.

Waddell, Steve R. *United States Army Logistics: The Normandy Campaign, 1944.* Westport, Conn.: Greenwood, 1994.

Weigley, Russell F. *Eisenhower's Lieutenants: The Campaign of France and Germany, 1944–1945.* Bloomington: Indiana University Press, 1981.

Whiting, Charles. *Death of a Division.* London: Frederick Warne, 1980.

Wilmot, Chester. *The Struggle for Europe.* New York: Harper, 1952.

Winterbotham, F. W. *The Ultra Secret.* London: Weidenfeld and Nicolson, 1974.

Articles

"Allen and His Men." *Time,* 9 August 1943.

Ambrose, Stephen. "Why We Won the War: The Politics of World War II." *Army,* June 1994, 12–18.

"Big Enough for Victory." *Kansas City Star,* 30 December 1942.

Blumenson, Martin. "America's World War II Leaders in Europe: Some Thoughts." *Parameters* 19, no. 4 (December 1989): 2–13.

Colby, Elbridge. "Replacements for a Field Army in Combat." *Infantry Journal* 60 (March 1947): 12–18.

Damon, W. F., and Claud P. Brownley. "9th Reconnaissance Troop on Maneuvers." *Cavalry Journal* 50, no. 5 (September–October 1941): 86–88.

Desch, John. "The 1941 German Army/The 1944–45 U.S. Army: A Comparative Analysis of Two Forces in Their Primes." *Command Magazine* 18 (September–October 1992): 54–63.

Ellis, Andrew G. "On Time—On Target: The Birth of Modern American Artillery." *Field Artillery* (August 1988): 26–30.

Fraser, L. V., and Oliver Steward. "Rocket Typhoons: Answer to German Panzers." *Armored Cavalry Journal* 53, no. 5 (September–October 1944): 8–11.

G-3 Section, Supreme Headquarters Allied Expeditionary Forces. "Employment of Tanks and Infantry in Normandy." *Military Review* 24, no. 9 (December 1944): 13–17.

Henry, Tom. "March of the Silent Men." *Washington Evening Star,* 30 September 1943.

Hillyard, H. L. "Employment of Tanks by the Infantry Division." *Military Review* 27, no. 3 (June 1947): 50–60.

Jacobs, Bruce. "Tensions between the Army National Guard and the Regular Army." *Military Review* 73 (October 1993): 5–17.

Kent, Frank R. "The Great Game of Politics." *Washington Evening Star,* 8 January 1943.

Lindley, Ernest K. "Size of the Army." *Washington Post,* 6 January 1943.

———. "So Large an Army." *Washington Post,* 18 December 1942.

McCarthy, Joe. "4th Armored Moved Suddenly and Fast." *Yank,* 21 January 1945, 26.

XIX Tactical Air Command. "Ground-Air Teamwork in France." *Military Review* 25, no. 2 (May 1945): 43–45.

Rodgers, David P. "The Camera Was Their Weapon." *Army* 47, no. 4 (April 1997): 50–54.

Sams, James D. "Ordnance Improvisation in the Combat Zone." *Military Review* 28, no. 2 (May 1948): 32–36.

Schute, Harry J., Jr. "Forgotten Principles: The 28th Division in the Huertgen Forest." *Armor* 102, no. 4 (July–August 1993): 40–44.

Smoler, Fredric. "The Secret of the Soldiers Who Didn't Shoot." *American Heritage,* March 1989, 37–45.

Spiller, Roger J. "S. L. A. Marshall and the Ratio of Fire." *RUSI Journal* 133, no. 4 (winter 1988): 63–71.

Stewart, Richard W. "The 'Red Bull' Division: The Training and Initial Engagements of the 34th Infantry Division, 1941–1943." *Army History* 25 (winter 1993): 1–10.

Index

European theater of operations (ETO), 5, 29, 36, 43, 67, 84, 110, 148, 178, 181, 184, 193–195, 200, 206, 208, 224, 230, 234–236, 252, 259, 262, 267, 272

FABIUS I, Exercise, 65–66
Falais Gap, 160, 170–172, 180, 256
Fedala, 85
Field Artillery Battery Test, 25
Field Artillery School, 24
Field manuals, 51
Field Manual 17–36, 161
Fire support: in amphibious operations, 52, 88, 175; during Battle of Metz, 205; during Battle of the Bulge, 221, 224–225, 228; during crossing of Rhine River, 243–244; German, 4, 92, 118, 120, 124, 171–172, 183, 190, 218, 232, 246; improvements in the interwar period, 121–123, 257; in Italy, 111, 121–124, 130–131, 246; massing of, 123, 145, 172, 180, 228, 242; in Normandy, 13, 133–137, 145, 149–150, 158, 297n5; in North Africa, 90, 96–98; during Operation COBRA, 161, 164–166, 169–171; during Operation GRENADE, 240; quality of American, 5, 7–8, 16, 111, 132, 171–172, 251, 257, 261–262; relation to combat effectiveness, 3; during seizure of Aachen, 183–185; in Sicily, 103, 107, 110; use against fortifications, 172, 183, 201, 212
Florence, 245
Floresta, 106
Fondouk Gap, 93
Formia, 174
Fort A. P. Hill, Va., 60–61
Fort Benning, Ga., 81
Fort Bliss, Tex., 75
Fort Bragg, N.C., 28, 54–56
Fort Dix, N.J., 77
FORTITUDE, Operation, 134, 272
Fort Jackson, S.C., 68, 75, 80–81, 209
Fort Knox, Ky., 28, 54
Fort Leavenworth, Kans., 17, 22, 24, 56, 62, 81, 102, 126
Fort Meade, Md., 59–61
Fort Sam Houston, Tex., 75
Fort Sill, Okla., 24, 54, 175

Forward observers, 123, 242, 257, 262
FOX, Exercise, 65–67
Fox Green Beach, 139
France, fall of, 14, 16–18, 102
Fredendall, Major General Lloyd R., 55, 90, 203
French Expeditionary Corps (FEC), 129

Gaffey, Major General Hugh J., 107
Gallipoli, 120, 295n40
Garda, Lake, 247
Gavin, Lieutenant General James M., 103, 114, 185
Geilenkirchen, 199–201
Gela, 100–101, 103, 108–109
General Headquarters (GHQ), 17, 19–21, 52, 55, 62, 272
Gerhardt, Major General Charles H., 62–67, 156, 194, 215, 279n19
Germany, tradition as a military state, 14
"Germany first" strategy, 11, 47–48, 272
Gerow, Major General Leonard T., 60–62, 188–189
GHQ maneuvers. See Maneuvers, army
GI. See Soldiers, American
Giles, James B., 218
Ginder, Colonel P. D., 147
Grand Wohekirkel, Fortress, 212
Great Britain: deployment of divisions to, 53, 71, 77, 87, 89, 116, 189, 199, 202, 204, 293n82; provision of lend-lease equipment to, 26; role in the Victory Program, 31; shortage of training areas in, 14, 50, 89
GRENADE, Operation, 240, 272
Group, 14th Cavalry, 220, 223
Guadalcanal, 80, 198
Gustav Line, 117–119, 129, 131
Guthrie, Brigadier General John S., 234

Haislip, Major General Wade H., 208, 232–233
Harmon, Major General Ernest N., 84, 94, 129–130
Harrison, Brigadier General William K., 68, 70–71, 153, 165, 301n20
Hastings, Max, 8, 259
Hawaiian Department, 56